The
State of Kuwait

George Gregory

The Birds of the State of Kuwait
by George Gregory

First published in Skegness, England in November 2005
by George Gregory, Gibraltar Point Field Station,
Gibraltar Road, Skegness, PE24 4SU, England.
Email: ggregory71@lycos.com

© George Gregory (text and photographs)
© Pekka Fagel (photographs)
© AbdulMuhsen Al-Suraye'a (photographs)
© Khalid Al-Nasrallah (photographs)
© Eisa Ramadan (photographs)
© Hussain Al-Qallaf (photographs)
© Khalid Al-Ghanim (photographs)

All rights reserved. No part of this publication may be reproduced or utilised in any form by any means, electronic, or mechanical, including photocopying, recording, or by any information or retrieval system, without prior written permission of the author and publisher.

While all reasonable care has been taken during the preparation of this edition, the author and publisher cannot accept responsibility for any consequences arising from the use thereof or from the information contained therein.

ISBN-10: 0-9551416-0-5
ISBN-13: 978-0-9551416-07.

Typeset and Design by Sam Ely Design and Illustration
Printed by Cupit Print, Horncastle, England.
Front Cover Picture: Crab Plover by Pekka Fagel

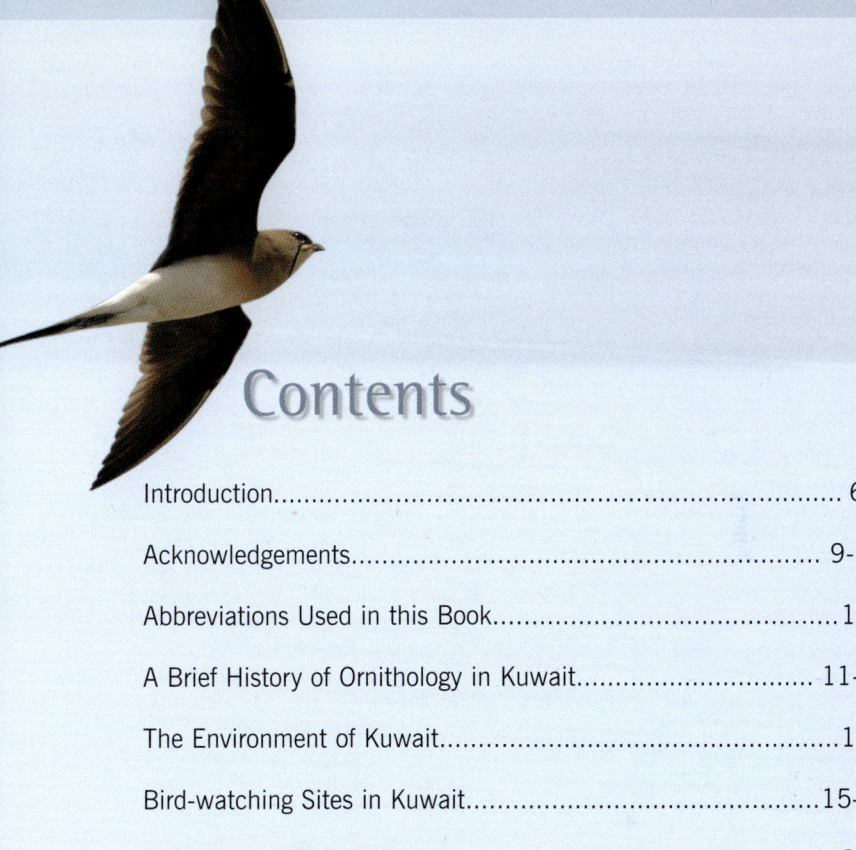

Contents

Introduction 6

Acknowledgements 9-10

Abbreviations Used in this Book 10

A Brief History of Ornithology in Kuwait 11-13

The Environment of Kuwait 14

Bird-watching Sites in Kuwait 15-27

Protection of Birds in Kuwait 32

Important Aspects of Kuwait's Birdlife 33

The Kuwait Bird List:

    a) The Main List of Species of Birds 34-184

    b) The Species of Birds of Captive Origin 184-187

    c) The Species of Birds Requiring Confirmation 188-197

References and Bibliography 204-211

Index of Common Names 212-215

Index of Scientific Names 216-219

INTRODUCTION

The main purpose of this book is to present an accurate status for each species of bird recorded in Kuwait, by reviewing and analysing all accessible records, both historical and recent. There is a great need for such a book. Kuwait occupies the south-eastern corner of the Western Palearctic Avifaunal Region, as delimited by *The Birds of the Western Palearctic* (Cramp, Simmons, and Perrins, 1977-1994), and by *The Birds of the Western Palearctic Concise Edition* (Snow and Perrins, 1998). It is one of the few remaining countries in this region not to have a modern and readily available book containing an up-to-date bird list. Field guides to birds in the region, such as those by H. Heinzel, R. Fitter and J. Parslow (1979), P. A. D. Hollom, R. F. Porter, S. Christensen and I. Willis (1988), L. Jonsson (1992), R. F. Porter, S. Christensen and P. Schiermacker-Hansen (1996), A. Harris, H. Shirihai and D. Christie (1996) and M. Beaman and S. Madge (1998) require accurate and up-to-date information about Kuwait's birds. Additionally, Kuwait is in the north-eastern corner of the Arabian peninsula as defined by *An Interim Atlas of Breeding Birds of Arabia* (Jennings, 1995), and has breeding bird species found nowhere else, or almost nowhere else, in the peninsula. All accessible evidence of birds breeding in Kuwait is presented in this book.

There have been previous lists of Kuwait birds. *Birds of Arabia* by R. Meinertzhagen (1954) lists many species of birds in the state. P. R. Haynes (1978) published his notes on the distribution and status of birds in Kuwait, followed shortly by his list of Kuwait's birds (Haynes, 1979). Next year, G. Bundy and F. E. Warr (1980) published *A Checklist of the Birds in the Arabian Gulf States*, which included Kuwait bird species. M. C. Jennings (1981) published *Birds of the Arabian Gulf*, which listed the bird species in Kuwait. Later, C. W. T. Pilcher (undated; 2000) provided lists and notes of Kuwait birds, essentially for *The Birds of the Western Palearctic Concise Edition* (Snow and Perrins, 1998). M. A. A. Al-Jraiwi (1999) published, in Arabic, *Kuwait Birds*, which included many photographs and a checklist of birds. A. S. Al-Haddad and F. A. Al-Sudairawi (2002) published a similar book, *Kuwait Birds - A Photographic Record*, again in Arabic and with photographs and a checklist of bird species. The *Annual Reports* of the Bird Monitoring and Protection Team (2000-2004) included lists of Kuwait birds. A. Al-Fadhel (2005) published *Birds of Kuwait - A Portrait*, mostly in Arabic, but with a largely correct checklist of bird species, showing the main status of each.

All of the above lists represented important stages in the development of the Kuwait bird list. However, all of them contain errors of commission and omission, many of which are serious. Many inaccuracies have clearly been perpetuated from work to work. Reviewing past data on birds in Kuwait has proven to be a very difficult task. The main problem is that most past records from the late 1970s to 1991 were destroyed during the Iraqi occupation, and many records from then to about 2002 are inaccessible for a number of other reasons. Nevertheless, all accessible records have been used in compiling this book; the inaccessibility of others is coped with as well as possible. If other records come to light in the future, they can be incorporated into new editions of this book.

ACKNOWLEDGEMENTS

I am most of all indebted to F. E. (Effie) Warr, who made available her notes on past records of birds in Kuwait, a mass of written communications, and a scarce copy of the *Computer List Of Bird Observations in Kuwait 1956-75* (Ahmadi Natural History and Field Studies Group, 1975). Without these, it would have been a much more difficult and time-consuming task for me to put this book together.

I am also much indebted to Mike Jennings for giving me a copy of the portion of his *Computer List of Breeding Bird Records in Arabia* (Jennings, undated) that covered Kuwait, and for much good advice and help concerning records of breeding birds in Kuwait.

Stan Howe was very helpful in providing details of past records and much useful information about the former Ahmadi Natural History and Field Studies Group.

Bill Bourne identified a number of specimens of gull wings that I sent to him.

The late Charles Pilcher, Mahmoud Shehab Al-Ahmed and Khalid Al-Nasrallah showed me a number of the best bird-watching sites in Kuwait.

Peter Robertson and Barry Thomas helped set up the short-lived Ornithological Society of Kuwait, helped with collection of bird specimens, and provided transport, which proved to be very useful in (re)discovering a number of important bird-watching sites in Kuwait.

The late Charles Pilcher, Thomas Spencer and Peter Cowan were of great assistance in the functioning of the Kuwait Ornithological Records Committee.

Gavin Rowlands and Zainab Khalil helped in typing up previous versions of the Kuwait Bird List.

David Hellam set up websites for the Ornithological Society of Kuwait and for the Bird Monitoring and Protection Team.

Su'ad Al-Ahmadi helped with translation and with transport.

The Kuwait Oil Company provided a permit to visit Umm Al-Aish Oil Camp.

The Kuwait Military Intelligence Department provided a permit to visit Bubiyan Island.

The Kuwait Coastguard provided transport to Bubiyan and Warba Islands.

The Emir of Kuwait, His Highness Shaikh Jaber Al-Ahmed Al-Jaber Al-Sabah, provided transport on his yacht to Kubbar Island.

Shaikha Amthal Al-Ahmed Al-Jaber Al-Sabah was instrumental in setting up the Bird Monitoring and Protection Team, and in arranging transport.

Shaikh Fahad Al-Sabah permitted me to visit his farm at Al-Abraq Al-Khabari, and, together with his son, Shaikh Sabah, often provided generous hospitality, and some valuable bird records.

Abdullah Al-Habashi permitted me to visit his farm at Jahra, provided generous hospitality, and, together with his employee Ali, provided important information about breeding birds.

Mohammed Al-Ajmi permitted me to visit his farm at Abdali and provided generous hospitality.

Sami Al-Daiji permitted me to visit his camp at Ratqa and provided generous hospitality.

Khalid Al-Ghanim, of the Environment Public Authority, permitted me to visit Jahra Pool Reserve and North Doha Nature Reserve, and provided many bird records and photographs.

The Kuwaiti members of the Bird Monitoring and Protection Team, namely Abdalla Al-Fadhel, Mish'al Al-Jeriwi, Fahad Al-Mansori, Khalid Al-Nasrallah, Hussain Al-Qallaf, Shaikha Amthal Al-Ahmed Al-Jaber Al-Sabah, Musaad Al-Saleh, AbdulRahman Al-

Sirhan, AbdulMuhsen Al-Sureye'a, Eisa Ramadan and Mahmoud Shehab, provided many bird records and photographs, and often helped with transport and generous hospitality.

Employees of the Kuwait Institute for Scientific Research who provided bird records, transport, advice and general help during the Bubiyan Project include Ronald Loughland, Edgardo Delima, Sara Al-Dosary, Matra Al-Mutairy and Jamal Dashti.

A number of expatriate residents of Kuwait, including members of the Bird Monitoring and Protection Team, made their bird records accessible and assisted with transport. These include Andrew Bailey, Shirley Carter-Brown, Mark Chichester, Guillaume Dallemagne, Pekka Fagel, Jeremy Gaskell, Harriet McCurdy, Helene Merlet, Gavin Rowlands, Barbara Settles, Jeffrey Shaw, Gary Walker and Rachel Williams.

Visiting bird-watchers who made their bird records available include Wolfgang Bindl, Hans-Martin Busch, Barrie Cooper, Steve Holliday, Philip Johnson, Andreas Lange, Franziska Lange, Charlie Moores, Gunhild Østerø, Johanna Rathgeber-Knan, Jo Seegers, Ole Schroeder, Solveig Schroeder, Clive Temple, Markku Varhimo and Graeme Wright.

John Middleton and Mike Reed, visiting bird-ringers, sent me all their bird records.

ABBREVIATIONS USED IN THIS BOOK

ANHFSG - Ahmadi Natural History and Field Studies Group
BMAPT - Bird Monitoring and Protection Team
EPA - Environment Public Authority
EPC - Environment Protection Council
KEPS - Kuwait Environment Protection Society
KISR - Kuwait Institute for Scientific Research
KNHG - Kuwait Natural History Group
KORC - Kuwait Ornithological Rarities Committee
OSK - Ornithological Society of Kuwait
OSME - Ornithological Society of the Middle East
PAAAFR - Public Authority for Agricultural Affairs and Fish Resources
VWC - Voluntary Work Centre

A BRIEF HISTORY OF ORNITHOLOGY IN KUWAIT

The bedouin, town dwellers, pearl divers and seafarers of Kuwait were, no doubt, familiar with many species of birds that they encountered. Kuwaiti falconers have long been able to identify prey species.
 The first European collectors of eggs and full-grown specimens from Kuwait included Colonel E.A. Butler and W. D. Cumming, who were resident at Basra in the late nineteenth and early twentieth centuries. Many of these eggs and specimens were donated to the British Museum and listed in their publications (British Museum, 1901, 1902). V. S. La Personne, an Indian collector, repeatedly visited the islands of Kuwait to obtain eggs and specimens for Major-General Sir Percy Cox and Major R. E. Cheesman, who were also resident at Basra. These specimens were instrumental in the publication of important articles on birds in Kuwait (Ticehurst, Buxton and Cheesman, 1921-1922; Ticehurst, Cox and Cheesman, 1925, 1926). Many of them are now in the British Museum (Warr, undated) or in the collection of the Bombay Natural History Society (Abdulali, 1968-1971).
 Colonel H. R. P. Dickson was resident in Kuwait from 1929 to 1951, kept a game register (Jennings, 1989) and provided much information about Kuwait birds in *The Arab of the Desert* (H. R. P. Dickson, 1949). His wife, Violet, wrote *Forty Years in Kuwait* (V. Dickson, 1970) and an article about a trip to Maskan and Auha Islands (V. Dickson, 1942). These works contain valuable data, especially about breeding birds.
 Colonel Richard Meinertzhagen visited Kuwait on his travels around Arabia. His book, *Birds of Arabia* (Meinertzhagen, 1954), is a source of much information on Kuwait birds.
 Victor Sales lived in Ahmadi for 16 years, from 1952 to 1968. His pioneering studies, involving bird-ringing and field observations, mostly at Ahmadi and Kuwait Bay, added many species to the Kuwait bird list. He worked in an era without proper identification guides for the region, something hard to imagine today, but worked hard to produce an extensive set of records.
 The ornithologists P. A. D. Hollom and R. D. Etchécopar visited Kuwait in 1965 and 1969, respectively.
 A number of expatriates and Kuwaitis employed in the oil industry formed the Ahmadi Natural History and Field Studies Group (ANHFSG), which functioned from 1970 to 1987. This was the first organisation of its kind in the region. John 'Bish' Brown, Stan Howe, Faisal Al-Ghanem, Tareq Rajab, Arthur Caldwell, Denis McQuaid, John Hunt, Roger Stafford, Bill Stuart and Michael Leven were prominent and active members of the group, which organised field trips, talks and slideshows, often involving visiting scientists and naturalists. It published a regular *Newsletter*, in which appeared bird lists and notes on the status and distribution of birds in Kuwait, e.g. by Anonymous (1972) and Paul Haynes (1974, 1978, 1979). It also produced an important computer printout of Kuwait bird records (Ahmadi Natural History and Field Studies Group, 1975). Books published by members of the ANHFSG that contained material on Kuwait birds were *Kuwait's Natural History - An Introduction* (Clayton and Pilcher, 1984) and *Discovering Kuwait's Wildlife* (Clayton and Wells, 1987).
 The Bird Recorders of the group were Bob and Margery Blacker, Paul Haynes and Charles Pilcher. Members functioning as Correspondents for *The Birds of the Western Palearctic* (Cramp, Simmons, and Perrins, 1977-1994) were Stan Howe, Paul Haynes and Charles Pilcher.
 For the purposes of recording birds, the group divided Kuwait into 20km x 20km squares, some with names such as Ash-Shiggayat, Umm Niqa, Umm Al-Aish, Umm

Ar-Rimam, Bahra, South Bubiyan/Subiya, Southeast Bubiyan, Mutla, Khadima, Kuwait City/Bay, Mischan/West Failaka, Auha/East Failaka, Khashman, Khaitan, Fintas, Minageesh, Abduliyah, Ahmadi, Mina, Sea Island/Kubr, South Minageesh, Burgan, Araifjan, Buqay and Mufattah. Some of these names are used when referring to past records.

During the functioning of the ANHFSG, past and recent records of rare bird species in Kuwait (and elsewhere in the Gulf region) were described on Rare Bird Report forms, and were judged by a panel, whose members included Mike Jennings, Graham Bundy, Duncan Brooks and David Scott.

In 1974 K. Nakamura, employed by the Tokyo University of Fisheries, recorded some birds in Kuwait's territorial waters (Nakamura, 1974).

The Kuwait Institute for Scientific Research (KISR) employed Fozia Al-Sudairawi to survey wintering birds on the mudflats (Al-Sudairawi, 1984).

From 1985 to 1987 a Kuwait government body, the Environment Protection Council (EPC), sponsored a survey of Kuwait's birds (Pilcher, 1987), which was carried out by Charles Pilcher, Alan Tye, George Gregory and Mahmoud Shehab. This survey added a number of species to the Kuwait bird list (Pilcher, Gregory, Tye and Ahmed, 1990). The EPC also provided assistance to two visiting ornithologists, Trevor Squires and Philip Jones, who carried out a programme of bird-ringing.

In 1987 the role of the ANHFSG was taken over by the Kuwait Natural History Group (KNHG). In 1994 it formed the Kuwait Ornithological Rarities Committee (KORC) to judge records of rare birds in the state. Participants in these two new organisations were Charles Pilcher, Peter Cowan, Bryon Wright, Thomas Spencer and George Gregory. These bodies ceased their work in the early 2000s.

Between 1990 and 2001, Peter Cowan, employed by Kuwait University and by the Kuwait Institute for Scientific Research (KISR), carried out a number of studies of birds in Kuwait, resulting in a number of important articles (Cowan, 1990, 2000a, 2000b; Cowan and Brown, 2001; Cowan and Newman, 1998; Cowan and Pilcher, 2003).

After the Iraqi occupation ended in 1991, the EPC sponsored studies of the environmental damage caused, including the effect on birds (Evans, Pilcher and Symens, 1991; Pilcher and Sexton, 1993). This body also sponsored programmes of bird-ringing, which Charles Pilcher helped to organise, carried out by Mike Reed, Tony Cross, John Middleton, Nigel Cleere and David Kelly (Reed and Cross, 1995; Cleere, Kelly and Pilcher, 2000a).

The role of the EPC was taken over in 1996 by a new body, the Environment Public Authority (EPA), which, amongst other functions, has been involved in the management of nature reserves in Kuwait. Khalid al-Ghanim, Manager of Reserves, has been very active in recording and photographing birds, particularly at Jahra Pool Reserve.

In early 2000 three expatriates, George Gregory, Peter Robertson and Barry Thomas, inaugurated the short-lived Ornithological Society of Kuwait.

Later in 2000, a number of Kuwaitis, led by Khalid Al-Nasrallah, with interests in bird protection and bird photography, set up the Bird Monitoring and Protection Team (BMAPT), which became an integral part of the Kuwait Environment Protection Society (KEPS). Other Kuwaiti members have been Shaikha Amthal Al-Ahmed Al-Jaber Al-Sabah, Mahmoud Shehab, Abdalla Al-Fadhel, Essa Ramadan, Fahad Al-Mansori, Mish'al Al-Jraiwi, Hussain Al-Qallaf, AbdulMuhsen Al-Sureye'a, Musaad Al-Saleh, Khalid al-Ghanim and AbdulRahman Al-Sirhan. Expatriate members have included George Gregory, Andrew Bailey, Shirley Carter-Brown, Su'ad Al-Ahmadi, Mark Chichester, Guillaume Dallemagne, Pekka Fagel, Brian Foster, Gavin Rowlands and Barbara Settles. The team has published an Annual Report from 2000 onwards, each including a bird list and brief notes on selected species, including several additions to the Kuwait bird list. It has also established a nature reserve at Sulaibikhat, and has escorted visiting bird-watchers around the state. In 2002 it carried out a survey of birds on Bubiyan Island, resulting in new discoveries (Al-Nasrallah and Gregory, 2003). The Secretaries of BMAPT have been George Gregory and Brian Foster.

From January 2004 to March 2005 KISR undertook a project to survey the environment of Bubiyan and Warba Islands, including a study of birds there. This was carried out by a Bird Team, which included Ron Loughland, Edgardo Delima, Sara Al-Dosary, Matra Al-Mutairy, George Gregory and Jamal Dashti, who made a number of important ornithological discoveries on the islands (Gregory, 2004b, 2005a; Loughland, 2004). This team also carried out a series of night surveys of birds at KISR's Agricultural Research Station at Kabd.

THE ENVIRONMENT OF KUWAIT

The State of Kuwait is an independent emirate situated at the north-western end of the Arabian Gulf, between Iraq and Saudi Arabia. Its land area is almost 18,000 square kilometers, and territorial waters cover about 5,500 square kilometers. The largest offshore islands are Bubiyan, Warba and Failaka; smaller ones are Auha, Mishkan, Umm Al-Nabel, Kubbar, Qaroh and Umm Al-Maradim.

The land slopes, mostly gradually, from the Arabian Gulf in the east up to about 300 metres in the western corner. There is one escarpment at Jal Az-Zor and some minor hillocks in the southeast, such as Jebel Al-Benayah, but most of the land is flat.

There are no natural rivers, but there are a few wadis, notably Wadi Al-Batin along the northwest border and the Wadi Ar-Rimam systems in the Sabah Al-Ahmed Natural Reserve (formerly the National Park). Most drainage is internal, resulting in a salinated soil. There are two short khors (inlets) in the southeast, Khor Al-Ala'ma and Khor Al-Mufateh.

Where grazing is prevented, the climax vegetation is that of semi-desert, with perennial shrubs, forbs and grasses, particularly **Stipagrostis, Cyperus, Haloxylon** and **Rhanterium**. There are occasional naturally-occurring trees such as **Acacia**. Near the shores and in the sabkha areas are halophytic plants, such as **Suaeda.** The blooming of ephemeral plants in the spring is dependent on adequate rainfall in the preceding winter. Prolonged overgrazing has exposed, in many areas, clayey, sandy and gravelly soil with some low outcrops of sandstone and limestone.

There are extensive mudflats, especially in Kuwait Bay and around Bubiyan and Warba Islands. Saltmarshes are found at Ras Subiya and east of Bahra.

Natural oases occur at Abdali, Jahra, Wafra, Al-Abraq Al-Khabari and other places, where small, tree-sheltered fields are irrigated by wells and tanks, and support various traditional crops. Modern greenhouse systems are extensively used in some of these areas. Sewage outflows feed reed beds, pools and marshy areas at Jahra, Doha and Sewer Plant Reeds near Zour.

There is extensive planting of trees, shrubs and herbs along urban roads and in various regional parks. Many villas, town parks and other areas support a variety of plants, so that many urban areas are quite green.

The human population is concentrated in the cities of Kuwait, Jahra and Ahmadi near the Gulf, so that much of the rest of the state is open. However, various oilfields are fenced off, and military areas and Bubiyan and Warba Islands have restricted access.

Although Kuwait is a small state with no spectacular scenery or habitats, it has a fairly rich avifauna. It is situated at a crossroads of two main migration routes, one between Eurasia and Africa, and another between Turkey and India, so most species recorded in Kuwait are passing through. Quite a few bird species breed in the urban areas. Various seabirds nest on offshore islands, and a surprising number of species breed, or are regularly found, in the reed beds and marshy areas.

BIRD-WATCHING SITES IN KUWAIT

Around the urban areas Laughing Dove (*Streptopelia senegalensis*), Eurasian Collared Dove (*Streptopelia decaocto*), Feral Pigeon (*Columba livia*), Common Mynah (*Acridotheres tristis*), White-eared Bulbul (*Pycnonotus leucogenys*), Red-vented Bulbul (*Pycnonotus cafer*), Rose-ringed Parakeet (*Psittacula krameri*) and House Sparrow (*Passer domesticus*) are regular resident breeders. Outside the urban areas Crested Lark (*Galerida cristata*) is the most frequently observed resident species. From the seafronts and beaches various gulls, terns and waders can usually be seen in most seasons. Many common migrants and winter visitors are frequently observed in many areas of Kuwait.

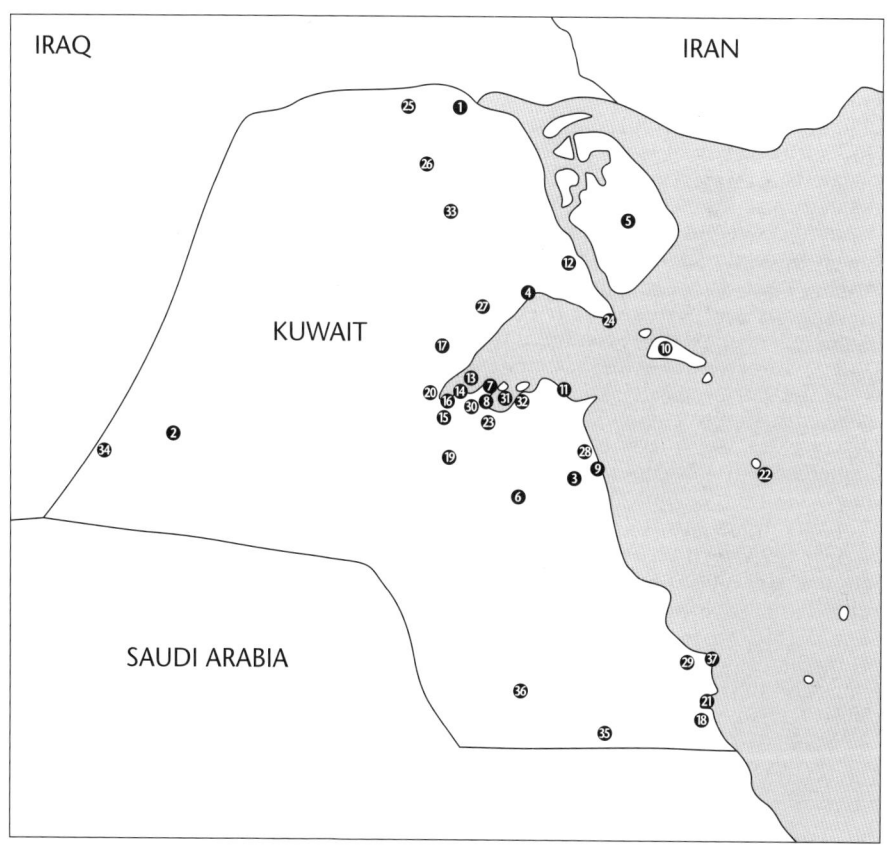

The most important particular bird-watching sites in Kuwait include:

(1) Abdali Farms
A large area of traditional farms next to the border with Iraq, to the east of the Basra Road. Access to individual farms is by private agreement with the owners.

Regularly-breeding species include Namaqua Dove (*Oena capensis*), Rufous-tailed Scrub Robin (*Cercotrichas galactotes*), Eastern Olivaceous Warbler (*Hippolais pallida*), White-eared Bulbul (*Pycnonotus leucogenys*) and Spanish Sparrow (*Passer hispaniolensis*). Other species that have bred are Red-wattled Lapwing (*Hoplopterus indicus*), Common Quail (*Coturnix coturnix*), Black-crowned Sparrow-lark (*Eremopterix nigriceps*) and Barn Owl (*Tyto alba*). Wintering species include Song Thrush (*Turdus philomelos*), European Robin (*Erithacus rubecula*) and occasionally Dark-throated Thrush (*Turdus ruficollis*). Egyptian Nightjar (*Caprimulgus aegyptius*) is present in the summer. Among many migrants have been Eurasian Wryneck (*Jynx torquilla*), White-throated Robin (*Irania gutturalis*), Syke's Warbler (*Hippolais rama*) and Basra Reed Warbler (*Acrocephalus griseldis*). Rarer species seen here have included Common Babbler (*Turdoides caudatus*).

(2) Al-Abraq Al-Khabari
An isolated small oasis in the western desert, including one traditional farm. Access is by private agreement with the owner.

Many migrants are attracted to the trees and bushes here, including Red-breasted Flycatcher (*Ficedula parva*), Semi-collared Flycatcher (*Ficedula semitorquata*), White-throated Robin (*Irania gutturalis*), River Warbler (*Locustella fluviatilis*), Thrush Nightingale (*Luscinia luscinia*), Rosy Starling (*Sturnus roseus*), Common Grasshopper Warbler (*Locustella naevia*), Levant Sparrowhawk (*Accipiter brevipes*), Shikra (*Accipiter badius*) and European Scops Owl (*Otus scops*). In winter Song Thrush (*Turdus philomelos*), European Robin (*Erithacus rubecula*), Common Blackbird (*Turdus merula*), European Siskin (*Carduelis spinus*) and Grey Hypocolius (*Hypocolius ampelinus*) can be found. A long list of rarer species that have found here includes Common Woodpigeon (*Columba palumbus*), Eversmann's Redstart (*Phoenicurus erythronotus*), Dusky Thrush (*Turdus naumanni*), Mistle Thrush (*Turdus viscivorus*), Ring Ouzel (*Turdus torquatus*), Richard's Pipit (*Anthus richardi*), Yellow-browed Warbler (*Phylloscopus inornatus*), Wood Lark (*Lullula arborea*), Zitting Cisticola (*Cisticola juncidis*), Great Snipe (*Gallinago media*), Desert Finch (*Rhodospiza obsoleta*), Olive-backed Pipit (*Anthus hodgsoni*), Great Spotted Cuckoo (*Clamator glandarius*), Black Stork (*Ciconia nigra*), Black-shouldered Kite (*Elanus caeruleus*) and Barbary Falcon (*Falco pelegrinoides*).

In the surrounding desert area, particularly from January to May, are many species of lark, including Temminck's Lark (*Eremophila bilopha*), Bimaculated Lark (*Melanocorypha bimaculata*), Dunn's Lark (*Eremalauda dunni*), Desert Lark (*Ammomanes deserti*) and Bar-tailed Lark (*Ammomanes cincturus*). Most of these species breed regularly. Also, sometimes present, mostly in winter, are Spotted Sandgrouse (*Pterocles senegallus*) and Pin-tailed Sandgrouse (*Pterocles alchata*).

(3) Ahmadi
An oil town south of Kuwait City, famous for its gardens and parks. The gardens around private houses require permission to be entered but much is visible from the numerous roads.

White-eared Bulbul (*Pycnonotus leucogenys*) and Red-vented Bulbul (*Pycnonotus cafer*) breed regularly, and Golden Oriole (*Oriolus oriolus*) and other species may do so. House Crow (*Corvus splendens*) and Black-crowned Sparrow-lark (*Eremopterix nigriceps*) have often been seen and there are many migrant and wintering species. Oriental Turtle Dove (*Streptopelia orientalis*), Purple Swamp-Hen (*Porphyrio porphyrio*), Mistle Thrush (*Turdus viscivorus*), Blyth's Reed Warbler (*Acrocephalus dumetorum*), Rook (*Corvus frugilegus*), Rock Bunting (*Emberiza cia*), Black-headed Bunting (*Emberiza melanocephala*) and Rustic Bunting (*Emberiza rustica*) have been recorded.

(4) Bahra

An area of open land, one small traditional farm, low cliffs, mudflats and oil lakes on the Subiya Road. Access is open except to the traditional farm, which requires private agreement with the owner.

Breeding species have included Eastern Olivaceous Warbler (*Hippolais pallida*) and Spanish Sparrow (*Passer hispaniolensis*). Regularly-occurring migrants are Red-breasted Flycatcher (*Ficedula parva*), European Scops Owl *(Otus scops)*, Caspian Plover (*Charadrius asiaticus*), Corn Crake (*Crex crex*) and Eurasian Golden Oriole (*Oriolus oriolus*), while others have included Macqueen's Bustard (*Chlamydotis macqueenii*), Shikra (*Accipiter badius*), Levant Sparrowhawk (*Accipiter brevipes*), Egyptian Nightjar (*Caprimulgus aegyptius*), Black-winged Pratincole (*Glareola nordmanni*), Black-headed Bunting (*Emberiza melanocephala*), Pale Rockfinch (*Petronia brachydactyla*) and Rosy Starling (*Sturnus roseus*). In winter Corn Bunting (*Milaria calandra*) and Skylark (*Alauda arvensis*) are regular. Rarer species have included Saker (*Falco cherrug*), Long-eared Owl (*Asio otus*) and Eversmann's Redstart (*Phoenicurus erythronotus*).

(5) Bubiyan and Warba Islands

Large islands in the north-east of Kuwait, next to Iraq. Access requires a permit from Military Intelligence for the main part of Bubiyan Island, and permission from the Kuwait Coastguard for visiting the small islets and Warba Island.

These islands are famous in the ornithological history of Kuwait, having first been visited and studied over one hundred years ago. Regularly-breeding species include Western Reef Egret (*Egretta gularis*), Grey Heron (*Ardea cinerea*), Eurasian Spoonbill (*Platalea leucorodia*), Crab Plover (*Dromas ardeola*), Slender-billed Gull (*Larus genei*), Gull-billed Tern (*Gelochelidon nilotica*), Greater Crested Tern (*Sterna bergii*), Caspian Tern (*Sterna caspia*) and Kentish Plover (*Charadrius alexandrinus*). Other breeding species have included Greater Flamingo (*Phoenicopterus roseus*), Great White Pelican (*Pelecanus onocrotalus*) and Lesser Crested Tern (*Sterna bengalensis*). Saunders's Tern (*Sterna saundersi*), Little Tern (*Sterna albifrons*), Sooty Falcon (*Falco concolor*) and other species may also breed. Many raptors, waders, gull, terns and terrestrial migrants pass across the islands in spring and summer. In winter Pallas's Gull (*Larus ichthyaetus*) is regular and rarer species such as Greylag Goose (*Anser anser*), Great Knot (*Calidris tenuirostris*) and Common Linnet (*Carduelis cannabina*) have been recorded.

(6) Burgan Oil Field

A fenced, large oil field mostly south of Kuwait International Airport and west of Ahmadi. Access is by permit only.

Several species of larks, including Black-crowned Sparrow-lark (*Eremophila nigriceps*), probably breed annually. Little Grebe (*Tachybaptus ruficollis*) is resident on small pools. Many migrants pass through in spring and summer. In winter Macqueen's Bustard

(*Chlamydotis macqueenii*), Stone-Curlew (*Burhinus oedicnemus*), Pin-tailed Sandgrouse (*Pterocles alchata*) and Spotted Sandgrouse (*Pterocles senegallus*) are sometimes present.

(7) Doha Peninsula

An area of harbours, mudflats and sabkha to the west of Kuwait City. This includes North Doha Nature Reserve, access to which requires a permit. Access to the rest of the peninsula is via the Doha Road next to Entertainment City

In winter there are many ducks, gulls, waders and other shorebirds, and Pallas's Gull (*Larus ichthyaetus*), Greater Sand Plover (*Charadrius leschenaultii*), Lesser Sand Plover (*Charadrius mongolus*), Eurasian Spoonbill (*Platalea leucorodia*) and Greater Flamingo (*Phoenicopterus roseus*) are regular, while Great White Pelican (*Pelecanus onocrotalus*) and Merlin (*Falco columbarius*) are occasionally recorded. Long-tailed Skua (*Stercorarius longicaudus*) and Mediterranean Gull (*Larus melanocephalus*) have been recorded here.

(8) East Doha

An area of sabkha, with a sewage stream, a sewage pool, reedbeds and planted trees east of the Doha Road. Graceful Prinia (*Prinia gracilis*), Little Crake (*Porzana parva*), Water Rail (*Rallus aquaticus*) and Common Moorhen (*Gallinula chloropus*) are resident. In summer European Reed Warbler (*Acrocephalus scirpaceus*) and probably other reedbed warblers are present. Wintering birds include Common Stonechat (*Saxicola torquatus*), Bluethroat (*Luscinia svecica*) and Water Pipit (*Anthus spinoletta*). Great White Pelican (*Pelecanus onocrotalus*) and Buff-bellied Pipit (*Anthus rubescens*) have been seen here.

(9) Fahaheel Park and Shore

The town of Fahaheel, south of Kuwait City, has a park and a shore several hundred metres south of the old Fish Market, where there is a car park. Access is open.

The park is used by many migrant species, particularly Eurasian Hoopoe (*Upupa epops*), warblers, Common Redstart (*Phoenicurus phoenicurus*) and Rufous-tailed Scrub Robin (*Cercotricas galactotes*). Wintering species have included European Siskin (*Carduelis spinus*) and Bluethroat (*Luscinia svecica*). Brown-necked Raven (*Corvus ruficollis*) has been recorded.

At low tide, the shore holds many waders, gulls and terns in winter, including Pallas's Gull (*Larus ichthyaetus*) and Lesser Crested Tern (*Sterna bengalensis*). Mediterranean Gull (*Larus melanocephalus*) has been recorded.

(10) Failaka Island

A medium-sized island, northeast of Kuwait City. It is largely deserted at present, but there are plans to redevelop it. Access is by ferry from the terminal at Ras Al-Ardh.

In the gardens of the abandoned houses many migrants can be found, Red-breasted Flycatcher (*Ficedula parva*) is regular and Northern Goshawk (*Accipiter gentilis*) has been recorded. Outside the town Graceful Prinia (*Prinia gracilis*) is usually seen. The beaches near the harbours hold many Pallas's Gulls (*Larus ichthyaetus*) in winter.

From the ferry Arctic Skua (*Stercorarius parasiticus*) and Pomarine Skua (*Stercorarius pomarinus*) can be seen in spring and autumn, and Pallas's Gull (*Larus ichthyaetus*) in winter.

(11) Green Island

An artificial island (actually a peninsula) off eastern Kuwait City, with many trees and bushes. Pedestrian access is by ticket.

Breeding birds include White-eared Bulbul (*Pycnonotus leucogenys*) and Red-vented Bulbul (*Pycnonotus cafer*). Many migrants stop here in spring and autumn, and regularly include Corn Crake (*Crex crex*), Great Reed Warbler (*Acrocephalus arundinaceus*), and Eurasian Golden Oriole (*Oriolus oriolus*). In winter groups of Black-necked Grebe (*Podiceps nigricollis*) can be seen offshore. Calandra Lark (*Melanocorypha calandra*) has been recorded nearby.

(12) Hujaijah

An avenue of trees near recent ruins north of Subiya, visible from the Umm Qasr Road. Access is open.

Although this is a bird-shooting site, many migrants can be seen in spring and autumn, including regular Lesser Kestrel (*Falco naumanni*), Oriental Skylark (*Alauda gulgula*), Rosy Starling (*Sturnus roseus*) and Grey Hypocolius (*Hypocolius ampelinus*). Rarer species that have been seen here are Crested Honey Buzzard (*Pernis ptilorhynchus*), Shikra (*Accipiter badius*), Northern Goshawk (*Accipiter gentilis*), Red-footed Falcon (*Falco vespertinus*) and Greenish Warbler (*Phylloscopus trochiloides*).

(13) Jahra Bay (part of Kuwait Bay)

A shallow bay with mudflats extending from Doha Port to Kadhma. There are various viewpoints accessible via dirt roads off the Jahra Expressway.

Large numbers of shorebirds, especially Greater Flamingo (*Phoenicopterus roseus*), Grey Heron (*Ardea cinerea*), Western Reef Egret (*Egretta gularis*), Great Egret (*Egretta alba*), Crab Plover (*Dromas ardeola*), Caspian Tern (*Sterna caspia*) and Slender-billed Gull (*Larus genei*), feed on the mudflats for most of the year. Many other species of waders, gulls and terns are regularly observed. Caspian Plover (*Charadrius asiaticus*) and Red-necked Phalarope (*Phalaropus lobatus*) are annually seen. Various species of ducks are often found near the shore in the winter. Raptors such as Short-toed Eagle (*Circaetus gallicus*), Osprey (*Pandion haliaetus*), Lesser Kestrel (*Falco naumanni*) and Pallid Harrier (*Circus macrourus*) fly overhead in spring and autumn. Peregrine (*Falco peregrinus*) has been recorded several times. Rarer birds that have been seen here include Greylag Goose (*Anser anser*), Common Crane (*Grus grus*), Ruddy Shelduck (*Tadorna ferruginea*), Spur-winged Lapwing (*Hoplopterus spinosus*), Slender-billed Curlew (*Numenius tenuirostris*), Red Knot (*Calidris canutus*) and Red-breasted Merganser (*Mergus serrator*).

(14) Jahra East Outfall

The most easterly sewage outfall from the Jahra area, near Judailiyat, with reed beds and a marshy area. Access is via dirt roads off the Jahra Expressway.

In summer European Reed Warbler (*Acrocephalus scirpaceus*), Great Reed Warbler (*Acrocephalus arundinaceus*), Common Moorhen (*Gallinula chloropus*) and Little Bittern (*Ixobrychus minutus*) breed here regularly. White-winged Tern (*Chlidonias leucopterus*) has bred several times, Black-crowned Night Heron (*Nycticorax nycticorax*) has bred once, and Water Rail (*Rallus aquaticus*), Graceful Prinia (*Prinia gracilis*), Savi's Warbler (*Locustella luscinioides*), Basra Reed Warbler (*Acrocephalus griseldis*), Clamorous Reed Warbler (*Acrocephalus stentoreus*), Moustached Warbler (*Acrocephalus melanopogon*), Squacco Heron (*Ardeola ralloides*), Little Crake (*Porzana parva*) and Spotted Crake (*Porzana porzana*) are suspected of doing so. Waders on migration include Little Ringed Plover (*Charadrius dubius*), White-tailed Lapwing (*Chettusia leucura*), Caspian Plover (*Charadrius asiaticus*), Wood Sandpiper (*Tringa glareola*) and Temminck's Stint (*Calidris temminckii*). Glossy Ibis (*Plegadis falcinellus*), Rufous-tailed Scrub Robin (*Cercotrichas galactotes*), Common Quail (*Coturnix coturnix*), Corn Crake (*Crex crex*), Collared Pratincole (*Glareola pratincola*) and Black-winged Pratincole (*Glareola nordmanni*) are regular. Rarer species that have been seen here include Pygmy Cormorant (*Phalacrocorax pygmeus*), White Stork (*Ciconia ciconia*), Greylag Goose (*Anser anser*), Rock Martin (*Hirundo fuligula*), Blyth's Pipit (*Anthus godlewskii*), Eurasian Dotterel (*Charadrius morinellus*), Spur-winged Lapwing (*Hoplopterus spinosus*) and Red-wattled Lapwing (*Hoplopterus indicus*).

(15) Jahra Farms

A group of traditional farms situated in the centre of Jahra City. Access to some of them is open but to others requires permission from the owners.

Regularly-breeding birds include Rose-ringed Parakeet (*Psittacula krameri*), White-eared Bulbul *(Pycnonotus leucogenys*), Common Myna (*Acridotheres tristis*), Bank Myna (*Acridotheres ginginianus*) and White-throated Kingfisher (*Halcyon smyrnensis*). Other species that have bred include Eurasian Golden Oriole (*Oriolus oriolus*), Red-vented Bulbul (*Pycnonotus cafer*), Chestnut-shouldered Sparrow (*Petronia xanthocollis*) and Spanish Sparrow (*Passer hispaniolensis*). Many migrants occur in spring and autumn, and these have included Great Snipe (*Gallinago media*), Wood Warbler (*Phylloscopus sibilitrax*), Icterine Warbler (*Hippolais icterina*), Syke's Warbler (*Hippolais rama*), River Warbler (*Locustella fluviatilis*), Thrush Nightingale (*Luscinia luscinia*), Semi-collared Flycatcher (*Ficedula semitorquata*), Pale Rockfinch (*Petronia brachydactyla*) and Basra Reed Warbler (*Acrocephalus griseldis*). Grey Hypocolius (*Hypocolius ampelinus*), Namaqua Dove (*Oena capensis*), Olive-backed Pipit (*Anthus hodgsoni*), and Dark-throated Thrush (*Turdus ruficollis*) are seen almost annually. Citrine Wagtail (*Motacilla citreola*), Common Chaffinch (*Fringilla coelebs*), Brambling (*Fringilla montifringilla*) and European Siskin (*Carduelis spinus*) have been recorded several times. Cattle Egret (*Bubulcus ibis*), Water Pipit (*Anthus spinoletta*) and Red-throated Pipit (*Anthus cervinus*) are present in winter. Rarer species that have been seen here include Desert Finch (*Rhodospiza obsoleta*), Ring Ouzel (*Turdus torquatus*) and Hume's Leaf Warbler (*Phylloscopus humei*).

(16) Jahra Pool Reserve

A fenced nature reserve, managed by the Environment Public Authority, consisting of a sewage outfall with reed beds and a pool surrounded by sabkha. Access is by permit only.

Species proven to have bred include Little Grebe (*Tachybaptus ruficollis*), Purple Swamp-Hen (*Porphyrio porphyrio*), European Reed Warbler (*Acrocephalus scirpaceus*), Rufous-tailed Scrub Robin (*Cercotrichas galactotes*) and Common Moorhen (*Gallinula chloropus*), while Great Reed Warbler (*Acrocephalus arundinaceus*), Basra Reed Warbler (*Acrocephalus griseldis*), Moustached Warbler (*Acrocephalus melanopogon*), Little Bittern (*Ixobrychus minutus*), Little Crake (*Porzana parva*), Water Rail (*Rallus aquaticus*), Spotted Crake (*Porzana porzana*) and Marbled Duck (*Marmaronetta angustirostris*) are suspected to have done so. Ducks, waders, Western Marsh Harrier (*Circus aeruginosus*), other raptors and Eurasian Penduline Tit (*Remiz pendulinus*) are regularly seen. Great White Pelican (*Pelecanus onocrotalus*), Common Crane (*Grus grus*), Macqueen's Bustard (*Chlamydotis macqueenii*), Black-bellied Sandgrouse (*Pterocles orientalis*), Pacific Golden Plover (*Pluvialis fulva*) and Levant Sparrowhawk

(*Accipiter brevipes*) have been observed here. Rarer species recorded here have included Spur-winged Lapwing (*Hoplopterus spinosus*), Fieldfare (*Turdus pilaris*), Common Babbler (*Turdoides caudatus*), Red Phalarope (*Phalaropus fulicaria*), Eurasian Woodcock (*Scolopax rusticola*), Dead Sea Sparrow (*Passer moabiticus*), Winter Wren (*Troglodytes troglodytes*), Dunnock (*Prunella modularis*), Black-throated Accentor (*Prunella atrogularis*), Zitting Cisticola (*Cisticola juncidis*), Greenish Warbler (*Phylloscopus trochiloides*), Mountain Chiffchaff (*Phylloscopus sindianus*), Ferruginous Duck (*Aythya nyroca*), Mute Swan (*Cygnus olor*), Stock Dove (*Columba oenas*), Sooty Falcon (*Falco concolor*) and Black-shouldered Kite (*Elanus caeruleus*).

(17) Jal Az-Zor

A limestone and sandstone escarpment extending from Al-Atraf to near Subiya. Open access points are via a tarmac road to Mutla Repeater Station and via dirt roads to the east of Bahra.

In spring and summer thousands of migratory raptors can be seen overhead, depending on weather conditions. Species regularly observed are Steppe Eagle (*Aquila nipalensis*), Imperial Eagle (*Aquila heliaca*), Greater Spotted Eagle (*Aquila clanga*), European Honey Buzzard (*Pernis apivorus*), Common Buzzard (*Buteo buteo*), Long-legged Buzzard *(Buteo rufinus*), Short-toed Eagle (*Circaetus gallicus*), Eurasian Sparrowhawk (*Accipiter nisus*), Common Kestrel (*Falco tinnunculus*), Lesser Kestrel (*Falco naumanni*), Eurasian Hobby (*Falco subbuteo*), Pallid Harrier (*Circus macrourus*), Western Marsh Harrier (*Circus aeruginosus*), Montagu's Harrier (*Circus pygargus*) and Black Kite (*Milvus migrans*). Less regular species include Levant Sparrowhawk (*Accipiter brevipes*), Lesser Spotted Eagle (*Aquila pomarina*), Egyptian Vulture (*Neophron percnopterus*), Eurasian Griffon Vulture (*Gyps fulvus*) and Hen Harrier (*Circus cyaneus*). Golden Eagle (*Aquila chrysaetos*), Lanner (*Falco biarmicus*) and Eurasian Black Vulture *(Aegypius monachus*) have also been recorded. Other migrant species, for example White Stork (*Ciconia ciconia*), Demoiselle Crane (*Anthropoides virgo*) and Black-winged Pratincole (*Glareola nordmanni*), are occasionally seen flying overhead. In winter Blue Rock Thrush (*Monticola solitarius*), Mourning Wheatear (*Oenanthe lugens*) and Finsch's Wheatear (*Oenanthe finschii*) are regular, and in various seasons White-crowned Wheatear (*Oenanthe leucopyga*), Hooded Wheatear (*Oenanthe monacha*), Kurdish Wheatear (*Oenanthe xanthoprymna*) and Red-tailed Wheatear (*Oenanthe chrysopygia*) have been seen several times.

(18) Jebel Al-Benayah

A low protruding hill near Khiran Town. Access is via dirt roads off the Khiran Road. This hill is a rock-climbing and picnicking site, but is a good viewpoint for migratory birds. Crag Martin (*Hirundo rupestris*), Steppe Eagle (*Aquila clanga*), Pallid Harrier (*Circus macrourus*) and Lesser Kestrel (*Falco naumanni*) have been seen flying overhead, and Kurdish Wheatear (*Oenanthe xanthoprymna*), Ortolan Bunting *(Emberiza hortulana*), Corn Crake (*Crex crex*) and Savi's Warbler (*Locustella luscinioides*) have been observed on the ground.

(19) Kabd (Sulaibiya Agricultural Research Station)

A large, fenced, ungrazed area south of Sulaibiya off the Kabd Road. Access is by permit from the Kuwait Institute for Scientific Research (KISR).

Species breeding on the vegetation-covered ground include Greater Hoopoe Lark (*Alaemon alaudipes*) and Crested Lark (*Galerida cristata*). Other species of lark and

Egyptian Nightjar (*Caprimulgus aegyptius*) have been suspected of doing so. Southern Grey Shrike (*Lanius meridionalis*), Black Redstart (*Phoenicurus ochruros*) and Long-legged Buzzard (*Buteo rufinus*) are regular in winter, and Merlin (*Falco columbarius*), Steppe Eagle (*Aquila nipalensis*), Northern Lapwing (*Vanellus vanellus*), White Stork (*Ciconia ciconia*) and Namaqua Dove (*Oena capensis*) have been recorded.

(20) Kadhmah Gardens (Qaisat)

A former oasis farm, north of Jahra City, with open water pools and wells, now abandoned and used as a picnic site. Access is via dirt road off the Subiya Road.

Many migrants stop here in spring and autumn, particularly warblers. Raptors recorded here include European Honey Buzzard (*Pernis apivorus*), Crested Honey Buzzard (*Pernis ptilorhynchus*), Shikra (*Accipiter badius*), Eurasian Griffon Vulture (*Gyps fulvus*), Egyptian Vulture (*Neophron percnopterus*) and Lesser Spotted Eagle (*Aquila pomarina*). Other species that have been seen are Alpine Swift (*Apus melba*), Crag Martin (*Ptyonoprogne rupestris*), White-tailed Lapwing (*Hoplopterus indicus*), Namaqua Dove (*Oena capensis*) and Little Bunting (*Emberiza pusilla*).

(21) Khor Ala'ma and Khor Al-Mufateh

Muddy inlets either side of Kiran Resort in the south-east of Kuwait. Access is by tarmac roads off the Nuwaisib Road.

Moderate numbers of migrant and wintering waders can be found. Caspian Plover (*Charadrius asiaticus*) is regular. Kentish Plover (*Charadrius alexandrinus*) breeds, and Cream-coloured Courser (*Cursorius cursor*) is often seen.

(22) Kubbar Island

A small sandy island off the south of Kuwait. Access is by small boat, but visitors must avoid disturbing the breeding colonies of terns.

Kubbar Island is historically famous for its colonies of breeding seabirds. Thousands of pairs of Bridled Tern (*Sterna anaethetus*) and White-cheeked Tern (*Sterna repressa*), and hundreds of pairs of Lesser Crested Tern (*Sterna bengalensis*), breed annually. Greater Crested Tern (*Sterna bergii*) used to breed until recently. A pair of House Crows (*Corvus splendens*) has nested on the communication tower. Migrant landbirds often stop on the island in spring and autumn, when Arctic Skua (*Stercorarius parasiticus*), Pomarine Skua (*Stercorarius pomarina*) and Socotra Cormorant (*Phalacrocorax nigrogularis*) can be seen offshore.

(No birds breed now on Qaroh Island and Umm Al-Maradim Island, although Socotra Cormorant (*Phalacrocorax nigrogularis*) and other species bred on both islands a long time ago, but migrant landbirds can sometimes be found on them.)

(23) Municipal Rubbish Tip

A large rubbish tip between Sulaibiya and Amghara, with brackish water pools and sandy banks. Access is by permit only.

In winter many Black Kites (*Milvus migrans*), Black-headed Gulls (*Larus ridibundus*), Caspian Gulls (*Larus cachinnans*) and Lesser Black-backed Gulls (*Larus fuscus*) are present. Sometimes waders, such as Green Sandpiper (*Tringa ochropus*) and Common Redshank (*Tringa totanus*), are found on the pools. Blue-cheeked Bee-eaters (*Merops superciliosus*) have bred in the sandy banks.

(24) Ras Subiya
An area of extensive saltmarshes and sandbars south and southeast of Subiya Power Station. Access is via dirt roads off the Subiya Road.
  Greater Flamingo (*Phoenicopterus roseus*), Grey Heron (*Ardea cinerea*), Western Reef Egret (*Egretta gularis*), waders, gulls and terns are present during most of the year. Osprey (*Pandion haliaetus*) is seen regularly. In winter flocks of Lesser Short-toed Larks (*Calandrella rufescens*) are usually present, and both Greylag Goose (*Anser anser*) and Greater White-fronted Goose (*Anser albifrons*) have been recorded.

(25) Ratqa
An area of semi-desert near the Iraq border, west of Abdali. Access is via dirt roads off the Abdali Road.
  In most winters Macqueen's Bustard (*Chlamydotis macqueenii*), Spotted Sandgrouse (*Pterocles senegallus*), Pin-tailed Sandgrouse (*Pterocles alchata*), Black-bellied Sandgrouse (*Pterocles orientalis*) and Stone-Curlew (*Burhinus oedicnemus*) are present, but most are shot, resulting in declining numbers. Other species recorded include Greylag Goose (*Anser anser*), Common Crane (*Grus grus*), Chestnut-bellied Sandgrouse (*Pterocles exustus*) and Thick-billed Lark (*Rhamphocoris clotbey*). Merlin (*Falco columbarius*) and Yellowhammer (*Emberiza citrinella*) have been seen nearby.

(26) Rawdatain
An oasis with a water-collection point south of Abdali, just west of the Basra Road. Access is open.
  The small trees and reeds attract migrants such as Corn Crake (*Crex crex*), Basra Reed Warbler (*Acrocephalus griseldis*) and Clamorous Reed Warbler (*Acrocephalus stentoreus*) in spring and autumn. Common Woodpigeon (*Columba palumbus*) is almost annual in spring. Shikra (*Accipiter badius*) and Oriental Turtle Dove (*Streptopelia orientalis*) have been recorded.

(27) Sabah Al-Ahmed Natural Reserve (formerly the National Park)
A 320 km^2 nature reserve to the north of Jahra City, on both sides of the Subiya Road. Access is by permit only. The north-western section contains a long stretch of the Jal Az-Zor escarpment, a series of small wadis including Wadi Ar-Rimam, an isolated group of trees at Tulha, and a large area of regenerating semi-desert. The south-eastern section consists of part of the shoreline of Jahra Bay, sabkha, areas of bushes, and another large area of regenerating semi-desert.
  Along the escarpment and in the wadis Little Owl (*Athene noctua*) breeds annually, Brown-necked Raven (*Corvus ruficollis*) and Eurasian Eagle Owl (*Bubo bubo*) have bred, and Trumpeter Finch (*Bucanetes githagineus*) is resident. Larks found regularly on the flat areas include Black-crowned Sparrow-lark (*Eremopterix nigriceps*), Greater Short-toed Lark (*Calandrella brachydactyla*), Lesser Short-toed Lark (*Calandrella rufescens*), Crested Lark (*Galerida cristata*), Greater Hoopoe Lark (*Alaemon alaudipes*), Desert Lark (*Ammomanes deserti*), Bar-tailed Lark (*Ammomanes cincturus*), Dunn's Lark (*Eremalauda dunni*), Temminck's Lark (*Eremophila bilopha*), Bimaculated Lark (*Melanocorypha bimaculata*), Eurasian Skylark (*Alauda arvensis*) and Oriental Skylark (*Alauda gulgula*). Many of these species definitely or probably breed. Spanish Sparrow (*Passer hispaniolensis*), Chestnut-shouldered Sparrow (*Petronia xanthocollis*) and Woodchat Shrike (*Lanius senator*) have bred in the trees at Tulha. In spring and autumn many migrant species stop in the reserve. Steppe Eagle (*Aquila nipalensis*), Greater Spotted Eagle (*Aquila clanga*), Imperial Eagle (*Aquila heliaca*), Short-toed

Eagle (*Circaetus gallicus*), Pallid Harrier (*Circus macrourus*), Montagu's Harrier (*Circus pygargus*), Lesser Kestrel (*Falco naumanni*), European Honey Buzzard (*Pernis apivorus*), European Scops Owl (*Otus scops*), Black-winged Pratincole (*Glareola nordmanni*), Collared Pratincole (*Glareola pratincola*), European Nightjar (*Caprimulgus europaeus*), Egyptian Nightjar (*Caprimulgus aegyptius*), Shikra (*Accipiter badius*), Ortolan Bunting (*Emberiza hortulana*), Cinereous Bunting (*Emberiza cineracea*) and Eastern Orphean Warbler (*Sylvia crassirostris*) are regular. Alpine Swift (*Apus melba*), Eurasian Griffon Vulture (*Gyps fulvus*), Bonelli's Eagle (*Hieraaetus fasciatus*), Northern Goshawk (*Accipiter gentilis*), Black-headed Bunting (*Emberiza melanocephala*), Common Rosefinch (*Carpodacus erythrinus*), Namaqua Dove (*Oena capensis*), Caspian Plover (*Charadrius asiaticus*), Red-wattled Lapwing (*Hoplopterus indicus*), Indian Silverbill (*Lonchura malabarica*) and Grey Hypocolius (*Hypocolius ampelinus*) are occasionally recorded. Rarer species that have been seen include Black Francolin (*Francolinus francolinus*), Great Spotted Cuckoo (*Clamator glandarius*), Stock Dove (*Columba oenas*), Greenish Warbler (*Phylloscopus trochiloides*), Desert Finch (*Rhodospiza obsoleta*), Hume's Wheatear (*Oenanthe alboniger*) and Red-headed Bunting (*Emberiza briniceps*). In winter there are many ducks present by the shore, several Long-legged Buzzards (*Buteo rufinus*) are usually present, Ménétries's Warbler (*Sylvia mystacea*) and Asian Desert Warbler (*Sylvia nana*) are regular, and Eurasian Dotterel (*Charadrius morinellus*) has been recorded.

(28) Sabah Al-Salem

An area of sabkha, a reed-fringed saline pool, two sewage-water pools, reed beds and bushes to the west of the Fahaheel Road opposite Messila, south of Kuwait City. Access is open.

Waders on the saline pool and sewage-water pools regularly include Broad-billed Sandpiper (*Limicola falcinellus*), Dunlin (*Calidris alpina*), Little Stint (*Calidris minuta*), Temminck's Stint (*Calidris temminckii*), Common Redshank (*Tringa totanus*), Spotted Redshank (*Tringa erythropus*), Common Greenshank (*Tringa nebularia*), Terek Sandpiper (*Xenus cinereus*), Wood Sandpiper (*Tringa glareola*), Green Sandpiper (*Tringa ochropus*), Common Sandpiper (*Actitis hypoleucos*), Marsh Sandpiper (*Tringa stagnatilis*), Ruff (*Philomachus pugnax*), Ruddy Turnstone (*Arenaria interpres*), Black-winged Stilt (*Himantopus himantopus*), Common Ringed Plover (*Charadrius hiaticula*), Little Ringed Plover (*Charadrius dubius*), Eurasian Curlew (*Numenius arquata*), Whimbrel (*Numenius phaeopus*), Kentish Plover (*Charadrius alexandrinus*) (which breeds regularly), Lesser Sand Plover (*Charadrius mongolus*) and Greater Sand Plover (*Charadrius leschenaultii*) (which has bred at least twice). Other species that have been observed on or over the saline pool include Glossy Ibis (*Plegadis falcinellus*), Little Gull (*Larus minutus*), Caspian Tern (*Sterna caspia*), Marbled Duck (*Marmaronetta angustirostris*), Whiskered Tern (*Chlidonias hybridus*), White-winged Tern (*Chlidonias leucopterus*), Peregrine (*Falco peregrinus*), Grey Heron (*Ardea cinerea*), and several species of gull. On the drier sabkha areas Common Quail (*Coturnix coturnix*), Corn Crake (*Crex crex*), Stone-Curlew (*Burhinus oedicnemus*), European Nightjar (*Caprimulgus europaeus*), Egyptian Nightjar (*Caprimulgus aegyptius*), Eurasian Skylark (*Alauda arvensis*), Oriental Skylark (*Alauda gulgula*), Tawny Pipit (*Anthus campestris*) and Ortolan Bunting (*Emberiza hortulana*) are regular on migration or in winter, and Chestnut-bellied Sandgrouse (*Pterocles exustus*) has been seen. Richard's Pipit (*Anthus richardi*), Dunnock (*Prunella modularis*) and Eversmann's Redstart (*Phoenicurus erythronotus*) have been recorded in nearby bushy areas.

Species known or suspected to breed in the reed beds and bushes next to the sewage-water pools include Little Bittern (*Ixobrychus minutus*), Squacco Heron (*Ardeola ralloides*), Little Crake (*Porzana parva*), Spotted Crake (*Porzana porzana*), Common Moorhen (*Gallinula chloropus*), Common Coot (*Fulica atra*), Water Rail (*Rallus aquaticus*), Namaqua Dove (*Oena capensis*), Moustached Warbler (*Acrocephalus melanopogon*), European Reed Warbler (*Acrocephalus scirpaceus*), Basra Reed Warbler (*Acrocephalus griseldis*), Great Reed Warbler (*Acrocephalus arundinaceus*), Rufous-tailed Scrub Robin (*Cercotrichas galactotes*), Indian Silverbill (*Lonchura malabarica*) and Streaked Weaver (*Ploceus manyar*). In these areas in autumn, winter and spring Little Egret (*Egretta garzetta*), Red-throated Pipit (*Anthus cervinus*), Water Pipit (*Anthus spinoletta*), Bluethroat (*Luscinia svecica*), European Robin (*Erithacus rubecula*), Song Thrush (*Turdus philomelos*), Eurasian Penduline Tit (*Remiz pendulinus*) and many shrikes are regularly seen. Northern Goshawk (*Accipiter gentilis*), Eurasian Woodcock (*Scolopax rusticola*), Great Bittern (*Botaurus stellaris*), Purple Swamp-Hen (*Porphyrio porphyrio*), Citrine Wagtail (*Motacilla citreola*), Winter Wren (*Troglodytes troglodytes*), Mountain Chiffchaff (*Phylloscopus sindianus*), Cetti's Warbler (*Cettia cetti*) and Syke's Warbler (*Sylvia rama*) have been recorded.

(29) Sewer Plant Reeds

A treated sewage-water outflow with a surrounding reed bed and pool, adjacent to the Zour road junction on the Nuwaisib Road. Access is via tarmac and dirt roads from the Nuwaisib Road.

In spring and summer Little Bittern (*Ixobrychus minutus*), Squacco Heron (*Ardeola ralloides*), Little Crake (*Porzana parva*), Common Moorhen (*Gallinula chloropus*), Black-crowned Sparrow-lark (*Eremopterix nigriceps*), European Reed Warbler (*Acrocephalus scirpaceus*), Great Reed Warbler (*Acrocephalus arundinaceus*), Clamorous Reed Warbler (*Acrocephalus stentoreus*), Basra Reed Warbler (*Acrocephalus griseldis*) and Graceful Prinia (*Prinia gracilis*) are present, and most of these species breed. Migrants include Great Bittern (*Botaurus stellaris*), Purple Heron (*Ardea purpurea*), Little Egret (*Egretta garzetta*), Montagu's Harrier (*Circus pygargus*), Western Marsh Harrier (*Circus aeruginosus*), Black-winged Stilt (*Himantopus himantopus*), Little Ringed Plover (*Charadrius dubius*), Corn Crake (*Crex crex*) and Common Quail (*Coturnix coturnix*). Citrine Wagtail (*Motacilla citreola*) has been recorded several times.

(Another small area of reeds and trees, called Power Plant Reeds, near Zour Power Station, sometimes holds migrants in spring and autumn.)

(30) South Doha Nature Reserve

An area of sabkha, scrub and artificial freshwater pools to the north of the Jahra Expressway. Access is by permit only.

Breeding species probably include European Reed Warbler (*Acrocephalus scirpaceus*), Great Reed Warbler (*Acrocephalus arundinaceus*) and Common Moorhen (*Gallinula chloropus*), while Common Coot (*Fulica atra*), Basra Reed Warbler (*Acrocephalus griseldis*), Clamorous Reed Warbler (*Acrocephalus stentoreus*) and Moustached Warbler (*Acrocephalus melanopogon*) possibly breed. In winter, ducks are sometimes found. A group of Purple Swamp-Hens (*Porphyrio porphyrio*) has become resident recently.

(31) Sulaibikhat Bay (part of Kuwait Bay)

A shallow bay with mudflats extending from Shuwaikh Port to the Doha Peninsula. There are various viewpoints accessible via car parks and dirt roads off Abu Dhabi Street.

Species here are similar to those in Jahra Bay. Large numbers of shorebirds, especially Greater Flamingo (*Phoenicopterus roseus*), Grey Heron (*Ardea cinerea*), Western Reef Egret (*Egretta gularis*), Great Egret (*Egretta alba*), Crab Plover (*Dromas ardeola*), Caspian Tern (*Sterna caspia*) and Slender-billed Gull *(Larus genei)*, feed on the mudflats. Many other species of waders, gulls and terns are regularly observed. Various species of ducks, especially Common Shelduck (*Tadorna tadorna*), are often found near the shore in the winter. Raptors such as Short-toed Eagle (*Circaetus gallicus*), Osprey (*Pandion haliaetus*), Lesser Kestrel (*Falco naumanni*) and Pallid Harrier (*Circus macrourus*) fly overhead in spring and autumn. White-throated Kingfisher (*Halcyon smyrnensis*) has bred. Rarer birds that have been seen here include Sacred Ibis (*Threskiornis aethiopicus*) and Ruddy Shelduck (*Tadorna ferruginea*).

(32) Sulaibikhat Nature Reserve

A small reserve, managed by the Kuwait Environment Protection Society (KEPS), along the shore of Sulaibikhat Bay just north of the Ministry of Health. Access is by permit only.

Species here are similar to those in Sulaibikhat Bay, and many of them roost on the land at high tide. In addition, the trees, bushes, ground vegetation and artificial freshwater pools attract many migrants in spring and summer, including regular Eastern Orphean Warbler (*Sylvia crassirostris*), Ménétries's Warbler (*Sylvia mystacea*), Semi-collared Flycatcher (*Ficedula semitorquata*), White-throated Robin (*Irania gutturalis*), Rufous-tailed Scrub Robin (*Cercotrichas galactotes*), Eurasian Wryneck (*Jynx torquilla*) and Squacco Heron (*Ardeola ralloides*). Kentish Plover (*Charadrius alexandrinus*), Graceful Prinia (*Prinia gracilis*) and White-eared Bulbul (*Pycnonotus leucogenys*) breed. A flock of up to one hundred Cream-coloured Coursers (*Cursorius cursor*) was present once. White-crowned Wheatear (*Oenanthe leucopygia*), Syke's Warbler (*Hippolais rama*) and Pale Rockfinch (*Petronia brachydactyla*) have been recorded.

(33) Umm Al-Aish Camp

An oil camp in the Rawdatain Oil Field, south of Abdali. Access, via a tarmac road off the Basra Road, is by permit only.

In spring and autumn many migrants stop in the bushes and trees in the camp. These usually include European Scops Owl *(Otus scops)*, Eurasian Wryneck (*Jynx torquilla*), White-throated Robin (*Irania gutturalis*), Common Grasshopper Warbler (*Locustella naevia*), Great Reed Warbler (*Acrocephalus arundinaceus*), Clamorous Reed Warbler (*Acrocephalus stentoreus*), Basra Reed Warbler (*Acrocephalus griseldis*), River Warbler (*Locustella fluviatilis*), Savi's Warbler (*Locustella luscinioides*), Semi-collared Flycatcher (*Ficedula semitorquata*), Chestnut-shouldered Sparrow (*Petronia xanthocollis*) and Common Rosefinch (*Carpodacus erythrinus*). Oriental Turtle Dove (*Streptopelia orientalis*), Long-eared Owl (*Asio otus*), Mistle Thrush (*Turdus viscivorus*), Cetti's Warbler (*Cettia cetti*), Olive-tree Warbler (*Hippolais olivetorum*) and Yellow-browed Warbler (*Phylloscopus inornatus*) have been recorded.

(34) Wadi Al-Batin

An internally-draining wadi forming the northwestern border with Iraq. Access is via dirt roads off the Salmi Road, but permission from the Kuwait Army or Kuwait Police is necessary.

Eurasian Eagle Owl (*Bubo bubo*) and Little Owl (*Athene noctua*) breed in the rocky sides of the wadi. In winter and spring Desert Lark (*Ammomanes deserti*), Bar-tailed Lark (*Ammomanes cinctorus*), Temminck's Lark (*Eremophila bilopha*) and Trumpeter Finch (*Bucanetes githagineus*) are often found, and probably breed in most years.

Thick-billed Lark (*Ramphocoris clotbey*) and Pale Rockfinch (*Petronia brachydactyla*) are sometimes observed.

(35) Wafra Farms

A large area of traditional farms on the southern border with Saudi Arabia. Access to individual farms is by private agreement with the owners.

Black-crowned Sparrow-lark (*Eremopterix nigriceps*) and White-eared Bulbul (*Pycnonotus leucogenys*) breed annually, and Blue-cheeked Bee-eater (*Merops persicus*) has bred. Migrants such as Basra Reed Warbler (*Acrocephalus griseldis*) and Egyptian Nightjar (*Caprimulgus aegyptius*) are regular. White-throated Kingfisher (*Halcyon smyrnensis*) usually occurs in winter.

(36) Wafra Oil Field

An oil field in the south of Kuwait, mostly northwest of Wafra Farms. Access is by permit only.

Several species of larks, including Black-crowned Sparrow-lark (*Eremopterix nigriceps*), breed annually. Many migrants pass through in spring and summer. Ring Ouzel (*Turdus torquatus*) and Greenish Warbler (*Phylloscopus trochiloides*) have been recorded.

(37) Zour Port

A fenced oil terminal with residences at Zour, on the Gulf south of Fahaheel. There are bushes, trees and a golf course on the land, and sand bars exposed at low tide offshore. Access is by permit only.

Chestnut-shouldered Sparrow (*Petronia xanthocollis*) breeds annually, Indian Silverbill (*Lonchura malabarica*) is often found and Common Babbler (*Turdoides caudatus*) was resident until recently. Many migrants stop here in spring and autumn, and Rosy Starling (*Sturnus roseus*), Grey Hypocolius (*Hypocolius ampelinus*), Eurasian Wryneck (*Jynx torquilla*), European Scops Owl (*Otus scops*), European Nightjar (*Caprimulgus europaeus*), Egyptian Nightjar (*Caprimulgus aegyptius*), Corn Crake (*Crex crex*), Common Quail (*Coturnix coturnix*) and Osprey (*Pandion haliaetus*) are regular. Socotra Cormorant (*Phalacrocorax nigrogularis*) is usually present offshore from March to September. Many terns, especially Lesser Crested Tern (*Sterna bengalensis*), Greater Crested Tern (*Sterna bergii*), White-cheeked Tern (*Sterna repressa*) and Caspian Tern (*Sterna caspia*), are present during most of the year. Alpine Swift (*Apus melba*), Little Bunting (*Emberiza pusilla*), Black-headed Bunting (*Emberiza melanocephala*), Red-headed Bunting (*Emberiza bruniceps*) and Trumpeter Finch (*Bucanetes githagineus*) have been recorded.

Channel (khor) at Bubiyan Island

Halophyte-covered banks of channel (khor) on Bubiyan Island

Sandy bank with nesting burrows of Crab Plover (*Dromas ardeola*) on Bubiyan Island

Low bank with *Suaeda* and nests of Western Reef Egret (*Egretta gularis*) and Grey Heron (*Ardea cinerea*) on Bubiyan Island

Saltmarsh at Ras Subiya

Beach and mudflats at Sulaibikhat Bay

Covered landfill and storm drain outlet at Sulaibikhat Bay

Sewage outflow and reeds at Jahra East Outfall

Shallow sewage pool at East Doha

Shallow sewage pool and reeds at Jahra East Outfall

Small reedbeds at East Doha

Evidence of over-hunting at East Doha

Brackish pool and regenerating reedbeds at Jahra Pool Reserve

Flooded sabkha and dry reedbed at North Doha Nature Reserve

Artificial freshwater pools with reeds at South Doha Nature Reserve

Interior of traditional well at Jahra Farms

Large irrigated plots and shelter belts at Abdali Farms

Planted Tamarisk trees near Jahra

Small irrigated plots and Date Palms at Jahra Farms

Lines of Date Palms at Abdali Farms

Isolated trees at Tulha in Sabah Al-Ahmed Natural Reserve

Bed of Dwarf Irises near Jebel Benayeh

Overgrazed desert near Subiya

Regenerating desert at Wadi Al-Batin

Small rocky outcrop at Jabel Al-Benayeh

Escarpment at Jal Az-Zor

Escarpment wadi at Sabah Al-Ahmed Natural Reserve

Escarpment wadi with spring flowers at Sabah Al-Ahmed Natural Reserve

Basin wadi cliff calving boulders at Wadi Ar-Rimam in the Sabah Al-Ahmed Natural Reserve

Basin wadi leading into basin at Wadi Ar-Rimam in the Sabah Al-Ahmed Natural Reserve

PROTECTION OF BIRDS IN KUWAIT

Efforts are being made in Kuwait to reduce the threats to birds, by organisations such as the Environment Public Authority (EPA), the Public Authority for Agricultural Affairs and Fish Resources (PAAAFR), the Voluntary Work Centre (VWC), the Kuwait Institute for Scientific Research (KISR) and the Kuwait Environment Protection Society (KEPS), one of whose constituent bodies, the Bird Monitoring and Protection Team (BMAPT), is actively and directly involved. Measures taken by these birds to conserve birdlife in Kuwait include:
(1) Limiting grazing to certain parts of the state.
(2) Establishing nature reserves in which grazing, hunting and disturbance are prevented.
(3) Greater enforcement of anti-hunting laws.
(4) Public education.
(5) Environmental clean-up operations.

So far, these measures have had some effect, but much remains to be done. Many Kuwaitis are now very aware of the need for protect not only birds, but also all of the natural environment. However, there are still many who are involved in their unnecessary destruction. It is hoped that this book will contribute to a better appreciation of birds and of the desirability of their conservation.

IMPORTANT ASPECTS OF KUWAIT'S BIRDLIFE

Kuwait is situated in the south-eastern corner of the Western Palearctic Avifaunal Region and many bird species regularly occurring in Kuwait cannot be seen easily elsewhere in this region. These include Socotra Cormorant (*Phalacrocorax nigrogularis*), Shikra (*Accipiter badius*), Crab Plover (*Dromas ardeola*), Pacific Golden Plover (*Pluvialis fulva*), Lesser Sand Plover (*Charadrius mongolus*), Caspian Plover (*Charadrius asiaticus*), Red-wattled Plover (*Hoplopterus indicus*), Great Knot (*Calidris tenuirostris*), Terek Sandpiper (*Xenus cinereus*), Saunders's Tern (*Sterna saundersi*), Indian Roller (*Coracias benghalensis*), Black-crowned Sparrow-lark (*Eremopterix nigriceps*), White-eared Bulbul (*Pycnonotus leucogenys*), Red-vented Bulbul (*Pycnonotus cafer*), Grey Hypocolius (*Hypocolius ampelinus*), Kurdish Wheatear (*Oenanthe xanthoprymna*), Red-tailed Wheatear (*Oenanthe chrysopygia*), Basra Reed Warbler (*Acrocephalus griseldis*), Syke's Warbler (*Hippolais rama*), Hume's Lesser Whitethroat (*Sylvia curruca althaea*), Desert Lesser Whitethroat (*Sylvia curruca minula*), Common Mynah (*Acridotheres tristis*), Bank Mynah (*Acridotheres ginginianus*), Isabelline Shrike (*Lanius isabellinus*), Steppe Grey Shrike (*Lanius meridionalis pallidirostris*) and Chestnut-shouldered Sparrow (*Petronia xanthocollis*).

Kuwait is also situated in the north-eastern corner of the Arabian peninsula, and many bird species have bred in Kuwait and nowhere else, or almost nowhere else, in the peninsula. These include Great White Pelican (*Pelecanus onocrotalus*), Grey Heron (*Ardea cinerea*), Greater Flamingo (*Phoenicopterus roseus*), Greater Sand Plover (*Charadrius leschenaultii*), Slender-billed Gull (*Larus genei*), Gull-billed Tern (*Gelochelidon nilotica*), White-winged Tern (*Chlidonias leucopterus*), Little Crake (*Porzana parva*), Purple Swamp-Hen (*Porphyrio porphyrio*), White-throated Kingfisher (*Halcyon smyrnensis*), Bimaculated Lark (*Melanocorypha bimaculata*) and Woodchat Shrike (*Lanius senator*).

The breeding population of Crab Plover (*Dromas ardeola*) on Bubiyan Island is probably the biggest in the world.

Several very rare bird species for the Western Palearctic avifaunal region have been recorded in Kuwait, including Sacred Ibis (*Threskiornis aethiopicus*), Slender-billed Curlew (*Numenius tenuirostris*), Chestnut-bellied Sandgrouse (*Pterocles exustus*) and Oriental Reed Warbler (*Acrocephalus orientalis*).

THE KUWAIT BIRD LIST

The Kuwait Bird List has been divided into:
(a) The Main List of Species of Birds,
(b) The Species of Birds of Captive Origin, and
(c) The Species of Birds Requiring Confirmation.

(a) THE MAIN LIST OF SPECIES OF BIRDS

The Main List of Species of Birds comprises those species of birds which are judged beyond reasonable doubt to have occurred in a wild state, or those species of birds originally of captive origin which have subsequently become established, in Kuwait.

SEASONAL STATUS:

The seasonal status of each species is judged to be one of the following categories:

Abundant: occurs annually in very large numbers (10,000+).

Very Common: occurs annually in large numbers (1,000 - 9,999).

Common: occurs annually in moderate numbers (100 - 999).

Uncommon: occurs annually in small numbers (10 - 99).

Scarce: occurs annually in very small numbers (1 - 9).

Rare: does not occur annually but has occurred more than 10 times in total.

Vagrant: has occurred less than 10 times in total.

Irregular: occurs, not necessarily every year, in very variable numbers.

Extinct: no longer exists.

SUBSPECIES:
The very difficult issue of subspecific identification is mostly only attempted for a few species which may be split in the near future.

STATISTICS:
In order to minimise bias due to uneven coverage, the highest daily count in each time period during the seven years from 1 July 1998 to 30 June 2005 is presented for all species except those that are entirely resident in Kuwait, those that are vagrant and those with no records during the seven years.

SPECIES:

Mute Swan *(Cygnus olor)*
Status: Vagrant (one record).
An immature bird, which was slightly oiled, was photographed at Jahra Pool Reserve by M. Al-Jraiwi in November 1997 (exact day unstated). The bird in the photograph clearly shows an immature swan with slightly off-white plumage, and a small knob at the base of the fairly dark bill (Al-Jraiwi, 1999).

Greater White-fronted Goose *(Anser albifrons)*
Status: Vagrant (at least one record).
 A description of a bird seen by L. Corrall at Jahra Pool Reserve on 22 December 1978 was written on a Rare Bird Report form, but the panel regarded it as inconclusive as to species. On 5 February 2005 G. Gregory saw a group of three birds fly west over Ras Subiya onto Bubiyan Island. He noted typical *Anser* shape, quite large size, strong blackish barring on the belly, white behind bill not noticeably extending backwards, and absence of an eye-ring.
 Local hunters have occasionally reported shooting this species in the area of Kuwait Bay in the winter. Using their own field guides, some of them distinguished the dead birds from Lesser White-fronted Goose (*A. erythropus*).

Greylag Goose *(Anser anser)*
Status: Rare winter visitor.
 Although not seen every year, this species has been recorded at numerous localities, including the coastal sites of Jahra East Outfall, Jahra Bay, Sulaibikhat Bay, Qaisat, Ahmadi, Ras Subiya, Bubiyan Island and Qaroh Island, mostly from November to March. There is one inland record of a bird shot and photographed by Kuwaiti hunters at Ratqa on 17 November 2001. Several other Kuwaiti hunters have reported shooting this species. The highest daily count is three seen on several occasions.

JAN 1-10	JAN 11-20	JAN 21-31	FEB 1-10	FEB 11-20	FEB 21-29	MAR 1-10	MAR 11-20	MAR 21-31	APR 1-10	APR 11-20	APR 21-30	MAY 1-10	MAY 11-20	MAY 21-31	JUN 1-10	JUN 11-20	JUN 21-30	JUL 1-10	JUL 11-20	JUL 21-31	AUG 1-10	AUG 11-20	AUG 21-31	SEP 1-10	SEP 11-20	SEP 21-30	OCT 1-10	OCT 11-20	OCT 21-31	NOV 1-10	NOV 11-20	NOV 21-30	DEC 1-10	DEC 11-20	DEC 21-31
3						1																							1	3					3

Ruddy Shelduck *(Tadorna ferruginea)*
Status: Rare winter visitor. Rare passage migrant.
 The first known record was a female seen by P. R. Haynes at Ras Al-Ardh from 5-8 August 1973. This observer stated that there was at least one other reliable summer record (Warr, undated), but details are not accessible. Recently this species has been seen almost every year, mostly at Jahra Bay and Sulaibikhat Bay, usually from November to April. The highest daily count is three seen by P. Fagel, B. Foster and G. Gregory at East Doha from 3 to 17 March 2005.

JAN 1-10	JAN 11-20	JAN 21-31	FEB 1-10	FEB 11-20	FEB 21-29	MAR 1-10	MAR 11-20	MAR 21-31	APR 1-10	APR 11-20	APR 21-30	MAY 1-10	MAY 11-20	MAY 21-31	JUN 1-10	JUN 11-20	JUN 21-30	JUL 1-10	JUL 11-20	JUL 21-31	AUG 1-10	AUG 11-20	AUG 21-31	SEP 1-10	SEP 11-20	SEP 21-30	OCT 1-10	OCT 11-20	OCT 21-31	NOV 1-10	NOV 11-20	NOV 21-30	DEC 1-10	DEC 11-20	DEC 21-31
1						3	3		2			2	1																	1					

Common Shelduck *(Tadorna tadorna)*
Status: Common winter visitor. Uncommon passage migrant.

Most birds seen in Kuwait have been at Sulaibikhat Bay and Jahra Bay. There is a scattering of records from the Gulf coast. There is one inland record of a bird seen by R. P. Blacker at Ahmadi on 21 April 1972. The highest count is 208 seen by S. T. Spencer from Sulaibikhat Bay to Jahra Bay on 1 January 2002.

JAN 1-10	JAN 11-20	JAN 21-31	FEB 1-10	FEB 11-20	FEB 21-29	MAR 1-10	MAR 11-20	MAR 21-31	APR 1-10	APR 11-20	APR 21-30	MAY 1-10	MAY 11-20	MAY 21-31	JUN 1-10	JUN 11-20	JUN 21-30	JUL 1-10	JUL 11-20	JUL 21-31	AUG 1-10	AUG 11-20	AUG 21-31	SEP 1-10	SEP 11-20	SEP 21-30	OCT 1-10	OCT 11-20	OCT 21-31	NOV 1-10	NOV 11-20	NOV 21-30	DEC 1-10	DEC 11-20	DEC 21-31
208	146	120	130	200	75	30	76	12	7	2		2	2	2		1	1									3			1	5	48	18	110	25	

Eurasian Wigeon *(Anas penelope)*
Status: Uncommon winter visitor. Uncommon passage migrant.

This species is most frequently observed at Jahra Bay and Sulaibikhat Bay. There are records from a number of other locations along the Gulf coast and from sewage-water and saline pools. The highest count is 300 seen between 1981 and 1993 (Pilcher, undated) but exact locations and dates are not accessible. During this period there was an apparently major increase in the numbers of many species of ducks in Kuwait, probably related to the destruction of marshland in southern Iraq. These numbers seem to have declined significantly in recent years.

JAN 1-10	JAN 11-20	JAN 21-31	FEB 1-10	FEB 11-20	FEB 21-29	MAR 1-10	MAR 11-20	MAR 21-31	APR 1-10	APR 11-20	APR 21-30	MAY 1-10	MAY 11-20	MAY 21-31	JUN 1-10	JUN 11-20	JUN 21-30	JUL 1-10	JUL 11-20	JUL 21-31	AUG 1-10	AUG 11-20	AUG 21-31	SEP 1-10	SEP 11-20	SEP 21-30	OCT 1-10	OCT 11-20	OCT 21-31	NOV 1-10	NOV 11-20	NOV 21-30	DEC 1-10	DEC 11-20	DEC 21-31
40		35	32			8	5	12	2	1		2	1													22		11		1	20		2		

Gadwall *(Anas strepera)*
Status: Uncommon passage migrant. Scarce winter visitor.

Gadwall has mostly been recorded at Jahra Bay and at Jahra Pool Reserve, with a scattering of records elsewhere along the coastline and on other pools. The highest count is 50 seen between 1981 and 1993 (Pilcher, undated) but exact locations and dates are not accessible.

JAN 1-10	JAN 11-20	JAN 21-31	FEB 1-10	FEB 11-20	FEB 21-29	MAR 1-10	MAR 11-20	MAR 21-31	APR 1-10	APR 11-20	APR 21-30	MAY 1-10	MAY 11-20	MAY 21-31	JUN 1-10	JUN 11-20	JUN 21-30	JUL 1-10	JUL 11-20	JUL 21-31	AUG 1-10	AUG 11-20	AUG 21-31	SEP 1-10	SEP 11-20	SEP 21-30	OCT 1-10	OCT 11-20	OCT 21-31	NOV 1-10	NOV 11-20	NOV 21-30	DEC 1-10	DEC 11-20	DEC 21-31
2			1	1	1																					2		1			12	2	1		

Common Teal *(Anas crecca)*
Status: Common passage migrant. Scarce winter visitor.

This species has been seen inland at Ahmadi, Burgan Oil Field and Abdali, as well as around the coastline and on pools. The highest count is 500 seen between 1981 and 1993 (Pilcher, undated) but exact locations and dates are not accessible.

JAN 1-10	JAN 11-20	JAN 21-31	FEB 1-10	FEB 11-20	FEB 21-29	MAR 1-10	MAR 11-20	MAR 21-31	APR 1-10	APR 11-20	APR 21-30	MAY 1-10	MAY 11-20	MAY 21-31	JUN 1-10	JUN 11-20	JUN 21-30	JUL 1-10	JUL 11-20	JUL 21-31	AUG 1-10	AUG 11-20	AUG 21-31	SEP 1-10	SEP 11-20	SEP 21-30	OCT 1-10	OCT 11-20	OCT 21-31	NOV 1-10	NOV 11-20	NOV 21-30	DEC 1-10	DEC 11-20	DEC 21-31
5	1	2	150	6	1		28																	7	3	3	6			8	2		1		3

Mallard *(Anas platyrhynchos)*
Status: Uncommon passage migrant. Scarce winter visitor.

Mallard has mostly been observed at Jahra Pool Reserve, South Doha Nature Reserve and at Jahra Bay. There are a few records elsewhere along the coastline and on other pools. The highest count is 53 seen by G. Rowlands at Sulaibikhat Bay on 10 February 2000.

JAN 1-10	JAN 11-20	JAN 21-31	FEB 1-10	FEB 11-20	FEB 21-29	MAR 1-10	MAR 11-20	MAR 21-31	APR 1-10	APR 11-20	APR 21-30	MAY 1-10	MAY 11-20	MAY 21-31	JUN 1-10	JUN 11-20	JUN 21-30	JUL 1-10	JUL 11-20	JUL 21-31	AUG 1-10	AUG 11-20	AUG 21-31	SEP 1-10	SEP 11-20	SEP 21-30	OCT 1-10	OCT 11-20	OCT 21-31	NOV 1-10	NOV 11-20	NOV 21-30	DEC 1-10	DEC 11-20	DEC 21-31
2	9	53	2	3		15	7		1		1							9									1		8			14		30	6

Northern Pintail *(Anas acuta)*
Status: Uncommon passage migrant. Uncommon winter visitor.

This species has mostly been observed at Jahra Bay and at Jahra Pool Reserve. Generally small numbers of birds have been seen on other pools and elsewhere along the coastline. The highest count is 150 seen between 1981 and 1993 (Pilcher, undated) but exact locations and dates are not accessible.

JAN 1-10	JAN 11-20	JAN 21-31	FEB 1-10	FEB 11-20	FEB 21-29	MAR 1-10	MAR 11-20	MAR 21-31	APR 1-10	APR 11-20	APR 21-30	MAY 1-10	MAY 11-20	MAY 21-31	JUN 1-10	JUN 11-20	JUN 21-30	JUL 1-10	JUL 11-20	JUL 21-31	AUG 1-10	AUG 11-20	AUG 21-31	SEP 1-10	SEP 11-20	SEP 21-30	OCT 1-10	OCT 11-20	OCT 21-31	NOV 1-10	NOV 11-20	NOV 21-30	DEC 1-10	DEC 11-20	DEC 21-31
7	9		7	3		16	39	20	6	10	4		4															1	1				3	4	

Garganey *(Anas querquedula)*
Status: Uncommon passage migrant.
 Most records of Garganey are from Jahra Pool Reserve and Jahra Bay, with others seen elsewhere along the coastline and on other pools. The highest count is 120 seen in spring or autumn between 1981 and 1993 (Pilcher, undated), but exact locations and dates are not accessible.

JAN 1-10	JAN 11-20	JAN 21-31	FEB 1-10	FEB 11-20	FEB 21-29	MAR 1-10	MAR 11-20	MAR 21-31	APR 1-10	APR 11-20	APR 21-30	MAY 1-10	MAY 11-20	MAY 21-31	JUN 1-10	JUN 11-20	JUN 21-30	JUL 1-10	JUL 11-20	JUL 21-31	AUG 1-10	AUG 11-20	AUG 21-31	SEP 1-10	SEP 11-20	SEP 21-30	OCT 1-10	OCT 11-20	OCT 21-31	NOV 1-10	NOV 11-20	NOV 21-30	DEC 1-10	DEC 11-20	DEC 21-31
			1	7	41	23	8	6	6															6	27	23	3	12	13	4					

Northern Shoveler *(Anas clypeata)*
Status: Uncommon passage migrant. Uncommon winter visitor.
 This species has mostly been recorded at Jahra Pool Reserve, at Sulaibikhat Bay and at Jahra Bay. Some records are from other coastal sites and from other pools. There are two inland records at Ahmadi seen by S. Howe on 6 April 1972 and 21 April 1972. The highest count is 150 seen between 1981 and 1993 (Pilcher, undated), but exact locations and dates are not accessible.

JAN 1-10	JAN 11-20	JAN 21-31	FEB 1-10	FEB 11-20	FEB 21-29	MAR 1-10	MAR 11-20	MAR 21-31	APR 1-10	APR 11-20	APR 21-30	MAY 1-10	MAY 11-20	MAY 21-31	JUN 1-10	JUN 11-20	JUN 21-30	JUL 1-10	JUL 11-20	JUL 21-31	AUG 1-10	AUG 11-20	AUG 21-31	SEP 1-10	SEP 11-20	SEP 21-30	OCT 1-10	OCT 11-20	OCT 21-31	NOV 1-10	NOV 11-20	NOV 21-30	DEC 1-10	DEC 11-20	DEC 21-31
65		2	100	3	7	56	64	8		4	3													1	1	2	15			48	1		15		

Marbled Duck *(Marmaronetta angustirostris)*
Status: Vagrant (three records).
 Two at Jahra Pool Reserve from 9 February 1995, three later, until at least December 1995, were seen by S. T. Spencer, C. W. Pilcher and M. Shehab. One of these was later seen and photographed by G. Gregory. The description noted a large head, longish pointed tail, a dark patch back from around the eye contrasting with white cheeks, large whitish spots on grayish brown back and upper wing, brown mottling on upper breast, grayish brown flanks, white rest of underparts, uniformly white under wing, and generally black bill with (unusually) a dull yellow area.
 One at Sabah Al Salem on 21-23 January 2000 was seen and described fully by J. Gaskell and M. O. Chichester.
 G. Gregory saw four flying off northeast at Sabah Al-Salem on 9 February 2001 and wrote a description that included the main identifying features.

Common Pochard *(Aythya ferina)*
Status: Rare winter visitor. Rare passage migrant.
Common Pochard has generally been a rare bird in Kuwait. It has mostly been recorded at Jahra Pool Reserve and on other sewage-water and saline pools. A few have been observed elsewhere along the coastline. The highest count is two seen at Jahra Pool Reserve by C. W. T. Pilcher, M. Shehab and G. Gregory on 3 March 1989. There were no accessible records between July 1998 and June 2005.

Ferruginous Duck *(Aythya nyroca)*
Status: Vagrant (at least two records).
Up to four at Jahra Pool Reserve on 5-24 September 1998 were seen and well described by S. T. Spencer, J. Gaskell and M. O. Chichester. This record was accepted by KORC. A. Bailey saw one at Jahra East Outfall on 30 June and 1 July 2005, noting all identificatory features. Several Kuwaiti photographers have photographs of individuals of this species taken on several occasions between 1990 and 2004 (exact dates not accessible) at several sites.

Tufted Duck *(Aythya fuligula)*
Status: Rare winter visitor. Rare passage migrant.
Most records of Tufted Ducks have been at Jahra Pool Reserve and at Jahra Bay, with low numbers seen on other pools and at various locations along the coastline. The highest count is 30 seen between 1981 and 1993 (Pilcher, undated), but exact locations and dates are not accessible.

JAN 1-10	JAN 11-20	JAN 21-31	FEB 1-10	FEB 11-20	FEB 21-29	MAR 1-10	MAR 11-20	MAR 21-31	APR 1-10	APR 11-20	APR 21-30	MAY 1-10	MAY 11-20	MAY 21-31	JUN 1-10	JUN 11-20	JUN 21-30	JUL 1-10	JUL 11-20	JUL 21-31	AUG 1-10	AUG 11-20	AUG 21-31	SEP 1-10	SEP 11-20	SEP 21-30	OCT 1-10	OCT 11-20	OCT 21-31	NOV 1-10	NOV 11-20	NOV 21-30	DEC 1-10	DEC 11-20	DEC 21-31
	2																								2										

Red-breasted Merganser *(Mergus serrator)*
Status: Vagrant (one record).
Two females/immatures were seen and described by S. T. Spencer and C. W. T. Pilcher at Kuwait Bay on 17-18 January 1997. The main features noted were: ginger, elongated, shaggy head, white patch on upperwing, grey brown upperparts, dark tail, whitish underparts and long thin orange-red bill.

Common Quail *(Coturnix coturnix)*
Status: Common passage migrant. Rare summer visitor. Has bred.
Common Quails are frequently flushed from the ground, in many locations in Kuwait, in spring and autumn. Many are shot by hunters. The highest daily count of migratory birds is six on several occasions.
Breeding possibly occurred in 1967, when V. A. D. Sales recorded one, probably near Ahmadi, during most of June and (probably same bird) on 18 and 20 July. R. Williams, G. Walker and G. Gregory heard a male singing on three occasions in four weeks in May 1995 at an area at Umm Al-Aish covered with spring ephemerals. Confirmation of breeding was first obtained in 'late spring' 2000, when seven tiny chicks were picked

up by farm workers from one spot, from which two adults flew, in a grass field near the Yaqoub Boodai Farm in southern Abdali. They were taken to Yaqoub Boodai for examination, and then returned whence they were found. On 18 March 2005 G. Gregory saw and heard a singing male at Kabd.

JAN 1-10	JAN 11-20	JAN 21-31	FEB 1-10	FEB 11-20	FEB 21-29	MAR 1-10	MAR 11-20	MAR 21-31	APR 1-10	APR 11-20	APR 21-30	MAY 1-10	MAY 11-20	MAY 21-31	JUN 1-10	JUN 11-20	JUN 21-30	JUL 1-10	JUL 11-20	JUL 21-31	AUG 1-10	AUG 11-20	AUG 21-31	SEP 1-10	SEP 11-20	SEP 21-30	OCT 1-10	OCT 11-20	OCT 21-31	NOV 1-10	NOV 11-20	NOV 21-30	DEC 1-10	DEC 11-20	DEC 21-31
1						2	1	6	5	2	1	2	1	2	1									1	2	1	2	3	1	2		2			1

Little Grebe *(Tachybaptus ruficollis)*
Status: Scarce resident. Scarce passage migrant. Scarce winter visitor. Has bred.

In winter, individuals or small groups of Little Grebes are occasionally observed in Kuwait Bay and the Gulf. They are more frequently recorded on the pools at Jahra Pool Reserve and at South Doha Nature Reserve, with up to nine (the highest daily count) seen at the latter site on many dates, mostly in the winter, in the 1990s.

C. W. T. Pilcher recorded single pairs breeding successfully at Jahra Pool Reserve, with not-fully-grown juveniles observed on 17 September 1993 and on an unrecorded date in 1996. Since at least 2003, small numbers of Little Grebes have been resident on pools in the recently-fenced Burgan Oil Field. However, access is difficult, and it has not been possible to prove breeding there. The table omits records of resident birds in Burgan Oil Field.

JAN 1-10	JAN 11-20	JAN 21-31	FEB 1-10	FEB 11-20	FEB 21-29	MAR 1-10	MAR 11-20	MAR 21-31	APR 1-10	APR 11-20	APR 21-30	MAY 1-10	MAY 11-20	MAY 21-31	JUN 1-10	JUN 11-20	JUN 21-30	JUL 1-10	JUL 11-20	JUL 21-31	AUG 1-10	AUG 11-20	AUG 21-31	SEP 1-10	SEP 11-20	SEP 21-30	OCT 1-10	OCT 11-20	OCT 21-31	NOV 1-10	NOV 11-20	NOV 21-30	DEC 1-10	DEC 11-20	DEC 21-31
	1					1	3		2															1	3	1								1	1

Great Crested Grebe *(Podiceps cristatus)*
Status: Rare winter visitor. Rare passage migrant.

Single birds or small groups are occasionally observed, but not every year, in Kuwait Bay, the Gulf or the pools at South Doha Nature Reserve, mostly from October to April. In most winters in the late 1990s one or two were present at Jahra Pool Reserve. The highest daily count is 9 seen by S. T. Spencer at Jahra Bay on 11 and 31 March 2000.

JAN 1-10	JAN 11-20	JAN 21-31	FEB 1-10	FEB 11-20	FEB 21-29	MAR 1-10	MAR 11-20	MAR 21-31	APR 1-10	APR 11-20	APR 21-30	MAY 1-10	MAY 11-20	MAY 21-31	JUN 1-10	JUN 11-20	JUN 21-30	JUL 1-10	JUL 11-20	JUL 21-31	AUG 1-10	AUG 11-20	AUG 21-31	SEP 1-10	SEP 11-20	SEP 21-30	OCT 1-10	OCT 11-20	OCT 21-31	NOV 1-10	NOV 11-20	NOV 21-30	DEC 1-10	DEC 11-20	DEC 21-31
5			8	6	9	8	9																									2			3

Horned Grebe *(Podiceps auritus)*
Status: Vagrant (one record).
An immature bird was seen at Jahra Pool Reserve in October 1988 (exact day not accessible) by G. Gregory, C. W. T. Pilcher, A. Tye and M. Shehab. The description noted the straight bill, white on head below eye level only and dusky fore-neck.

Black-necked Grebe *(Podiceps nigricollis)*
Status: Uncommon passage migrant. Uncommon winter visitor.
Rafts of Black-necked Grebes can sometimes be seen at Kuwait Bay and along the Gulf from September to April, with a highest daily count of about 35 seen on several dates. Occasionally in recent years intact corpses have been found on tidelines, with no apparent cause of death. Smaller numbers are occasionally found on the pools at South Doha Nature Reserve. In most winters in the late 1990s up to six used to be present at Jahra Pool Reserve. There is one inland record of a bird in Wafra Oil Field seen by M. O. Chichester on 28 September 2002.

JAN 1-10	JAN 11-20	JAN 21-31	FEB 1-10	FEB 11-20	FEB 21-29	MAR 1-10	MAR 11-20	MAR 21-31	APR 1-10	APR 11-20	APR 21-30	MAY 1-10	MAY 11-20	MAY 21-31	JUN 1-10	JUN 11-20	JUN 21-30	JUL 1-10	JUL 11-20	JUL 21-31	AUG 1-10	AUG 11-20	AUG 21-31	SEP 1-10	SEP 11-20	SEP 21-30	OCT 1-10	OCT 11-20	OCT 21-31	NOV 1-10	NOV 11-20	NOV 21-30	DEC 1-10	DEC 11-20	DEC 21-31
7		1	2	1	13	4	22	35	4					1					1	2	1		2	1								5	3		

Audubon's Shearwater *(Puffinus lherminieri)*
Status: Vagrant (one or two records).
The first record of this species in Kuwait was by V. A. D. Sales on 9 May 1957. His description, on a Rare Bird Report form, reads as follows:
'Groups of 2, 18 and 5 birds observed from the beach south of Shuaiba flying in a southerly direction in an easy low gliding manner just above the sea with an occasional wing beat.
Their general appearance were [sic] darkish/black brown upts with whitish unpts. Tips of wings & center of back on some birds appeared darker or black. The underwing & sides of body not so dark as upts. & not so white as belly. Bill darkish - legs & feet not really seen. Length probably between 12-15 inches.
Birds obs through a 10 x 50 binoculars & x 50 prismoscale.
I believe R. D. Etchécopar recorded this bird a week or so after I left Kuwait during his brief visit in 1965.'
V. A. D. Sales' record was accepted by the panel. Comments below on the Rare Bird Report read:
'This is the only record from the inner Gulf apart from a record of nine seen "off Basra" 18th June 1965 by K. Salwegter which we are unable to question.'
It would be extremely difficult now to access details of the record by R. D. Etchécopar. Both Kuwait records were omitted from the list of the ANHFSG (1975) for unknown reasons. However, P. R. Haynes (1979) and C. W. T. Pilcher (undated) listed this species as accidental in Kuwait.
On 29 May 2003, M. O. Chichester observed what was probably an Audubon's Shearwater 2-3km offshore of Zour Port. His description is below:
'The bird was viewed from behind and only dark grey to black upperparts were

observed. Underparts were not observable. The short intervals of flapping alternating with long glides were distinctly *Puffinus* shearwater. The bird was more compact than the Sooty Shearwater I am most familiar with - shorter wings and thicker bodied.'

Very little sea-watching is done in Kuwait and occurrences of this and other marine species are likely to have been missed.

All these records are of the subspecies *P. lherminieri persicus*, which is sometimes regarded as a species in its own right.

Red-billed Tropicbird *(Phaethon aethereus)*
Status: Vagrant (at least four records).

R. Meinertzhagen (1954) recorded this species in 'March, Sea-Island/Kubr', and in 'April, Mufattah'. He also stated that it 'breeds ... certainly on ... Um-al-Maradim and Kubbar'. However, this report of breeding was 'probably hearsay and in error' (Gallagher, Scott, Ormond, Connor and Jennings, 1984).

K. Nakamura (1974) observed three at sea, position 29°15N, 48°13'E, which is within Kuwait territorial waters, on 5th December 1968. (Another bird that he observed on the same day, position c28°27'N, 48°33'E, is actually in Saudi Arabian territorial waters.)

R.D. Etchécopar stated that this species was 'twice seen flying on 26th April 1969 between Um al Maradhim and Garu (perhaps same bird)' (Warr, undated).

Great Cormorant *(Phalacrocorax carbo)*
Status: Very common winter visitor. Common passage migrant.

Great Cormorants are generally distributed around the bays and the Gulf, mostly from October to March. Up to 1600 birds used to roost on the wrecked ships near the harbours at Shuwaikh and Doha every winter for at least 20 years after 1981, but these ships have now been removed. On 20 January 2005 about 2000 birds (the highest daily count) were seen by B. Foster to fly towards what must have a roost near Shuwaikh Port, but its exact location was not determined. The same number of birds was seen by G. Gregory, B. Foster and P. Fagel standing on the shore at North Doha on 4 February 2005. Some birds have reportedly remained during the summer in the past. L. Cornwallis reported that a bird found dead in Kuwait in May 1955 was ringed as a juvenile on 2 November 1954 at Astrakhan (44°55'N, 47°45'E) (Warr, undated).

JAN 1-10	JAN 11-20	JAN 21-31	FEB 1-10	FEB 11-20	FEB 21-29	MAR 1-10	MAR 11-20	MAR 21-31	APR 1-10	APR 11-20	APR 21-30	MAY 1-10	MAY 11-20	MAY 21-31	JUN 1-10	JUN 11-20	JUN 21-30	JUL 1-10	JUL 11-20	JUL 21-31	AUG 1-10	AUG 11-20	AUG 21-31	SEP 1-10	SEP 11-20	SEP 21-30	OCT 1-10	OCT 11-20	OCT 21-31	NOV 1-10	NOV 11-20	NOV 21-30	DEC 1-10	DEC 11-20	DEC 21-31
450	2000	145	2000	1600	1000	600	850	150	15	4	2		1	5		1			3			6	15							2	25	1000	60	50	1200

Socotra Cormorant *(Phalacrocorax nigrogularis)*
Status: Uncommon disperser in spring, summer and autumn. Has bred.

This species is declining throughout its limited world range. It used to breed on some of Kuwait's islands, but no longer does so. P. Cox visited Umm Al-Maradim Island on 11 June 1905, finding 'corpses of young Cormorants', and later that day on Qaroh Island he reported that 'A flock of Cormorants were seen and the island was strewn with dried-up corpses of half-grown young' (Ticehurst, Cox and Cheesman, 1925).

V. Dickson (1949) wrote that 'many eggs (cormorant and seagull) were collected by fishermen' on the deserted islands of Warba, Auha, Maskan and Umm Al-Maradim in late May and early June. She also stated that 'On the islands of Auha and Kubbar in late May and early June many sea birds nest. Many eggs, both of the gull type and a chalky white kind, probably the cormorant' (V. Dickson, undated).

In all the above cases it is reasonably assumed that the species involved is Socotra Cormorant (*P. nigrogularis*) and not Great Cormorant (*P. carbo*), whose nearest breeding area is northern Syria.

In recent years single birds or small groups are regularly seen, mostly from April to September, on the Gulf coast. The highest recent daily count is 40 seen by M. O. Chichester at Bnaider and Zour on 18 August 2000.

JAN 1-10	JAN 11-20	JAN 21-31	FEB 1-10	FEB 11-20	FEB 21-29	MAR 1-10	MAR 11-20	MAR 21-31	APR 1-10	APR 11-20	APR 21-30	MAY 1-10	MAY 11-20	MAY 21-31	JUN 1-10	JUN 11-20	JUN 21-30	JUL 1-10	JUL 11-20	JUL 21-31	AUG 1-10	AUG 11-20	AUG 21-31	SEP 1-10	SEP 11-20	SEP 21-30	OCT 1-10	OCT 11-20	OCT 21-31	NOV 1-10	NOV 11-20	NOV 21-30	DEC 1-10	DEC 11-20	DEC 21-31
1	1			2	2				6	1	4	4	6	3	4	7	4	8	9	17	10	40	10	18	15	5	2	2	1		1	4			

Pygmy Cormorant *(Phalacrocorax pygmeus)*
Status: Vagrant (one record).

Two birds were seen at Jahra East Outfall by O. Schroeder, S. Schroeder and G. Østerø on 10 March 2001.

Their description is as follows:

'OS, SS and GØ were observing birds in the Jahra Bay area, next to Jahra East Outfall, in the afternoon of 10 March 2001, when they observed two very small cormorants standing near where the outfall entered the sea. They were identified as Pygmy Cormorants after observation with binoculars and telescopes.

Size and Shape: Very small cormorants. The bill was short and the tail was long, in comparison to nearby Cormorants.

Plumage and Exposed Parts: Generally all-dark plumage, except for brown head. No white was observed in the plumage. The bill was short and fairly pale. Leg colour not observed.

Range: About 100m.

Time of Observation: About 15 minutes.

Previous Experience: All the observers have seen this species before in Hungary.'

Great White Pelican *(Pelecanus onocrotalus)*
Status: Rare disperser in all seasons. Has bred.

C. B. Ticehurst, P. Cox and R. E. Cheesman (1926) reported that 'According to Arab testimony Pelicans used to breed on ... Warba Island' in about 1903. They also stated that on 18 April 1922 V. S. La Personne visited Bubiyan Island and found adult White Pelicans and a few downy young. However, he also observed that 'On one part of the island the carcasses of about 100 adults and twenty young were found and it appeared that some epidemic had swept off most of the colony. On another islet near by more dead adults and young were discovered.' He revisited the island on 1 April 1923 and reported that the 'pelicans were nesting; very slight nests were made. A good many eggs and young were seen and again a number of dead birds. Two adults were obtained for identification ...'. These specimens and three eggs, together with three eggs from 18 April 1922, were later donated to the British Museum (Warr, undated). There have been no further records of White Pelicans breeding in Kuwait.

In more recent times this species has been observed occasionally, though not annually, and some birds have been present in the breeding season.

Recent records include one on Bubiyan Island on an unstated date (Al-Haddad and Al-Sudairawi, 2000), 2 at Sulaibikhat Bay in October 1987; one moribund bird at Jahra Pool Reserve in autumn 1998 (exact date not accessible), later found dead on the adjacent road; two at Ras Subiya on 5 May 2000; one at Sulaibikhat Bay on 29 November 2002; one at East Doha on 28 January 2005; and one at Jahra East Outfall on 17 June 2005.

JAN 1-10	JAN 11-20	JAN 21-31	FEB 1-10	FEB 11-20	FEB 21-29	MAR 1-10	MAR 11-20	MAR 21-31	APR 1-10	APR 11-20	APR 21-30	MAY 1-10	MAY 11-20	MAY 21-31	JUN 1-10	JUN 11-20	JUN 21-30	JUL 1-10	JUL 11-20	JUL 21-31	AUG 1-10	AUG 11-20	AUG 21-31	SEP 1-10	SEP 11-20	SEP 21-30	OCT 1-10	OCT 11-20	OCT 21-31	NOV 1-10	NOV 11-20	NOV 21-30	DEC 1-10	DEC 11-20	DEC 21-31
1											2				1																	1			

Dalmatian Pelican *(Pelecanus crispus)*
Status: Vagrant (four records).

An exhausted bird was picked up and given to V. A. D. Sales at Ahmadi on 30 March 1968. It was provided with water and eventually it recovered. A description and some measurements were recorded on a Rare Bird Report form. After five days it was released in the desert a few miles away and flew strongly towards the coast.

The description noted: 'Plumage white with greyish tinge to upperparts. Pale yellow patch on breast. Slight crest on back of head. Primaries blackish, also primary coverts. Secondaries white with pale grey wash. Bill yellowish grey with redish [sic] edges. Pouch yellow with orange tinge. Legs and feet dull dirty grey. Iris pale yellow.' The measurements were: wing 690mm, tail 220mm, bill 400mm and tarsus 115mm. This record was accepted by the panel.

One was seen by C. W. T. Pilcher at Sulaibikhat Bay on 28 November 1981. Three were seen at Subiya on 5 April 1999 by H-M. Busch, J. Rathberger-Knan and W. Bindl. One was found dead at Jahra East Outfall by G. Gregory on 6 March 2005.

Great Bittern *(Botaurus stellaris)*
Status: Scarce passage migrant. Rare winter visitor.

This secretive species is, no doubt, seriously under-recorded. Most sightings are of passage birds at or near reedbeds, the highest daily count being a group of six birds observed and photographed by G. Gregory, M. Shehab and C. W. T. Pilcher, flying from the north into reeds at Jahra Pool Reserve in autumn 1995 (exact date not accessible). Usually, however, only one or two together have been recorded in recent years, and some birds have been found shot dead.

JAN 1-10	JAN 11-20	JAN 21-31	FEB 1-10	FEB 11-20	FEB 21-29	MAR 1-10	MAR 11-20	MAR 21-31	APR 1-10	APR 11-20	APR 21-30	MAY 1-10	MAY 11-20	MAY 21-31	JUN 1-10	JUN 11-20	JUN 21-30	JUL 1-10	JUL 11-20	JUL 21-31	AUG 1-10	AUG 11-20	AUG 21-31	SEP 1-10	SEP 11-20	SEP 21-30	OCT 1-10	OCT 11-20	OCT 21-31	NOV 1-10	NOV 11-20	NOV 21-30	DEC 1-10	DEC 11-20	DEC 21-31
1									1																										2

Little Bittern *(Ixobrychus minutus)*
Status: Uncommon passage migrant. Scarce summer visitor. Breeds.

Most birds seen are passage migrants, usually single birds, at or near reedbeds. Several have been discovered in the early morning perched on railings of small balconies of blocks of flats, presumably having roosted overnight.

This species has probably bred undetected for many years in reedbeds in Kuwait. Confirmation of breeding was first obtained at Jahra East Outfall by G. Gregory and P. Robertson on 12 June 2000, when two adults and two very juvenile birds were forced to the edge of the reeds by a massive fire. One flushed from reeds at Jahra East Outfall on 1 June 2001 was a possible breeder. Breeding was proven again at Jahra East Outfall on 31 May 2002 when S. T. Spencer observed a juvenile with adults. A pair was observed in reeds at Sabah Al-Salem for weeks from 23 May 2002, and one male was in suitable breeding habitat in reeds there from 23 May 2003 to 9 June 2003. In 2004 three pairs were at Sabah Al-Salem in the breeding season, breeding being confirmed by on 8 June, and at least one pair was at Sewer Plant Reeds, with breeding confirmed on 14 June. In both cases not-fully-grown juveniles were observed. In 2005 up to nine at Doha South and Jahra East Outfall were the highest daily count, and two juveniles with two adults at a reed-fringed pool at Wafra on 21 June confirmed breeding.

JAN 1-10	JAN 11-20	JAN 21-31	FEB 1-10	FEB 11-20	FEB 21-29	MAR 1-10	MAR 11-20	MAR 21-31	APR 1-10	APR 11-20	APR 21-30	MAY 1-10	MAY 11-20	MAY 21-31	JUN 1-10	JUN 11-20	JUN 21-30	JUL 1-10	JUL 11-20	JUL 21-31	AUG 1-10	AUG 11-20	AUG 21-31	SEP 1-10	SEP 11-20	SEP 21-30	OCT 1-10	OCT 11-20	OCT 21-31	NOV 1-10	NOV 11-20	NOV 21-30	DEC 1-10	DEC 11-20	DEC 21-31
					1		2	1	1	1	2	2	9	6	6	6	4					1		1	2	1			1						

Black-crowned Night Heron *(Nycticorax nycticorax)*
Status: Scarce passage migrant. Rare summer visitor. Rare winter visitor. Has bred.

This is a secretive species and is undoubtedly under-recorded. Most birds observed have been on passage in spring and autumn, with a highest daily count of ten seen by V. A. D. Sales at an unstated location on 6 April 1968.

The first and only confirmed occurrence of breeding in Kuwait was at Jahra East Outfall on 12 June 2000, when two weakly-flying juveniles were observed by G. Gregory and P. Robertson. The adults may have died in a massive reedbed fire, or abandoned these youngsters. Two adults flushed from reeds at Jahra East Outfall on 1 June 2001 were possible breeders. An adult in reeds at South Doha Nature Reserve on 23 June 2005 was also a possible breeder.

JAN 1-10	JAN 11-20	JAN 21-31	FEB 1-10	FEB 11-20	FEB 21-29	MAR 1-10	MAR 11-20	MAR 21-31	APR 1-10	APR 11-20	APR 21-30	MAY 1-10	MAY 11-20	MAY 21-31	JUN 1-10	JUN 11-20	JUN 21-30	JUL 1-10	JUL 11-20	JUL 21-31	AUG 1-10	AUG 11-20	AUG 21-31	SEP 1-10	SEP 11-20	SEP 21-30	OCT 1-10	OCT 11-20	OCT 21-31	NOV 1-10	NOV 11-20	NOV 21-30	DEC 1-10	DEC 11-20	DEC 21-31
2						7		2	1	1	2		2	2	2	1			1		1			9	2			1							

Squacco Heron *(Ardeola ralloides)*
Status: Uncommon passage migrant. Rare summer visitor.

Squacco Herons are much more readily observed than the two preceding species, except perhaps in the breeding season. They are often seen in the open at the edge of reedbeds and on mudflats and in ditches. The great majority of records are of passage migrants, with a highest daily count of about 60 seen by L. Corrall at Jahra Pool Reserve on 15 September 1981.

Meinertzhagen (1954) recorded breeding by this species in Kuwait, but this claim, although possibly correct, is not supported by good evidence. In 2001 there was a maximum of 12 at Sabah Al-Salem on 29 March, with some remaining into the breeding season, and six flushed from reeds at Jahra East Outfall on 1 June were possible breeders. Up to four were in reeds at Sabah Al-Salem from 25 April 2002. In 2003 a pair was present for months at Sabah Al-Salem from February onwards. An adult was seen carrying food into a reedbed at Sewer Plant Reeds on 8 June 2004. All of these recent observations suggest breeding occurs, but it has never been confirmed.

JAN 1-10	JAN 11-20	JAN 21-31	FEB 1-10	FEB 11-20	FEB 21-29	MAR 1-10	MAR 11-20	MAR 21-31	APR 1-10	APR 11-20	APR 21-30	MAY 1-10	MAY 11-20	MAY 21-31	JUN 1-10	JUN 11-20	JUN 21-30	JUL 1-10	JUL 11-20	JUL 21-31	AUG 1-10	AUG 11-20	AUG 21-31	SEP 1-10	SEP 11-20	SEP 21-30	OCT 1-10	OCT 11-20	OCT 21-31	NOV 1-10	NOV 11-20	NOV 21-30	DEC 1-10	DEC 11-20	DEC 21-31
						3	5	12	14	25	4	6	8	3	8	6	1		1	1				9	13	4	1	1		8		2	1		

Cattle Egret *(Bubulcus ibis)*
Status: Uncommon disperser in autumn, winter and spring.

Either singly or in groups, Cattle Egrets can be seen during most of the year in a wide variety of habitats, including small farm plots, sewage outfalls, traffic roundabouts, roadside grassy patches and both saline and freshwater pools. The KISR Bird Team observed three birds present amongst breeding Western Reef Egrets (*Egretta gularis*) and Grey Herons (*Ardea cinerea*) on Bubiyan Island on 25 March 2004, but breeding has never been proven anywhere in Kuwait. The highest daily count is 30 at East Doha on 20 December 2004, seen by P. Fagel.

JAN 1-10	JAN 11-20	JAN 21-31	FEB 1-10	FEB 11-20	FEB 21-29	MAR 1-10	MAR 11-20	MAR 21-31	APR 1-10	APR 11-20	APR 21-30	MAY 1-10	MAY 11-20	MAY 21-31	JUN 1-10	JUN 11-20	JUN 21-30	JUL 1-10	JUL 11-20	JUL 21-31	AUG 1-10	AUG 11-20	AUG 21-31	SEP 1-10	SEP 11-20	SEP 21-30	OCT 1-10	OCT 11-20	OCT 21-31	NOV 1-10	NOV 11-20	NOV 21-30	DEC 1-10	DEC 11-20	DEC 21-31
17	12	26	23	26	7	8	21	26	5	10	4	3	6	5	1	1					1	5	9	5	5	9	2		1					30	25

Western Reef Egret *(Egretta gularis)*
Status: Very common resident. Breeds.

White, pale grey and dark grey birds are present throughout most of the year along much of the coastline, most frequently wading on mudflats, where they hunt mainly for mudskippers, but also perched on hadras (fish traps), sandy beaches and muddy inlets. Small numbers are occasionally observed up to one kilometre inland at Sabah Al-Salem and Jahra Pool Reserve. From March to July most birds are concentrated around Bubiyan and Warba Islands. Occasional grey birds with some white feathers, and white birds with some grey feathers, are observed.

This species was first recorded as breeding in Kuwait on 3 May 1878, when five eggs were collected on Warba Island and were later donated to the British Museum. This institution also has eggs collected in April 1879, April 1884, May 1884 and April 1899, all definitely or probably from Warba Island. The names of the actual collectors of the eggs are unknown, but E. A. Butler, D. Hume, W. D. Cumming and S. Baker were involved in receiving them and in donating them as part of various collections (British Museum, 1902).

On 30 May 1906 P. Cox observed breeding colonies of this species on Warba Island (Ticehurst, Cox and Cheesman, 1926). V. S. La Personne visited Kubbar Island on 24 April 1921, collecting three eggs from some of the 6-8 nests that he observed (Ticehurst, Cox and Cheesman, 1925) He also visited Bubiyan Island on 25 April and 28 June 1922, collecting three eggs and three adults from some of the 25 nests in one colony (Ticehurst, Cox and Cheesman, 1926). All of these eggs are also now in the British Museum, as are the specimens of adults (Warr, undated).

V. Dickson (1942) found five nests on Auha Island on 9 May 1942, with four nests containing one egg and one nest containing three eggs. N. Muddiman reported nesting 'herons sp.' on Bubiyan Island in May/June 1983 (Warr, undated).

Four pairs were found nesting on a wrecked ship in Khor Subiya (not Khor Bubiyan as reported) in March 2001 (Al-Nasrallah, Al-Ahmed and Al-Fadhel, 2001). In 2002 members of BMAPT, namely K. Al-Nasrallah, E. Ramadan, M. Shehab, G. Gregory, F. Al-Mansori, A. Al-Sureye'a, A. Bailey and M. Al-Saleh, found about 300 pairs breeding on Bubiyan Island, including c10 pairs on a wrecked ship in Khor Subiya. Eggs were recorded from 4 March, and pulli from 4 April.

In 2004 the KISR Bird Team observed this species nesting on Bubiyan Island from 18 March, with eggs and pulli observed from 25 March. They estimated about 450 breeding pairs on Bubiyan Island. In 2005 they observed adults on nests from the early date of 10 February.

The colonies on the islands are on low shrubby ridges next to the khors (channels). They are mixed, the accompanying species being Grey Heron (*Ardea cinerea*) and Eurasian Spoonbill (*Platalea leucorodia*), with up to 40 nests of Western Reef Egret in each colony. The nests on the islands are built on the ground or on top of low shrubs, are up to one metre tall and are made of sticks of Suaeda, often fouled with droppings. Eggs number from two to four, are unmarked pale/medium blue, and are often encrusted with muddy deposits. The nests on the wrecked ship were mostly on the deck fittings, were also made of sticks of *Suaeda*, and were mixed with those of Grey Heron (*Ardea cinerea*) only. Seven old nests were found on Warba Island, but future breeding seemed unlikely there, due to disturbance.

Little Egret *(Egretta garzetta)*
Status: Uncommon passage migrant. Uncommon winter visitor.

This species is usually observed on sewage-water or saline pools, less so on the coastline, and occasionally inland. Due to apparent confusion with the white phase of Western Reef Heron (*E. gularis*), some high counts in the past are probably erroneous. The highest reliable daily count is 13 seen by M. O. Chichester at Wafra Oil Field on 27 March 2001.

A bird found dead in August 1964 at Ahmadi had been ringed as a pullus five kilometres north of Koktyubet, Tarumouka District, Dagestan, U. S. S. R. on 12 June 1961 (Sales, undated).

JAN 1-10	JAN 11-20	JAN 21-31	FEB 1-10	FEB 11-20	FEB 21-29	MAR 1-10	MAR 11-20	MAR 21-31	APR 1-10	APR 11-20	APR 21-30	MAY 1-10	MAY 11-20	MAY 21-31	JUN 1-10	JUN 11-20	JUN 21-30	JUL 1-10	JUL 11-20	JUL 21-31	AUG 1-10	AUG 11-20	AUG 21-31	SEP 1-10	SEP 11-20	SEP 21-30	OCT 1-10	OCT 11-20	OCT 21-31	NOV 1-10	NOV 11-20	NOV 21-30	DEC 1-10	DEC 11-20	DEC 21-31
3	6	7	6	1	4	4	12	13		2	1	4	2	9							2	7	2		6	4	1		1				1	4	1	1

Great Egret *(Egretta albus)*
Status: Uncommon winter visitor. Uncommon passage migrant.

Small numbers of Great Egrets are sometimes seen around the coasts or on pools on passage or in winter. There are no inland records. A moderately-sized wintering group has in recent years been observed in Jahra Bay, often near Jahra East Outfall, with a highest daily count of 34 seen there by S. T. Spencer on 2 January 2002.

JAN 1-10	JAN 11-20	JAN 21-31	FEB 1-10	FEB 11-20	FEB 21-29	MAR 1-10	MAR 11-20	MAR 21-31	APR 1-10	APR 11-20	APR 21-30	MAY 1-10	MAY 11-20	MAY 21-31	JUN 1-10	JUN 11-20	JUN 21-30	JUL 1-10	JUL 11-20	JUL 21-31	AUG 1-10	AUG 11-20	AUG 21-31	SEP 1-10	SEP 11-20	SEP 21-30	OCT 1-10	OCT 11-20	OCT 21-31	NOV 1-10	NOV 11-20	NOV 21-30	DEC 1-10	DEC 11-20	DEC 21-31
34	1	12	7	2	9	9	16	7		17		3		1	1				1					3	5		1	17	3		10	2	15	3

Grey Heron *(Ardea cinerea)*
Status: Very common winter visitor. Common passage migrant. Common resident. Breeds.

This species is mostly found outside the breeding season along the coastline, feeding especially on mudskippers. Some also are often observed on sewage-water and saline pools. Birds have repeatedly been seen roosting on disused lampposts at Salwa and in trees at Shuwaikh. The highest daily count is 650 seen by G.Gregory at Sulaibikhat Nature Reserve on 23 November 2004. From March to July most birds remaining in Kuwait are concentrated around Bubiyan and Warba Islands.

The first known breeding evidence for Kuwait involves an egg collected from Abdullah Bank (Warba/Bubiyan Islands) on 24 April 1884, received by W. D. Cumming, and donated to the British Museum (British Museum, 1902). P. Cox visited Warba Island in May 1906 and found Grey Herons breeding there. On 19 May 1921, V. S. La Personne observed several nests with three or four eggs on Warba Island on 19 May. He also visited Bubiyan Island on 21 May 1921, 30 May 1922 and 1 April 1923, finding nesting birds, and recording that 'The birds had just begun to lay, two nests containing single eggs' on the latter date (Ticehurst, Cox and Cheesman, 1926).

Nine pairs were found nesting on a wrecked ship in Khor Subiya (not Khor Bubiyan as reported) in March 2001 (Al-Nasrallah, Al-Ahmed and Al-Fadhel, 2001). In 2002 members of BMAPT found about 100 pairs breeding on Bubiyan Island, including five pairs on a wrecked ship in the Khor Subiya. Eggs were recorded from 4 March, and pulli from 4 April.

In 2004 the KISR Bird Team observed this species nesting on Bubiyan Island from 18 March 2004, with eggs and pulli observed from 25 March. They estimated about 150 breeding pairs on Bubiyan Island. In 2005 they observed birds on nests from 10 February, and at one site they found two nests with two eggs each and two nests with three eggs each.

The colonies on the islands are on low shrubby ridges next to the khors (channels). They are mixed, the accompanying species being Western Reef Egret (*Egretta gularis*) and Eurasian Spoonbill (*Platalea leucorodia*), with up to 40 nests of Grey Heron in each colony. The nests are built on the ground or on top of low shrubs, are up to one metre tall (but bigger than those of Western Reef Egret) and are made of sticks of *Suaeda*, often fouled with droppings. Eggs number from two to four, are unmarked pale/medium blue, and are often encrusted with muddy deposits. The nests on the wrecked ship were mostly on the deck fittings, were also made of sticks of *Suaeda*, and were mixed with those of Western Reef Egret (*Egretta gularis*) only. Three old nests were found on Warba Island, but future breeding seemed unlikely there, due to disturbance.

JAN 1-10	JAN 11-20	JAN 21-31	FEB 1-10	FEB 11-20	FEB 21-29	MAR 1-10	MAR 11-20	MAR 21-31	APR 1-10	APR 11-20	APR 21-30	MAY 1-10	MAY 11-20	MAY 21-31	JUN 1-10	JUN 11-20	JUN 21-30	JUL 1-10	JUL 11-20	JUL 21-31	AUG 1-10	AUG 11-20	AUG 21-31	SEP 1-10	SEP 11-20	SEP 21-30	OCT 1-10	OCT 11-20	OCT 21-31	NOV 1-10	NOV 11-20	NOV 21-30	DEC 1-10	DEC 11-20	DEC 21-31
150	150	50	450	300	200	150	350	300	124	75	15	17	25	27	4	8	1		5		9	11		30	65	100	150	200	45	150	100	650	40	170	350

Purple Heron *(Ardea purpurea)*
Status: Uncommon passage migrant. Rare summer visitor. Rare winter visitor.

Purple Herons are usually observed in migratory flight, but grounded birds are mostly found around reedbeds, or sewage-water or saline pools. Usually small numbers are involved, but occasionally fair-sized groups are observed on passage. Due to apparent confusion with Grey Heron (*A. cinerea*), some high counts in the past are probably erroneous. The highest reliable daily count is 22 seen by M. O. Chichester at Zour Port on 14 September 2004.

W. D. Cumming received three eggs from Fao, two on 24 April 1884 and one on an unstated date also in April 1884, and donated them to the British Museum, which erroneously labelled them as from 'Koeit' (Warr, undated). M. C. Jennings, in a personal communication to G. Gregory, confirmed that he believed that the eggs were not from Kuwait.

JAN 1-10	JAN 11-20	JAN 21-31	FEB 1-10	FEB 11-20	FEB 21-29	MAR 1-10	MAR 11-20	MAR 21-31	APR 1-10	APR 11-20	APR 21-30	MAY 1-10	MAY 11-20	MAY 21-31	JUN 1-10	JUN 11-20	JUN 21-30	JUL 1-10	JUL 11-20	JUL 21-31	AUG 1-10	AUG 11-20	AUG 21-31	SEP 1-10	SEP 11-20	SEP 21-30	OCT 1-10	OCT 11-20	OCT 21-31	NOV 1-10	NOV 11-20	NOV 21-30	DEC 1-10	DEC 11-20	DEC 21-31
						3	6	7	5	1	1		1								9	1	20	22	14		7	1							

Black Stork *(Ciconia nigra)*
Status: Vagrant (three records).

A sub-adult, with 'legs reddish, bill not', was seen all day at Jahra Pool Reserve by L. Corrall on 13 June 1980.

One was seen and well described by S. T. Spencer in the Jahra/Jal Az-Zor area in about 1993/1994 (exact date not accessible).

An immature bird was shot by hunters at Al-Abraq Al-Khabari on 2 November 2001 and was later photographed by M. Shehab. The following description is from the photograph:

'Size and Shape: Clearly a big bird with long, slightly upcurved bill, long legs and neck. Wing and tail tips together approximately, at rest.

Plumage: Head and upper neck brownish-grey, merging to greyish feathers with brownish edges on breast. Rest of visible underbody white. Mantle and upperwing coverts dark greyish with thin brown edges to feathers. Primaries dark, appearing blackish-grey. Visible part of tail blackish-grey.

Exposed Parts:
Bill: upper-mandible fairly pale greyish-brown with reddish tint. Lower mandible more reddish-brown. Thick eye-ring: brownish-grey. Legs: pale yellowish.'

White Stork *(Ciconia ciconia)*
Status: Rare passage migrant.

Almost all records of White Stork are of one or two birds passing overhead on spring or autumn migration. Birds have been sighted at many locations. The highest daily count is 65 - 70 birds seen by V. A. D. Sales near Ahmadi, flying north and then landing to drink at an irrigation point, in April 1957 (exact day unstated). On 14/15 March 2005, 19 birds roosted overnight on a long wheeled irrigation arm at Kabd.

Glossy Ibis *(Plegadis falcinellus)*
Status: Uncommon passage migrant.
This species is usually seen in migratory flight or at sewage-water or saline pools. Most records are of singles but some fairly large groups have been observed, the highest daily count being 60 seen by M. O. Chichester at Zour Port on 22 August 1999.

Sacred Ibis *(Threskiornis aethiopicus)*
Status: Vagrant (one record).
From about 1980 to at least 1989 a single bird, presumably the same one, wintered at Sulaibikhat Bay. It was usually present between September and March, and was seen by many observers, including C. W. T. Pilcher, G. Gregory and M. Shehab. It, no doubt, was part of the breeding population in the marshes of southern Iraq. The black head and neck, generally white plumage except for black untidy-looking feathers at the rear at rest, dark down-curved bill and dark legs were well observed.

Eurasian Spoonbill *(Platalea leucorodia)*
Status: Common resident. Breeds.
This species is mostly found, outside the breeding season, in small numbers along the coastline. From March to July most birds in Kuwait are concentrated around Bubiyan and Warba Islands.
The first known breeding evidence for Kuwait involved four eggs collected on Bubiyan Island on 25 May 1878 and 17 eggs collected at Abdullah Bank (Warba/Bubiyan Islands) on 24 April 1884, received by W. D. Cumming, and donated to the British Museum (British Museum, 1902). EurasianSpoonbills were observed by P. Cox to be breeding on Warba Island on 19 May 1907 (Ticehurst, Cox and Cheesman, 1926). V. S. La Personne collected an unknown number of eggs on 20 May 1922, and three on 1 June 1922, on Bubiyan Island (Ticehurst, Buxton and Cheesman 1921-22). N. Muddiman reported this species breeding on Bubiyan Island in May/June 1983 (Warr, undated).
In 2002 members of BMAPT found about 50 pairs breeding on Bubiyan Island. Eggs were recorded from 4 April, and pulli from 17 May. In 2004 the KISR Bird Team

observed this species nesting on Bubiyan Island from 18 March, with eggs and pulli observed from 15 April. They estimated about 75 breeding pairs on Bubiyan Island. The colonies on the islands are on low shrubby ridges next to the khors (channels). They are mixed, the accompanying species being Western Reef Egret (*Egretta gularis*) and Grey Heron (*Ardea cinerea*), with up to six nests of Eurasian Spoonbill in each colony. The nests are built on the ground or on top of low shrubs, are up to one and a half metres tall and are made of sticks of *Suaeda*, sometimes fouled with droppings. Eggs usually number three, are unmarked white, and often encrusted with muddy deposits.

Greater Flamingo *(Phoenicopterus roseus)*
Status: Very common resident. Very common disperser in all seasons. Has bred.

Throughout the year, though more commonly in winter, large flocks of Greater Flamingoes are easily seen at Sulaibikhat Bay and Jahra Bay. Smaller numbers are seen regularly at Ras Subiya, and sometimes on Bubiyan Island and along the Gulf coast. A flock of up to 75 was present on the sewage-water pool at Jahra Pool Reserve from January to March 1996. Inland records include those of five found long dead by G. Gregory and P. Robertson under electricity transmission lines in what is now the Sabah Al-Ahmed Natural Reserve in April 1995 (exact day not accessible), and one seen by M. O. Chichester at Wafra Oil Field on 27 March 2001. Most of the birds seen in Kuwait presumably spend the summer in breeding colonies in Turkey, Iran or elsewhere. Only a small proportion of birds observed after the breeding season are juveniles, and almost none are observed in some years. The highest daily count is 3000 seen by S. T. Spencer at Sulaibikhat Bay on 8 February 2001.

This species was first recorded as breeding in Kuwait on 25 May 1878, when 71 eggs were collected on Bubiyan Island and were later donated to the British Museum. This institution also has eggs collected on Bubiyan Island on 25 May 1879 and on Abdullah Bank (Warba/Bubiyan Island) on 24 April 1884 and on an unrecorded date. The names of the actual collectors of the eggs are unknown, but E. A. Butler, D. Hume, W. D. Cumming and S. Baker were involved in receiving them, and in donating them as part of various collections (British Museum, 1902). C. B. Ticehurst P. A. Buxton and R. E. Cheesman (1921-22) wrote that 'According to Cumming it breeds on the Koweit side of the head of the Gulf, whence I believe he obtained from the Arabs many eggs which are now in the Karachi Museum'.

V. S. La Personne visited Bubiyan Island in 1921, 1922 and 1923. C. B. Ticehurst, P. Cox and R. E. Cheesman (1926) wrote about his observations: 'On May 21, 1921. Flamingoes were breeding on Bubyan Island and a rotten egg was picked up. On April 7, 1922, a colony of about 500 pairs was located on Bubyan ... nesting on a slightly raised stretch of sand covered with low scrub. The nests, situated on bare dry sand within a foot of each other and just above high water mark, were either mounds of sand raised above the level or else the egg was laid on the level sand and the surrounding sand scooped away leaving the egg on the mound. The nests measured one foot in diameter and contained one egg, rarely two. ... Subsequently the colony deserted and by May 30, had laid again in another part of the Khor but most of the eggs had been washed away by a big tide. The young in down swims with ease. On April 1, 1923, no Flamingoes were seen on Bubyan.' Two eggs and an adult specimen collected on the 15 April 1922 visit are now in the British Museum, as is an egg collected by an unknown person on Bubiyan Island on 16 April 1923 (Warr, undated).

Captain Salem Al-Mulla of the Kuwait Coastguard, in a personal communication to G. Gregory, related that in several of the ten years 1994-2003 he and his men had observed small colonies of Greater Flamingoes breeding on Bubiyan Island. A maximum of 65 nests were built in one year, and some had eggs and young. On other occasions the birds built nests but then abandoned them. In 2004 the KISR Bird Team recorded small numbers of Greater Flamingoes on Bubiyan Island from March to June but found no evidence of breeding. This species is best described as an irregular breeder in Kuwait.

JAN 1-10	JAN 11-20	JAN 21-31	FEB 1-10	FEB 11-20	FEB 21-29	MAR 1-10	MAR 11-20	MAR 21-31	APR 1-10	APR 11-20	APR 21-30	MAY 1-10	MAY 11-20	MAY 21-31	JUN 1-10	JUN 11-20	JUN 21-30	JUL 1-10	JUL 11-20	JUL 21-31	AUG 1-10	AUG 11-20	AUG 21-31	SEP 1-10	SEP 11-20	SEP 21-30	OCT 1-10	OCT 11-20	OCT 21-31	NOV 1-10	NOV 11-20	NOV 21-30	DEC 1-10	DEC 11-20	DEC 21-31
950	800	1500	3000	1000	1000	2500	2200	1400	600	150	18	300	400	25	50	400		48			5	200	300	450	500	25	600	1000	1200	600	800	2000			

European Honey Buzzard *(Pernis apivorus)*
Status: Scarce passage migrant.

Small numbers are normally seen on migratory flight in spring and autumn. Records have been from many sites. It is possible that some past records refer to Crested Honey Buzzard (*P. ptilorhynchus*), a species that has only recently been realised to occur in Kuwait. The highest daily count is three seen by G. Rowlands at Bneid Al-Gar on 17 April 2001. A partially oiled juvenile was cleaned, ringed and released by V. A. D. Sales at Ahmadi on 8 October 1967 (Sales, undated).

JAN 1-10	JAN 11-20	JAN 21-31	FEB 1-10	FEB 11-20	FEB 21-29	MAR 1-10	MAR 11-20	MAR 21-31	APR 1-10	APR 11-20	APR 21-30	MAY 1-10	MAY 11-20	MAY 21-31	JUN 1-10	JUN 11-20	JUN 21-30	JUL 1-10	JUL 11-20	JUL 21-31	AUG 1-10	AUG 11-20	AUG 21-31	SEP 1-10	SEP 11-20	SEP 21-30	OCT 1-10	OCT 11-20	OCT 21-31	NOV 1-10	NOV 11-20	NOV 21-30	DEC 1-10	DEC 11-20	DEC 21-31
					1			3	1	1	1	1													1	1	2								

Crested Honey Buzzard *(Pernis ptilorhynchus)*
Status: Scarce passage migrant.

This species was first discovered to occur in Kuwait when S. T. Spencer observed three at Jal Az-Zor on 21 September 2001. Since then it has been recorded annually in Kuwait. A juvenile, about two weeks dead, was found at Qaisat on 4 October 2002. Singles were found fairly recently dead at Hujaijah on 31 May 2003 and at Bubiyan Bridge on 27 September 2003. One was seen at Abdali Farms on 12 April 2004. A juvenile was seen in the Sabah Al-Ahmed Natural Reserve on 22 September 2004. An adult was found about two months dead near Al-Abraq Al-Khabari on 7 January 2005. Some past records of Honey Buzzards (*P. apivorus*) probably refer to this species. Accordingly, the status given above is probably the best one.

JAN 1-10	JAN 11-20	JAN 21-31	FEB 1-10	FEB 11-20	FEB 21-29	MAR 1-10	MAR 11-20	MAR 21-31	APR 1-10	APR 11-20	APR 21-30	MAY 1-10	MAY 11-20	MAY 21-31	JUN 1-10	JUN 11-20	JUN 21-30	JUL 1-10	JUL 11-20	JUL 21-31	AUG 1-10	AUG 11-20	AUG 21-31	SEP 1-10	SEP 11-20	SEP 21-30	OCT 1-10	OCT 11-20	OCT 21-31	NOV 1-10	NOV 11-20	NOV 21-30	DEC 1-10	DEC 11-20	DEC 21-31
								1			1															3	1								

Black-shouldered Kite *(Elanus caeruleus)*
Status: Vagrant (two records).

One was caught in a baited raptor trap, and later was photographed by M. Shehab, at Al-Abraq Al-Khabari on 28 February 2002. The description is below:
'On 28 February 2002 Shaikh Fahd's employees at Al-Abraq Al-Khabari found an unfamiliar raptor in a live-baited raptor trap in an open area at the farm. They brought the bird to Shaikh Fahd, who was unable to identify it either. The bird was tethered and kept for training as a falconer's bird.

A few days later, MS visited Al-Abraq Al-Khabari, and was shown the bird by Shaikh Fahd and was asked to identify it. MS identified it as a Black-shouldered Kite and photographed it. G. Gregory wrote the description from the photograph.
Size and Shape: Clearly a small Kite, with a fairly small bill and notched tail at rest.
Plumage: Head white, merging into pale grey of upper body. Thin blackish line through eye. Upper wings pale grey with darker primaries and blackish area on lesser coverts and forward edge of inner wing. Three generations of feathers, on wear and colour, apparent on primaries, secondaries and tertials. Upper tail paler grey. Under parts all white.
Exposed Parts: Bill dark grey. Eye bright scarlet. Legs yellowish. Claws dark.'

One was seen and photographed by Khalid Al-Ghanim at Jahra Pool Reserve on 28 June 2003; the photograph shows the main identificatory features.

Black Kite *(Milvus migrans)*
Status: Common passage migrant. Common winter visitor.

Black Kites are frequently seen in migratory flight over all areas of Kuwait, even over Kuwait City, in spring and autumn, with a highest daily count of about 500 seen by V. A. D. Sales at Ahmadi on 24 March 1966. The rubbish tip near Sulaibiya has held a wintering flock of up to 150 in recent years.

JAN 1-10	JAN 11-20	JAN 21-31	FEB 1-10	FEB 11-20	FEB 21-29	MAR 1-10	MAR 11-20	MAR 21-31	APR 1-10	APR 11-20	APR 21-30	MAY 1-10	MAY 11-20	MAY 21-31	JUN 1-10	JUN 11-20	JUN 21-30	JUL 1-10	JUL 11-20	JUL 21-31	AUG 1-10	AUG 11-20	AUG 21-31	SEP 1-10	SEP 11-20	SEP 21-30	OCT 1-10	OCT 11-20	OCT 21-31	NOV 1-10	NOV 11-20	NOV 21-30	DEC 1-10	DEC 11-20	DEC 21-31
6	70	10	60	150	30	35	54	28	7	2	7	5	2		1							1	3	2	2	145	1	15	11	19	2	18	2		

Egyptian Vulture *(Neophron percnopterus)*
Status: Scarce passage migrant.

This species probably occurs on passage every year in small numbers. It has been recorded at many sites, including Ahmadi, Jal Az-Zor, Qaisat, the Sabah Al-Ahmed Natural Reserve, Jahra Pool Reserve and Abdali Farms. The highest daily count is two seen at various locations on many dates in the past.

JAN 1-10	JAN 11-20	JAN 21-31	FEB 1-10	FEB 11-20	FEB 21-29	MAR 1-10	MAR 11-20	MAR 21-31	APR 1-10	APR 11-20	APR 21-30	MAY 1-10	MAY 11-20	MAY 21-31	JUN 1-10	JUN 11-20	JUN 21-30	JUL 1-10	JUL 11-20	JUL 21-31	AUG 1-10	AUG 11-20	AUG 21-31	SEP 1-10	SEP 11-20	SEP 21-30	OCT 1-10	OCT 11-20	OCT 21-31	NOV 1-10	NOV 11-20	NOV 21-30	DEC 1-10	DEC 11-20	DEC 21-31
						1		1			1									1															

Eurasian Griffon Vulture *(Gyps fulvus)*
Status: Scarce disperser in autumn, winter and spring.
Small numbers of Eurasian Griffon Vultures are probably present annually. On several occasions photographs of captured roosting birds have appeared in local newspapers, and Kuwaiti hunters have reported several birds shot in recent years. The highest recorded daily count is five seen by K. Al-Nasrallah, A. Al-Suraye'a and others in what is now the Sabah Al-Ahmed Natural Reserve on several dates in November and December 2001. This species has also been recorded at Qaisat, Jal Az-Zor and near Umm Qasr recently.

JAN 1-10	JAN 11-20	JAN 21-31	FEB 1-10	FEB 11-20	FEB 21-29	MAR 1-10	MAR 11-20	MAR 21-31	APR 1-10	APR 11-20	APR 21-30	MAY 1-10	MAY 11-20	MAY 21-31	JUN 1-10	JUN 11-20	JUN 21-30	JUL 1-10	JUL 11-20	JUL 21-31	AUG 1-10	AUG 11-20	AUG 21-31	SEP 1-10	SEP 11-20	SEP 21-30	OCT 1-10	OCT 11-20	OCT 21-31	NOV 1-10	NOV 11-20	NOV 21-30	DEC 1-10	DEC 11-20	DEC 21-31
								3			2															1				5	5	5			

Eurasian Black Vulture *(Aegypius monachus)*
Status: Rare disperser in autumn, winter and spring.
The first known record is of one seen and photographed by P. R. Haynes and W. A. Stuart over the Salmi Road on 10 March 1978. P. R. Haynes observed and photographed one at Jal Az-Zor on 18 November 1978. One was seen at Wafra Oil Field by M. O. Chichester on 28 September 2002. M. Al-Jeriwi photographed one at Jahra Pool Reserve in early March 2005. There are four other sightings recorded by C. W. T. Pilcher (2000), but details are not accessible. Additionally, there are an unknown number of records, backed by good verbal descriptions and at least one photograph, of birds seen by several Kuwaiti photographers and hunters, but the dates and locations are not accessible. In the circumstances, the status given above is probably the best one.

JAN 1-10	JAN 11-20	JAN 21-31	FEB 1-10	FEB 11-20	FEB 21-29	MAR 1-10	MAR 11-20	MAR 21-31	APR 1-10	APR 11-20	APR 21-30	MAY 1-10	MAY 11-20	MAY 21-31	JUN 1-10	JUN 11-20	JUN 21-30	JUL 1-10	JUL 11-20	JUL 21-31	AUG 1-10	AUG 11-20	AUG 21-31	SEP 1-10	SEP 11-20	SEP 21-30	OCT 1-10	OCT 11-20	OCT 21-31	NOV 1-10	NOV 11-20	NOV 21-30	DEC 1-10	DEC 11-20	DEC 21-31
						1																								1					

Short-toed Eagle *(Circaetus gallicus)*
Status: Uncommon passage migrant. Rare winter visitor.
Short-toed Eagles pass through in spring and autumn in relatively small numbers. The highest daily count is six seen at several locations on several dates, mostly in the past. In the Ahmadi Natural History and Field Studies Group *Newsletter* 17 (1977), P. R. Haynes related how one at Manageesh on 9 March 1977 'caused a power failure in the oilfield by electrocuting itself at 1 a.m. when the snake it had in its bill touched a live power cable.'

Western Marsh Harrier *(Circus aeruginosus)*
Status: Uncommon passage migrant. Scarce winter visitor. Rare summer visitor.

Most records of this species are of passage birds, though it is annual in winter and occasional birds have recently remained until early summer around Jahra East Outfall and Jahra Pool Reserve. It could potentially breed at these sites or at South Doha Nature Reserve.

The highest daily count is 8 seen by M. O. Chichester at Jahra Pool Reserve on 17 September 1998.

Hen Harrier *(Circus cyaneus)*
Status: Rare passage migrant.

The numerous records of this species up to 1983 show it to have been apparently more common than Pallid Harrier (*C. macrourus*), and P. R. Haynes (1979) listed it as a 'Common Passage Migrant'. There was clearly thorough confusion with Pallid Harrier and possibly also with Montagu's Harrier (*C. pygargus*). It probably occurred on at least several occasions, but there is no practical method of determining which of these records are reliable and which are not, even though some of the observers were probably familiar with all the species concerned. Accordingly, it is probably best to disregard all of these records.

More recent records that carefully distinguished this species include: a male and a ringtail seen by G. Gregory, C. W. T. Pilcher and M. Shehab on separate but inaccessible dates between 1985 and 1989; a ringtail seen by G. Rowlands at Doha on 11 February 2000; an adult male seen by G. Gregory in the Sabah Al-Ahmed Natural Reserve on 8 September 2004; an adult male seen by J. Dashti and G. Gregory on Bubiyan Island on 21 September 2004; and two (the highest daily count) seen by P. Fagel and M. Varhimo near Ras Al-Ardh on 5 April 2005. In the circumstances, the status given above is probably the best one.

Pallid Harrier *(Circus macrourus)*
Status: Common passage migrant.

Pallid Harriers are a common sight on spring and autumn migration in almost all areas. The highest daily count is 35 seen by the KISR Bird Team at Bubiyan Island on 21 September 2004.

JAN 1-10	JAN 11-20	JAN 21-31	FEB 1-10	FEB 11-20	FEB 21-29	MAR 1-10	MAR 11-20	MAR 21-31	APR 1-10	APR 11-20	APR 21-30	MAY 1-10	MAY 11-20	MAY 21-31	JUN 1-10	JUN 11-20	JUN 21-30	JUL 1-10	JUL 11-20	JUL 21-31	AUG 1-10	AUG 11-20	AUG 21-31	SEP 1-10	SEP 11-20	SEP 21-30	OCT 1-10	OCT 11-20	OCT 21-31	NOV 1-10	NOV 11-20	NOV 21-30	DEC 1-10	DEC 11-20	DEC 21-31
		1				2	4	5	10	2	1													3	6	35	2	3	1	2					1

Montagu's Harrier *(Circus pygargus)*
Status: Uncommon passage migrant.

Individuals are occasionally observed in migratory flight in many areas, or quartering around reedbeds. Some previous records, including some high counts, are unreliable, and probably involve confusion with Pallid Harrier (*C. macrourus*). The highest daily count of reliably identified birds is apparently two seen at many locations on many dates.

JAN 1-10	JAN 11-20	JAN 21-31	FEB 1-10	FEB 11-20	FEB 21-29	MAR 1-10	MAR 11-20	MAR 21-31	APR 1-10	APR 11-20	APR 21-30	MAY 1-10	MAY 11-20	MAY 21-31	JUN 1-10	JUN 11-20	JUN 21-30	JUL 1-10	JUL 11-20	JUL 21-31	AUG 1-10	AUG 11-20	AUG 21-31	SEP 1-10	SEP 11-20	SEP 21-30	OCT 1-10	OCT 11-20	OCT 21-31	NOV 1-10	NOV 11-20	NOV 21-30	DEC 1-10	DEC 11-20	DEC 21-31
						1	1		1	2	2	1									2	1	1		1										

Northern Goshawk *(Accipiter gentilis)*
Status: Rare passage migrant and winter visitor.

The first known record for Kuwait is of a female seen by M. Shehab at Jahra on 25 An September 1992. An immature male was seen by C. W. T. Pilcher, G. Gregory and S. T. Spencer at Jahra Pool Reserve in 1995, and the latter observer also had at least one record in 1993-1994, but the details are not accessible.

Other recent accessible records include: an immature male seen and photographed by G. Gregory at Jahra Farms on 5 February 1996; an adult female found dead and photographed by P. Robertson and G. Gregory in what is now the Sabah Al-Ahmed Natural Reserve on 19 October 1998; a female seen by G. Gregory on Failaka Island on 8 February 2001; a first-year male found dead by A. Bailey and G. Gregory at Sabah Al-Salem on 16 January 2002; an immature male found dead by G. Gregory at Hujaijah on 16 April 2004: and a female seen by M. Al-Jeriwi at Jahra Pool Reserve on 17 March 2005. There are at least several more records of Northern Goshawk in Kuwait, supported by some good verbal descriptions and at least one photograph, of birds seen by several Kuwaiti bird-watchers and photographers, and of birds shot by hunters, but the dates are not accessible. In the circumstances, the status given above is probably the best one. All birds seen have been singles.

It must be noted that some of these records, and those of other species of raptors, may refer to escaped falconers' birds.

JAN 1-10	JAN 11-20	JAN 21-31	FEB 1-10	FEB 11-20	FEB 21-29	MAR 1-10	MAR 11-20	MAR 21-31	APR 1-10	APR 11-20	APR 21-30	MAY 1-10	MAY 11-20	MAY 21-31	JUN 1-10	JUN 11-20	JUN 21-30	JUL 1-10	JUL 11-20	JUL 21-31	AUG 1-10	AUG 11-20	AUG 21-31	SEP 1-10	SEP 11-20	SEP 21-30	OCT 1-10	OCT 11-20	OCT 21-31	NOV 1-10	NOV 11-20	NOV 21-30	DEC 1-10	DEC 11-20	DEC 21-31
1	1		1			1	1																	1											

Eurasian Sparrowhawk *(Accipiter nisus)*
Status: Uncommon passage migrant. Uncommon winter visitor.
Eurasian Sparrowhawks are seen on passage and in winter at many sites in Kuwait, always in small numbers. Some past records may refer to Shikra (*A. badius*). The highest daily count is four seen at several locations on several dates.

JAN 1-10	JAN 11-20	JAN 21-31	FEB 1-10	FEB 11-20	FEB 21-29	MAR 1-10	MAR 11-20	MAR 21-31	APR 1-10	APR 11-20	APR 21-30	MAY 1-10	MAY 11-20	MAY 21-31	JUN 1-10	JUN 11-20	JUN 21-30	JUL 1-10	JUL 11-20	JUL 21-31	AUG 1-10	AUG 11-20	AUG 21-31	SEP 1-10	SEP 11-20	SEP 21-30	OCT 1-10	OCT 11-20	OCT 21-31	NOV 1-10	NOV 11-20	NOV 21-30	DEC 1-10	DEC 11-20	DEC 21-31
1	1	1	1	1	1	1	2	2	1	3	1	1												1	2	1	1	1	1	4			2	1	2

Shikra *(Accipiter badius)*
Status: Scarce passage migrant. Scarce winter visitor.
The first record of Shikra in Kuwait was that of a juvenile male found dead, described, measured and photographed by G. Gregory, C. W. T. Pilcher and M. Shehab at Al-Abraq Al-Khabari on 30 September 1988. This was followed by a juvenile female found dead on 14 November 1996, and a juvenile female found dead on 1 October 1999, both in what is now the Sabah Al-Ahmed Natural Reserve; and an adult female found dead at Hujaijah on 22 October 1999. Increased awareness of this species resulted in a second-year male being found dead at Hujaijah on 3 May 2001 and an adult male being seen at Mishref on 7 December 2001.

2002 records involved single immatures at Rawdatain on 26 April, at Salmi (caught in a baited raptor trap) on 10 September, and at Qaisat on 13 December; all of these birds were photographed. In 2003 there were a second-year bird seen at Jahra Pool Area on 28 February, a second-year bird seen near Salmi on 11 March, and a first-year male found dead in what is now the Sabah Al-Ahmed Natural Reserve on 16 October.

There were even more records in 2004: a juvenile male found dead at Hujaijah on 1 October, a juvenile female found dead at Hujaijah on 15 October, a juvenile male seen in the Sabah Al-Ahmed Natural Reserve on 16 October, two juveniles found dead at Al-Abraq Al-Khabari on 22 October and a juvenile male seen at Sabriya Farm on 19 November.

In 2005 a second-year male was seen at Abdali Farms on 14 January.

The observers involved in the records since 1996 were G. Gregory, P. Robertson, V. Robertson, K. Al-Nasrallah, M. Shehab, A. Al-Sureye'a, M. Al-Saleh, F. Al-Mansori, A. Bailey and B. Foster.

It is clear that this species occurs annually in Kuwait as a passage migrant and winter visitor, and that it was no doubt overlooked in the past.

JAN 1-10	JAN 11-20	JAN 21-31	FEB 1-10	FEB 11-20	FEB 21-29	MAR 1-10	MAR 11-20	MAR 21-31	APR 1-10	APR 11-20	APR 21-30	MAY 1-10	MAY 11-20	MAY 21-31	JUN 1-10	JUN 11-20	JUN 21-30	JUL 1-10	JUL 11-20	JUL 21-31	AUG 1-10	AUG 11-20	AUG 21-31	SEP 1-10	SEP 11-20	SEP 21-30	OCT 1-10	OCT 11-20	OCT 21-31	NOV 1-10	NOV 11-20	NOV 21-30	DEC 1-10	DEC 11-20	DEC 21-31
1				1		1		1	1																	1		2		1			1	1	

Levant Sparrowhawk *(Accipiter brevipes)*
Status: Rare passage migrant and winter visitor.

The only accessible records of this species are: a juvenile female found dead at Al-Abraq Al-Khabari on 7 November 1996; a juvenile female found dead at Al-Abraq Al-Khabari on 30 September 1988; an adult male seen at Jahra Farms 5 January and (probably the same bird) 23 February 1996; one seen at Jahra on 8 March 2000; one seen at Khiran on 12 March 2000; five (the highest daily count) seen at Jal Az-Zor on 29 September 2000; a juvenile seen at Shaab on 4 October 2001; two seen on Bubiyan Island on 21 September 2004; an adult male seen at Sabriya Farm on 1 October 2004; and a juvenile male found dead at Al-Abraq Al-Khabari on 15 November 2004. Observers involved in these records were C. W. T. Pilcher, M. Shehab, G. Gregory, S. T. Spencer, A. Bailey, J. Dashti, S. Al-Dosary, M. Al-Mutairy, E. Delima and B. Foster.

There are known to be other records. Pilcher (undated) stated 'Single birds recorded late September-early November and two records February'. These additional records are not accessible.

JAN 1-10	JAN 11-20	JAN 21-31	FEB 1-10	FEB 11-20	FEB 21-29	MAR 1-10	MAR 11-20	MAR 21-31	APR 1-10	APR 11-20	APR 21-30	MAY 1-10	MAY 11-20	MAY 21-31	JUN 1-10	JUN 11-20	JUN 21-30	JUL 1-10	JUL 11-20	JUL 21-31	AUG 1-10	AUG 11-20	AUG 21-31	SEP 1-10	SEP 11-20	SEP 21-30	OCT 1-10	OCT 11-20	OCT 21-31	NOV 1-10	NOV 11-20	NOV 21-30	DEC 1-10	DEC 11-20	DEC 21-31
1				1	1																					5	1				1				

Common Buzzard *(Buteo buteo)*
Status: Common passage migrant. Scarce winter visitor.

Common Buzzards are widespread in Kuwait on spring and autumn migration. All records probably involve just the migratory subspecies, ***B. b. vulpinus*** (Steppe Buzzard), which has very variable plumage, sometimes resembling the nominate subspecies. The highest daily count is 'literally hundreds' seen by L. Corrall between Jal Az-Zor and Qaisat on 21 September 1978. A few are observed in winter each year, usually at coastal sites.

JAN 1-10	JAN 11-20	JAN 21-31	FEB 1-10	FEB 11-20	FEB 21-29	MAR 1-10	MAR 11-20	MAR 21-31	APR 1-10	APR 11-20	APR 21-30	MAY 1-10	MAY 11-20	MAY 21-31	JUN 1-10	JUN 11-20	JUN 21-30	JUL 1-10	JUL 11-20	JUL 21-31	AUG 1-10	AUG 11-20	AUG 21-31	SEP 1-10	SEP 11-20	SEP 21-30	OCT 1-10	OCT 11-20	OCT 21-31	NOV 1-10	NOV 11-20	NOV 21-30	DEC 1-10	DEC 11-20	DEC 21-31
1	3	2	1			1	2	48	3			1	1	1										1	2	35	5		6	1	2	1	1	1	

Long-legged Buzzard *(Buteo rufinus)*
Status: Uncommon winter visitor. Scarce passage migrant.
This species has been recorded at many sites, but always in small numbers. Some past records may involve confusion with Steppe Buzzard (*B. buteo vulpinus*). The highest daily count is six seen at the Sabah Al-Ahmed Natural Reserve and at Bahra on many dates in winter. An adult at Jahra Farms on 11 June 2004 was present in the breeding season.

JAN 1-10	JAN 11-20	JAN 21-31	FEB 1-10	FEB 11-20	FEB 21-29	MAR 1-10	MAR 11-20	MAR 21-31	APR 1-10	APR 11-20	APR 21-30	MAY 1-10	MAY 11-20	MAY 21-31	JUN 1-10	JUN 11-20	JUN 21-30	JUL 1-10	JUL 11-20	JUL 21-31	AUG 1-10	AUG 11-20	AUG 21-31	SEP 1-10	SEP 11-20	SEP 21-30	OCT 1-10	OCT 11-20	OCT 21-31	NOV 1-10	NOV 11-20	NOV 21-30	DEC 1-10	DEC 11-20	DEC 21-31
2	6	6	6	2	1	1	1	1	3						1	1						2					1			1	1	6	6	1	6	6

Lesser Spotted Eagle *(Aquila pomarina)*
Status: Vagrant (at least six records).
Single Lesser Spotted Eagles were recorded by V. A. D. Sales, probably at Ahmadi, on 25 September 1967 and on 24 March 1968. P. R. Haynes, in a personal communication to F. E. Warr, wrote: 'Between 60 and 80 in the space of 1 1/2 hours near Jahra on 7th November, in two parties of about 20 and numbers of single and strung-out birds. 17 were counted on the ground, the rest flying overhead. A further 60+ in one flock, together with a few Steppe Eagles were overhead in the same place 8th November 1977 moving along the line of the Zor Hills, i.e. westwards. There were also 2 singles, one of which landed briefly.' F. E. Warr (undated) appended the comment: 'Ian Willis identified photo as *A. clanga* and Richard Porter "inclined to *A. pomarina*." ' Similar numbers of either species have not been observed recently.
A. Tye observed and well described a single bird during the Avifaunal Survey 1985-1987 but the location and exact date are not accessible. One was seen by H-M. Busch, J. Rathberger-Knan and W. Bindl near Jahra on 1 April 1999. Two were seen by H-M. Busch, J. Rathberger-Knan, F. Lange and A. Lange near Jahra on 8 March 2000. One was seen by G. Gregory, A. Bailey and H. McCurdy at Qaisat on 5 April 2002. G. Gregory, A. Bailey and B. Foster saw one at Jahra East Outfall on 25 March 2005. There are known to be other records but details of them are not accessible. This species is almost certainly under-recorded.

Greater Spotted Eagle *(Aquila clanga)*
Status: Uncommon passage migrant. Scarce winter visitor.
When conditions are right, 'kettles' of up to 100 or more large eagles pass along over Kuwait on spring and autumn migration. Almost all of these are Steppe Eagles (*A. nipalensis*), the remainder including Greater Spotted Eagles and Imperial Eagles (*A. heliaca*), and sometimes other species. Jal Az-Zor, Qaisat, Kabd and Bubiyan Island are the best places to see this spectacular visible migration, although it is very unpredictable.
The highest daily count of Greater Spotted Eagle is probably amongst inaccessible data from the period 1979-1990, but is likely to be about 10 on at least several occasions. Juveniles in *fulvescens* plumage are observed in most years.
Wintering birds are usually seen around the Jahra Bay and Bahra areas.

Steppe Eagle *(Aquila nipalensis)*
Status: Very common passage migrant. Scarce winter visitor.
This is the most common large eagle seen in Kuwait. Almost all birds are passage migrants. The highest daily count is about 770 seen by P. J. Cowan at Kabd on 28 February 2002. Wintering birds are recorded annually, mostly at coastal sites, in small numbers.

Imperial Eagle *(Aquila heliaca)*
Status: Uncommon passage migrant. Rare winter visitor.
Relatively small numbers of migrating Imperial Eagles usually accompany the other species of large eagles, and a few have been recorded in winter. The highest daily count is probably amongst inaccessible data from the period 1979-1990, but is likely to be about 5 on at least several occasions.

Golden Eagle *(Aquila chrysaetos)*
Status: Vagrant (four records).
A sub-adult was seen and photographed by P. R. Haynes near Bahra on 19 November 1977. The slide was identified by I. Willis and R. F. Porter, and British Museum skins were checked (Warr, undated). One was observed by A. Tye at an unstated location on 26 March 1986. One was seen and well described by M. O. Chichester on the Wafra-Nuwaisib Road on 22 February 1998. A second-year bird was seen, distantly photographed and described by G. Gregory and several non-birders at Dibdibah on 2 March 1995.

There have been other reports, by several Kuwaiti hunters and photographers, of the occurrence of this species in Kuwait, but with insufficient supporting evidence.

Booted Eagle *(Hieraaetus pennatus)*
Status: Scarce passage migrant.
 Small numbers of Booted Eagles are seen passing through on migration every year, with a few observed in winter. The highest daily count is two at several locations on several dates in the past. Light and dark phases are seen in roughly equal proportions.

Bonelli's Eagle *(Hieraaetus fasciatus)*
Status: Rare disperser in autumn, winter and spring.
 This species is only occasionally observed, with as many as four seen in one year in the past and none in others. All records are of single birds, seen at various locations, including Jal Az-Zour, Umm Al-Aish, Mina, Qaisat, Burgan Oil Field and the Sabah Al-Ahmed Natural Reserve.

Osprey *(Pandion haliaetus)*
Status: Scarce passage migrant. Rare winter visitor.
 Most records of this species are from coastal locations and pools, with inland records of single birds seen by G. B. Stafford at Umm Ar-Rimam on 31 March 1972, by S. Howe at Burgan Oil Field on 17 September 1971, and, found dead, by G. Gregory at Al-Abraq Al-Khabari on 18 October 2002. The highest daily count is two on several dates.

Lesser Kestrel *(Falco naumanni)*
Status: Common passage migrant. Rare winter visitor.

Lesser Kestrels are now mostly seen singly or in small groups on spring migration over all areas of Kuwait. Fewer are seen in autumn, and there have been some winter records. This species has decreased significantly in numbers since V. Dickson ((1949) wrote that this species 'in some years appears in tens of thousands over Kuwait town during the end of March and April'. These rather imprecise figures represent the highest daily count. In the 1960s V. A. D. Sales considered it to be common from March to May, seeing 'hundreds daily with 1000 to 2000+ not uncommon', while P. R. Haynes, in the 1970s, recorded 'small groups and flocks of 50 or so' during this period (Warr, undated). By the late 1990s a count of 50 in a day in spring was unusual. In 2003 the highest daily count was 11, in 2004 it was five, and in 2005 it was 22. This species is, unfortunately, often found dead at a number of shooting sites.

JAN 1-10	JAN 11-20	JAN 21-31	FEB 1-10	FEB 11-20	FEB 21-29	MAR 1-10	MAR 11-20	MAR 21-31	APR 1-10	APR 11-20	APR 21-30	MAY 1-10	MAY 11-20	MAY 21-31	JUN 1-10	JUN 11-20	JUN 21-30	JUL 1-10	JUL 11-20	JUL 21-31	AUG 1-10	AUG 11-20	AUG 21-31	SEP 1-10	SEP 11-20	SEP 21-30	OCT 1-10	OCT 11-20	OCT 21-31	NOV 1-10	NOV 11-20	NOV 21-30	DEC 1-10	DEC 11-20	DEC 21-31
1	1					25	22	8	30	14	50	1	15	2	1									1	2	3		3		1					

Common Kestrel *(Falco tinnunculus)*
Status: Uncommon passage migrant. Uncommon winter visitor. Uncommon resident. Has bred.

Common Kestrels are present throughout the year at various sites in Kuwait, but most birds are passage migrants or winter visitors. V. A. D. Sales recorded about 150 (the highest daily count) at Ahmadi on 7 April 1956 (Sales, undated), but there has clearly been a reduction in numbers since then. Many birds are shot or captured by hunters, and live birds are often on sale in the main bird market at Al-Rai.

The first breeding record is of a pair observed by W. A. Stuart on a 'cliff nest' at Jal Az-Zor on 1 March 1977 (Jennings, undated). The only other record of breeding was by K. Al-Nasrallah, who photographed three young on a nest just south of Kuwait City in May 2003.

JAN 1-10	JAN 11-20	JAN 21-31	FEB 1-10	FEB 11-20	FEB 21-29	MAR 1-10	MAR 11-20	MAR 21-31	APR 1-10	APR 11-20	APR 21-30	MAY 1-10	MAY 11-20	MAY 21-31	JUN 1-10	JUN 11-20	JUN 21-30	JUL 1-10	JUL 11-20	JUL 21-31	AUG 1-10	AUG 11-20	AUG 21-31	SEP 1-10	SEP 11-20	SEP 21-30	OCT 1-10	OCT 11-20	OCT 21-31	NOV 1-10	NOV 11-20	NOV 21-30	DEC 1-10	DEC 11-20	DEC 21-31
3	2	3	1	2	1	3	22	10	25	8	2	1	15	7	2	1	2	2	1	1		1			1	2		2	2	1	2	3	3	2	2

Red-footed Falcon *(Falco vespertinus)*
Status: Vagrant (one record).

The only Kuwait record is that of a second-year female found dead by G. Gregory and H. Merlet at Hujaijah on 9 May 2002. The description is as follows:
'At about 12.30 p.m. GG and HM were checking for dead birds at the avenue of trees at Hujaijah, when GG found an obvious female Red-footed Falcon, dead about one week. It was bagged, taken to Salwa, described, measured and photographed.
Plumage: Forehead and crown buffish orange. Rest of upper body barred mid grey and black, with some pale rufous admixed. All remiges, primary coverts and alula dark brownish grey. Secondary coverts and scapulars basically grey with darker centres to feathers. Upper tail grey with numerous blackish bands and pale rufousy white tips (3 innermost) or rufousy white with dark brown bands and off-white narrow tips (3 outermost).
Blackish marks around eye. Chin and half-collar white. Breast and belly buffish orange with thin blackish streaks on upper breast and flanks. Under tail coverts pale buffish white. Under tail greyish white with greyish brown bars. Under remiges dark grey with large white spots/bars on inner webs. Under coverts off-white, centrally and barred dark greyish brown, with some buffish orange admixed.
Exposed Parts: Bill - bluish grey. Cere - yellowish with some grey tints. Eye - decayed. Legs - brownish red. Claws - greyish horn.
Measurements: Wing - 235. Tail - 123. Bill - 11.9. Tarsus - 30. Hind claw - 8.6.
Primaries:

1	2	3	4	5	6
-13	L	-11	-27	-44	-65

Emargination: OUTER P2 and P3 (slightly).
INNER P1 (30 from tip).
Tail difference: 12.
Age
Brownish grey upper remiges with somewhat worn tips; absence of buffish orange (except for some admixed) extensively on under wing coverts; and dark streaks on upper breast and flanks indicate a 2Y bird. This is confirmed by rufous admixed on upper body.'

Merlin *(Falco columbarius)*
Status: Rare winter visitor. Rare passage migrant.

Merlins have been seen at both coastal and inland sites in almost every recent year. Some birds have stayed for prolonged periods, such as a female wintering at Kabd from October 2004 to February 2005. All records have been of single birds.

JAN 1-10	JAN 11-20	JAN 21-31	FEB 1-10	FEB 11-20	FEB 21-29	MAR 1-10	MAR 11-20	MAR 21-31	APR 1-10	APR 11-20	APR 21-30	MAY 1-10	MAY 11-20	MAY 21-31	JUN 1-10	JUN 11-20	JUN 21-30	JUL 1-10	JUL 11-20	JUL 21-31	AUG 1-10	AUG 11-20	AUG 21-31	SEP 1-10	SEP 11-20	SEP 21-30	OCT 1-10	OCT 11-20	OCT 21-31	NOV 1-10	NOV 11-20	NOV 21-30	DEC 1-10	DEC 11-20	DEC 21-31
1	1	1	1	1	1																					1	1		1	1		1	1	1	1

Eurasian Hobby *(Falco subbuteo)*
Status: Uncommon passage migrant.
This species is widespread on spring and autumn migration, but is seen only in small numbers. Occasionally individuals have bewen found in winter in the past. The highest daily count is five seen by V. A. D. Sales at Ahmadi on 24 April 1968, and by G. Rowlands at Sabah Al-Salem on 17 April 2001.

JAN 1-10	JAN 11-20	JAN 21-31	FEB 1-10	FEB 11-20	FEB 21-29	MAR 1-10	MAR 11-20	MAR 21-31	APR 1-10	APR 11-20	APR 21-30	MAY 1-10	MAY 11-20	MAY 21-31	JUN 1-10	JUN 11-20	JUN 21-30	JUL 1-10	JUL 11-20	JUL 21-31	AUG 1-10	AUG 11-20	AUG 21-31	SEP 1-10	SEP 11-20	SEP 21-30	OCT 1-10	OCT 11-20	OCT 21-31	NOV 1-10	NOV 11-20	NOV 21-30	DEC 1-10	DEC 11-20	DEC 21-31
						1			3	5	1	1	1	1	1				1					1	1	1									

Sooty Falcon *(Falco concolor)*
Status: Vagrant (at least six records).
The rejected records of Eleonora's Falcon (*F. eleonorae*) in 1966 and 1975 probably referred to Sooty Falcons.
The first definite record was of a second-year bird seen and filmed by K. Al-Nasrallah at Jahra Pool Area on 21 April 1999. The description is below:
'On 21 April 1999, KN found a falcon sitting in a tamarisk tree in Jahra Pool Area. He videoed it with his shoulder-held video camera. After watching the video clip, about 1 minute long, he identified the bird as a Sooty Falcon. He gave G. Gregory a copy of the video clip. G. Gregory confirmed identification as a Sooty Falcon, and wrote the following description.
Size and Shape: Size not easy to judge, but appears as a medium/small falcon. Typical falcon shape. Wing just extend beyond tail at rest.
Plumage: Upper head and visible parts of upper body medium grey. Upper wing with darker primaries. Prominent dark greyish black mark extending forward and downward in front of eye, and back through eye. Chin and throat off white. Breast and belly mid grey. Under tail coverts appear dull greyish. Under wing brownish grey with darker barring, not greatly contrasting. Under tail similar pattern to under wing, with broader band at tip.
Exposed Parts: Bill dark, with paler cere. Eye dark. Legs yellowish.
Identification
Clearly moulting body from juvenile to adult, but wing and tail feathers not yet replaced. 2Y male Red-footed Falcon would have more contrasting under wing pattern and would have bright rufous on under tail coverts and flanks, as well as red legs. Body too pale for dark phase Eleonora's Falcon. Sooty Falcon is known to perch in trees outside of breeding season.'

In 2002 two were seen by S. T. Spencer at Jabriya on 21 April. Later in the year a pair of unspecified falcons were seen repeatedly, by several observers, visiting a possible nest site between boulders in a sea wall close to where two juveniles were photographed by M. Al-Saleh at Shuwaikh on 19 June 2002. This possible nest site did not seem very suitable for Kestrel (*F. tinnunculus*).

Records in 2004 were of singles seen on a wrecked ship off Bubiyan Island on 29 April, at Fintas on 31 May and at Jahra Farms on 8 October; observers included R. Loughland, J. Dashti, G. Gregory, S. Al-Dosary and B. Foster.

The pattern of records and the evidence from Shuwaikh indicate that Sooty Falcons may breed at least occasionally in Kuwait.

Lanner *(Falco biarmicus)*
Status: Rare disperser in autumn, winter and spring.

It would be extremely difficult to determine the exact number of reliable records of wild birds of this species in Kuwait.

L. Corrall observed one on 14 April 1978 near Wadi Al-Batin, but stated: 'As the bird allowed me to approach so close I'm inclined to think it was an escape' (Warr, undated). P. R. Haynes (1979) commented: 'Some, if not all records are of escaped falconers' birds.' This clearly implies that other birds had been seen, but no details are accessible. G. Gregory and C. W. T. Pilcher had good views of one flying south near Jal Az-Zor in autumn 1995 but the exact date is not accessible. Several Kuwaiti hunters have reported seeing this species, and it has recently been caught for falconry about once every three years. However, exact dates and locations are not accessible. All records refer to single birds. In the circumstances, the status given above is probably the best one.

Saker *(Falco cherrug)*
Status: Rare passage migrant and winter visitor.

Sakers are much prized in Kuwait as falconers' birds, and there are some impressive private collections. Presumed-wild birds are not recorded annually, and all records are of single birds. P. R. Haynes (1979) considered this species an uncommon passage migrant, but also noted that 'Escaped falconers' birds also seen quite frequently.' The only accessible records from that period are singles seen at Mufattah on 18 September 1974 and at Kadhima on 2 January 1975 (ANHFSG, 1975).

More recent records include single birds at Sulaibikhat on an unknown date in January 1987; at Sulaibikhat Bay on 10 February and (probably the same bird) at Bahra on 31 March 2000; at Salmi on 6 September 2002; at Ratqa on 19 November 2002; and (trapped for falconry) at Adaira on 6 October 2004. Also, Kuwaiti hunters have reported seeing or capturing other individuals of this species about once every two years, but dates and locations are not accessible. All birds seen have been singles.

JAN 1-10	JAN 11-20	JAN 21-31	FEB 1-10	FEB 11-20	FEB 21-29	MAR 1-10	MAR 11-20	MAR 21-31	APR 1-10	APR 11-20	APR 21-30	MAY 1-10	MAY 11-20	MAY 21-31	JUN 1-10	JUN 11-20	JUN 21-30	JUL 1-10	JUL 11-20	JUL 21-31	AUG 1-10	AUG 11-20	AUG 21-31	SEP 1-10	SEP 11-20	SEP 21-30	OCT 1-10	OCT 11-20	OCT 21-31	NOV 1-10	NOV 11-20	NOV 21-30	DEC 1-10	DEC 11-20	DEC 21-31
1			1																					1			1			1					

Peregrine *(Falco peregrinus)*
Status: Rare disperser in all seasons. Rare resident.

Presumed-wild Peregrines, always seen singly, have been recorded in almost every year for which there are accessible records. Definite escapes, bearing jesses etc, are also occasionally seen. Most records have been at coastal sites, including two on Failaka Island, but birds have also been seen at Manageesh Oil Field, Wadi Al-Batin and Ahmadi. All records have involved single birds. From 2000-2003 a Peregrine, photographed occasionally, roosted on a tall bank building at Qibla in Kuwait City. Presumably it fed mostly on Feral Pigeons (*Columba livia*).

JAN 1-10	JAN 11-20	JAN 21-31	FEB 1-10	FEB 11-20	FEB 21-29	MAR 1-10	MAR 11-20	MAR 21-31	APR 1-10	APR 11-20	APR 21-30	MAY 1-10	MAY 11-20	MAY 21-31	JUN 1-10	JUN 11-20	JUN 21-30	JUL 1-10	JUL 11-20	JUL 21-31	AUG 1-10	AUG 11-20	AUG 21-31	SEP 1-10	SEP 11-20	SEP 21-30	OCT 1-10	OCT 11-20	OCT 21-31	NOV 1-10	NOV 11-20	NOV 21-30	DEC 1-10	DEC 11-20	DEC 21-31
1	1	1	1	1	1	1	1	1	1	1	1	1	1	1	1	1	1	1	1	1	1	1	1	1	1	1	1	1	1	1	1	1	1	1	1

Barbary Falcon *(Falco pelegrinoides)*
Status: Vagrant (at least four records).
  Single birds seen by M. Shehab on 15 February and 15 September (locations and years not accessible), and at Al-Abraq Al-Khabari on 19 May 2001, showed no sign of captivity. Features observed included: pale blue back and inner wing, large rufous patch on back of head and neck, large white cheek patch and very pale underparts. B. Foster and A. Bailey saw one at East Doha on 17 June 2005, noting the main identificatory features. Also, Kuwaiti hunters have reported seeing or capturing other individuals of this species on several occasions, but dates and locations are not accessible. Escaped falconers' birds have also been seen occasionally by several observers.

Water Rail *(Rallus aquaticus)*
Status: Uncommon resident. Uncommon passage migrant. Scarce winter visitor. Has bred.
  Up to ten pairs of Water Rails are known or suspected to be resident in reedbeds at Sabah Al-Salem, Jahra East Outfall, Sewer Plant Reeds, South Doha Nature Reserve, East Doha and Jahra Pool Reserve. Other birds occur on passage or in winter, at the above sites and elsewhere, as evidenced by past records at Umm-Al-Aish, Mina Ahmadi and Burgan Oil Field. The highest daily count outside the breeding season is 10+ seen by M. Reed and T. Cross at Jahra Pool Reserve on 13 November 1991. From June to early September there has been little recent coverage of reedbeds, but birds are presumed to be present but skulking.
  Breeding was confirmed for the first and only time when G. Gregory found a not-fully-grown juvenile near two adults at Sabah Al-Salem on 5 May 2002. Song was heard by B. Settles, S. Carter-Brown and G. Gregory at Jahra East Outfall on 2 May 2003.

JAN 1-10	JAN 11-20	JAN 21-31	FEB 1-10	FEB 11-20	FEB 21-29	MAR 1-10	MAR 11-20	MAR 21-31	APR 1-10	APR 11-20	APR 21-30	MAY 1-10	MAY 11-20	MAY 21-31	JUN 1-10	JUN 11-20	JUN 21-30	JUL 1-10	JUL 11-20	JUL 21-31	AUG 1-10	AUG 11-20	AUG 21-31	SEP 1-10	SEP 11-20	SEP 21-30	OCT 1-10	OCT 11-20	OCT 21-31	NOV 1-10	NOV 11-20	NOV 21-30	DEC 1-10	DEC 11-20	DEC 21-31
2	3	1	1	2	2	3	4	1	1	1		3	2	1	1								1			1			2		2	1	1	2	

Spotted Crake *(Porzana porzana)*
Status: Uncommon resident. Uncommon passage migrant. Rare winter visitor.
  Up to five pairs of Spotted Crakes are known or suspected to be resident in reedbeds at Sabah Al-Salem, Jahra East Outfall, Jahra Pool Reserve and Sewer Plant Reeds. Others may also be resident in other reedbeds at South Doha Nature Reserve and East Doha. Passage migrants have also been seen at Burgan Oil Field and Failaka Island. A wintering bird was seen by S. Howe at Burgan Oil Field on 24 January 1972. The

highest daily count is nine seen by B. Foster, P. Fagel and M. Varhimo at Doha East on 9 April 2005. From June to early September there has been little recent coverage of reedbeds, but birds are presumed to be present but skulking.

Breeding has never been proven in Kuwait. However, in the spring and early summer of 2003 birds were heard singing at Sabah Al-Salem, by R. Bridle and G. Gregory, several times from 9 May, and responded to a taped song once. In the same year a bird was heard, by B. Settles and G. Gregory, responding to a human imitation at Jahra East Outfall on 4 April. On 24 February 2005 a bird was heard singing at Jahra Pool Reserve.

JAN 1-10	JAN 11-20	JAN 21-31	FEB 1-10	FEB 11-20	FEB 21-29	MAR 1-10	MAR 11-20	MAR 21-31	APR 1-10	APR 11-20	APR 21-30	MAY 1-10	MAY 11-20	MAY 21-31	JUN 1-10	JUN 11-20	JUN 21-30	JUL 1-10	JUL 11-20	JUL 21-31	AUG 1-10	AUG 11-20	AUG 21-31	SEP 1-10	SEP 11-20	SEP 21-30	OCT 1-10	OCT 11-20	OCT 21-31	NOV 1-10	NOV 11-20	NOV 21-30	DEC 1-10	DEC 11-20	DEC 21-31
1			1		1	2	2	6	9	5	5	1	3	1										1	2	1	1			1					1

Little Crake *(Porzana parva)*
Status: Uncommon resident. Uncommon passage migrant. Rare winter visitor. Breeds.

At least 10 pairs, possibly many more, of Little Crakes are known or suspected to be resident in reedbeds at Sabah Al-Salem, Sewer Plant Reeds, East Doha, Jahra Pool Reserve and Jahra East Outfall. Others may also be resident in other reedbeds at South Doha Nature Reserve. Passage migrants have also been seen at Manageesh Oil Field, Araifjan, Jahra Farms, Ahmadi and Umm Al-Aish. A wintering bird was seen by G. Gregory at Jahra Farms on 11 December 2003. The highest daily count is 10+ seen by M. Reed and T. Cross at Jahra Pool Reserve on 13 November 1991.

The first confirmed breeding record for Kuwait was at Sabah Al-Salem on 16 February 2001, when G. Rowlands observed a not-fully-grown juvenile near to an adult female. Song was heard, by number of observers, at Jahra East Outfall, Sabah Al-Salem and Sewer Plant Reeds, on several occasions in the spring and early summer of 2002, and a bird responded to a taped song at the first location once that year. Singing birds were also heard at Jahra East Outfall and at Sabah Al-Salem in the spring and early summer of 2003. Confirmation of breeding was obtained twice in 2004, when G. Gregory observed not-fully-grown juveniles at Sabah Al-Salem on 31 May and on 14 September. In 2005, singing birds were heard at East Doha and Jahra Pool Reserve from February onwards. From June to early September there has been little recent coverage of reedbeds, but birds are presumed to be present but skulking.

JAN 1-10	JAN 11-20	JAN 21-31	FEB 1-10	FEB 11-20	FEB 21-29	MAR 1-10	MAR 11-20	MAR 21-31	APR 1-10	APR 11-20	APR 21-30	MAY 1-10	MAY 11-20	MAY 21-31	JUN 1-10	JUN 11-20	JUN 21-30	JUL 1-10	JUL 11-20	JUL 21-31	AUG 1-10	AUG 11-20	AUG 21-31	SEP 1-10	SEP 11-20	SEP 21-30	OCT 1-10	OCT 11-20	OCT 21-31	NOV 1-10	NOV 11-20	NOV 21-30	DEC 1-10	DEC 11-20	DEC 21-31
1	1		2	4	7	5	5	8	5	1	1		2	1										1	3		1	4			7			1	3

Baillon's Crake *(Porzana pusilla)*
Status: Scarce passage migrant.

This is a secretive species which is no doubt seriously under-recorded in Kuwait. All records are of passage migrants, seen mostly at Jahra Pool Reserve, with birds also recorded at Ahmadi, Kuwait City and what is now the Sabah Al-Ahmed Natural Reserve. The highest daily count is two seen on 2 September 1977 by P. R. Haynes.

Corn Crake *(Crex crex)*
Status: Uncommon passage migrant. Rare winter visitor.

Corn Crakes are regularly seen on migration every year, with records from Abdali, Umm Al-Aish, Qaisat, Jahra Pool Reserve, Jahra East Outfall, Sabah Al-Salem, Zour Port, Subiya, Bubiyan Island (including one on a wrecked ship offshore), Sabah Al-Ahmed Natural Reserve, Rawdatain, Mufattah, Ahmadi, Manageesh Oil Field, Al-Abraq Al-Khabari, Jahra Farms and Green Island. Unfortunately, the remains of birds shot by hunters are often found. The highest daily count is three seen by V. A. D. Sales at Ahmadi on 11 May 1961. A bird ringed as an adult by V. A. D. Sales at Ahmadi on 16 April 1968 was later killed near Oktemberyan, Armenia (Sales, undated).

Common Moorhen *(Gallinula chloropus)*
Status: Uncommon resident. Scarce passage migrant. Scarce winter visitor. Breeds.

Common Moorhens are at present known or suspected to be resident breeders at Jahra East Outfall, Jahra Pool Reserve, Sabah Al-Salem, Sewer Plant Reeds, East Doha and South Doha Nature Reserve; numbers at these sites are augmented by passage migrants and winter visitors. Migrants have been recorded at Umm Al-Aish, Mina Ahmadi and Burgan Oil Field. From June to early September there has been little recent coverage of reedbeds, but birds are presumed to be present but skulking. The highest daily count is 50 on several occasions.

Breeding was first recorded in Kuwait at the old Sulaibiya Prison Pool by an unknown Kuwaiti, who reported observing chicks to P. R. Haynes on an unstated date in the 1970s (Warr, undated). Confirmation of breeding was obtained at Jahra Pool Reserve on 18 April 1985 by C. W. T. Pilcher, who observed '2 or 3 day old chicks seen as late as 1 July', on 6 May 2005 by B. Foster and P. Fagel, who observed three juveniles with an adult at Sabah Al-Salem, and on 19 May 2005 by B. Foster and P. Fagel, who observed four juveniles with an adult at East Doha.

JAN 1-10	JAN 11-20	JAN 21-31	FEB 1-10	FEB 11-20	FEB 21-29	MAR 1-10	MAR 11-20	MAR 21-31	APR 1-10	APR 11-20	APR 21-30	MAY 1-10	MAY 11-20	MAY 21-31	JUN 1-10	JUN 11-20	JUN 21-30	JUL 1-10	JUL 11-20	JUL 21-31	AUG 1-10	AUG 11-20	AUG 21-31	SEP 1-10	SEP 11-20	SEP 21-30	OCT 1-10	OCT 11-20	OCT 21-31	NOV 1-10	NOV 11-20	NOV 21-30	DEC 1-10	DEC 11-20	DEC 21-31
11	30	50	15	15	12	9	15	11	9	9	3	4	8	4	4	15			3			1		3	4	3	7	1	15		15		4	8	8

Purple Swamp-Hen *(Porphyrio porphyrio)*
Status: Scarce resident. Has bred

The first record was of a bird captured in Ahmadi by V. A. D. Sales on 16 October 1958, and an account and photograph of this bird appeared in the local press (Sales, undated).

In September 1992 (exact date not accessible) S. T. Spencer found a pair of Purple Swamp-Hens at Jahra Pool Reserve, and birds were resident there for years afterwards, being seen also by C. W. T. Pilcher, M. Shehab, G. Gregory, M. O. Chichester, J. Gaskell, K. Al-Ghanim, K. Al-Nasrallah and possibly others. An immature bird was observed from May 1994, but this was not considered proof of breeding. Three chicks were found by C. W. T. Pilcher on an unknown date in 1996, confirming breeding for the first time in Kuwait. The last known sighting was of one bird seen by K. Al-Nasrallah on 23 October 2000. About this time the pool began to dry up and conditions became unsuitable for this species. Full descriptions of the birds were written, noting all identificatory features.

One was seen and described by G. Gregory at Sabah Al-Salem on 29 December 2001, and footprints of this bird were seen later also by A. Bailey.

On 12 May 2005 P. Fagel discovered a Purple Swamp-Hen at South Doha Nature Reserve, and it was quickly established that at least six birds were present in the reeds there, forming a small resident population.

Eurasian Coot *(Fulica atra)*
Status: Uncommon winter visitor. Uncommon passage migrant. Scarce summer visitor. Breeds.

In the winter groups of Eurasian Coots, often mixed with other species, can sometimes be seen in Jahra Bay. Smaller numbers have been recorded offshore elsewhere, including Kuwait Bay, Failaka Island and Fintas. Wintering birds have also been recorded on pools at Jahra Pool Reserve, South Doha Nature Reserve, Sabah Al-Salem, and Sewer Plant Reeds. Inland records include one seen by S. Howe at Burgan Oil Field on 21 November 1971, and one found dead by M. O. Chichester in Wafra Oil Field on 14 November 2001. The highest daily count is 300+ seen by C. W. T. Pilcher, S.T. Spencer and M. Shehab at Jahra Pool Reserve on several dates in December 1993 and January 1994.

Breeding was first confirmed at Jahra Pool Reserve by C. W. T. Pilcher on an unknown date in 1996, with three downy chicks observed. Breeding was also confirmed at Sabah Al-Salem by G. Gregory on 14 May 2004, with two non-flying juveniles seen.

JAN 1-10	JAN 11-20	JAN 21-31	FEB 1-10	FEB 11-20	FEB 21-29	MAR 1-10	MAR 11-20	MAR 21-31	APR 1-10	APR 11-20	APR 21-30	MAY 1-10	MAY 11-20	MAY 21-31	JUN 1-10	JUN 11-20	JUN 21-30	JUL 1-10	JUL 11-20	JUL 21-31	AUG 1-10	AUG 11-20	AUG 21-31	SEP 1-10	SEP 11-20	SEP 21-30	OCT 1-10	OCT 11-20	OCT 21-31	NOV 1-10	NOV 11-20	NOV 21-30	DEC 1-10	DEC 11-20	DEC 21-31
6	8	7	25	11	8	14	7	2			2		2	2		1												1		4	25		4	4	

Common Crane *(Grus grus)*
Status: Vagrant (three records).
The first record was of two birds seen flying over Jahra Pool Reserve by C. W. T. Pilcher, M. Shehab and G. Gregory on 13 November 1987. Features observed included: mainly grey body, black primaries and secondaries, black on head and upper neck only, and white streak back from center of head.
One was found by G. Rowlands, and also seen by M. O. Chichester, S. T. Spencer and G. Gregory, at Sulaibikhat Bay from 30 December 2000 to March 2001. A full description was written, noting all features.
Two were shot at Habari Al-Awazem on 17 February 2001 by Kuwaiti hunters, and later seen by K. Al-Nasrallah, who observed the identificatory features.
Several reports of other birds of this species seen by various Kuwaiti hunters have not excluded Demoiselle Crane (*Anthropoides virgo*).

Demoiselle Crane *(Anthropoides virgo)*
Status: Vagrant (at least four records).
The first record was of a 'small flock' seen at Khadima in January, exact date not stated (Meinertzhagen, 1954). On 8 September 1977 P. R. Haynes observed six at Kuwait City coast. A. Tye saw a small flock on 17 March 1986, but the exact location is not accessible. Two birds were shot by Hamad Al-Baqr, a Kuwaiti hunter, at Ratqa on 24 March 2000. Photographs of the birds were shown to G. Gregory, who noted black on neck extending to upper breast, thin white streak behind eye, grey body and blackish on wings.
Additionally, there are at least several records, backed by good verbal descriptions and a distant photograph, of birds seen by several Kuwaiti photographers and hunters, but the dates and locations are not accessible.

Macqueen's Bustard *(Chlamydotis macqueenii)*
Status: Irregular winter visitor. Has bred.
The former Houbara Bustard (*Chlamydotis undulata*) has recently been split into two species and Macqueen's Bustard (*C. macqueenii*) is the one occurring in Kuwait. It has always been the much-prized prey of falconers and hunters.
This species used to be common in Kuwait. H. R. P. Dickson (1949) wrote that birds 'arrive about October each year on the E. and N.E. seaboard on the Persian Gulf and continue to come till about April', and 'In Kuwait the sheikh bags about 2000 each winter'. In his game register he records a maximum of 103 shot or taken by falcons on one day between 1933 and 1936 by one hunting party (Jennings, 1989). V. Dickson (undated) stated that they 'arrive late September and depart end March.' Since then numbers of birds seen in Kuwait clearly decreased, and P. R. Haynes (1979) described Houbara Bustard as an uncommon winter visitor. In recent years it is still annually recorded, in variable numbers: in some winters just one, in others 'many' are reported by Kuwaiti hunters and falconers. Precise numbers and dates are, however, difficult to obtain.
The first record of confirmed breeding by this species in Kuwait is uncertain. C. B. Ticehurst, P. A. Buxton and R. E. Cheesman (1921-22) stated that eggs received by W. D. Cumming in Kuwait were then in the British Museum. However, the only such egg registered by this institution, in 1890, may not have been of this species, and it was not found there in April 1978 (Warr, undated). V. Dickson (undated) wrote that the 'Houbara or Lesser Bustard occasionally nests in the N.W. of the state and Badawins sometimes bring in an egg to His Highness the Sheikh, though I myself have not seen

one.' Colonel H. R. P. Dickson (1949) said that on 15 March 1935 Houbara Bustard eggs were found '40 miles south of Kuwait [City], also mid May from 80 miles W. of Kuwait [City]'. According to R. Meinertzhagen (1954) this species 'breeds regularly from Kuwait ... '. J. D. Silsby (1980) stated that it was believed to breed still in Kuwait, but this seems unlikely due to pressure of hunters using four-wheel-drive vehicles.

JAN 1-10	JAN 11-20	JAN 21-31	FEB 1-10	FEB 11-20	FEB 21-29	MAR 1-10	MAR 11-20	MAR 21-31	APR 1-10	APR 11-20	APR 21-30	MAY 1-10	MAY 11-20	MAY 21-31	JUN 1-10	JUN 11-20	JUN 21-30	JUL 1-10	JUL 11-20	JUL 21-31	AUG 1-10	AUG 11-20	AUG 21-31	SEP 1-10	SEP 11-20	SEP 21-30	OCT 1-10	OCT 11-20	OCT 21-31	NOV 1-10	NOV 11-20	NOV 21-30	DEC 1-10	DEC 11-20	DEC 21-31
1	1																							1	2					2	1		1		4

Eurasian Oystercatcher *(Haematopus ostralegus)*
Status: Common passage migrant. Common winter visitor.
Eurasian Oystercatchers have in the past been observed in all months, though not recently. All records are from coastal sites and pools. The highest daily count is 250 seen by H-M. Busch, J. Rathberger-Knan and W. Bindl at Doha on 6 April 1999.

JAN 1-10	JAN 11-20	JAN 21-31	FEB 1-10	FEB 11-20	FEB 21-29	MAR 1-10	MAR 11-20	MAR 21-31	APR 1-10	APR 11-20	APR 21-30	MAY 1-10	MAY 11-20	MAY 21-31	JUN 1-10	JUN 11-20	JUN 21-30	JUL 1-10	JUL 11-20	JUL 21-31	AUG 1-10	AUG 11-20	AUG 21-31	SEP 1-10	SEP 11-20	SEP 21-30	OCT 1-10	OCT 11-20	OCT 21-31	NOV 1-10	NOV 11-20	NOV 21-30	DEC 1-10	DEC 11-20	DEC 21-31
40	4	2	175	70	50	10	150	154	250				52								2	2	2	5	9	7	25	3	2	17	12	2	4	30	11

Black-winged Stilt *(Himantopus himantopus)*
Status: Common passage migrant. Uncommon summer visitor. Scarce winter visitor. Has bred.
This species is mostly observed on spring or autumn passage, although sometimes it is seen in winter. Almost all records are from coastal sites or pools, but a few have been recorded well inland at Burgan Oil Field, Ahmadi, Abdali Farms, Al-Abraq Al-Khabari and Umm Al-Aish. The highest daily count is 390 seen by S. T. Spencer at Jahra Bay on 26 August 1999.
The first recorded breeding of this species in Kuwait was at Jahra Pool Reserve in 1993. C. W. T. Pilcher wrote of this discovery: 'On 11 June 3 nests at Jahra Pool and by 18 June this had increased to 8. Two of the more accessible were examined; both had two eggs and one nest contained virtually no materials whilst the other had 2 eggs and fragments of reed stems. Of the 38 birds present 14 were juveniles, some or all of which may have been born elsewhere on the site' (Jennings, undated). On 19 May 1998, M. A. A. Al-Jraiwi found and photographed eight birds on nests at a now-dry reservoir about one kilometer east of Jahra Pool Reserve (Al-Jraiwi, 1999). These birds were later photographed by M. Shehab. On 1 June 2004 two recently-fledged juveniles were at Sewer Plant Reeds but they must have hatched elsewhere. On 20 May 2005 B. Foster and P. Fagel observed distraction display by parents at South Doha Nature Reserve and saw 16 newly-fledged juveniles at Jahra East Outfall with 46 adults.

	JAN 1-10	JAN 11-20	JAN 21-31	FEB 1-10	FEB 11-20	FEB 21-29	MAR 1-10	MAR 11-20	MAR 21-31	APR 1-10	APR 11-20	APR 21-30	MAY 1-10	MAY 11-20	MAY 21-31	JUN 1-10	JUN 11-20	JUN 21-30	JUL 1-10	JUL 11-20	JUL 21-31	AUG 1-10	AUG 11-20	AUG 21-31	SEP 1-10	SEP 11-20	SEP 21-30	OCT 1-10	OCT 11-20	OCT 21-31	NOV 1-10	NOV 11-20	NOV 21-30	DEC 1-10	DEC 11-20	DEC 21-31
	5	6	8	20	49	14	33	74	26	14	7	7	8	16	16	70	62	22			5	1	32	390	4	5		2			1					3

Pied Avocet *(Recurvirostra avosetta)*
Status: Common winter visitor. Uncommon passage migrant.
  Pied Avocets are observed mostly at coastal sites and pools. However, there is one inland record of a bird seen at Ahmadi by S. Howe on 6 April 1972. The highest daily count is 160 seen by G. Rowlands at Sulaibikhat Bay on 10 February 2000. A full-winged juvenile seen by B. Foster and A. Bailey at East Doha on 17 June was evidence of breeding in Kuwait, but the exact ABBA square is uncertain.

	JAN 1-10	JAN 11-20	JAN 21-31	FEB 1-10	FEB 11-20	FEB 21-29	MAR 1-10	MAR 11-20	MAR 21-31	APR 1-10	APR 11-20	APR 21-30	MAY 1-10	MAY 11-20	MAY 21-31	JUN 1-10	JUN 11-20	JUN 21-30	JUL 1-10	JUL 11-20	JUL 21-31	AUG 1-10	AUG 11-20	AUG 21-31	SEP 1-10	SEP 11-20	SEP 21-30	OCT 1-10	OCT 11-20	OCT 21-31	NOV 1-10	NOV 11-20	NOV 21-30	DEC 1-10	DEC 11-20	DEC 21-31
	9	3	1	160	42	50	18		10	2	54	3	4	9	9	1									40	25	8		6	4						16

Crab Plover *(Dromas ardeola)*
Status: Very common summer visitor. Common resident. Breeds.
  The first evidence of breeding of Crab Plovers in Kuwait concerns two eggs received by W. D. Cumming on 20 May 1900 and later donated to the British Museum. Although they are labelled 'Fao', E. C. S. Baker wrote that they were 'not I believe at Fao but from some islands further south in the Persian Gulf ... 40 miles south of Fao' (Warr, undated). C. B. Ticehurst, P. A. Buxton and R. E. Cheesman (1922) wrote ' at Fao Cumming obtained specimens in October and eggs from the district. Probably these came from the Khor Abdulla, as Armstrong, while at Fao, ascertained that it breeds there in large numbers and had eggs brought to him on May 20th from there.'
  P. Cox visited Umm Al-Maradim Island on 11 June 1905 and recorded that 'A small group of Crab Plover, *Dromas ardeola* were seen'. On 24 April 1921, V. S. La Personne visited Kubbar Island and saw 'a flock' of Crab Plovers and 'Many holes on the higher ground' (Ticehurst, Cox and Cheesman, 1925). V. S. La Personne also visited Bubiyan Island on 15 April 1922 and collected three specimens of adult Crab Plovers, which are now in the British Museum (Warr, undated). C. B. Ticehurst, P. Cox and R. E. Cheesman (1926) stated of this species: 'It also nests freely on Warba Island.' One undated adult specimen from there was donated to the collection of the Bombay Natural History Society (Abdulali, 1970).
  V. S. La Personne also visited Auha Island on 12 June 1923, finding that Crab Plover 'Breeds in numbers. The parent birds were seen carrying pulped crabs to young in the holes; the young in down walk with difficulty and make a noise like the young of chickens.' Four adult specimens that he obtained on this visit are now in the British Museum (Warr, undated). On a visit to Auha Island on 9 May 1942, V. Dickson

collected 74 Crab Plover eggs, including one 'lying at the entrance to one of the holes, and another ... some way off.' She wrote that ' The mouth of the holes was about six inches across ... The egg lay at the far end of the burrow, which was sometimes as much as four and a half feet long dug obliquely in the ground, others were slightly shorter', 'The usual number of eggs laid was one, but very occasionally two were found in one burrow', and 'the eggs have not a fishy taste and are much sought after by the Arabs.' On 16 August 1970 W. D. Gallagher (1971) observed 'Young birds being fed and learning to fly' on Failaka Island. S. Howe, probably in the 1970s, stated that Crab Plover 'Breeds Failaka and Auha. Eggs are still taken by fishermen on Auha and frantic cries of adults in May along southern beach of Failaka' (Warr, undated).

It is possible that there were undiscovered nest burrows on the north side of Kuwait Bay in about the 1960s. In May, probably in 1968, V. A. D. Sales observed a 'Young bird, too young to have been far from the nest' there, but stated that 'a search could not find any nest holes' (Jennings, undated). However, it must be noted that courtship and feeding of begging juveniles often occur far from breeding sites (Wright, 1995; G. Gregory, personal observations). They are not, of themselves, evidence of nearby breeding. There are still remote and largely undisturbed areas in the north of Kuwait Bay where breeding could still occur.

N. Muddiman recorded this species on Bubiyan Island in May/June 1983 (Warr, undated). In 2002 members of BMAPT found Crab Plovers breeding on Bubiyan Island. About 1000 adults with two food-begging juveniles were observed on 4 April. About 100 active burrows were discovered on 17 May, with many adults and two second-year birds (not newly hatched birds) emerging. Some eggs were found outside burrows, including one on an islet with no nest burrows. E. Ramadan recorded the air temperature inside a nest burrow as being 10°C lower than the air temperature just outside. About 50 old nesting burrows were also found. In 2004 the KISR Bird Team found about 1500 active nest burrows on Bubiyan Island, making a total of about 1600 known active nest holes - probably the largest breeding concentration in the world. They found two nest burrows sharing a common entrance. A number of old nest burrows were discovered on Warba Island, being eroded away by the sea. Future breeding seemed unlikely on this island, due to disturbance. It also seems unlikely on Auha, Umm Al-Maradim and Kubbar Islands for the same reason. In 2005, B. Foster and P. Fagel observed 2500 adults at nest holes on Bubiyan Island on 28 April.

Approximately half of the Kuwait breeding population remains in the state outside the breeding season, some remaining on Bubiyan Island, and almost all the others on Warba Island, and at Jahra Bay and Sulaibikhat Bay. At the latter location up to 450 can be seen in some winters, though most daily counts are lower (Cowan, 1990). The rest of the breeding population presumably disperses to the rest of the Gulf or even beyond, and returns mostly in March. V. A. D. Sales (undated) wrote that 'In 1968 between 21st and 30th March between 07.15 & 09.00 over 800 birds were observed flying in a N-N.N.W. direction over Ahmadi (7 miles inland) with 440 on the first day. A visit to Kuwait Bay on the 30th March & 9th April only about 50 & 30 birds respectively were recorded.' It is unknown whether this remarkable overland route is of regular occurrence, due to paucity of coverage.

JAN 1-10	JAN 11-20	JAN 21-31	FEB 1-10	FEB 11-20	FEB 21-29	MAR 1-10	MAR 11-20	MAR 21-31	APR 1-10	APR 11-20	APR 21-30	MAY 1-10	MAY 11-20	MAY 21-31	JUN 1-10	JUN 11-20	JUN 21-30	JUL 1-10	JUL 11-20	JUL 21-31	AUG 1-10	AUG 11-20	AUG 21-31	SEP 1-10	SEP 11-20	SEP 21-30	OCT 1-10	OCT 11-20	OCT 21-31	NOV 1-10	NOV 11-20	NOV 21-30	DEC 1-10	DEC 11-20	DEC 21-31
104	300	221	107	350	25	150	300	1500	1002	3000	2500	3	200	1000	75	53		20	10		1	20	10	55	30	150	450	30	5	60	5	20			300

Stone-Curlew *(Burhinus oedicnemus)*
Status: Uncommon passage migrant. Rare winter visitor.
Stone-Curlew is a somewhat secretive species in Kuwait, sometimes even hiding under trees. It has been seen in many areas in the state. Occasional birds are flushed from low cover during spring and autumn. There are a few winter records from the past. This species is a prized prey of Kuwaiti falconers. During his years in Kuwait, H. R. P. Dickson bagged a total of 16 birds (Jennings, 1989), so it has probably never been common. The highest daily count is four, recorded on several occasions.

H.R.P. Dickson (1949) listed this species as breeding on the ridge near Ahmadi. However, M. C. Jennings, in a personal communication to G. Gregory, considered this claim to be in error.

JAN 1-10	JAN 11-20	JAN 21-31	FEB 1-10	FEB 11-20	FEB 21-29	MAR 1-10	MAR 11-20	MAR 21-31	APR 1-10	APR 11-20	APR 21-30	MAY 1-10	MAY 11-20	MAY 21-31	JUN 1-10	JUN 11-20	JUN 21-30	JUL 1-10	JUL 11-20	JUL 21-31	AUG 1-10	AUG 11-20	AUG 21-31	SEP 1-10	SEP 11-20	SEP 21-30	OCT 1-10	OCT 11-20	OCT 21-31	NOV 1-10	NOV 11-20	NOV 21-30	DEC 1-10	DEC 11-20	DEC 21-31
		1				4	2		1																1	1					4				

Cream-coloured Courser *(Cursorius cursor)*
Status: Common disperser in spring, summer and autumn. Breeds.
This species has probably always bred regularly in the more remote areas of Kuwait, but eggs or flightless chicks have only rarely been found. The first record of breeding was on 11 March 1937 near Ahmadi by V. Dickson, who wrote: 'we found 2 chicks just hatched, but not in any nest, they crouched when we approached and shutting their eyes exactly resembled a pebble.' In the same area on 1 March 1939, she found two eggs that were probably of this species, recording: 'No nest, slight depression (hoof-mark), eggs pale buff covered all over in small blotches of grey and brown and measuring about 39mm. Many pairs about. Later on 17-3-99 [clearly intended to be 39] we actually caught one young one of about 4 or 5 days old. There were two of them. Still covered in down but could run very fast' (V. Dickson, undated). On 14 April 1977 W. A. Stuart found an adult with two chicks near Salmi.

From early June onwards, family parties start wandering around, and it is not easy to know if observations of them constitute proof of breeding in the area where they are seen. Such parties have been observed at Umm Al-Aish, the Sabah Al-Ahmed Natural Reserve, Khor Ala'ma, Bahra and Subiya. Later, larger groups of adults and juveniles often form, and may be found far from breeding areas. Examples are 161 (the highest daily count) seen by V. A. D. Sales at Kuwait Bay on 15 July 1956, and up to 100 seen by many observers at Sulaibikhat Nature Reserve in September 2003. Many of these birds have probably dispersed from outside of Kuwait.

JAN 1-10	JAN 11-20	JAN 21-31	FEB 1-10	FEB 11-20	FEB 21-29	MAR 1-10	MAR 11-20	MAR 21-31	APR 1-10	APR 11-20	APR 21-30	MAY 1-10	MAY 11-20	MAY 21-31	JUN 1-10	JUN 11-20	JUN 21-30	JUL 1-10	JUL 11-20	JUL 21-31	AUG 1-10	AUG 11-20	AUG 21-31	SEP 1-10	SEP 11-20	SEP 21-30	OCT 1-10	OCT 11-20	OCT 21-31	NOV 1-10	NOV 11-20	NOV 21-30	DEC 1-10	DEC 11-20	DEC 21-31
	1							1				5	3	6	3	36	2	7	5	9	70	100	80	4			1								

Collared Pratincole *(Glareola pratincola)*
Status: Common passage migrant. Scarce summer visitor.

Collared Pratincoles may have bred in Kuwait. On 12 June 2000, G. Gregory and P. Robertson observed two agitated adults flying slowly around and making wailing sounds after a massive fire at Jahra East Outfall; possibly a nest or young were destroyed by heat. Otherwise this species occurs mostly on passage in spring and autumn, with a few present in summer every year. Records are from many areas in the state. The highest daily count is 110+ seen by V. A. D. Sales at Kuwait Bay on 23 April 1956.

JAN 1-10	JAN 11-20	JAN 21-31	FEB 1-10	FEB 11-20	FEB 21-29	MAR 1-10	MAR 11-20	MAR 21-31	APR 1-10	APR 11-20	APR 21-30	MAY 1-10	MAY 11-20	MAY 21-31	JUN 1-10	JUN 11-20	JUN 21-30	JUL 1-10	JUL 11-20	JUL 21-31	AUG 1-10	AUG 11-20	AUG 21-31	SEP 1-10	SEP 11-20	SEP 21-30	OCT 1-10	OCT 11-20	OCT 21-31	NOV 1-10	NOV 11-20	NOV 21-30	DEC 1-10	DEC 11-20	DEC 21-31
						3	37	50	2	2	10	6	35		2	1			1		3			1	6	4	1								

Black-winged Pratincole *(Glareola nordmanni)*
Status: Uncommon passage migrant.

This species is usually much less frequently observed than the previous one. All records have been of passage birds, usually seen at coastal sites but sometimes well inland. The highest daily count is 57 seen at Jahra East Outfall by G. Gregory on 24 March 2000.

JAN 1-10	JAN 11-20	JAN 21-31	FEB 1-10	FEB 11-20	FEB 21-29	MAR 1-10	MAR 11-20	MAR 21-31	APR 1-10	APR 11-20	APR 21-30	MAY 1-10	MAY 11-20	MAY 21-31	JUN 1-10	JUN 11-20	JUN 21-30	JUL 1-10	JUL 11-20	JUL 21-31	AUG 1-10	AUG 11-20	AUG 21-31	SEP 1-10	SEP 11-20	SEP 21-30	OCT 1-10	OCT 11-20	OCT 21-31	NOV 1-10	NOV 11-20	NOV 21-30	DEC 1-10	DEC 11-20	DEC 21-31
						25	57	1	8		6	1		1							2			1											

Little Ringed Plover *(Charadrius dubius)*
Status: Uncommon passage migrant. Scarce summer visitor. Scarce winter visitor.

Little Ringed Plovers are most commonly observed, in fairly small numbers, in spring, mostly on sewage-water pools. Some are recorded in autumn and a few in summer. There is one record of a bird far inland near Wadi Al-Batin seen by P. R. Haynes on 4 April 1974. This species has never been known to breed in Kuwait, despite there being apparently suitable sites. There have been several extremely high counts in the past, clearly indicating confusion with other species of waders. The highest reliable daily count is 20 seen at Jahra East Outfall by H-M. Busch, J. Rathberger-Knan, F. Lange and A. Lange on 15 March 2000.

JAN 1-10	JAN 11-20	JAN 21-31	FEB 1-10	FEB 11-20	FEB 21-29	MAR 1-10	MAR 11-20	MAR 21-31	APR 1-10	APR 11-20	APR 21-30	MAY 1-10	MAY 11-20	MAY 21-31	JUN 1-10	JUN 11-20	JUN 21-30	JUL 1-10	JUL 11-20	JUL 21-31	AUG 1-10	AUG 11-20	AUG 21-31	SEP 1-10	SEP 11-20	SEP 21-30	OCT 1-10	OCT 11-20	OCT 21-31	NOV 1-10	NOV 11-20	NOV 21-30	DEC 1-10	DEC 11-20	DEC 21-31
					1	8	20	13	13	1	1	5	1		2	1	3				3	9	4		1	3	8	1							

Common Ringed Plover *(Charadrius hiaticula)*
Status: **Common passage migrant. Common winter visitor. Rare summer visitor.**

This species has been recorded in all months, but only a few birds have been observed in summer. All birds seen have been at coastal sites, except for several seen at Umm Al-Aish and at Ahmadi. The highest reliable daily count is 240 seen by B. Foster and P. Fagel at Jahra East Outfall on 6 May 2005.

JAN 1-10	JAN 11-20	JAN 21-31	FEB 1-10	FEB 11-20	FEB 21-29	MAR 1-10	MAR 11-20	MAR 21-31	APR 1-10	APR 11-20	APR 21-30	MAY 1-10	MAY 11-20	MAY 21-31	JUN 1-10	JUN 11-20	JUN 21-30	JUL 1-10	JUL 11-20	JUL 21-31	AUG 1-10	AUG 11-20	AUG 21-31	SEP 1-10	SEP 11-20	SEP 21-30	OCT 1-10	OCT 11-20	OCT 21-31	NOV 1-10	NOV 11-20	NOV 21-30	DEC 1-10	DEC 11-20	DEC 21-31
35	40	15	45	57	5	40	2	20	25	6	8	240	50	4		6					4		20	45	5	20	20	5	4	3	1		2		28

Kentish Plover *(Charadrius alexandrinus)*
Status: **Very common resident. Breeds.**

Breeding by this species in Kuwait was first recorded on Maskan Island on 7 May 1942 by V. Dickson. She wrote: 'Kentish Plover, 'Garawi' were nesting. Their nests were usually on the dry hard patches of earth away from the shore, and were just a circular depression lined with chips of dry mud and pieces of broken sea shell. I found two nests containing three eggs and one nest with one egg. One bird was seen running ahead of us trailing her wing and taking a zigzag shoreward course. She probably had young, but I could not find them' (V. Dickson, 1942). Since then breeding has been recorded at many coastal sites from Bubiyan Island to the south-east coast, and at a saline pool at Sabah Al-Salem. The building of chalets along much of the coastline in recent years has, no doubt, reduced the number of breeding pairs. At some sites there is a fairly high breeding concentration. At Sulaibikhat Nature Reserve 39 nests were discovered in 2003 along a one kilometre stretch of bay, with some nests 50 metres from the tide-line. Unfortunately, the eggs in 12 nests were eaten by Long-eared Hedgehogs (*Hemiechinus auritus*) (Al-Nasrallah, 2004).

Outside of the breeding season quite large flocks form. The highest daily count is 'thousands' along Kuwait Bay seen by V. A. D. Sales on 15 July 1958. Recent maxima have been lower.

Lesser Sand Plover *(Charadrius mongolus)*
Status: **Common passage migrant. Common winter visitor. Uncommon summer visitor.**

This species is usually observed in moderate numbers, in all seasons, but some quite big flocks are occasionally found. At high tide quite large groups can be observed near the shore. All birds seen have been at coastal sites or pools. The highest reliable daily count is 500 seen on several occasions. This species has clearly been thoroughly confused with Greater Sand Plover (*C. leschenaultii*), mostly in the past but also recently. Accordingly, some editing of records has been necessary in producing the table.

JAN 1-10	JAN 11-20	JAN 21-31	FEB 1-10	FEB 11-20	FEB 21-29	MAR 1-10	MAR 11-20	MAR 21-31	APR 1-10	APR 11-20	APR 21-30	MAY 1-10	MAY 11-20	MAY 21-31	JUN 1-10	JUN 11-20	JUN 21-30	JUL 1-10	JUL 11-20	JUL 21-31	AUG 1-10	AUG 11-20	AUG 21-31	SEP 1-10	SEP 11-20	SEP 21-30	OCT 1-10	OCT 11-20	OCT 21-31	NOV 1-10	NOV 11-20	NOV 21-30	DEC 1-10	DEC 11-20	DEC 21-31
300	200	15	7	60	5	500	180	6	500		7	42	3	4	75	30		1	4	9		30	1	14	9	30	50	15	40	21	50	1	400	90	60

Greater Sand Plover *(Charadrius leschenaultii)*
Status: Common passage migrant. Common winter visitor. Uncommon summer visitor. Has bred.

Greater Sand Plovers are usually more common than the previous species. They are usually found in similar habitats, but sometimes in sand dunes near the shore. The highest daily count is 'several thousand' seen by P. A. D. Hollom and V. A. D. Sales along Kuwait Bay on 20 November 1965. This species has clearly been thoroughly confused with Lesser Sand Plover (*C. mongolus*), mostly in the past but also recently. Accordingly, some editing of records has been necessary in producing the table.

This species is known to have bred twice in Kuwait. On 22 May 2000 G. Rowlands found a downy chick, accompanied by a parent, on an area of inland saltpans at Sabah Al-Salem. He reported the observation to G. Gregory, who visited the site on 25 May and relocated the chick accompanied by an adult female of the subspecies *C. l. columbinus*. The parent moved away rapidly, partly drooping one wing, apparently injury feigning. The chick ran several metres, and then hid by crouching in a dry, flat patch of Salsola-type vegetation. Nearby there were three other columbinus-type Greater Sand Plovers, including a male in rather poor plumage. Breeding in the same place was confirmed again in 2001, with G. Rowlands finding two downy chicks on 12 May. From 2002 onwards the late spring flock of Greater Sand Plovers did not form at Sabah Al-Salem, possibly due to disturbance and dieback of vegetation, and breeding was not recorded again. This remarkable incidence of breeding was probably opportunistic.

JAN 1-10	JAN 11-20	JAN 21-31	FEB 1-10	FEB 11-20	FEB 21-29	MAR 1-10	MAR 11-20	MAR 21-31	APR 1-10	APR 11-20	APR 21-30	MAY 1-10	MAY 11-20	MAY 21-31	JUN 1-10	JUN 11-20	JUN 21-30	JUL 1-10	JUL 11-20	JUL 21-31	AUG 1-10	AUG 11-20	AUG 21-31	SEP 1-10	SEP 11-20	SEP 21-30	OCT 1-10	OCT 11-20	OCT 21-31	NOV 1-10	NOV 11-20	NOV 21-30	DEC 1-10	DEC 11-20	DEC 21-31
50	150	200	2	150	150	10	700	200		2000		6	1	4		4	40	14	9	2	5	6	10	6	10	15	50	5	12	4	100	2		5	450

Caspian Plover *(Charadrius asiaticus)*
Status: Uncommon passage migrant.

Migrating Caspian Plovers pass through Kuwait in spring and autumn. However, they are no doubt under-recorded, since they often move through well inland, as evidenced by hunters shooting them occasionally at desert shooting camps and near isolated inland farms such as Al-Abraq Al-Khabari. Some are observed at coastal sites and at the saline pool at Sabah Al-Salem. The highest reliable daily count is 13 seen by M. O. Chichester at Khor Ala'ma on 16 August 2000. Records of much higher numbers, even in winter, along the coastline, clearly involve confusion with other species of waders.

JAN 1-10	JAN 11-20	JAN 21-31	FEB 1-10	FEB 11-20	FEB 21-29	MAR 1-10	MAR 11-20	MAR 21-31	APR 1-10	APR 11-20	APR 21-30	MAY 1-10	MAY 11-20	MAY 21-31	JUN 1-10	JUN 11-20	JUN 21-30	JUL 1-10	JUL 11-20	JUL 21-31	AUG 1-10	AUG 11-20	AUG 21-31	SEP 1-10	SEP 11-20	SEP 21-30	OCT 1-10	OCT 11-20	OCT 21-31	NOV 1-10	NOV 11-20	NOV 21-30	DEC 1-10	DEC 11-20	DEC 21-31
								9		2		10	1		3	13					2	13	2		1	5									

Eurasian Dotterel *(Charadrius morinellus)*
Status: Rare winter visitor and passage migrant.
This species has been recorded mainly from inland sites, including Rawdatain, Wadi Al-Batin and Haswan. Other birds have been seen nearer the coast at Judailiyat and in the coastal section of the Sabah Al-Ahmed Natural Reserve. The highest reliable daily count is 15 seen by V. A. D. Sales near Ahmadi on 30 November 1962.

JAN 1-10	JAN 11-20	JAN 21-31	FEB 1-10	FEB 11-20	FEB 21-29	MAR 1-10	MAR 11-20	MAR 21-31	APR 1-10	APR 11-20	APR 21-30	MAY 1-10	MAY 11-20	MAY 21-31	JUN 1-10	JUN 11-20	JUN 21-30	JUL 1-10	JUL 11-20	JUL 21-31	AUG 1-10	AUG 11-20	AUG 21-31	SEP 1-10	SEP 11-20	SEP 21-30	OCT 1-10	OCT 11-20	OCT 21-31	NOV 1-10	NOV 11-20	NOV 21-30	DEC 1-10	DEC 11-20	DEC 21-31
7																													12		5				

Pacific Golden Plover *(Pluvialis fulva)*
Status: Scarce passage migrant and winter visitor.
Pacific Golden Plovers are recorded every year in small numbers at coastal sites. All or nearly all of the records of European Golden Plover (*P. apricaria*) in Kuwait clearly refer to this species. The highest reliable daily count is three seen on several occasions.

JAN 1-10	JAN 11-20	JAN 21-31	FEB 1-10	FEB 11-20	FEB 21-29	MAR 1-10	MAR 11-20	MAR 21-31	APR 1-10	APR 11-20	APR 21-30	MAY 1-10	MAY 11-20	MAY 21-31	JUN 1-10	JUN 11-20	JUN 21-30	JUL 1-10	JUL 11-20	JUL 21-31	AUG 1-10	AUG 11-20	AUG 21-31	SEP 1-10	SEP 11-20	SEP 21-30	OCT 1-10	OCT 11-20	OCT 21-31	NOV 1-10	NOV 11-20	NOV 21-30	DEC 1-10	DEC 11-20	DEC 21-31
1			1			3	3														1				1					1					

Grey Plover *(Pluvialis squatarola)*
Status: Common winter visitor. Uncommon passage migrant. Scarce summer visitor.
All records of Grey Plovers have been along the coastline or at pools except for singles seen at Ahmadi by J. Webb and B. Brown on 5 and 13 May 1972. The highest reliable daily count is 340 seen by B. Foster and P. Fagel at East Doha on 29 April 2005.

JAN 1-10	JAN 11-20	JAN 21-31	FEB 1-10	FEB 11-20	FEB 21-29	MAR 1-10	MAR 11-20	MAR 21-31	APR 1-10	APR 11-20	APR 21-30	MAY 1-10	MAY 11-20	MAY 21-31	JUN 1-10	JUN 11-20	JUN 21-30	JUL 1-10	JUL 11-20	JUL 21-31	AUG 1-10	AUG 11-20	AUG 21-31	SEP 1-10	SEP 11-20	SEP 21-30	OCT 1-10	OCT 11-20	OCT 21-31	NOV 1-10	NOV 11-20	NOV 21-30	DEC 1-10	DEC 11-20	DEC 21-31
4	20	27	22	25	15	120	140	23	50	8	340	15	50	2	4	6		6		8	4	30	9	15	4	20	6	16	15	5	7	20	2	6	44

Spur-winged Lapwing *(Hoplopterus spinosus)*
Status: Vagrant (four records).

The first one recorded in Kuwait was seen by V. A. D. Sales at Ahmadi on 29 November 1958. His description, which was written on a Rare Bird Report form and accepted by the panel, is as follows:
'Lapwing like and size. Black and white with pale back and wing. Head and nape jet black. Mantle and back brownish. Upper tail coverts white. Sides of head and neck including ear coverts white. Under parts: chin, centre of breast and flanks black, belly and under tail coverts white. Tail black. Wings pale brown but in flight primaries blackish. Under wing coverts white giving a black and white appearance. Bill, legs and feet black. Iris reddish.
Three Lapwings had been seen 10 days before on the 19th November so the contrast between these birds was quite striking.'

A single bird was seen by M. Shehab at Jahra Bay on 16 October 1992. The main features were observed.

One was seen by P. Jones and T. Squire at Jahra Pool Reserve on 13 March 1996. The description, which was accepted by KORC, included the main identificatory features.

One was seen by S. T. Spencer and M. O. Chichester at Jahra Bay on 7.1.2000. A full description was written and accepted by KORC.

Red-wattled Lapwing *(Hoplopterus indicus)*
Status: Scarce disperser in autumn, winter and spring. Rare summer visitor. Has bred.

At least one Red-wattled Lapwing has been observed every year recently, usually singly at coastal sites and pools. This species has bred once in Kuwait. In 2003 at the Yacoub Boodai Farm at Abdali, there was a maximum of 15 (the highest daily count) in January, usually beside artificial freshwater ponds. One pair remained to breed in June, when a flightless chick was found, examined by Yacoub Boodai, and then returned whence it was found, while the adults flew overhead calling frantically. In 2004 there were seven at the same farm on 18 March, but there was no further evidence of breeding.

JAN 1-10	JAN 11-20	JAN 21-31	FEB 1-10	FEB 11-20	FEB 21-29	MAR 1-10	MAR 11-20	MAR 21-31	APR 1-10	APR 11-20	APR 21-30	MAY 1-10	MAY 11-20	MAY 21-31	JUN 1-10	JUN 11-20	JUN 21-30	JUL 1-10	JUL 11-20	JUL 21-31	AUG 1-10	AUG 11-20	AUG 21-31	SEP 1-10	SEP 11-20	SEP 21-30	OCT 1-10	OCT 11-20	OCT 21-31	NOV 1-10	NOV 11-20	NOV 21-30	DEC 1-10	DEC 11-20	DEC 21-31
7	15	8	2	2	2	2	7	2	2	2	2	2	2	3				1			1				1			1				1	1	

Sociable Lapwing *(Chettusia gregaria)*
Status: Vagrant (two records).

One was seen at Subiya by J. Webb (and possibly also J. H. B. Brown) on 19 March 1971. This record was accepted by P. R. Haynes (1979) and by C. W. T. Pilcher (undated). The description is not accessible.

One was seen at Bharat Ali, near the Salmi Road, on 12 December 1999 by M. Shehab, who noted a black cap surrounded by white, brown body with white belly, and black and white on wings and tail.

Two birds possibly of this species were observed briefly by M. O. Chichester as they were flushed from an area just northwest of Wafra Oil Field and flew to the northwest on 15 January 2000.

White-tailed Lapwing *(Chettusia leucura)*
Status: Uncommon passage migrant.
 White-tailed Plovers are mostly observed from February to April, with lower numbers in November, mostly at sewage-water and saline pools. There are inland records at Umm Ar-Rimam, seen by S. Howe on 27 February 1971, at Umm Al-Aish, seen by L. Corrall on 12 November 1978, and Ratqa, seen by S. Al-Awadi on 5 March 2002. Numbers in spring have clearly increased recently, with sizable flocks observed. The highest daily count is 57 seen by S. T. Spencer at Jahra East Outfall on 26 February 1999.

JAN 1-10	JAN 11-20	JAN 21-31	FEB 1-10	FEB 11-20	FEB 21-29	MAR 1-10	MAR 11-20	MAR 21-31	APR 1-10	APR 11-20	APR 21-30	MAY 1-10	MAY 11-20	MAY 21-31	JUN 1-10	JUN 11-20	JUN 21-30	JUL 1-10	JUL 11-20	JUL 21-31	AUG 1-10	AUG 11-20	AUG 21-31	SEP 1-10	SEP 11-20	SEP 21-30	OCT 1-10	OCT 11-20	OCT 21-31	NOV 1-10	NOV 11-20	NOV 21-30	DEC 1-10	DEC 11-20	DEC 21-31
			1	57	30	5	4	1	2																						1	1			

Northern Lapwing *(Vanellus vanellus)*
Status: Scarce winter visitor. Scarce passage migrant.
 Recently, Northern Lapwings have been recorded every year, usually in small numbers. Birds have been seen at both coastal and inland locations. The highest daily count is an exceptional flock of 43 seen by G. Gregory flying south over Kabd on 24 January 2005.

JAN 1-10	JAN 11-20	JAN 21-31	FEB 1-10	FEB 11-20	FEB 21-29	MAR 1-10	MAR 11-20	MAR 21-31	APR 1-10	APR 11-20	APR 21-30	MAY 1-10	MAY 11-20	MAY 21-31	JUN 1-10	JUN 11-20	JUN 21-30	JUL 1-10	JUL 11-20	JUL 21-31	AUG 1-10	AUG 11-20	AUG 21-31	SEP 1-10	SEP 11-20	SEP 21-30	OCT 1-10	OCT 11-20	OCT 21-31	NOV 1-10	NOV 11-20	NOV 21-30	DEC 1-10	DEC 11-20	DEC 21-31
	43	2																										2		6	6		6		

Great Knot *(Calidris tenuirostris)*
Status: Uncommon winter visitor.
 The first described record for Kuwait was a group of 11 birds seen and photographed by G. Gregory, S. Al-Dosary and J. Dashti at Ras Al-Gaid, on the eastern side of Bubiyan Island on 11 March 2004. The description is below:
'At about 11am on 11 March 2004, GG, AD and JD were searching through a large mixed flock of gulls, terns and waders at Ras Al-Gaid on the eastern side of Bubiyan Island. Waders in the flock included Redshanks, Curlews, Grey Plovers and Bar-tailed Godwits. In amongst a group of the latter, at a range of about 75 metres from the observers, were three smaller waders, which were not immediately identified. However, two of them took off and one chased the other around within about 40 metres of the observers, who were able to obtain excellent views of all features in flight in excellent light conditions. They were clearly identified as Great Knot. They settled back next to the Bar-tailed Godwits and were compared with nearby Grey Plovers and Redshanks. About 15 metres to the north of them, also amongst Bar-tailed Godwits, were eight

more Great Knot, for a total of eleven. About ten photographs of them were taken using a large digital camera. The birds were under observation for about 30 minutes, mostly on the muddy shore, but also two were well observed in flight several more times.
Size and Shape: Noticeably smaller than nearby Bar-tailed Godwits, about size of nearby Redshanks, and less chunky than nearby Grey Plovers. Generally resembled outsize Dunlin in shape rather than Knot, from memory.
Plumage at rest: Most of head grayish with a whitish supercilium and a whitish throat. Dark, almost blackish centers to feathers on nape, back and breast (forming a semi-distinct breast band), with off-white edges. Rest of upper feathering had grayish centers and off-white edges. Belly generally white with some darker marking on flanks.
Additional plumage features in flight: Upperwings mostly mid-grey with a thin wing bar and noticeably dark primary coverts. Entire underwing and axillaries whitish. Rump white with a small amount of admixed pale grey marking, contrasting with medium/dark grey back and tail.
Exposed parts: Bill blackish, moderately long and slightly decurved (quite Dunlin-shaped). Eye not distinguished. Legs dirty greenish-grey.'

On 25 March 2004 the same observers saw 19 Great Knot on the western side of Bubiyan Island. G. Gregory then observed seven at Ras Al-Gaid on 18 October 2004. The KISR Bird Team recorded eight on the western side of Bubiyan Island on 10 February 2005. G. Gregory saw a single bird at Jahra East Outfall on 6 March 2005.

Observers in the past were, no doubt, unaware that this species could occur in Kuwait (it has recently been observed regularly in Bahrain and elsewhere in the Gulf). In the rest of the Gulf, Red Knot (*C. canuta*) is extremely rare, and Purple Sandpiper (*C. maritima*) is unrecorded and most unlikely to occur. Probably the observers then had no field guides or other books showing this species, which they might well have identified as these other species.

All or most of the following past records of Red Knot, regarded as rejected by F. E. Warr (undated), more likely refer to Great Knot than to Red Knot: 18 January 1963 (one), 25 May 1963 (one), 17 January 1964 (one), 8 October 1965 (three), 12 April 1966 (one), 29 December 1966 (two), 29 October 1971 (one) and 29 April 1974 (a few). All these birds were seen in Kuwait Bay and the observers were V. A. D. Sales and P. R. Haynes.

Additionally, all or most of the past records of Purple Sandpiper (*C. maritima*), regarded as rejected by F. E. Warr (undated), most likely refer to Great Knot: 18 January 1963 (one), 2 February 1967 (one), 21 April 1969 (one), an unstated date in 1970 (one) and 15 March 1972 (one). All of these birds were seen in Kuwait Bay; the observers were J. Webb, J. D. Etchécopar and V. A. D. Sales.

The above observers in the past also had no access to Bubiyan Island. In these circumstances, the status given above for Great Knot is probably the best one.

JAN 1-10	JAN 11-20	JAN 21-31	FEB 1-10	FEB 11-20	FEB 21-29	MAR 1-10	MAR 11-20	MAR 21-31	APR 1-10	APR 11-20	APR 21-30	MAY 1-10	MAY 11-20	MAY 21-31	JUN 1-10	JUN 11-20	JUN 21-30	JUL 1-10	JUL 11-20	JUL 21-31	AUG 1-10	AUG 11-20	AUG 21-31	SEP 1-10	SEP 11-20	SEP 21-30	OCT 1-10	OCT 11-20	OCT 21-31	NOV 1-10	NOV 11-20	NOV 21-30	DEC 1-10	DEC 11-20	DEC 21-31
					8		1	11	19																			7							

Red Knot *(Calidris canutus)*
Status: Vagrant (one record).

The only acceptable record of Red Knot in Kuwait is of one in summer plumage seen by V. A. D. Sales at Kuwait Bay on 26 July 1962, described on a Rare Bird Report form and accepted by the panel. His description is below:

'Wind slight N.E. Bright and sunny. Kuwait Bay. 07.45 - 10.15 hrs, during last hour slight heat haze with increase humidity and incoming tide.
Description: plumpish, speckled brown upper parts, and chestnut breast and belly. Under tail whitish. Crown black, brown streaks extended over nape a light chestnut/cinnamon. Mantle more spotted - feathers black/brown with light brown edges and light tips.
Side of Head: pale chestnut eye stripe, lores darker slight streaking. Ear coverts as lores.
Under parts: chin, breast and belly, pale chestnut lights on flanks. Under tail whitish ? some darker streaking.
Wing: primaries black brown with lighter edges to inner primaries. Secondaries dark brown with light brown or chestnut-brownish fringes. Coverts and scapulars similar with narrower fringes.
Bare Parts: bill, black similar to Reeve. Iris darkish. Legs dull green.
Bird with Oyster Catchers. Tail brownish with light edges, a little longer than wing tips ? squarish. Plumpish like Turnstone but larger, bill longer and narrower. Bird perching in the soft mud.'

The same observer also recorded one on 24 August 1962; this was most likely the same bird.

All or most of the other records of Red Knot between 1963 and 1974 more likely refer to Great Knot (*C. tenuirostris*) than to Red Knot (see the above account for Great Knot).

More recent records, some involving high counts, of Red Knot in Kuwait clearly involve confusion with other species of waders.

Sanderling *(Calidris alba)*
Status: Common passage migrant. Common winter visitor.

Sanderlings are usually present in small flocks at most coastal sites and occasionally on saline pools. There is one inland record of a bird seen at Ahmadi by J. Webb and B. Brown on 13 May 1972. The highest daily count is 'several thousand' recorded by V. A. D. Sales on 15 July 1958 and on 7 February 1964 at Kuwait Bay. Recent yearly maxima have been much lower.

JAN 1-10	JAN 11-20	JAN 21-31	FEB 1-10	FEB 11-20	FEB 21-29	MAR 1-10	MAR 11-20	MAR 21-31	APR 1-10	APR 11-20	APR 21-30	MAY 1-10	MAY 11-20	MAY 21-31	JUN 1-10	JUN 11-20	JUN 21-30	JUL 1-10	JUL 11-20	JUL 21-31	AUG 1-10	AUG 11-20	AUG 21-31	SEP 1-10	SEP 11-20	SEP 21-30	OCT 1-10	OCT 11-20	OCT 21-31	NOV 1-10	NOV 11-20	NOV 21-30	DEC 1-10	DEC 11-20	DEC 21-31
3	130	9	15	38	1	40	60	128	20	9	4	18	7		4	3				1	6	21	4	8	30	4	8	18	6	12					50

Little Stint *(Calidris minuta)*
Status: Very common passage migrant. Common winter visitor.
 This species is widespread along the coast and on pools, but the only inland record is a single at Umm Al-Aish seen by S. Howe and A. Caldwell on 21 September 1972. The highest reliable daily count is 1000 seen by P. Fagel and B. Foster at East Doha on 11 March 2005.

JAN 1-10	JAN 11-20	JAN 21-31	FEB 1-10	FEB 11-20	FEB 21-29	MAR 1-10	MAR 11-20	MAR 21-31	APR 1-10	APR 11-20	APR 21-30	MAY 1-10	MAY 11-20	MAY 21-31	JUN 1-10	JUN 11-20	JUN 21-30	JUL 1-10	JUL 11-20	JUL 21-31	AUG 1-10	AUG 11-20	AUG 21-31	SEP 1-10	SEP 11-20	SEP 21-30	OCT 1-10	OCT 11-20	OCT 21-31	NOV 1-10	NOV 11-20	NOV 21-30	DEC 1-10	DEC 11-20	DEC 21-31
5	100	20	28	75	30	100	1000	114	300	16	68	658	302	100	11	9	9				9	15	18	150	22	200	20	20	15	8	15	14	11		5

Temminck's Stint *(Calidris temminckii)*
Status: Uncommon passage migrant. Uncommon winter visitor.
 Temminck's Stints are much less common than the previous species but have probably been much overlooked. The first, and only inland, record is of two seen by R. Meinertzhagen 'in flooded cropland' in January 1951. The highest daily count is 10+ seen by P. Fagel and M. Varhimo at Jahra East Outfall on 6 April 2005.

JAN 1-10	JAN 11-20	JAN 21-31	FEB 1-10	FEB 11-20	FEB 21-29	MAR 1-10	MAR 11-20	MAR 21-31	APR 1-10	APR 11-20	APR 21-30	MAY 1-10	MAY 11-20	MAY 21-31	JUN 1-10	JUN 11-20	JUN 21-30	JUL 1-10	JUL 11-20	JUL 21-31	AUG 1-10	AUG 11-20	AUG 21-31	SEP 1-10	SEP 11-20	SEP 21-30	OCT 1-10	OCT 11-20	OCT 21-31	NOV 1-10	NOV 11-20	NOV 21-30	DEC 1-10	DEC 11-20	DEC 21-31
1	2	1	1	4	5	2	3		10	1	1	3									1			2	3		2								4

Curlew Sandpiper *(Calidris ferruginea)*
Status: Common passage migrant.
 Either singly or in small groups, this species is fairly regularly recorded in spring and autumn on the coast or on pools. There are a few inland records at Umm Al-Aish and Ahmadi. The highest reliable daily count is 254 seen at Jahra East Outfall and East Doha by B. Foster and P. Fagel on 5 May 2005.

JAN 1-10	JAN 11-20	JAN 21-31	FEB 1-10	FEB 11-20	FEB 21-29	MAR 1-10	MAR 11-20	MAR 21-31	APR 1-10	APR 11-20	APR 21-30	MAY 1-10	MAY 11-20	MAY 21-31	JUN 1-10	JUN 11-20	JUN 21-30	JUL 1-10	JUL 11-20	JUL 21-31	AUG 1-10	AUG 11-20	AUG 21-31	SEP 1-10	SEP 11-20	SEP 21-30	OCT 1-10	OCT 11-20	OCT 21-31	NOV 1-10	NOV 11-20	NOV 21-30	DEC 1-10	DEC 11-20	DEC 21-31
	2		4	3	86	20	40	254	203	8	6	8	22	6	1		11	20	14	30	8	10	1	4		3	4	3							

Dunlin *(Calidris alpina)*
Status: Very common passage migrant. Common winter visitor.

Dunlins are regularly observed, mostly on passage, on the coast or on pools, with a few inland records at Ahmadi and Umm Al-Aish. The highest daily count is 5000 along Jahra Bay seen by H-M. Busch, J. Rathberger-Knan, F. Lange and A. Lange on 19 March 2000.

JAN 1-10	JAN 11-20	JAN 21-31	FEB 1-10	FEB 11-20	FEB 21-29	MAR 1-10	MAR 11-20	MAR 21-31	APR 1-10	APR 11-20	APR 21-30	MAY 1-10	MAY 11-20	MAY 21-31	JUN 1-10	JUN 11-20	JUN 21-30
25	500	220	350	200	150	1000	5000	200	2500	65	35	50	6	4		60	

JUL 1-10	JUL 11-20	JUL 21-31	AUG 1-10	AUG 11-20	AUG 21-31	SEP 1-10	SEP 11-20	SEP 21-30	OCT 1-10	OCT 11-20	OCT 21-31	NOV 1-10	NOV 11-20	NOV 21-30	DEC 1-10	DEC 11-20	DEC 21-31
1	9	7	40	40	80	45	52	25		60	20	5					400

Broad-billed Sandpiper *(Limicola falcinellus)*
Status: Uncommon winter visitor. Uncommon passage migrant.

This species has probably been much overlooked in the past. It is found occasionally in winter or on passage, all records being at coastal sites or on pools. The highest daily count is 124 seen by B. Foster and P. Fagel at East Doha on 5 May 2005.

JAN 1-10	JAN 11-20	JAN 21-31	FEB 1-10	FEB 11-20	FEB 21-29	MAR 1-10	MAR 11-20	MAR 21-31	APR 1-10	APR 11-20	APR 21-30	MAY 1-10	MAY 11-20	MAY 21-31	JUN 1-10	JUN 11-20	JUN 21-30
55	30									2		1	124	2		2	

JUL 1-10	JUL 11-20	JUL 21-31	AUG 1-10	AUG 11-20	AUG 21-31	SEP 1-10	SEP 11-20	SEP 21-30	OCT 1-10	OCT 11-20	OCT 21-31	NOV 1-10	NOV 11-20	NOV 21-30	DEC 1-10	DEC 11-20	DEC 21-31
			4	2	1	4				17	4				5		

Ruff *(Philomachus pugnax)*
Status: Uncommon passage migrant. Rare winter visitor.

Ruffs, usually in groups, are occasionally observed, mostly on passage at sewage-water or saline pools. The highest reliable daily count is 150 seen at Jahra East Outfall and East Doha by P. Fagel on 12 May 2005.

JAN 1-10	JAN 11-20	JAN 21-31	FEB 1-10	FEB 11-20	FEB 21-29	MAR 1-10	MAR 11-20	MAR 21-31	APR 1-10	APR 11-20	APR 21-30	MAY 1-10	MAY 11-20	MAY 21-31	JUN 1-10	JUN 11-20	JUN 21-30
4	2	14	14	50	80	37	40	17	22	49	150	6	3	2		1	2

JUL 1-10	JUL 11-20	JUL 21-31	AUG 1-10	AUG 11-20	AUG 21-31	SEP 1-10	SEP 11-20	SEP 21-30	OCT 1-10	OCT 11-20	OCT 21-31	NOV 1-10	NOV 11-20	NOV 21-30	DEC 1-10	DEC 11-20	DEC 21-31
1	2	1	4	2	1	30	4		2	1	1		1				

Jack Snipe *(Lymnocryptes minimus)*
Status: Scarce winter visitor. Scarce passage migrant.

This species has, no doubt, been much overlooked in Kuwait. It probably occurs every year in small numbers, with a highest daily count of three seen on several occasions. All records have been from pools or marshy areas.

JAN 1-10	JAN 11-20	JAN 21-31	FEB 1-10	FEB 11-20	FEB 21-29	MAR 1-10	MAR 11-20	MAR 21-31	APR 1-10	APR 11-20	APR 21-30	MAY 1-10	MAY 11-20	MAY 21-31	JUN 1-10	JUN 11-20	JUN 21-30	JUL 1-10	JUL 11-20	JUL 21-31	AUG 1-10	AUG 11-20	AUG 21-31	SEP 1-10	SEP 11-20	SEP 21-30	OCT 1-10	OCT 11-20	OCT 21-31	NOV 1-10	NOV 11-20	NOV 21-30	DEC 1-10	DEC 11-20	DEC 21-31
1		3	1						2	1																1		1			1				1

Common Snipe *(Gallinago gallinago)*
Status: Common passage migrant. Uncommon winter visitor.

Common Snipes are regularly flushed from reedbeds or marshy ground. Some passage birds have been seen in drier habitats. The highest daily count is 40 seen at Jahra East Outfall by P. Fagel on 20 March 2005.

JAN 1-10	JAN 11-20	JAN 21-31	FEB 1-10	FEB 11-20	FEB 21-29	MAR 1-10	MAR 11-20	MAR 21-31	APR 1-10	APR 11-20	APR 21-30	MAY 1-10	MAY 11-20	MAY 21-31	JUN 1-10	JUN 11-20	JUN 21-30	JUL 1-10	JUL 11-20	JUL 21-31	AUG 1-10	AUG 11-20	AUG 21-31	SEP 1-10	SEP 11-20	SEP 21-30	OCT 1-10	OCT 11-20	OCT 21-31	NOV 1-10	NOV 11-20	NOV 21-30	DEC 1-10	DEC 11-20	DEC 21-31
3	8	16	30	1	23	24	40	12	3	2		2	1											1	3	9	3	27	2	1	25	5	20	2	4

Great Snipe *(Gallinago media)*
Status: Rare passage migrant.

This species is, no doubt, under-recorded. Single birds have been observed at Ahmadi, Mina, Umm Al-Aish, Al-Abraq Al-Khabari and Jahra Farms. Some other records are not accessible, but the pattern is of a passage migrant not seen every year.

JAN 1-10	JAN 11-20	JAN 21-31	FEB 1-10	FEB 11-20	FEB 21-29	MAR 1-10	MAR 11-20	MAR 21-31	APR 1-10	APR 11-20	APR 21-30	MAY 1-10	MAY 11-20	MAY 21-31	JUN 1-10	JUN 11-20	JUN 21-30	JUL 1-10	JUL 11-20	JUL 21-31	AUG 1-10	AUG 11-20	AUG 21-31	SEP 1-10	SEP 11-20	SEP 21-30	OCT 1-10	OCT 11-20	OCT 21-31	NOV 1-10	NOV 11-20	NOV 21-30	DEC 1-10	DEC 11-20	DEC 21-31
																							1												

Eurasian Woodcock *(Scolopax rusticola)*
Status: Rare winter visitor.

The first Woodcock recorded in Kuwait was collected by V. Dickson on 1 February 1951, at an unknown location, and donated to the British Museum (Warr, undated). This was followed by one found dead on the shore, exact site not stated, by R.

Meinertzhagen, on 12 February 1951. Singles were seen at Ahmadi by V. A. D. Sales on 20 January 1964 and by G. Stafford on 30 January 1972. G. Gregory observed one at Al-Abraq Al-Khabari in December 1986. AbdulRahman Al-Sirhan photographed one at Jahra Pool Reserve on 23 November 2001. A. Bailey and G. Gregory found one at Sabah Al-Salem on 24 December 2001. Other birds arrived and a maximum of three was seen several times. At least one remained until 31 January 2002, being seen also by M. O. Chichester and S. T. Spencer. In addition there are known to be several more records that are not accessible. Accordingly, the status given above is probably the best one.

JAN 1-10	JAN 11-20	JAN 21-31	FEB 1-10	FEB 11-20	FEB 21-29	MAR 1-10	MAR 11-20	MAR 21-31	APR 1-10	APR 11-20	APR 21-30	MAY 1-10	MAY 11-20	MAY 21-31	JUN 1-10	JUN 11-20	JUN 21-30	JUL 1-10	JUL 11-20	JUL 21-31	AUG 1-10	AUG 11-20	AUG 21-31	SEP 1-10	SEP 11-20	SEP 21-30	OCT 1-10	OCT 11-20	OCT 21-31	NOV 1-10	NOV 11-20	NOV 21-30	DEC 1-10	DEC 11-20	DEC 21-31
3	2	3																																	1	1

Black-tailed Godwit *(Limosa limosa)*
Status: Uncommon passage migrant. Rare winter visitor.

Black-tailed Godwits are occasionally observed at coastal sites and at pools. Numbers have always been low, with the highest reliable daily count being seven seen on several occasions. There is one inland record of a single bird seen at Ahmadi on 13 May 1972 by J. Webb and B. Brown.

JAN 1-10	JAN 11-20	JAN 21-31	FEB 1-10	FEB 11-20	FEB 21-29	MAR 1-10	MAR 11-20	MAR 21-31	APR 1-10	APR 11-20	APR 21-30	MAY 1-10	MAY 11-20	MAY 21-31	JUN 1-10	JUN 11-20	JUN 21-30	JUL 1-10	JUL 11-20	JUL 21-31	AUG 1-10	AUG 11-20	AUG 21-31	SEP 1-10	SEP 11-20	SEP 21-30	OCT 1-10	OCT 11-20	OCT 21-31	NOV 1-10	NOV 11-20	NOV 21-30	DEC 1-10	DEC 11-20	DEC 21-31
						1	5	2	3						1	1					4	1	3				1			1					

Bar-tailed Godwit *(Limosa lapponica)*
Status: Common passage migrant. Uncommon winter visitor.

This species is much more commonly observed than the preceding one. All records have been from coastal sites. The highest daily count is an exceptional 2000 seen at Sulaibikhat Bay on 6 April 1999 by H-M. Busch, J. Rathberger-Knan and W. Bindl.

JAN 1-10	JAN 11-20	JAN 21-31	FEB 1-10	FEB 11-20	FEB 21-29	MAR 1-10	MAR 11-20	MAR 21-31	APR 1-10	APR 11-20	APR 21-30	MAY 1-10	MAY 11-20	MAY 21-31	JUN 1-10	JUN 11-20	JUN 21-30	JUL 1-10	JUL 11-20	JUL 21-31	AUG 1-10	AUG 11-20	AUG 21-31	SEP 1-10	SEP 11-20	SEP 21-30	OCT 1-10	OCT 11-20	OCT 21-31	NOV 1-10	NOV 11-20	NOV 21-30	DEC 1-10	DEC 11-20	DEC 21-31
50	120	4	18			200	300	300	250	2000	2	6	12								3	2		2	1	12	6		1		3				17

Whimbrel *(Numenius phaeopus)*
Status: Common passage migrant. Rare winter visitor.
Whimbrels pass through in spring and autumn, and there are a few winter records. Most records are of single birds or small groups, but the highest reliable daily count is 123 seen by B. Foster and P. Fagel on 29 April 2005 at East Doha.

JAN 1-10	JAN 11-20	JAN 21-31	FEB 1-10	FEB 11-20	FEB 21-29	MAR 1-10	MAR 11-20	MAR 21-31	APR 1-10	APR 11-20	APR 21-30	MAY 1-10	MAY 11-20	MAY 21-31	JUN 1-10	JUN 11-20	JUN 21-30	JUL 1-10	JUL 11-20	JUL 21-31	AUG 1-10	AUG 11-20	AUG 21-31	SEP 1-10	SEP 11-20	SEP 21-30	OCT 1-10	OCT 11-20	OCT 21-31	NOV 1-10	NOV 11-20	NOV 21-30	DEC 1-10	DEC 11-20	DEC 21-31
					17		6	25	55	123	26	4	5			1	2	1	6	6	5	6	3		2										2

Slender-billed Curlew *(Numenius tenuirostris)*
Status: Vagrant (one record).
A record of five birds seen by V. A. D. Sales at Kuwait Bay on 12 January 1967 was described on a Rare Bird Report form and accepted by the referees. (The date is incorrectly given as 15 January 1967 on the form.) The description is as follows:
'Description: Five birds the size of Whimbrel but paler and lacking the broad dark brown streaks on the head easily distinctive in the Whimbrel present, more like the Curlew also present but much smaller. Under parts white with larger darker irregular shaped spots on the lower breast and sides of belly making them easily distinguishable from the Whimbrel. These five birds kept together unlike the Curlew which were spread out over the Bay. Three Whimbrel nearby, but two and three others also present. Legs, dark grey. Under tail coverts, white. Iris, dark-brown. Bill, brown, lighter at the base of lower mandible.
53 Curlew and 8 Whimbrel observed the same day, which my field notes are dated the 12th not the 15th January 1967. A further visit was made to Kuwait Bay on the 14th January but no Slender-Bill Curlew were observed, only 3 Curlew and 1 Whimbrel were observed.'
A record of a bird seen by 'DAWM' at Mischan/Failaka on 10 May 1974 appeared on the computer list of the ANHFSG (1975). P. R. Haynes stated that they had been 'Seen by Mike and Angela Newhouse', but later added 'Something of a puzzle. The Newhouses deny all knowledge' (Warr, undated). This record clearly cannot be accepted without elucidation of this problem.

Eurasian Curlew *(Numenius arquata)*
Status: Very common winter visitor. Common passage migrant.
Eurasian Curlews are a common sight for most of the year at coastal locations. A few are occasionally seen on saline pools, and one was seen on the sewage-water pools at Jahra Pool Reserve by I. Corrall on 27 June 1981. The highest daily count is 1500 seen by H-M. Busch, J. Rathberger-Knan and W. Bindl at Doha on 6 April 1999.

JAN 1-10	JAN 11-20	JAN 21-31	FEB 1-10	FEB 11-20	FEB 21-29	MAR 1-10	MAR 11-20	MAR 21-31	APR 1-10	APR 11-20	APR 21-30	MAY 1-10	MAY 11-20	MAY 21-31	JUN 1-10	JUN 11-20	JUN 21-30	JUL 1-10	JUL 11-20	JUL 21-31	AUG 1-10	AUG 11-20	AUG 21-31	SEP 1-10	SEP 11-20	SEP 21-30	OCT 1-10	OCT 11-20	OCT 21-31	NOV 1-10	NOV 11-20	NOV 21-30	DEC 1-10	DEC 11-20	DEC 21-31
200	80	500	1150	150	15	600	400	400	1500	35	50	32	5	35	50	30	11	2	5	6	7	8	6	15	15	25	6	75	55	24	75	40	3	4	150

Spotted Redshank *(Tringa erythropus)*
Status: Scarce passage migrant. Rare winter visitor.
This species is seen in very small numbers, mostly on spring and autumn migration, usually at coastal sites and on pools. There are four inland records, all at Ahmadi. The highest daily count is three seen at Jahra Bay by O. Schroeder, S. Schroeder and G. Østerø on 21 March 2001.

JAN 1-10	JAN 11-20	JAN 21-31	FEB 1-10	FEB 11-20	FEB 21-29	MAR 1-10	MAR 11-20	MAR 21-31	APR 1-10	APR 11-20	APR 21-30	MAY 1-10	MAY 11-20	MAY 21-31	JUN 1-10	JUN 11-20	JUN 21-30	JUL 1-10	JUL 11-20	JUL 21-31	AUG 1-10	AUG 11-20	AUG 21-31	SEP 1-10	SEP 11-20	SEP 21-30	OCT 1-10	OCT 11-20	OCT 21-31	NOV 1-10	NOV 11-20	NOV 21-30	DEC 1-10	DEC 11-20	DEC 21-31
	1		1			3	2	2					2						1															1	

Common Redshank *(Tringa totanus)*
Status: Very common passage migrant. Very common winter visitor.
Common Redshanks are frequently seen and heard for most of the year along the coastline and on pools, with a highest daily count of 1000 seen by B. Foster at Sulaibikhat Bay on 20 January 2005. There are inland records at Ahmadi, Qaisat, Umm Al-Aish and Jahra Farms.

JAN 1-10	JAN 11-20	JAN 21-31	FEB 1-10	FEB 11-20	FEB 21-29	MAR 1-10	MAR 11-20	MAR 21-31	APR 1-10	APR 11-20	APR 21-30	MAY 1-10	MAY 11-20	MAY 21-31	JUN 1-10	JUN 11-20	JUN 21-30	JUL 1-10	JUL 11-20	JUL 21-31	AUG 1-10	AUG 11-20	AUG 21-31	SEP 1-10	SEP 11-20	SEP 21-30	OCT 1-10	OCT 11-20	OCT 21-31	NOV 1-10	NOV 11-20	NOV 21-30	DEC 1-10	DEC 11-20	DEC 21-31
250	1000	400	210	450	200	500	200	100	200	90	15	6	4		3	12	30	8	47	35	18	40	45	50	35	30	20	62	40	25	28	35	60	1	450

Marsh Sandpiper *(Tringa stagnatilis)*
Status: Common passage migrant. Uncommon winter visitor.
This species is often seen on mudflats or on sewage-water or saline pools, mostly in spring and autumn. There are no inland records. Most observations are of single birds or small groups, but the highest daily count is 63 seen by S. Holliday on 28 March 2000 at Sulaibikhat Bay.

JAN 1-10	JAN 11-20	JAN 21-31	FEB 1-10	FEB 11-20	FEB 21-29	MAR 1-10	MAR 11-20	MAR 21-31	APR 1-10	APR 11-20	APR 21-30	MAY 1-10	MAY 11-20	MAY 21-31	JUN 1-10	JUN 11-20	JUN 21-30	JUL 1-10	JUL 11-20	JUL 21-31	AUG 1-10	AUG 11-20	AUG 21-31	SEP 1-10	SEP 11-20	SEP 21-30	OCT 1-10	OCT 11-20	OCT 21-31	NOV 1-10	NOV 11-20	NOV 21-30	DEC 1-10	DEC 11-20	DEC 21-31
1	30	4	2	4		12	58	63	25	6	12	10	1		7		2				3	1	3	1		4	3	2	3				2	1	1

Common Greenshank *(Tringa nebularia)*
Status: Common passage migrant. Uncommon winter visitor.

Common Greenshanks are seen in autumn, winter and spring along the coastline or on pools. There is one inland record of one seen at Ahmadi by J. Webb and B. Brown on 13 May 1972. The highest daily count is 80 - 90 seen by V. A. D. Sales on 11 March 1966 at Kuwait Bay. Recent annual maxima have been much lower, and some very high counts recorded indicate confusion with other species of waders.

JAN 1-10	JAN 11-20	JAN 21-31	FEB 1-10	FEB 11-20	FEB 21-29	MAR 1-10	MAR 11-20	MAR 21-31	APR 1-10	APR 11-20	APR 21-30	MAY 1-10	MAY 11-20	MAY 21-31	JUN 1-10	JUN 11-20	JUN 21-30	JUL 1-10	JUL 11-20	JUL 21-31	AUG 1-10	AUG 11-20	AUG 21-31	SEP 1-10	SEP 11-20	SEP 21-30	OCT 1-10	OCT 11-20	OCT 21-31	NOV 1-10	NOV 11-20	NOV 21-30	DEC 1-10	DEC 11-20	DEC 21-31
1	8	10	8	1	7	8	7	7	20	1	6	1	8	1			1	4	16	15	4	2	5	4	2	2	2	4	3	1	1	3			

Green Sandpiper *(Tringa ochropus)*
Status: Uncommon winter visitor. Uncommon passage migrant.

This species is most commonly seen on pools, near reedbeds and in marshy areas, mostly between September and May. There are many inland records from Manageesh Oil Field, Wadi al-Batin, Ahmadi, Umm Al-Aish, Burgan Oil Field and Jahra Farms. The highest daily count is 11 seen on several occasions.

JAN 1-10	JAN 11-20	JAN 21-31	FEB 1-10	FEB 11-20	FEB 21-29	MAR 1-10	MAR 11-20	MAR 21-31	APR 1-10	APR 11-20	APR 21-30	MAY 1-10	MAY 11-20	MAY 21-31	JUN 1-10	JUN 11-20	JUN 21-30	JUL 1-10	JUL 11-20	JUL 21-31	AUG 1-10	AUG 11-20	AUG 21-31	SEP 1-10	SEP 11-20	SEP 21-30	OCT 1-10	OCT 11-20	OCT 21-31	NOV 1-10	NOV 11-20	NOV 21-30	DEC 1-10	DEC 11-20	DEC 21-31
4	11	11	5	6	8	11	9	9	5	6	1	4		1		2	5		3	1	3	3	1	2	2	4	1		1	1	1	3	11		1

Wood Sandpiper *(Tringa glareola)*
Status: Common passage migrant. Rare winter visitor.

Wood Sandpipers are regularly observed, in spring and autumn, on saline and sewage-water pools. There are some inland records from Ahmadi, Umm Al-Aish, Manageesh Oil Field and Jahra Farms. The highest daily count is 482 seen by B. Foster and P. Fagel on 6 May 2005 at Sabah Al-Salem, Jahra East Outfall and East Doha.

JAN 1-10	JAN 11-20	JAN 21-31	FEB 1-10	FEB 11-20	FEB 21-29	MAR 1-10	MAR 11-20	MAR 21-31	APR 1-10	APR 11-20	APR 21-30	MAY 1-10	MAY 11-20	MAY 21-31	JUN 1-10	JUN 11-20	JUN 21-30	JUL 1-10	JUL 11-20	JUL 21-31	AUG 1-10	AUG 11-20	AUG 21-31	SEP 1-10	SEP 11-20	SEP 21-30	OCT 1-10	OCT 11-20	OCT 21-31	NOV 1-10	NOV 11-20	NOV 21-30	DEC 1-10	DEC 11-20	DEC 21-31
4	1	2	5	11	1	3	15	15	20	482	20	3	4	1				6	1	2		1	1	2	5	1		5			1	1			

Terek Sandpiper *(Xenus cinereus)*
Status: Common winter visitor. Common passage migrant.

This species occurs in winter and on passage, in fairly high numbers, at Warba and Bubiyan Islands and at Kuwait Bay. Smaller numbers are observed elsewhere at coastal sites and on pools. There are no inland records. The highest daily count is 1000+ seen on 7 February 1964 at Kuwait Bay by V. A. D. Sales. Recent annual maxima have been lower.

JAN 1-10	JAN 11-20	JAN 21-31	FEB 1-10	FEB 11-20	FEB 21-29	MAR 1-10	MAR 11-20	MAR 21-31	APR 1-10	APR 11-20	APR 21-30	MAY 1-10	MAY 11-20	MAY 21-31	JUN 1-10	JUN 11-20	JUN 21-30	JUL 1-10	JUL 11-20	JUL 21-31	AUG 1-10	AUG 11-20	AUG 21-31	SEP 1-10	SEP 11-20	SEP 21-30	OCT 1-10	OCT 11-20	OCT 21-31	NOV 1-10	NOV 11-20	NOV 21-30	DEC 1-10	DEC 11-20	DEC 21-31
45	2	270	152	40	40	300	70	160	400	10	150	332	18	15	35	1		10	7	11	11	25	2	10	31	20	2		20						65

Common Sandpiper *(Actitis hypoleucos)*
Status: Uncommon passage migrant. Scarce winter visitor.

Common Sandpipers are observed mostly at coastal sites and on pools, but there are many inland records from Ahmadi and one from Umm Al-Aish. The highest daily count is about 100 seen on 10 April 1959 by V. A. D. Sales at Kuwait Bay.

JAN 1-10	JAN 11-20	JAN 21-31	FEB 1-10	FEB 11-20	FEB 21-29	MAR 1-10	MAR 11-20	MAR 21-31	APR 1-10	APR 11-20	APR 21-30	MAY 1-10	MAY 11-20	MAY 21-31	JUN 1-10	JUN 11-20	JUN 21-30	JUL 1-10	JUL 11-20	JUL 21-31	AUG 1-10	AUG 11-20	AUG 21-31	SEP 1-10	SEP 11-20	SEP 21-30	OCT 1-10	OCT 11-20	OCT 21-31	NOV 1-10	NOV 11-20	NOV 21-30	DEC 1-10	DEC 11-20	DEC 21-31
1	1	1			1	2	8	6	25	5	3	7	3	1		3			6	14	1	1	1		3	1	2	2	2				1	1	

Ruddy Turnstone *(Arenaria interpres)*
Status: Common passage migrant. Uncommon winter visitor.

This species is often observed in autumn, winter and spring at coastal locations and on pools. The only inland record is of a bird seen at Umm Al-Aish from 6 to 8 September 1972 by S. Howe and A. Caldwell. Small groups are most usual, but the highest daily count is 150 seen at Jahra Bay by O. Schroeder, S. Schroeder and G. Østerø on 21 March 2001.

JAN 1-10	JAN 11-20	JAN 21-31	FEB 1-10	FEB 11-20	FEB 21-29	MAR 1-10	MAR 11-20	MAR 21-31	APR 1-10	APR 11-20	APR 21-30	MAY 1-10	MAY 11-20	MAY 21-31	JUN 1-10	JUN 11-20	JUN 21-30	JUL 1-10	JUL 11-20	JUL 21-31	AUG 1-10	AUG 11-20	AUG 21-31	SEP 1-10	SEP 11-20	SEP 21-30	OCT 1-10	OCT 11-20	OCT 21-31	NOV 1-10	NOV 11-20	NOV 21-30	DEC 1-10	DEC 11-20	DEC 21-31
10	2	1	2	13	20	100	150	80	3	60	70	53	35	1		25				2	7	15	18	5	2	10	8	6							

Red-necked Phalarope *(Phalaropus lobatus)*
Status: Uncommon passage migrant.

In Kuwait Red-necked Phalaropes have mostly been seen swimming on pools or off the coastline or islands. There is one inland record of a bird found on a small pool near the Traffic Department at Ahmadi by L. Corrall on 17 April 1978. This species is probably heavily under-recorded. The highest daily count is 35 seen at Jahra East Outfall and Doha East by B. Foster and P. Fagel on 5 May 2005.

JAN 1-10	JAN 11-20	JAN 21-31	FEB 1-10	FEB 11-20	FEB 21-29	MAR 1-10	MAR 11-20	MAR 21-31	APR 1-10	APR 11-20	APR 21-30	MAY 1-10	MAY 11-20	MAY 21-31	JUN 1-10	JUN 11-20	JUN 21-30	JUL 1-10	JUL 11-20	JUL 21-31	AUG 1-10	AUG 11-20	AUG 21-31	SEP 1-10	SEP 11-20	SEP 21-30	OCT 1-10	OCT 11-20	OCT 21-31	NOV 1-10	NOV 11-20	NOV 21-30	DEC 1-10	DEC 11-20	DEC 21-31
						11	22	28	1	35	17		5			5								1			1								

Red Phalarope *(Phalaropus fulicaria)*
Status: Vagrant (one record).

One was photographed by G. Gregory, videoed by S. T. Spencer and also seen by C. W. T. Pilcher at Jahra Pool in October 1994, the exact date not being accessible. This bird was retroactively identified by G. Kirwan from S. T. Spencer's video. G. Gregory, who was present at the pool and took photographs before the others arrived, then searched his photographs and found an undated one of an adult Red Phalarope from that period. The photograph and video show a swimming phalarope with white underparts, pale grey back, white head with a dark cap, hindneck and line behind the eye, and a relatively thick, blunt-tipped bill compared to the needle-like bills on photographs and videos of Red-necked Phalaropes (*P. lobatus*) taken around that time.

Pomarine Skua *(Stercorarius pomarinus)*
Status: Uncommon passage migrant. Scarce winter visitor. Rare summer visitor.

Like most seabirds, Pomarine Skuas are, no doubt, seriously under-recorded in Kuwait. On boat trips offshore, they can often be seen in small numbers in spring and autumn. There are a few records from summer and winter. The highest daily count is five seen on many occasions. Skuas presumably migrate overland between their breeding grounds in the north and the Gulf. However, there are no inland records in Kuwait.

JAN 1-10	JAN 11-20	JAN 21-31	FEB 1-10	FEB 11-20	FEB 21-29	MAR 1-10	MAR 11-20	MAR 21-31	APR 1-10	APR 11-20	APR 21-30	MAY 1-10	MAY 11-20	MAY 21-31	JUN 1-10	JUN 11-20	JUN 21-30	JUL 1-10	JUL 11-20	JUL 21-31	AUG 1-10	AUG 11-20	AUG 21-31	SEP 1-10	SEP 11-20	SEP 21-30	OCT 1-10	OCT 11-20	OCT 21-31	NOV 1-10	NOV 11-20	NOV 21-30	DEC 1-10	DEC 11-20	DEC 21-31
1	1		2	1																							1								

Arctic Skua *(Stercorarius parasiticus)*
Status: Uncommon passage migrant. Scarce winter visitor. Rare summer visitor.

Arctic Skua is more commonly observed than the preceding species, but otherwise records of this species show a similar pattern. The highest daily count is 16 seen off Kuwait City on 13 April 1971 by T. Inskipp.

JAN 1-10	JAN 11-20	JAN 21-31	FEB 1-10	FEB 11-20	FEB 21-29	MAR 1-10	MAR 11-20	MAR 21-31	APR 1-10	APR 11-20	APR 21-30	MAY 1-10	MAY 11-20	MAY 21-31	JUN 1-10	JUN 11-20	JUN 21-30	JUL 1-10	JUL 11-20	JUL 21-31	AUG 1-10	AUG 11-20	AUG 21-31	SEP 1-10	SEP 11-20	SEP 21-30	OCT 1-10	OCT 11-20	OCT 21-31	NOV 1-10	NOV 11-20	NOV 21-30	DEC 1-10	DEC 11-20	DEC 21-31
1	1	2	2			5	5	6																2											

Long-tailed Skua *(Stercorarius longicaudus)*
Status: Vagrant (one record).
A written description of an adult Long-tailed Skua seen by S. T. Spencer and C. W. T. Pilcher on 27 May 1994 at Doha Point was accepted by KORC. The description noted pale grey back and upperwing, slim, tapering body, fairly long tail projection, long, narrow wings with barely noticeable white flashes, white neck (creamy near crown and nape) and lighter jizz compared to nearby Arctic Skuas (*S. parasiticus*).
Records of single birds seen by J. Bishop in Kuwait Bay on 13 June 1987 and on 29 May 1990 were rejected by KORC on the grounds of insufficient description.

Pallas's Gull *(Larus ichthyaetus)*
Status: Common winter visitor. Uncommon passage migrant.
Pallas's Gulls occur in variable numbers each year. In some recent winters a group of over 100 has been present near the ferry harbour on Failaka Island. All records have been from coastal sites, except for groups of up to 14 birds observed on flooded sabkha on Bubiyan Island on several dates in March 2004 by the KISR Bird Team. The highest daily count is an exceptional 542 seen by O. Schroeder, S. Schroeder and G. Østerø on 12 March 2001 at Doha.

JAN 1-10	JAN 11-20	JAN 21-31	FEB 1-10	FEB 11-20	FEB 21-29	MAR 1-10	MAR 11-20	MAR 21-31	APR 1-10	APR 11-20	APR 21-30	MAY 1-10	MAY 11-20	MAY 21-31	JUN 1-10	JUN 11-20	JUN 21-30	JUL 1-10	JUL 11-20	JUL 21-31	AUG 1-10	AUG 11-20	AUG 21-31	SEP 1-10	SEP 11-20	SEP 21-30	OCT 1-10	OCT 11-20	OCT 21-31	NOV 1-10	NOV 11-20	NOV 21-30	DEC 1-10	DEC 11-20	DEC 21-31
40	117	135	60	32	15	30	542	2	1																			4		4	6	20			49

Mediterranean Gull *(Larus melanocephalus)*
Status: Vagrant (four records).
The first record was that of a bird seen by V. A. D. Sales at Kuwait Bay on 17 February 1961, which F. E. Warr accepted (Warr, undated). A second-year was observed in flight by G. Gregory, C. W. T. Pilcher and M. Shehab at Jahra Pool Reserve in January 1989, but the exact date is not accessible. Features noted included an almost white mantle and centre of wing, contrasting strongly with dark on wing coverts and primaries and a dark bar along secondaries. G. Gregory (and three non-birders) observed an adult at Doha Harbour on 2 March 1995. J. Gaskell saw an adult at Fahaheel Sea Club on 28 January 2000. The descriptions for the latter two records covered the main identificatory features and were accepted by KORC.

Little Gull *(Larus minutus)*

Status: Vagrant (at least three records).

The first record was of five birds seen by V. A. D. Sales at Kuwait Bay on 17 August 1978. A description was written on a Rare Bird Report form. This is now not accessible, but the record was accepted by the panel.

One was photographed by W. A. Stuart at Messila on 26 February or 26 March 1978 (his notes record the former date, his slide the latter.)

A description of a second-year bird seen by P. R. Haynes at Messila on 1 and 15 April 1979 was written on a Rare Bird Report form and accepted by the panel. Photographic slides were taken. The description is as follows:

'Upper Parts: Forehead white, top of head smudged grey-black and black smudge/large spot on side of nape. Mantle soft grey with dark greyish-black line along wing at rest, showing as broad band in flight from body to leading edge of wing at wrist. Black wing tips and tail tip. Tail white.

Under Parts: Uniform white.

Flight Pattern and Under Wing: Under wing white, greyer on primaries.

Bare Parts: Bill black, legs orange.

Shape and Size: Overall looked very similar to small Black-headed Gull (*L. ridibundus*) and seen together with that species for size comparison.

Voice: Silent.

Behaviour: Mostly standing at edge of water (small pool of sewage/irrigation outlet) but in flight very buoyant and graceful.

Range: Seen at 20-30m at rest and at times even closer in flight. Present on both occasions for at least 1/2 hour in very good light.

Experience: First sighting of this species, but of course B-h Gull is familiar.

C. W. T. Pilcher wrote of this species: 'Accidental. Eight records' (Pilcher, undated). However, details of the additional records are not accessible, and some may involve confusion with other species.

Black-headed Gull *(Larus ridibundus)*

Status: Abundant passage migrant. Abundant winter visitor. Uncommon summer visitor.

This species is widespread at coastal sites and pools during most of the year. Some immatures over-summer. Many flocks are seen flying inland, but not usually more than 30 kilometres from the coast. The highest daily count is 5000 observed on several occasions.

JAN 1-10	JAN 11-20	JAN 21-31	FEB 1-10	FEB 11-20	FEB 21-29	MAR 1-10	MAR 11-20	MAR 21-31	APR 1-10	APR 11-20	APR 21-30	MAY 1-10	MAY 11-20	MAY 21-31	JUN 1-10	JUN 11-20	JUN 21-30	JUL 1-10	JUL 11-20	JUL 21-31	AUG 1-10	AUG 11-20	AUG 21-31	SEP 1-10	SEP 11-20	SEP 21-30	OCT 1-10	OCT 11-20	OCT 21-31	NOV 1-10	NOV 11-20	NOV 21-30	DEC 1-10	DEC 11-20	DEC 21-31
100	500	600	5000	400	350	1200	1000	1000	200	14	2	12	25		1	1	40	2	1						50		50	15	50	120	700	600	8	1250	

Slender-billed Gull *(Larus genei)*
Status: Abundant passage migrant. Common resident. Breeds.

Slender-billed Gulls are most commonly observed in spring and autumn, with exceptional flocks of about 20,000 (the highest daily count) observed in Kuwait Bay on several occasions. Smaller numbers are found in winter. Most birds are at coastal sites, but some are found on pools. There are no inland records. In spring almost all birds leave most of the coastline and concentrate on breeding grounds on Bubiyan Island, and in Iraq and Iran.

This species was first recorded as breeding in Kuwait in 1884, when five eggs were collected on 24 April and one on an unstated date in May, on Abdullah Bank (Warba/Bubiyan Islands). These eggs were received by W. D. Cumming and were later donated to the British Museum (British Museum, 1901).

On 30 May 1906 P. Cox visited Warba Island, and recorded that 'this gull was found breeding with Caspian Terns ... a few had then incubated eggs, most had hatched' (Ticehurst, Cox and Cheesman, 1926).

In 1921 V. S. La Personne collected, on Warba Island, an adult specimen on 19 May, and two eggs and an adult specimen on 20 May, and, on Bubiyan Island, one egg and an adult specimen on 20 May (Warr, undated). On his 19 May visit to Warba Island he recorded that Slender-billed Gulls were 'Breeding freely there with Gull-billed Terns on the N.E. side ... laying had just begun and 31 nests of the two species were counted in an area of 5 yards square. On April 5, 1921 the birds had just arrived for breeding purposes. The nests are made of the twigs of a salt bush (Sueda?) ... The Arab name for this gull is 'Simachi Harmi', i.e. forbidden by the Quran to be 'halaled' (Ticehurst, Cox and Cheesman, 1926).

In 1922, V. S. La Personne collected two eggs and an adult specimen from Warba Island on 26 May, a pullus specimen from Bubiyan Island on 26 May and three pullus specimens from Bubiyan Island on 27 May. All these eggs and specimens are now in the British Museum (Warr, undated).

This species was not discovered breeding again until 2002, when members of BMAPT found it breeding on Bubiyan Island, with about 200 agitated and vocal adults flying slowly overhead at one site on 4 April, and about 50 agitated adults and four well-feathered pulli found at another site on 17 May (Al-Nasrallah and Gregory, 2003).

On 28 May 2004 the KISR Bird Team recorded, in one area of Bubiyan Island, about 1500 pulli in crèches (each of up to several hundred pulli), 250 attending adults, 100 nests and 15 eggs. Several similar finds were made at other sites in June 2004. The breeding population was estimated as 1600 pairs, nesting in colonies of 10-250 pairs, usually somewhat apart from other species, in two-dimensional clusters with nests up to one metre apart.

Each nest is a shallow depression, lined with *Suaeda* twigs, normally heavily fouled with droppings, on the substratum, 10-50m from khors. Eggs number 2-4, and are speckled off-white or pale colour. No nests were found on Warba Island, and future breeding seems unlikely there, due to disturbance.

JAN 1-10	JAN 11-20	JAN 21-31	FEB 1-10	FEB 11-20	FEB 21-29	MAR 1-10	MAR 11-20	MAR 21-31	APR 1-10	APR 11-20	APR 21-30	MAY 1-10	MAY 11-20	MAY 21-31	JUN 1-10	JUN 11-20	JUN 21-30	JUL 1-10	JUL 11-20	JUL 21-31	AUG 1-10	AUG 11-20	AUG 21-31	SEP 1-10	SEP 11-20	SEP 21-30	OCT 1-10	OCT 11-20	OCT 21-31	NOV 1-10	NOV 11-20	NOV 21-30	DEC 1-10	DEC 11-20	DEC 21-31
80	300	400	500	300	250	500	800	300	2500	120	2003	164	550	1750	40	350	1	80	6	23	30	90	500	5000	4000	20000	800	450	250	500	40	400	25	5000

Mew Gull *(Larus canus)*
Status: Scarce winter visitor.
This species is, no doubt, under-recorded in Kuwait, but it probably occurs annually in very small numbers. All reliable recent records have involved just single birds. Some high and very high counts, both past and recent, indicate confusion with Caspian Gull (*L. cachinnans*). The same probably applies to past records from May to August.

JAN 1-10	JAN 11-20	JAN 21-31	FEB 1-10	FEB 11-20	FEB 21-29	MAR 1-10	MAR 11-20	MAR 21-31	APR 1-10	APR 11-20	APR 21-30	MAY 1-10	MAY 11-20	MAY 21-31	JUN 1-10	JUN 11-20	JUN 21-30	JUL 1-10	JUL 11-20	JUL 21-31	AUG 1-10	AUG 11-20	AUG 21-31	SEP 1-10	SEP 11-20	SEP 21-30	OCT 1-10	OCT 11-20	OCT 21-31	NOV 1-10	NOV 11-20	NOV 21-30	DEC 1-10	DEC 11-20	DEC 21-31
1						1	1																												1

Lesser Black-backed Gull *(Larus fuscus)*
Status: Common winter visitor. Common passage migrant.
Lesser Black-backed Gulls are easily seen at coastal sites and pools in autumn, winter and spring. Some birds fly inland for some considerable distance. Past records of this species in Kuwait probably did not include some *L. f. barabensis* (Baraba Gull) and are therefore unreliable. The highest reliable daily count is 1000 seen by P. Fagel and B. Foster at East Doha on 11 March 2005.
Recent field observations, examination of wings sent to W. R. P. Bourne by G. Gregory and consideration of records produce the following conclusions:
(i) *L. f. fuscus* (Baltic Gull) is an uncommon passage migrant and winter visitor, occurring mostly from October to March.
(ii) *L. f. heuglini* (Heuglin's/Siberian Gull) is a common passage migrant and winter visitor, occurring mostly from October to March.
(iii) *L. f. barabensis* (Baraba Gull) is a common passage migrant and winter visitor, occurring mostly from October to March, with some immatures arriving as early as September and not departing until April. Wings were from birds found dead on 15 September and 7 December.
(iv) Recent possible records of *L. f. intermedius* and/or *L. f. graellsii* most probably referred to Heuglin's/Siberian Gull (*L. f. heuglini*).
(v) The records of *L. marinus* (Greater Black-backed Gull) from 1964 to 1984 almost certainly referred to *L. f. fuscus* (Baltic Gull).

JAN 1-10	JAN 11-20	JAN 21-31	FEB 1-10	FEB 11-20	FEB 21-29	MAR 1-10	MAR 11-20	MAR 21-31	APR 1-10	APR 11-20	APR 21-30	MAY 1-10	MAY 11-20	MAY 21-31	JUN 1-10	JUN 11-20	JUN 21-30	JUL 1-10	JUL 11-20	JUL 21-31	AUG 1-10	AUG 11-20	AUG 21-31	SEP 1-10	SEP 11-20	SEP 21-30	OCT 1-10	OCT 11-20	OCT 21-31	NOV 1-10	NOV 11-20	NOV 21-30	DEC 1-10	DEC 11-20	DEC 21-31
4	20	25	500	45	2	15	1000	17	6	1		1									1	1	1	3	9	11	25			400	14	14	45	60	2

Caspian Gull *(Larus cachinnans)*
Status: Very common winter visitor. Very common passage migrant.

Until recently, all Eurasian forms of large, pale-backed, white-headed gulls were considered to belong to one species, Herring Gull (*L. argentatus*). Then Yellow-legged Gull (*L. cachinnans*, including *L. c. cachinnans, L. c. michahellis* etc.) and Armenian Gull (*L. armenicus*) were split off. Now, many taxonomists regard Yellow-legged Gull (*L. michahellis*) and Caspian Gull (*L. cachinnans*) to be distinct species, and this work treats them as such. Almost all Kuwait records, apart from some recent ones, of large, pale-backed, white-headed gulls were listed as 'Herring Gulls' or as 'Yellow-legged Gulls'. Most such records probably included some *L. f. barabensis* (Baraba Gull) and are therefore unreliable. The highest reliable daily count is 700 seen by M. O. Chichester at Zour Port on 20 October 2000.

As a result of recent field observations, consideration of past records, and of examination of wings sent to W. R. P. Bourne by G. Gregory, the following conclusions are produced:

(i) *L. cachinnans* (Caspian Gull) is a very common winter visitor and passage migrant, occurring mostly from October to March, with some immature birds remaining in the summer, or possibly arriving as early as August/September. Wings were from birds found dead on 13 September, 15 September, 20 March and 23 March.

(ii) There are no acceptable records in Kuwait of the modern *L. argentatus* (Herring Gull), *L. (vegae) mongolicus* (Mongolian Gull), *L. michahellis* (Yellow-legged Gull) or *L. armenicus* (Armenian Gull).

JAN 1-10	JAN 11-20	JAN 21-31	FEB 1-10	FEB 11-20	FEB 21-29	MAR 1-10	MAR 11-20	MAR 21-31	APR 1-10	APR 11-20	APR 21-30	MAY 1-10	MAY 11-20	MAY 21-31	JUN 1-10	JUN 11-20	JUN 21-30	JUL 1-10	JUL 11-20	JUL 21-31	AUG 1-10	AUG 11-20	AUG 21-31	SEP 1-10	SEP 11-20	SEP 21-30	OCT 1-10	OCT 11-20	OCT 21-31	NOV 1-10	NOV 11-20	NOV 21-30	DEC 1-10	DEC 11-20	DEC 21-31
300	250	215	500	80	25	150	300	35	500	3		15		6	1						6	3	4	4	20	40	15	700	75	250	65	6	350	300	30

Gull-billed Tern *(Gelochelidon nilotica)*
Status: Very common summer visitor. Common resident. Breeds.

The first evidence of breeding by this species in Kuwait involved 300 eggs and an adult specimen collected on Warba Island on 3 April 1878 by a Mr. Huskisson. This collector observed that 'the nests, which were very abundant, were built about a foot apart and consisted of a small mound of sand scraped together by the birds, from 3 to 5 inches high, with small twigs and sticks laid on the top for the eggs to rest upon. Most of the nests contained three eggs, all more or less incubated' (Hume, 1890). The eggs and adult specimen were received by Colonel E. A. Butler at Basra. The eggs were donated to the British Museum (British Museum, 1901).

In 1921 V. S. La Personne collected an adult specimen on Warba Island on 18 May, two eggs and two adult specimens on Warba Island on 19 May, and an egg on Bubiyan Island on 20 May. In 1922 he collected three eggs and an adult specimen on 7 April, and an adult and an immature specimens on 25 April, all on Bubiyan Island. All of these eggs and specimens were donated to the British Museum (Warr, undated). In addition, the collection of the Bombay Natural History Society contains undated adult specimens, one from Warba Island and one from Bubiyan Island (Abdulali, 1970).

Of V. La Personne's observations, C. B. Ticehurst, P. Cox and R. E. Cheesman

(1926) wrote: 'On 21 May, 1921, the Gull-billed Tern was found nesting on open flat ground or slightly raised ridges along the border of a creek [on Bubiyan Island]. Another colony was nesting amongst the Pelican skeletons and on April 18, 1922, some had already hatched. On Warba Island it was breeding with Slender-billed Gulls on the edge of shingle and scrub, and on May 19, 1921 the nests held 2 to 3 mostly 2, fresh eggs; a slight nest of twigs is made.'

This species was not discovered breeding again until 2002, when members of BMAPT found 69 nests with eggs at a few sites on Bubiyan Island on 4 April 2002. Many other nests and pulli were found later that year at other sites. One nest contained two eggs of Gull-billed Tern and one of Western Reef Egret (*Egretta gularis*); possibly egg retrieval was involved.

In 2004 the KISR Bird Team found 617 nests, many with eggs and young, at various sites on Bubiyan and Warba Islands on 25 March. Many other nests were later found at other sites. The breeding population was estimated as about 800 pairs, nesting in colonies of 10-50 pairs, often near to Western Reef Egret, Grey Herons (*Ardea cinerea*) and Eurasian Spoonbills (*Platalea leucorodia*), usually in lines, but sometimes in small two-dimensional clusters, with nests up to 10 metres apart. In 2005 employees of KISR observed birds giving alarm calls overhead from 10 February.

The nest is a shallow depression, lined with *Suaeda* twigs, reed stems or small pieces of driftwood, on the substratum, from 10 to 50 metres from khors. It is almost always clean and free from droppings. Eggs number from two to four, and are speckled off-white or pale colour.

Outside the breeding season some birds remain in Kuwait, being found mostly at coastal sites, although there are inland records at Ahmadi, Wafra Oil Field and the Sabah Al-Ahmed Natural Reserve. The remainder presumably disperses to the rest of the Gulf or beyond.

JAN 1-10	JAN 11-20	JAN 21-31	FEB 1-10	FEB 11-20	FEB 21-29	MAR 1-10	MAR 11-20	MAR 21-31	APR 1-10	APR 11-20	APR 21-30	MAY 1-10	MAY 11-20	MAY 21-31	JUN 1-10	JUN 11-20	JUN 21-30	JUL 1-10	JUL 11-20	JUL 21-31	AUG 1-10	AUG 11-20	AUG 21-31	SEP 1-10	SEP 11-20	SEP 21-30	OCT 1-10	OCT 11-20	OCT 21-31	NOV 1-10	NOV 11-20	NOV 21-30	DEC 1-10	DEC 11-20	DEC 21-31
10	30	55	250	120	30	100	90	1234	138	250	64	35	100	270	12	32	1		5		1		2	15	20	8	4	35	12	6	4	9	4	3	35

Caspian Tern *(Sterna caspia)*
Status: Common resident. Breeds.

Caspian Terns were first recorded breeding in Kuwait on 3 April 1878, when a Mr. Huskisson collected 97 eggs and an adult specimen on Warba Island. These were received by Colonel E. A. Butler at Basra, and the eggs were later donated to the British Museum (British Museum, 1901). This institution also contains 14 eggs collected on Warba Island on 6 April 1979, and one collected on Abdulla Bank (Warba/Bubiyan Islands) on 24 April 1884 (Warr, undated). The collection of the Bombay Natural History Society contains two undated adult specimens from Warba Island (Abdulali, 1970). C. B. Ticehurst, P. Cox and R. E. Cheesman (1926) wrote: 'A few pairs bred on Warba Island in 1906, where on May 30, most had hatched. None there in 1907, 1921 or 1922.'

V. Dickson (1942) related that 'Last year [1941] there had been many nests of Terns on the shore [of Auha Island] which he [Ibrahim, a Kuwaiti fisherman] called 'Hamr

Mangar' (the red-beaked one)'. These must have been Caspian Terns.

Of his visit to Kubbar Island on 11 July 1958, V. A. D. Sales (1965) wrote: 'Caspian Terns, of which there were 300-350 birds, were nesting in the centre of the island on a clear sandy patch, and it was possible to count all nests. There were three colonies. The largest contained 180 nests with a single egg each and one nest with 2 eggs. The second largest colony contained 44 nests with one egg, 5 nests with 2 eggs and one nest with the only chick of the species seen. The smallest bird colony contained 25 nests with 1 egg, 14 nests with 2 eggs and 7 other scattered nests with 1 egg each. Nests in each colony were very close together averaging 8 to 12 inches apart, and in general nests contained no nesting material.' He later stated that 'In August 1959 on Kubbar Island not one bird was observed or any evidence of nesting in the area of the previous year' (Warr, undated). M. Dryden (1982) that this species was nesting with eggs on Kubbar Island.

In 2002 members of BMAPT observed 30 agitated and vocal adults flying slowly overhead at one site on Bubiyan Island on 4 April. At another site they found about 25 adults and seven nests with apparently predated eggs.

On 15 April 2004 the KISR Bird Team saw about 300 adults with 250 nests containing eggs and a few chicks, in a colony, overlapping one of Greater Crested Terns (*S. bergii*), on Bubiyan Island.

In Kuwait this species nests in colonies of up to 250 pairs, usually apart from other species except sometimes Greater Crested Terns. The colonies do not regularly or persistently form at any one site. The nest is a shallow depression, usually lined with pebbles or Suaeda twigs, on the substratum, 10-50m from khors. Eggs usually number two, and are speckled off-white or pale colour.

Outside of the breeding season the birds spread out over the Kuwait coastline, and a few may be seen on pools. There are no records from more than about one kilometer inland.

JAN 1-10	JAN 11-20	JAN 21-31	FEB 1-10	FEB 11-20	FEB 21-29	MAR 1-10	MAR 11-20	MAR 21-31	APR 1-10	APR 11-20	APR 21-30	MAY 1-10	MAY 11-20	MAY 21-31	JUN 1-10	JUN 11-20	JUN 21-30	JUL 1-10	JUL 11-20	JUL 21-31	AUG 1-10	AUG 11-20	AUG 21-31	SEP 1-10	SEP 11-20	SEP 21-30	OCT 1-10	OCT 11-20	OCT 21-31	NOV 1-10	NOV 11-20	NOV 21-30	DEC 1-10	DEC 11-20	DEC 21-31
2	6	5	65	65	60	63	300	25	70	300	60	45	25	40	8	11	40		8					1	6	3	120	40	65	15	2	5	10	8		6	6	2

Greater Crested Tern *(Sterna bergii)*

Status: Common summer visitor. Uncommon resident. Breeds.

The first evidence of this species breeding in Kuwait involved two eggs collected on Kubbar Island by P. Cox on 11 June 1905. V. S. La Personne collected an adult specimen on Auha Island on 13 June 1923. The eggs and specimen were donated to the British Museum (Warr, undated). M. Dryden (1982) wrote that this species was nesting with eggs on Kubbar Island. C. W. T. Pilcher and N. Downing recorded 14 nests on 22 July 1983, none on 25 July 1984, 11 nests on 3 August 1985, two nests on 22 July 1986 and one nest on 9 August 1987, all on Kubbar Island (Pilcher, 1989a).

At one site on Bubiyan Island, members of BMAPT found seven eggs and many agitated adults on 4 March 2002, and about 300 agitated adults, 100 eggs and four downy pulli on 4 April. At the same site in 2004 the KISR Bird Team discovered a colony, overlapping one of Caspian Terns (*S. caspia*), of about 600 nests with eggs and a few young on 15 April.

In Kuwait this species nests in colonies of up to 600 pairs, usually apart from other species except sometimes Caspian Terns. There is no real nest: the single egg is laid directly on the substratum or in a shallow unlined depression in the substratum. The egg is speckled or scrawled off-white or pale colour.

After breeding most of the birds disperse down the Gulf, but a few, mostly immature birds, remain throughout the winter. All records are from coastal sites.

JAN 1-10	JAN 11-20	JAN 21-31	FEB 1-10	FEB 11-20	FEB 21-29	MAR 1-10	MAR 11-20	MAR 21-31	APR 1-10	APR 11-20	APR 21-30	MAY 1-10	MAY 11-20	MAY 21-31	JUN 1-10	JUN 11-20	JUN 21-30	JUL 1-10	JUL 11-20	JUL 21-31	AUG 1-10	AUG 11-20	AUG 21-31	SEP 1-10	SEP 11-20	SEP 21-30	OCT 1-10	OCT 11-20	OCT 21-31	NOV 1-10	NOV 11-20	NOV 21-30	DEC 1-10	DEC 11-20	DEC 21-31
5	7	5	18	28	2	25	40	75	300	1200	3	5	5	25	6		1					1												1	6

Lesser Crested Tern *(Sterna bengalensis)*
Status: Common summer visitor. Uncommon resident. Breeds.

Lesser Crested Terns were first recorded in Kuwait as breeding 'in numbers' on Kubbar Island by P. Cox on 9 June 1905. He also recorded 'small colonies' of this species on Umm Al-Maradim Island on 11 June 1905. He visited Qaroh Island on the same day, seeing this species there, but noting that the island 'was apparently not used as a breeding ground' (Ticehurst, Buxton and Cheesman, 1925). In 1922 V. S. La Personne collected, on Warba Island, two pullus specimens on 26 May, five eggs on 27 May, and three adult specimens dated 26 May and 26 June [possibly an error]. Notes accompanying three of the eggs read: 'All laid on sand with no nest and sometimes only a scratching for the eggs. A few eggs were laid on rocks, also without any attempt being made to form a nest' (Warr, undated). C. B. Ticehurst, P. Cox and R. E. Cheesman (1926) wrote of V. S. La Personne's observations: 'colonies exist on Bubiyan Island ... and on Warba Island ... where on May 26, 1922, a few had hatched. Of these eggs the collectors took both single and two eggs in the clutch, but in no case three, and probably clutches of this number are very exceptional'. This collector also found this species breeding 'in great numbers' on Auha Island on 12th June 1923 (Ticehurst, Cox and Cheesman, 1925).

V. A. D. Sales (undated) listed this species as breeding on Kubbar Island, but with no details. C. W. T. Pilcher and N. Downing recorded 100 nests on 22 July 1983, an unknown number of nests on 25 July 1984, 404 nests on 3 August 1985, 166 nests on 22 July 1986 and 493 nests on 9 August 1987, all on Kubbar Island (Pilcher, 1989a). In 1993, C. W. T. Pilcher counted 136 nests on Kubbar Island on 26 June, and on 6 July observed some chicks there (Jennings, undated). Members of BMAPT recorded about 600 adults at the breeding colony on Kubbar Island on 9 June 2001. In 2003 counts on Kubbar Island were 180 birds and 22 eggs on 15 May, recorded by M. O. Chichester, and c150 pairs on 10 June, recorded by K. Al-Nasrallah and A. Al-Fadhel. The KISR Bird Team recorded a maximum of 320 birds on Bubiyan Island on 4 February 2004, but no evidence of breeding was found that year.

After breeding, many birds scatter along the coastline, with a maximum of 450 seen by M. O. Chichester between Bnaider and Zour Port on 18 August 2000. Later all seem to disperse down the Gulf or even beyond; those observed in January and February are mostly juveniles. There are no inland records.

	JAN 1-10	JAN 11-20	JAN 21-31	FEB 1-10	FEB 11-20	FEB 21-29	MAR 1-10	MAR 11-20	MAR 21-31	APR 1-10	APR 11-20	APR 21-30	MAY 1-10	MAY 11-20	MAY 21-31	JUN 1-10	JUN 11-20	JUN 21-30	JUL 1-10	JUL 11-20	JUL 21-31	AUG 1-10	AUG 11-20	AUG 21-31	SEP 1-10	SEP 11-20	SEP 21-30	OCT 1-10	OCT 11-20	OCT 21-31	NOV 1-10	NOV 11-20	NOV 21-30	DEC 1-10	DEC 11-20	DEC 21-31
	1	4		320	150		28	150	60	2	7	30	25	180	35	600	1		11	8	7	35	450	45	15	30	40	120								

Sandwich Tern *(Sterna sandvicensis)*
Status: Uncommon passage migrant. Uncommon winter visitor. Scarce summer visitor.

This species has been recorded in all months in Kuwait, but it is least common in the summer. All records are from coastal sites. The highest daily count is an exceptional 200 seen by M. O. Chichester at Zour Port on 14 January 1999. Members of BMAPT observed three adults (one dead) in possible breeding habitat on Bubiyan Island on 4 April 2002, but this species has never been recorded breeding in Kuwait.

	JAN 1-10	JAN 11-20	JAN 21-31	FEB 1-10	FEB 11-20	FEB 21-29	MAR 1-10	MAR 11-20	MAR 21-31	APR 1-10	APR 11-20	APR 21-30	MAY 1-10	MAY 11-20	MAY 21-31	JUN 1-10	JUN 11-20	JUN 21-30	JUL 1-10	JUL 11-20	JUL 21-31	AUG 1-10	AUG 11-20	AUG 21-31	SEP 1-10	SEP 11-20	SEP 21-30	OCT 1-10	OCT 11-20	OCT 21-31	NOV 1-10	NOV 11-20	NOV 21-30	DEC 1-10	DEC 11-20	DEC 21-31
	20	200	30	10		6	15	80	10	20	8	7	6	1	2	2			1	9	1		3					10	45		4			12		1

Common Tern *(Sterna hirundo)*
Status: Scarce passage migrant.

Common Terns have been recorded in all months in the past, but many of these records probably involved confusion with White-cheeked Tern (*S. repressa*). The highest reliable daily count is 6 seen by B. Foster and A. Bailey at Jahra East Outfall on 17 June 2005. There are no inland records. In the Ahmadi Natural History and Field Studies Group *Newsletter* 14: 9 (1973) it was reported that this species was breeding in large numbers on Kubbar Island in late July and August 1973. However, there clearly was confusion with White-cheeked Terns (*S. repressa*), which was not listed as being recorded there that day. In 2002 members of BMAPT observed two adults in possible breeding habitat on Bubiyan Island on 17 May, but found no later evidence of possible breeding there. There are two undated adult specimens from Warba Island in the collection of the Bombay Natural History Society (Abdulali, 1970).

	JAN 1-10	JAN 11-20	JAN 21-31	FEB 1-10	FEB 11-20	FEB 21-29	MAR 1-10	MAR 11-20	MAR 21-31	APR 1-10	APR 11-20	APR 21-30	MAY 1-10	MAY 11-20	MAY 21-31	JUN 1-10	JUN 11-20	JUN 21-30	JUL 1-10	JUL 11-20	JUL 21-31	AUG 1-10	AUG 11-20	AUG 21-31	SEP 1-10	SEP 11-20	SEP 21-30	OCT 1-10	OCT 11-20	OCT 21-31	NOV 1-10	NOV 11-20	NOV 21-30	DEC 1-10	DEC 11-20	DEC 21-31
			1				2			2	4			6	2								2													

Arctic Tern *(Sterna paradisaea)*
Status: Vagrant (one record).
On 2 June 2005, A. Al-Sirhan photographed an adult Arctic Tern in summer plumage at Jahra East Outfall. The photograph was published on his website at www.al-sirhan.com. It shows a fairly small *Sterna* tern with a neat black cap, slightly grayish white underparts, pale grey wings and mantle, short dark red legs, and a uniformly red, relatively thick and short bill.

White-cheeked Tern *(Sterna repressa)*
Status: Very common summer visitor. Breeds.
The first evidence of breeding by this species in Kuwait involved four eggs collected at Khor Abdulla (Warba/Bubiyan Islands) on an unrecorded date in 1893 by an unknown collector, received by E. A. Butler, and donated to the British Museum (Warr, undated). On 9 June 1905 P. Cox visited Kubbar Island, finding White-cheeked Terns breeding, and noting: 'Small separate colonies in the open; some attempt was made at a nest; two eggs seemed the usual number and they varied much in colour in the same nest.' On 11 June 1905 he found this species breeding also on Umm Al-Maradim Island on 11 June 1905, recording that 'In one or two cases a small colony of *repressa* [White-cheeked Terns] were nesting in the middle of colonies of *bengalensis* [Lesser Crested Terns (*S. bengalensis*)].' He visited Qaroh Island on the same day, seeing this species there, but noting that the island 'was apparently not used as a breeding ground' (Ticehurst, Buxton and Cheesman, 1925). He also noted that 'In 1906 and 1907 it bred on Warba Is., fresh eggs being found on May 19, but it is unrecorded thence in 1921 and 1922' (Ticehurst, Cox and Cheesman, 1926). V. S. La Personne visited Auha Island on 12 June 1923 and found White-cheeked Terns 'Breeding in great numbers' (Ticehurst, Cox and Cheesman, 1925). There is one undated adult specimen from Kubbar Island in the collection of the Bombay Natural History Society (Abdulali, 1970).
V. A. D. Sales (1965) wrote: 'It was estimated that there were 1000 to 1500 of these terns on Khubbar Island 11th June 1958, with nests and young. All nests appeared to be on open ground and no bird was seen to leave the shrubs. Nesting material was used though less than in those nests of the Brown-winged Terns [Bridled Terns (*S. anaethetus*)] on the open ground. A casual count of nests revealed 14 with 1 egg, 5 with 2 eggs and 3 with one chick.'
C. W. T. Pilcher and N. Downing recorded 200 nests on 22 July 1983, an unknown number of nests on 25 July 1984, 295 nests on 3 August 1985, 462 nests on 22 July 1986 and 570 nests on 9 August 1987, all on Kubbar Island (Pilcher, 1989a). Members of BMAPT saw about 4000 birds on Kubbar Island, mostly breeding, on 9 June 2001. On 15 May 2003 M. O. Chichester estimated 2000 pairs on Kubbar Island, noting that most nests had two eggs and some had a single egg in a scrape near cover or in the open space between vegetation. K. Al-Nasrallah and A. Al-Fadhel recorded the same number of pairs there on 10 June 2003.
After breeding some birds spread to the southeast coast, and occasionally elsewhere. A total of 700 at Zour Port on 5 September 2003 was notable. In September all birds leave Kuwait, presumably moving down the Gulf and beyond, and do not usually return until March at the earliest. There have been no inland records in Kuwait.

JAN 1-10	JAN 11-20	JAN 21-31	FEB 1-10	FEB 11-20	FEB 21-29	MAR 1-10	MAR 11-20	MAR 21-31	APR 1-10	APR 11-20	APR 21-30	MAY 1-10	MAY 11-20	MAY 21-31	JUN 1-10	JUN 11-20	JUN 21-30	JUL 1-10	JUL 11-20	JUL 21-31	AUG 1-10	AUG 11-20	AUG 21-31	SEP 1-10	SEP 11-20	SEP 21-30	OCT 1-10	OCT 11-20	OCT 21-31	NOV 1-10	NOV 11-20	NOV 21-30	DEC 1-10	DEC 11-20	DEC 21-31
					2	1		3	45	40	4000	200	4000	22	6	36	20	60	70	30	90		700	50	200	40		1							

Bridled Tern *(Sterna anaethetus)*
Status: Very common summer visitor. Breeds.

Bridled Tern was first recorded as breeding in Kuwait on 9 June 1905, when P. Cox visited Kubbar Island and found it 'Breeding in small colonies and also scattered singly all over the island.' On 11 June he found it nesting on Umm Al-Maradim Island, noting: 'Here and there among small colonies of *bengalensis* [Lesser Crested Tern (*S. bengalensis*)] was a nest of *fuligula* [Bridled Tern] under any little bush which happened to be in the former's territory.' He also visited Qaroh Island on the same day, recording this species there, but noting that the island 'was apparently not used as a breeding ground'. V. S. La Personne visited Auha Island on 12 June 1923 and found Bridled Terns there 'Nesting in disused holes of *Dromas ardeola* [Crab Plovers], the single egg being placed about six inches down the hole. The eggs were fresh' (Ticehurst, Cox and Cheesman, 1925).

V. A. D. Sales (1965) wrote of his observations of this species on Kubbar Island on 11 July 1958: 'The most numerous species and 2000-2500 birds on the island. Nests were all over the island, frequently beneath the shrubs. Nests in exposed positions contained nesting material and were generally well made, but those under the shrubs contained no nesting material and were merely shallow scrapes. A sample count of 50 nests taken at random revealed 29 with 1 egg, 13 with 2 eggs, 7 with 1 chick, and the remaining nest with 2 chicks.' In the Ahmadi Natural History and Field Studies Group Newsletter 7 (1971) and in V. A. D. Sales (undated), he added that at the end of August 1958 500-600 were still present on Kubbar Island, and that on 6 August 1959 approximately 1600 adults with young were there, but no eggs were found. The young were 'at various stages though all over a week to ten days old, majority between three-four weeks.' The Ahmadi Natural History and Field Studies Group *Newsletter* 11 (1972) noted Bridled Terns breeding on Umm Al-Maradim Island on 15 June 1972, while number 14 (1974) of the same publication stated that it was nesting on Kubbar Island in late July/early August 1973.

P. R. Haynes (1978) noted of this species that 'What used to be a very large breeding colony on Kubr Island is being shot out of existence by whole boatloads of gunmen.' M. Dryden (1982) noted that it was breeding on Bubiyan Island, and that eggs were observed, probably in July. N. Muddiman stated that it was probably nesting there in May/June 1983 (Warr, undated).

C. W. T. Pilcher and N. Downing counted 650 nests on 22 July 1983, 884 nests on 25 July 1984, 869 nests on 3 August 1985, 916 nests on 22 July 1986 and 1612 nests on 9 August 1987, all on Kubbar Island (Pilcher, 1989a). Members of BMAPT saw about 4000 breeding birds on Kubbar Island on 9 June 2001. In 2002 they also saw four adults at one site on Bubiyan Island on 4 April and two adults at a different site there on 17 May, but recorded no other possible evidence of breeding. On 15 May 2003 M. O. Chichester counted about 2200 pairs on Kubbar Island, noting that most nests had a single egg in a scrape near or under scant vegetation. K. Al-Nasrallah and A. Al-Fadhel observed 2000 pairs there on 10 June 2003.

Before and after breeding some birds are present on the southeast coast and occasionally elsewhere in Kuwait, but there are no inland records. In late August almost all birds appear to leave Kuwait, dispersing down the Gulf and beyond, but some remain in winter. Others start to arrive back in April.

JAN 1-10	JAN 11-20	JAN 21-31	FEB 1-10	FEB 11-20	FEB 21-29	MAR 1-10	MAR 11-20	MAR 21-31	APR 1-10	APR 11-20	APR 21-30	MAY 1-10	MAY 11-20	MAY 21-31	JUN 1-10	JUN 11-20	JUN 21-30	JUL 1-10	JUL 11-20	JUL 21-31	AUG 1-10	AUG 11-20	AUG 21-31	SEP 1-10	SEP 11-20	SEP 21-30	OCT 1-10	OCT 11-20	OCT 21-31	NOV 1-10	NOV 11-20	NOV 21-30	DEC 1-10	DEC 11-20	DEC 21-31
16	3						13	50	2	4400	2400	4000		4000		2	3	11	45		1													7	

Little Tern *(Sterna albifrons)*
Status: Uncommon passage migrant. Rare summer visitor. Rare winter visitor.

Past records of this species are likely to include some of Saunders's Tern (*S. saundersi*). Little Terns, according to V. A. D. Sales (undated) had been recorded in every month, but most now occur in spring and autumn. The highest recorded daily count is 300 seen by V. A. D. Sales at Kuwait Bay on 10 April 1959. These, however, were likely to have included some Saunders's Terns. All records are from coastal sites and pools.

This species has never been proven to breed in Kuwait. V. Dickson (1942) recorded that on Failaka Island on 9 May 1942 'The small terns, 'Juwaida' were also nesting and flew over-head screeching.' However, it is not certain to which species these birds belonged, and they could have been Saunders' Terns. In 2002 members of BMAPT observed four adults on 4 April and two adults on 17 May in possible breeding habitat on Bubiyan Island, but there was no further indication of breeding, and these birds were probably just passage migrants.

Most or all birds in Kuwait show pale grey rumps. There has been some discussion whether this species intergrades with Saunders's Tern in the northwestern Gulf.

JAN 1-10	JAN 11-20	JAN 21-31	FEB 1-10	FEB 11-20	FEB 21-29	MAR 1-10	MAR 11-20	MAR 21-31	APR 1-10	APR 11-20	APR 21-30	MAY 1-10	MAY 11-20	MAY 21-31	JUN 1-10	JUN 11-20	JUN 21-30	JUL 1-10	JUL 11-20	JUL 21-31	AUG 1-10	AUG 11-20	AUG 21-31	SEP 1-10	SEP 11-20	SEP 21-30	OCT 1-10	OCT 11-20	OCT 21-31	NOV 1-10	NOV 11-20	NOV 21-30	DEC 1-10	DEC 11-20	DEC 21-31
					5	1	60	20	35	10	52	196		44				22	1						3			2							

Saunders's Tern *(Sterna saundersi)*
Status: Uncommon passage migrant and summer visitor.

This species, no doubt, has always occurred in Kuwait annually, but has often been overlooked as Little Tern (*S. albifrons*). Many previous records were probably lumped under that species.

C. J. O. Harrison (1983) wrote that 'Ticehurst et al were in error in stating that these [records of Little/Saunders's Terns in southern Iraq] were all referable to the Little Tern. Both species were present at Fao when W. D. Cumming collected specimens there in 1886.' The reference is to C. B. Ticehurst, P. A. Buxton and R. E. Cheesman (1921-22). Fao is just across the Khor Abdulla from Warba Island, and the Saunders's Terns collected must surely have passed through Kuwait territorial waters.

V. A. D. Sales and one other unstated observer recorded this species at Kuwait Bay on 29 and 30 April 1963, at Kuwait City on 30 April 1963 and on 4 April 1970, at Mina on 15 May 1970 and at Kuwait Bay on 24 April 1973.

C. W. T. Pilcher (undated) wrote of this species: 'Scarce/uncommon passage migrant. Recorded rarely in summer but no evidence of breeding.' However, the additional records referred to are not accessible.

Jeremy Gaskell and M. O. Chichester observed one well at Khor Ala'ma on 4 September 1998. The latter observer frequently watched birds offshore near his home at Zour Port from late 1998 to late 2003. He recorded many Little Terns there during this period. In addition, small terns that he (sometimes with S. T. Spencer, J. Gaskell and C. W. T. Pilcher) did not specifically identify he recorded as 'Little/Saunders's Tern' on the grounds of caution. These records are as follows:

In 1999: 8 April (5), 21 May (1+), 16 July (2), 6 August (1) and 20 August (2).
In 2000: 13 April (18), 27 April (30), 28 April (60), 11 May (1), 22 May (200+), 25 May (70), 29 May (20), 2 June (90), 9 July (1), 20 July (9), 22 July (2 adults feeding a begging fledgling), 27 July (15), 28 July (20), 31 July (2), 3 August (1), 10 August (14), 11 August (3), 18 August (1), 14 September (6) and 5 October (2).
In 2001: 26 April (2), 24 May (30, 28 June (3), 19 July (1), 20 July (1) and 3 August (2).
In 2002: 1 June (20), 13 June (22) and 14 June (2).
In 2003: 25 April (3), 1 May (5), 2 May (10), 9 May (3), 29 May (22), 5 June (1), 6 June (15), 27 June (6), 4 July (21), 22 August (2) and 5 September (9).
He also recorded similar birds at other locations, including Shaab and Khor Ala'ma, on 22 April 1999 (1+), 27 July 2000 (6), 2 August 2000 (5), 18 August 2000 (1) and 25 August 2000 (1).
Of the 21 birds that he observed at Zour Port on 4 July 2003, one had 'nice orange legs' and 'head markings' that 'were more consistent with Little [Tern] - white point extended just behind the eye.' The other 20 had 'dark' legs. The majority of these birds 'had broader white areas that didn't form a peak at the centre of the forehead. It was more square in front and looked like a receding hairline. It didn't go behind the eye viewed from the side.' 'The majority' of these birds clearly were Saunders's Terns. Some of the other birds that he recorded as 'Little/Saunders's Terns' were probably Saunders's Terns also. The fledgling observed on 22 July 2000 cannot be definitely considered as a local breeding record, since very young terns are known move considerable distances away from breeding areas accompanied by adults.
On 12 June 2002 A. Al-Sirhan photographed one at Shuwaikh. On 20 and 27 May 2005 B. Foster and A. Bailey observed at least 6 Saunders's Terns amongst Little Terns at Jahra East Outfall.
The table is of definite Saunders's Terns only. It clearly does not represent the true status of Saunders's Tern in Kuwait.

JAN 1-10	JAN 11-20	JAN 21-31	FEB 1-10	FEB 11-20	FEB 21-29	MAR 1-10	MAR 11-20	MAR 21-31	APR 1-10	APR 11-20	APR 21-30	MAY 1-10	MAY 11-20	MAY 21-31	JUN 1-10	JUN 11-20	JUN 21-30	JUL 1-10	JUL 11-20	JUL 21-31	AUG 1-10	AUG 11-20	AUG 21-31	SEP 1-10	SEP 11-20	SEP 21-30	OCT 1-10	OCT 11-20	OCT 21-31	NOV 1-10	NOV 11-20	NOV 21-30	DEC 1-10	DEC 11-20	DEC 21-31
													6	6	1		20							1											

Black Tern *(Chlidonias niger)*

P. R. Haynes (1979) stated that there were 'One or two unconfirmed records' of this species in Kuwait. However, no details are accessible, and confusion with White-winged Tern (*C. leucopterus*) or Whiskered Tern (*C. hybridus*) is possible for these records.
On 23 July 2005 A. Al-Sirhan photographed an adult Black Tern in summer plumage at Jahra East Outfall. He published the photograph on his website at www.al-sirhan.com. The photograph shows a *Chlidonias* tern with generally mid to dark grey plumage except for paler wings and mantle, white vent and undertail coverts (the tail and rump are covered by the wings), mostly pale dusky underwing and darker crown.

Whiskered Tern *(Chlidonias hybridus)*
Status: Uncommon passage migrant. Rare winter visitor.

Whiskered Terns are occasionally found in spring and autumn mostly at coastal sites and pools. There are occasional winter records. There is one inland record of a bird seen by L. Corrall over a small pool near Ahmadi Traffic Department from 25 April to 18 May 1978. The highest daily count is about 15 at Jahra Pool Reserve seen by L. Corrall on 6 June 1980. The juvenile seen together with 6 adults by B. Foster and A. Bailey at East Doha on 17 June 2005 does not constitute proof of local breeding since young terns are known to move considerable distances just after fledging.

JAN 1-10	JAN 11-20	JAN 21-31	FEB 1-10	FEB 11-20	FEB 21-29	MAR 1-10	MAR 11-20	MAR 21-31	APR 1-10	APR 11-20	APR 21-30	MAY 1-10	MAY 11-20	MAY 21-31	JUN 1-10	JUN 11-20	JUN 21-30	JUL 1-10	JUL 11-20	JUL 21-31	AUG 1-10	AUG 11-20	AUG 21-31	SEP 1-10	SEP 11-20	SEP 21-30	OCT 1-10	OCT 11-20	OCT 21-31	NOV 1-10	NOV 11-20	NOV 21-30	DEC 1-10	DEC 11-20	DEC 21-31
		1													7	2		2	6	1	1			2				2							

White-winged Tern *(Chlidonias leucopterus)*
Status: Uncommon passage migrant. Scarce summer visitor. Breeds.

This species is mostly a passage migrant in Kuwait, seen at coastal locations and pools. Inland records include single birds observed at Ahmadi on three occasions and at Jahra Ponds once. The highest daily count is 246 recorded by B. Foster and P. Fagel on 22 June 1956 at East Doha and Sabah Al-Salem.

In recent years White-winged Terns have been discovered to breed in Kuwait. In May and June 1999, two first-summer birds were observed by G. Gregory, P. Robertson and the Eliassen family to linger around Jahra East Outfall, but by 11 June they had gone. On 5 May 2000, G. Gregory and P. Robertson found four adults flying around Jahra East Outfall. On 12 June 2000 they found seven birds: two pairs of adults and three very juvenile birds, not quite fully grown, flying semi-weakly around the marshy area at the outfall. One of the juveniles perched on a nest, made of greenish plant material and situated in the marshy area, and then two adults followed. The presence of a second nest could not be established with certainty, so only one pair was proven to breed, though it is possible that both pairs did.

In 2001 two pairs of this species were found breeding at Jahra East Outfall on 25 May, and eventually raised one juvenile each. Unfortunately, one of these juveniles and an adult were shot by hunters. In 2002 it bred again at Jahra East Outfall, with a maximum of 12 adults and second-year birds seen on 17 May, but only one juvenile on 14 June. There was a maximum of four birds at Jahra East Outfall on 2 October 2003. Breeding was not proven that year, but could have occurred at the then inaccessible South Doha Nature Reserve, where the habitat was suitable and there was no disturbance. Seven birds at Jahra East Outfall on 21 May 2004 included a juvenile that must have hatched nearby, possibly at South Doha Nature Reserve.

JAN 1-10	JAN 11-20	JAN 21-31	FEB 1-10	FEB 11-20	FEB 21-29	MAR 1-10	MAR 11-20	MAR 21-31	APR 1-10	APR 11-20	APR 21-30	MAY 1-10	MAY 11-20	MAY 21-31	JUN 1-10	JUN 11-20	JUN 21-30	JUL 1-10	JUL 11-20	JUL 21-31	AUG 1-10	AUG 11-20	AUG 21-31	SEP 1-10	SEP 11-20	SEP 21-30	OCT 1-10	OCT 11-20	OCT 21-31	NOV 1-10	NOV 11-20	NOV 21-30	DEC 1-10	DEC 11-20	DEC 21-31
									4	1	246	35	8		6	8	2		1					1			10	30	4						

Spotted Sandgrouse *(Pterocles senegallus)*
Status: Irregular winter visitor and passage migrant. Rare summer visitor. Has bred.
Most recent records of sandgrouse in Kuwait involve birds shot by hunters without precise numbers and dates being available. Very few live birds are seen by ornithologists. Accordingly, precise tables are very difficult to produce.
The first records of Spotted Sandgrouse in Kuwait were by Colonel H. R. P. Dickson, who mentions two snared near Kuwait City on 16 September 1934, three seen fighting at Shuwaikh on 19 September 1934 and one shot, location and date unstated (H. R. P. Dickson, 1949; Game Register). The first recorded breeding by this species in Kuwait was described by V. Dickson. On 4 May 1935 she found several nests of this species, together with several of Pin-tailed Sandgrouse (*P. alchata*), on the Dhahar Ridge some 15 miles south of Kuwait City (V. Dickson, 1970). For unknown reasons these records seem to have been overlooked or rejected, and this species was omitted from the Kuwait list by P. R. Haynes (1979) and C. W. T. Pilcher (undated).
From at least the 1960s onwards many Kuwaiti hunters have shot individuals in various parts of the state, and have sometimes caged wounded ones. M. Shehab, G. Gregory, K. Al-Nasrallah and others have seen such birds in at least four collections at Al-Abraq Al-Khabari, Kuwait City and Zour. Pairs in captivity have even bred on several occasions. Many Kuwaiti hunters are familiar with this species.
There was no grazing or disturbance in the Demilitarised Zone, next to the Iraqi border, for years after the end of the Iraqi occupation in 1991, allowing suitable conditions for breeding to develop. From 1994 to 2000, hundreds of pairs of this species, together with similar numbers of Pin-tailed Sandgrouse, bred in the zone at Bharat Haushan, Habari Al-Awazim and Umm Esdair. Adults were present from March, nests were observed in April, and the first young flew on 1 July. During these months adults were repeatedly seen and heard in the evening obtaining water from sites at Abdali Farms, at least ten kilometers from the nearest nests. In February 2001, restrictions were lifted, and hunters entered the Demilitarised Zone, shooting hundreds of birds and preventing breeding. Some wounded birds were caged, three being observed in a collection at Zour by members of BMAPT later in the year. On an unstated date in 2000, Shaikh Sabah captured one north of Al-Abraq Al-Khabari. Small numbers were shot by Kuwaiti hunters in northern Kuwait from January to March 2002, from February to March 2003, and in January 2005.

Chestnut-bellied Sandgrouse *(Pterocles exustus)*
Status: Vagrant (two records).
This species is now only rarely recorded in the Western Palearctic region. The first Kuwait record is fully documented in the description below:
'One Friday in February 1999, Sami Al-Awadi and other hunters shot 13 out of a flock of about 30 similar sandgrouse at Ratqa. Of these 13, three birds (two males and a female) survived their wounds and were caged at Sami Al-Awadi's villa in Rawda, Kuwait City. He and other hunters were familiar with Pin-tailed, Spotted and Black-bellied Sandgrouse, but could not identify these birds. K. Al-Nasrallah and G. Gregory were contacted, and they visited the villa to photograph and examine the birds in the hand, identifying them as Chestnut-bellied Sandgrouse (the first for Kuwait and an important Western Palearctic record). The birds were still alive in early 2002.
Shape and Size: Typical sandgrouse shape. Size about that of accompanying caged Spotted, smaller than Pin-tailed and much smaller than Black-bellied, all of which were examined in the hand. Males had a pin tail; females a pointed tail.
Plumage of Males: Upper body and breast paleish greyish brown generally, with dark

brown tips to feathers scapulars and mantle. Thin black line between breast and upper belly. Belly paleish greyish brown anteriorly, but posteriorly merged into chestnutty brown which extended to flanks and lower tail coverts. Most upper coverts paleish yellowish brown with thin very dark brown tips. Primaries and secondaries mostly quite dark greyish brown with paler tips to inner feathers. Leg feathering pale whitish brown. Under wing all dark greyish brown.

Plumage of Females: Head paleish yellowish brown. Upper parts generally barred dark and pale brownish. Some paler spots on scapulars and wing coverts. Primaries and secondaries mid greyish brown. Breast basically pale yellowish brown, with dark brown streaks extending to broken dark brown line between breast and belly. Anterior belly very pale brownish white. Posterior belly, flanks and lower tail coverts closely barred dark and mid brownish. Under wing dark greyish brown.

Exposed Parts: Bill blueish grey. Eye very dark. Toes dark.

(Note: Some fading of colours may have occurred in captivity.)'

The second Kuwait record was of a female seen and photographed by P. Fagel, B. Foster, A. Bailey and G. Gregory at Sabah Al-Salem on 4 March 2005.

Black-bellied Sandgrouse *(Pterocles orientalis)*

Status: Rare winter visitor.

Small numbers of Black-bellied Sandgrouse have been recorded from October to April, though not every year. The highest daily count is seven seen flying south at Jahra Pool Reserve by C. W. T. Pilcher, G. Gregory and M. Shehab on 13 November 1987. This species is a prized prey of Kuwaiti hunters, and some are familiar with it. Some birds that survive their injuries are caged, but these birds have never bred in captivity. Between 1929 and 1951 H. R. P. Dickson recorded, in his Game Register, a total of 234 birds shot or taken in Kuwait. The only precise recent records are of seven shot at Ratqa on 17 December 2001 and three seen at Ratqa on 5 March 2002. In most recent years small numbers have been reported shot in November and December.

Pin-tailed Sandgrouse *(Pterocles alchata)*

Status: Irregular winter visitor and passage migrant. Rare summer visitor. Has bred.

The first recorded occurrence and breeding of this species in Kuwait were described by V. Dickson. On 4 May 1935 she found several nests of this species, together with several of Spotted Sandgrouse (*P. senegallus*), on the Dhahar Ridge some 15 miles south of Kuwait City. She wrote: 'On 4 & 11 May, sandgrouse nests on the Dhahar ridge (stony/pebbly) each containing 2 or 3 eggs. Good rains that year but no rains to the north. Nests mostly on top of mounds covered in shrub and pebbles. Nests = hollow cavities, unlined, dug in gravelly soil. Some nests in open, some under small shrub. Many other nests reported that year. Adult left nest at 30 yds and sat watching the author. Then flew off uttering a curious alarm call' (Warr, undated; V. Dickson, 1970). Colonel H. R. P. Dickson shot one at Khaitan on 11 May of the same year (H. R. P. Dickson, 1949).

There have been large irruptions of this species in Kuwait. V. A. D. Sales (undated) wrote of one such event: 'Large eruption 1968 between 24 March and 25 May, numbers varying between 20 and 900 birds a day. Peak days 2 & 3 April, 900 and 896 birds. Main movement in a northerly direction between 0700 and 0900 occasionally between 1600 and 1700.' P. R. Haynes described another: 'Flock after flock going overhead March 1978. According to a Kuwaiti they're regular on migration but no longer breed here, although they apparently do just over the Saudi border where there are less population pressures' (Warr, undated). The highest daily count is the 900 birds seen by V. A. D. Sales near Ahmadi on 2 April 1968.

From at least the 1960s onwards many Kuwaiti hunters have shot individuals in various parts of the state, and have sometimes caged wounded ones. G. Gregory, K. Al-Nasrallah, A. Bailey and others have seen such birds in at least five collections at Sabriya, Kuwait City and Zour. Captive pairs have bred on many occasions.

M. Dryden (1982) wrote of this species: 'Formerly common breeding bird which rapidly declined in numbers in the 1960s and early 1970s. In recent years sightings have become more frequent; the birds have been seen feeding off insects that collect around camel dung and it has been suggested that the increase in sandgrouse is related to a corresponding increase in domestic camels.'

There was no grazing or disturbance in the Demilitarised Zone, next to the Iraqi border, for years after the end of the Iraqi occupation in 1991, allowing suitable conditions for breeding to develop. From 1994 to 2000, hundreds of pairs of this species, together with similar numbers of Spotted Sandgrouse, bred in the zone at Bharat Haushan, Habari Al-Awazim and Umm Esdair. Adults were present from March, nests were observed in April, and the first young flew on 1 July. During these months adults were repeatedly seen and heard in the evening obtaining water from sites at Abdali Farms, at least ten kilometers from the nearest nests. In February 2001, restrictions were lifted, and hunters entered the Demilitarised Zone, shooting hundreds of birds and preventing breeding. Some wounded birds were caged, eight birds were observed in a collection at Zour by members of BMAPT later in the year.

Hundreds were shot by Kuwaiti hunters in northern Kuwait from January to April 2002. Members of BMAPT visited a hunting camp at Ratqa in February 2002 and examined hundreds of fresh and fairly fresh wings of this species. Fair numbers were shot by Kuwaiti hunters in northern Kuwait from February to March 2003, and in January 2005. The only precise recent records are of ten seen in February and one in June.

Rock Dove *(Columba livia)*

Status: No acceptable records of wild Rock Doves, but Feral Pigeons, Tumblers etc are abundant breeding residents.

Past records of birds believed to be wild Rock Doves include two at Jal Az-Zor on 30 March 1968, one at Ahmadi on 6 March 1969, one (captured) at Manageesh on 22 April 1970, one at Ahmadi on 3 July 1970, one at Umm Ar-Rimam on 14 November 1971 and one at Jal Az-Zor on 21 April 1972. The observers included V. A. D. Sales, S. Howe, M. Leven and J. Hunt. On the basis of these records P. R. Haynes (1979) listed it as 'Accidental in wild form'. However, L. Corrall noted that 'We have seen them well away from human habitation but cannot be certain they were not feral' (Warr, undated). It is best to regard all these records as referring to Feral Pigeons.

Feral Pigeons are present in all urban areas of Kuwait, and thousands can often be seen together in the centre of Kuwait City. They roost and breed on tall buildings. Some birds occur around desert camps, isolated farms and other places outside of the cities. Tumblers and other varieties are on sale in the main bird market at Al-Rai and in other markets. Some individuals fetch high prices. Possession of a flock of Tumblers is a status symbol. There are dovecotes for these birds, some elaborate, in many locations in Kuwait. Other varieties are kept in collections.

Stock Dove *(Columba oenas)*

Status: Vagrant (three records).

A single bird was recorded at Jaber Al-Ali Farm, near Umm Ar-Rimam, by M. Shehab in March 1998. He noted the grey rump and back, short blackish bars on the inner wings and mostly grey underwing.

A record of one seen at Jahra on 15 October 1999 by S. T. Spencer was accepted by KORC.

G. Gregory observed a single bird at Umm Al-Aish on 30 November 2004, and noted the important identificatory features.

Common Woodpigeon *(Columba palumbus)*
Status: Scarce disperser in spring and autumn.

The first record of Common Woodpigeon in Kuwait was that of one seen by L. Corrall at Umm Al-Aish on 10 April 1981. This was followed by two more seen by the same observer at Jahra Pool Reserve on 20 April 1981. There were then two more records up to about 1995 but details are not accessible (Pilcher, undated). Further records were one at Al-Abraq Al-Khabari on 23 March 1998, one at Jahra Farms on 13 May 2004 and four (the highest daily count) at Abdali Farms on 17 September 2004. The observers included M. Shehab, S. T. Spencer, G. Gregory and A. Al-Suraye'a.

In every recent year at least one individual of this species has been shot or observed by Kuwaiti hunters in north Kuwait, usually at Rawdatain, but definite dates are not accessible. M. Shehab and G. Gregory have been shown some of these shot birds, in order to confirm their identity. Accordingly, the status given above is probably the best one.

JAN 1-10	JAN 11-20	JAN 21-31	FEB 1-10	FEB 11-20	FEB 21-29	MAR 1-10	MAR 11-20	MAR 21-31	APR 1-10	APR 11-20	APR 21-30	MAY 1-10	MAY 11-20	MAY 21-31	JUN 1-10	JUN 11-20	JUN 21-30	JUL 1-10	JUL 11-20	JUL 21-31	AUG 1-10	AUG 11-20	AUG 21-31	SEP 1-10	SEP 11-20	SEP 21-30	OCT 1-10	OCT 11-20	OCT 21-31	NOV 1-10	NOV 11-20	NOV 21-30	DEC 1-10	DEC 11-20	DEC 21-31
						1			1															4											

Eurasian Collared Dove *(Streptopelia decaocto)*
Status: Common resident. Uncommon disperser in spring and autumn. Breeds.

This species was first recorded in Kuwait on 21 March 1960 by V. A. D. Sales, who saw a single bird at Ahmadi. The number of sightings then gradually increased until a population became established in about 1970. The first record of breeding by this species in Kuwait (and in the Arabian peninsula) was by P. A. D. Hollom at Kuwait City on 29 April 1963 (Jennings, 1986b). The only other definite record of breeding in the state was by W. A. Stuart at Jahra on an unstated date in 1977. On several other occasions nest-building has been observed but without further proof of breeding. At present birds are resident in most areas of Kuwait with trees or bushes, and presumably breed there. The highest daily count is 50 seen by V. A. D. Sales at Ahmadi on 21 November 1965. There appears to be some movement in spring and autumn.

JAN 1-10	JAN 11-20	JAN 21-31	FEB 1-10	FEB 11-20	FEB 21-29	MAR 1-10	MAR 11-20	MAR 21-31	APR 1-10	APR 11-20	APR 21-30	MAY 1-10	MAY 11-20	MAY 21-31	JUN 1-10	JUN 11-20	JUN 21-30	JUL 1-10	JUL 11-20	JUL 21-31	AUG 1-10	AUG 11-20	AUG 21-31	SEP 1-10	SEP 11-20	SEP 21-30	OCT 1-10	OCT 11-20	OCT 21-31	NOV 1-10	NOV 11-20	NOV 21-30	DEC 1-10	DEC 11-20	DEC 21-31
6	10	35	14	6	8	6	10	11	15	4	25	8	10	10	6	14		4	9	1	10	6	4	2	15	30	35	8	4	8	15	9	15	6	6

African Collared Dove *(Streptopelia roseogrisea)*
Status: Scarce resident. Scarce disperser in spring and autumn.
(Escaped Barbary Doves (which have bred) and Albinos are sometimes seen.)
   Wild-type African Collared Doves breed in southwest Arabia, and are spreading north. They have bred in the Riyadh area and have reached Bahrain and Israel. This species is likely to establish itself as a breeder in Kuwait in the near future. All wild-type birds recorded in Kuwait were presumed until recently to be of captive origin. They are on sale in bird markets and are kept in many private collections. However, in recent years long-staying birds have been observed in several locations. Although not yet proven to be an established breeder, this species has established a presence in Kuwait.
   The first wild-type bird recorded in Kuwait was seen by G. Gregory at Salmiya in March 2001. Later that year, members of BMAPT found a pair of Barbary Doves breeding at Wafra on 31 May.
   In 2002 there were up to seven or more wild-type birds at Sabah Al-Salem, three at Abu Halifa, and one each at Mahboula, Messila and Salwa. Two Barbary Doves were with the three African Collared Doves at Abu Halifa on 23 May. Single mongrels were seen at Mahboula on 29 March and at Jahra Farms on 14 June. An Albino was present at Salwa from October to December.
   In 2003 the highest counts of wild-type birds were two at Sabah al-Salem and one at Mahboula on several dates. Single presumed mongrels were at Sabah Al-Salem on 15 March and at Jahra Farms on 11 April.
   In 2004 two wild-type birds were present in the Sabah Al-Ahmed Natural Reserve throughout the year, and at least until early 2005, but there was no observed evidence of breeding. One was at Sabah Al-Salem on 14 May. At least two were present at Kabd from 1 September and were still present in early 2005.
   There appears to be some movement in spring and autumn.

JAN 1-10	JAN 11-20	JAN 21-31	FEB 1-10	FEB 11-20	FEB 21-29	MAR 1-10	MAR 11-20	MAR 21-31	APR 1-10	APR 11-20	APR 21-30	MAY 1-10	MAY 11-20	MAY 21-31	JUN 1-10	JUN 11-20	JUN 21-30	JUL 1-10	JUL 11-20	JUL 21-31	AUG 1-10	AUG 11-20	AUG 21-31	SEP 1-10	SEP 11-20	SEP 21-30	OCT 1-10	OCT 11-20	OCT 21-31	NOV 1-10	NOV 11-20	NOV 21-30	DEC 1-10	DEC 11-20	DEC 21-31
4	6	6	9	5	4	4	4	4	2	2	4	3	5	4	2	2	2	2	2	2	2	2	5	6	4	4	4	4	4	4	4	4	4	4	4

European Turtle Dove *(Streptopelia turtur)*
Status: Common passage migrant. Rare winter visitor. Has bred.
   European Turtle Doves are mostly passage migrants in Kuwait. They are one of the favourite prey species of shooters, netters and falconers. V. Dickson (undated) wrote that they were 'Shot for food by local people. Owners of falcons keep as many as 100 of those netted in cool rooms as food for their birds during the summer months. P. R. Haynes (1978) wrote that 'The locals make sure that far fewer leave the country than enter.' The highest daily count is 480 seen at Ahmadi by V. A. A. D. Sales 27 April 1958. Recently, numbers have been much lower, no doubt due to over-hunting. Many birds are still shot, but precise dates are not accessible. Relatively few birds are seen alive by ornithologists.
   Most birds seen are of the nominate subspecies *S. t. turtur*, but roughly one in five is of the paler subspecies *S. t. arenicola*. There is one winter record of a bird 'obtained' by R. Meinertzhagen on 16 January 1951, but no location was stated (Meinertzhagen,

1954). Both this specimen and another collected by V. Dickson on 12 April 1947 were identified as *S. t. arenicola*, and were donated to the British Museum (Warr, undated). An adult ringed by V. A. D. Sales at Ahmadi on 5 May 1966 was found on 18 September 1967 near Paytok, Andizhanskaya, Uzbekistan (40°54'N, 72°15'E) (Sales, undated). The only breeding record involved a very young bird found at the Ahmadi stables in July 1971 by an unstated observer, as reported in the ANHFSG Newsletter 14 (1972).

JAN 1-10	JAN 11-20	JAN 21-31	FEB 1-10	FEB 11-20	FEB 21-29	MAR 1-10	MAR 11-20	MAR 21-31	APR 1-10	APR 11-20	APR 21-30	MAY 1-10	MAY 11-20	MAY 21-31	JUN 1-10	JUN 11-20	JUN 21-30	JUL 1-10	JUL 11-20	JUL 21-31	AUG 1-10	AUG 11-20	AUG 21-31	SEP 1-10	SEP 11-20	SEP 21-30	OCT 1-10	OCT 11-20	OCT 21-31	NOV 1-10	NOV 11-20	NOV 21-30	DEC 1-10	DEC 11-20	DEC 21-31
20						2	6	2	1	6	8	2	1	1				5			4	2	1	45	1					4					

Oriental Turtle Dove *(Streptopelia orientalis)*
Status: Rare passage migrant.

It would be very difficult to determine the exact number of reliable records of this species in Kuwait.

A record of two birds seen by V. A. D. Sales at Ahmadi on 6 June 1956 was described on a Rare Bird Report form and was accepted by the panel. On the same form the observer also described birds that he had also seen at Ahmadi on 14 June 1956 (one), 27 September 1957 (three), 26 October 1964 (one), 14 September 1967 (one), 29-30 April 1968 (two) and 10 May 1969 (two). The panel rejected all of these records. A record of one bird seen by S. Howe at Umm Al-Aish on 14 September 1972 was described on a Rare Bird Report form but was rejected by the panel. At that time, identification was based mainly on the colour of the tail tip and of the neck patch, and not on other features later discovered to be valid. Prolonged discussions followed amongst the panel and with the observers about these rejected records, but they remained rejected. In reconsidering them, it is difficult to come to come to any conclusion except that at least some of these records could have been of Oriental Turtle Doves.

A group of six birds was observed by Kuwaiti hunters at Sulaibiya on 1 October 2001. One bird was shot and wounded, and was caged in Kuwait City. K. Al-Nasrallah and G. Gregory observed and photographed this bird, which was a juvenile/first-year of the subspecies *S. o. meena*. Another bird was wounded and captured at Zour on 12 April 2002. It was identified as an Oriental Turtle Dove using a field guide by the hunters, who were familiar with European Turtle Dove (*S. turtur*). Other Kuwaiti hunters have reported shooting individuals of this species, but exact dates and locations are not accessible.

G. Gregory, A. Bailey and B. Foster had good views of a juvenile/first-year at Rawdatain on 17 September 2004. The KISR Bird Team saw another on Bubiyan Island on 21 September 2004.

In the circumstances, the status given above is probably the best one.

JAN 1-10	JAN 11-20	JAN 21-31	FEB 1-10	FEB 11-20	FEB 21-29	MAR 1-10	MAR 11-20	MAR 21-31	APR 1-10	APR 11-20	APR 21-30	MAY 1-10	MAY 11-20	MAY 21-31	JUN 1-10	JUN 11-20	JUN 21-30	JUL 1-10	JUL 11-20	JUL 21-31	AUG 1-10	AUG 11-20	AUG 21-31	SEP 1-10	SEP 11-20	SEP 21-30	OCT 1-10	OCT 11-20	OCT 21-31	NOV 1-10	NOV 11-20	NOV 21-30	DEC 1-10	DEC 11-20	DEC 21-31
											1													1	1	6									

Laughing Dove *(Streptopelia senegalensis)*
Status: Abundant resident. Breeds.

Laughing Dove was first observed in Kuwait by G. Nicholls at an unstated location on 23 April 1975. It was not recorded again until M. Shehab found one in Kuwait City on an unstated date in 1981. Since then it has become an established resident in all areas of Kuwait with houses and trees. It is now the second most common resident breeding wild bird in the state, after House Sparrow (***Passer domesticus***). The highest daily count is 100+ recorded on many occasions.

Breeding was first recorded in 1983, when C. W. T. Pilcher found a nest five metres up a date palm at Jahra. The female was incubating a second clutch of eggs in the nest when the fully-fledged young of the first brood were still returning to the nest (Pilcher, 1994b). Breeding has also been proven in Kuwait City several times. It has not been found definitely to breed at Abdali Farms, Al-Abraq Al-Khabari, the Sabah Al-Ahmed Natural Reserve, Zour Port or Wafra Farms, but it surely must do so. Some nests have been made almost entirely of pieces of wire (Pilcher, 1994b; Jennings, undated).

Namaqua Dove *(Oena capensis)*
Status: Uncommon resident. Scarce disperser in spring and autumn. Breeds.

This rather elusive species was first recorded in Kuwait on 4 August 1978, when L. Corrall and another unstated observer found two birds at Jahra Pool Reserve. Since then there have been many records from all sites with trees and bushes in Kuwait.

Breeding was first confirmed when M. Shehab and other observers photographed a female with two newly-fledged juveniles at Jahra Pool Reserve on 27 June 2002. Breeding was also proven at the Mohammed Al-Ajmi Farm at Abdali on 31 May 2003, when G. Gregory, B. Settles and S. Carter-Brown observed a pair on a nest. It has, no doubt, bred elsewhere in Kuwait, since juvenile birds are sometimes seen from July onwards. B. Foster and P. Fagel observed two pairs at East Doha on 6 May 2005. Namaqua Doves are now regarded as an established resident in Kuwait, with numbers augmented by occasional birds dispersing from outside the state. The highest daily count is ten seen by P. Fagel and M. Varhimo at Jahra East Outfall, Jahra Farms and Qaisat on 10 April 2005.

JAN 1-10	JAN 11-20	JAN 21-31	FEB 1-10	FEB 11-20	FEB 21-29	MAR 1-10	MAR 11-20	MAR 21-31	APR 1-10	APR 11-20	APR 21-30	MAY 1-10	MAY 11-20	MAY 21-31	JUN 1-10	JUN 11-20	JUN 21-30	JUL 1-10	JUL 11-20	JUL 21-31	AUG 1-10	AUG 11-20	AUG 21-31	SEP 1-10	SEP 11-20	SEP 21-30	OCT 1-10	OCT 11-20	OCT 21-31	NOV 1-10	NOV 11-20	NOV 21-30	DEC 1-10	DEC 11-20	DEC 21-31
1	1		1			2	4	10	1	2	4	1	2		1	3		1			1	2	1				1	1	1	2	1				1

Rose-ringed Parakeet *(Psittacula krameri)*
Status: Common winter visitor. Uncommon resident. Has bred.

Rose-ringed Parakeets have been recorded at Kuwait City and its suburbs, Jahra, Ahmadi, Fahaheel, Zour Port, Abdali Farms and Umm Al-Aish. Numbers are highest in winter, but some birds remain all year. The biggest known winter roost was, in the mid 1990s, at Salmiya, with about 250 birds (the highest daily count) present on many occasions. However, it has not formed recently. Other temporary roosts formed in the past.

Breeding has long been suspected in Kuwait, but confirmation was first obtained when G. Gregory observed a bird on a nest at Abu Halifa several times in May 2004. A newly-fledged juvenile, accompanied by a parent, seen at Jahra Farms on 6, 10 and 16 June 2004 by G. Gregory, constituted the second confirmed breeding record.

JAN 1-10	JAN 11-20	JAN 21-31	FEB 1-10	FEB 11-20	FEB 21-29	MAR 1-10	MAR 11-20	MAR 21-31	APR 1-10	APR 11-20	APR 21-30	MAY 1-10	MAY 11-20	MAY 21-31	JUN 1-10	JUN 11-20	JUN 21-30	JUL 1-10	JUL 11-20	JUL 21-31	AUG 1-10	AUG 11-20	AUG 21-31	SEP 1-10	SEP 11-20	SEP 21-30	OCT 1-10	OCT 11-20	OCT 21-31	NOV 1-10	NOV 11-20	NOV 21-30	DEC 1-10	DEC 11-20	DEC 21-31
36	20	15	4	7	4	25	7	8	2	15	4	3	5	3	3	6					1	1	7	1	10	5	9	15	12	5	30	9	7	11	4

Great Spotted Cuckoo *(Clamator glandarius)*
Status: Rare passage migrant.

The first record of this species in Kuwait was on 28 June 1956, when V. A. D. Sales saw two birds at Ahmadi. This observer also recorded single birds there on 22 June 1957, 26 September 1961, 5 April 1963, 14 January 1965 (caught and ringed) and 18 September 1967. M. Shehab, C. W. T. Pilcher and G. Gregory saw one at Al-Abraq Al-Khabari in 1988, but the exact date is inaccessible. The latter observer observed one at Salmiya on 14 April 1999. S. T. Spencer recorded one at an unstated location on 9 March 2000. In 2004 members of BMAPT saw and photographed a single bird in the Sabah Al-Ahmed Natural Reserve on 19 March. It was later joined by a second bird, and they remained there until at least 26 March. There have been several other sightings of this species by Kuwaiti photographers and hunters, but the dates and locations are not accessible.

JAN 1-10	JAN 11-20	JAN 21-31	FEB 1-10	FEB 11-20	FEB 21-29	MAR 1-10	MAR 11-20	MAR 21-31	APR 1-10	APR 11-20	APR 21-30	MAY 1-10	MAY 11-20	MAY 21-31	JUN 1-10	JUN 11-20	JUN 21-30	JUL 1-10	JUL 11-20	JUL 21-31	AUG 1-10	AUG 11-20	AUG 21-31	SEP 1-10	SEP 11-20	SEP 21-30	OCT 1-10	OCT 11-20	OCT 21-31	NOV 1-10	NOV 11-20	NOV 21-30	DEC 1-10	DEC 11-20	DEC 21-31
								1	2	1																									

Common Cuckoo *(Cuculus canorus)*
Status: Uncommon passage migrant.

Common Cuckoos pass through Kuwait in spring, usually in very small numbers. Recently there have been no autumn records. The highest daily count is four seen by V. A. D. Sales at Ahmadi on 11 May 1961. This species has been seen at most locations with trees and bushes. Known records of hepatic females include 28 April 1955, 26 February 1962, 27 September 1965, 10 September 1981, 12 March 1999 and 3 May 2001.

JAN 1-10	JAN 11-20	JAN 21-31	FEB 1-10	FEB 11-20	FEB 21-29	MAR 1-10	MAR 11-20	MAR 21-31	APR 1-10	APR 11-20	APR 21-30	MAY 1-10	MAY 11-20	MAY 21-31	JUN 1-10	JUN 11-20	JUN 21-30	JUL 1-10	JUL 11-20	JUL 21-31	AUG 1-10	AUG 11-20	AUG 21-31	SEP 1-10	SEP 11-20	SEP 21-30	OCT 1-10	OCT 11-20	OCT 21-31	NOV 1-10	NOV 11-20	NOV 21-30	DEC 1-10	DEC 11-20	DEC 21-31
1						1	1		3	1	2	1	1																						

Barn Owl *(Tyto alba)*
Status: Scarce disperser in all seasons. Has bred.

This species has been recorded at many sites, including Ahmadi, Qaisat, the Sabah Al-Ahmed Natural Reserve, Wafra, Abdali Farms, Judailiyat, Jahra and Salmiya. Unfortunately many birds have been found shot dead. Yaqoub Boodai and others observed this species nesting in 2001 and 2002 at the Yaqoub Boodai Farm at Abdali. The nest site was in a cavity inside a well and several young (with 'monkey-like' faces) were observed. The table omits these breeding records, for which precise dates are not available.

European Scops Owl *(Otus scops)*
Status: Uncommon passage migrant.

European Scops Owls, being active mostly nocturnally, are no doubt under-recorded. They mostly pass through on migration, but there is one winter record of a bird seen in Kuwait City by 'DTY' and 'RDY' on 22 December 1973 (ANHFSG, 1975). This species has been recorded at most sites with trees in Kuwait. Both grey and brown phases are observed, but the former is much more common. A bird ringed by V. A. D. Sales at Ahmadi on 3 April 1966 was later killed on 23 April 1967 at Diana, Ruwandiz, Iraq (36°41'N, 44°35') (Sales, undated). The highest daily count is three seen on several occasions.

Eurasian Eagle Owl *(Bubo bubo)*
Status: Scarce resident. Breeds.

The first known record of this species in Kuwait involved a bird found slightly injured in the north of Kuwait on 1 January 1972 by Captain Faisal Al-Ghanim (ANHFSG *Newsletter* 8 (1972): 5). A bird was seen at Ahmadi on 13 December, and captured there on 25 December, 1972 by 'GT' and 'EA' (ANHFSG, 1975; Haynes, 1978).

Since at least 1978 a pair has nested, or attempted to nest, in Wadi Al-Batin. In mid-February 1978 two eggs were observed at a nest, but both nest and eggs were found destroyed later (Haynes, 1978). In 1979 breeding was successful, and W. A. Stuart photographed a nest with three chicks on 23 March. M. D. Gallagher saw an adult and a clutch of three eggs on 6 March 1981 (Warr, undated). M. Dryden (1982) observed a pair on a nest in spring, but it was later found destroyed. Nests and eggs were observed almost every year from then until the late 1990s. Some previous nest sites became unusable due to erosion, but at least one other was used. After the Iraqi occupation the Wadi Al-Batin area has been inaccessible for many years, but breeding is believed to occur there annually.

From 1999 to 2001 Eurasian Eagle Owls were present in what is now the Sabah Al-Ahmed Natural Reserve. One was seen and photographed by G. Gregory in Wadi Ar-Rimam on 14 October 1999. Pellets were found at Wadi Ar-Rimam on 14 January 2000. In March and June 2001 birds were recorded several times by members of BMAPT at Wadi Ar-Rimam and on the escarpment, and a used nest with nearby pellets was found.

All birds seen have been of the subspecies *B. b. ascalaphus*.

Little Owl *(Athene noctua)*
Status: Uncommon resident. Breeds.

There are three known breeding areas in Kuwait for this species.

The first is along the Jal Az-Zor escarpment, about half of which is in the Sabah Al-Ahmed Natural Reserve. Here, pairs visiting nesting holes with white droppings outside were recorded by W. A. Stuart on 13 May 1978, and by C. W. T. Pilcher on 20 April 1985. In June 1987 D. A. Clayton carried out a study of breeding Little Owls there. He found several pairs nesting, usually not less than one kilometre apart. One nest had two disembowelled down-covered chick corpses outside the nesting burrow - possibly the result of predation by Desert Monitor (*Varanus grisens*) [called 'Worral' locally] as there were tracks of this species near to the corpses and the nest hole. 97 pellets were examined and the prey items identified inside included invertebrates, reptiles, birds and mammals (Clayton, 1991).

The second is at Wadi Ar-Rimam inside the Sabah Al-Ahmed Natural Reserve. Here, birds visiting nest holes were observed by G. Gregory and P. Robertson on 29 January 1998, and by G. Gregory, B. Settles and S. Carter-Brown on 6 June 2003.

The third is at Wadi Al-Batin, when C. W. T. Pilcher observed a pair visiting a nest hole on 25 January 1985.

Outside of the breeding season Little Owls are occasionally recorded at these three sites, with a maximum of 5+ seen at Jal Az-Zor by G. Rowlands on 4 January 2001.

Long-eared Owl *(Asio otus)*
Status: Vagrant (two records).

One was seen and photographed by C. W. T. Pilcher and M. Shehab at Umm Al-Aish on 18 January and 8 February 1985. The photographs clearly showed the long ear tufts, orange eyes, and rufous on the face mask.

One found about two months dead at Sabriya on 26 December 2001 by G. Gregory, A. Bailey and K. Al-Nasrallah. The description is below:

'GG and AB were walking around the rows of trees of Sabriya Farm, when they found a dead owl stuck in the branches of an *Acacia*. It was shown to KN, and then bagged. Back at Salwa, the bird was described, measured and photographed. It was mostly decayed.

Shape and Form: Medium-sized, fairly slender owl with long ear tufts.
Upperparts: Upper head and body brown with blackish streaks. Forehead buff streak dark brown. Off-white long crescents between bill and eyes. Upper bill largely surrounded by bristly off-white feathers. Face mask buff, tinged rufous; surrounded by dark brown line with white additionally at sides of chin. Tail and wing coverts mid

brown barred darker brown. Dark brown patches at carpel. Primaries and secondaries faded orangey and pale brown with darker brown barring distally.
Underparts: Underbody buff with dark brown streaks. Under wing mostly buffish white with pale brown barring on primaries and a dark brown crescent on median coverts. Tail mid brown with darker brown bars.
Exposed Parts: Bill greyish-black. Cere - mid brown Eye - decayed. Toes - with darker soles. Claws - dark grey, curved.
Measurements: Wing: 296mm. Bill to feathers: 26.8mm. Tail: damaged. Tarsus: 38.5mm. Ear tufts: 52mm to skull, but may be short due to decay.
Identification: Only similar species is Short-eared Owl. Wing, bill to feathers, tarsus within range of Long-eared, but too small for Short-eared. Long ear tufts and rufous tinge to face mask are features of Long-eared.'

Short-eared Owl *(Asio flammeus)*
Status: Rare winter visitor.

Short-eared Owls are present in most winters in Kuwait. One was recorded by R. S. Wolstenholme on 9 November 1983 in the suburbs of Kuwait City at Mishref. Otherwise, it has been recorded at numerous coastal and inland sites away from urban areas. This largely diurnal species is, unfortunately, often shot dead by hunters. Most of the dates of these shootings are not accessible. The highest daily count is five, all shot, found by P. R. Haynes at an unstated location in early January 1978 (Warr, undated).

JAN 1-10	JAN 11-20	JAN 21-31	FEB 1-10	FEB 11-20	FEB 21-29	MAR 1-10	MAR 11-20	MAR 21-31	APR 1-10	APR 11-20	APR 21-30	MAY 1-10	MAY 11-20	MAY 21-31	JUN 1-10	JUN 11-20	JUN 21-30	JUL 1-10	JUL 11-20	JUL 21-31	AUG 1-10	AUG 11-20	AUG 21-31	SEP 1-10	SEP 11-20	SEP 21-30	OCT 1-10	OCT 11-20	OCT 21-31	NOV 1-10	NOV 11-20	NOV 21-30	DEC 1-10	DEC 11-20	DEC 21-31
3		3																								2	1	1							

European Nightjar *(Caprimulgus europaeus)*
Status: Uncommon passage migrant.

This nocturnal species occurs on spring and autumn passage through Kuwait, but is no doubt under-recorded. During the day it remains concealed on branches or on the ground, and can easily be overlooked. Some past records in summer and winter may have involved confusion with Egyptian Nightjar (*C. aegyptius*). The highest daily count is six recorded by V. A. D. Sales at Ahmadi on 7 May 1961. Less than half of birds examined are of the subspecies *C. e. unwini*.

JAN 1-10	JAN 11-20	JAN 21-31	FEB 1-10	FEB 11-20	FEB 21-29	MAR 1-10	MAR 11-20	MAR 21-31	APR 1-10	APR 11-20	APR 21-30	MAY 1-10	MAY 11-20	MAY 21-31	JUN 1-10	JUN 11-20	JUN 21-30	JUL 1-10	JUL 11-20	JUL 21-31	AUG 1-10	AUG 11-20	AUG 21-31	SEP 1-10	SEP 11-20	SEP 21-30	OCT 1-10	OCT 11-20	OCT 21-31	NOV 1-10	NOV 11-20	NOV 21-30	DEC 1-10	DEC 11-20	DEC 21-31
						1			1	1	1			1							1	1	2												

Egyptian Nightjar *(Caprimulgus aegyptius)*
Status: Uncommon passage migrant. Uncommon summer visitor. Uncommon winter visitor.

Egyptian Nightjars have clearly been under-recorded in Kuwait, and some past records of European Nightjar (*C. europaeus*) may actually have been of this species. Only two sightings appear on the computer list of the ANHFSG (1975). P. R. Haynes (1979) listed it as an accidental or rare passage migrant. There was clearly little night bird-watching done during that period.

Recent observations have shown that this species is mostly a passage migrant through Kuwait. Most birds in spring and autumn are presumably from populations which breed to the north and east of Kuwait and winter in Africa. The highest daily count of passage birds is 15, unfortunately all found shot dead, by G. Gregory and B. Thomas, in what is now the Sabah Al-Ahmed Natural Reserve, on 17 September 1999. There was no drinking pool there at that time.

However, in addition, Egyptian Nightjars have recently been proven to be present in both winter and summer in Kuwait, but not in large numbers. In fairly recent years there have been records from November to February at locations such as Qaisat and Kuwait City, involving birds seen after sunset. Members of BMAPT saw at least one in the Sabah Al-Ahmed Natural Reserve after dark on 7 June 2001. This was the first year that fresh water was supplied throughout the summer in a drinking pool there. M. O. Chichester observed a single bird at Zour Port, where there are freshwater ponds, on 15 and 16 July 2001. The KISR Bird Team has carried out night surveys at the Agricultural Research Station at Kabd, where there is available fresh water, several times every month since January 2004. They have recorded this species every month there, seeing upto six birds during almost every survey. G. Gregory, who lived there from September 2004 to April 2005, frequently saw Egyptian Nightjars there after dark in each of these months. During this period, he also occasionally observed one or two individuals, again after dark, at Qaisat, where there are open freshwater pools, and in the area around Jahra Pool Reserve, where there is standing sewage water. Burgan Oil Field, where there are freshwater pools, is clearly also likely to hold birds in winter and summer, but there is no access there at night. Yaqoub Boodai and others have seen up to six almost every night throughout the summer, feeding on insects visible in the light from the house, at the Yaqoub Boodai Farm at Abdali, for many years. There are freshwater pools there and breeding must surely occur there.

JAN 1-10	JAN 11-20	JAN 21-31	FEB 1-10	FEB 11-20	FEB 21-29	MAR 1-10	MAR 11-20	MAR 21-31	APR 1-10	APR 11-20	APR 21-30	MAY 1-10	MAY 11-20	MAY 21-31	JUN 1-10	JUN 11-20	JUN 21-30	JUL 1-10	JUL 11-20	JUL 21-31	AUG 1-10	AUG 11-20	AUG 21-31	SEP 1-10	SEP 11-20	SEP 21-30	OCT 1-10	OCT 11-20	OCT 21-31	NOV 1-10	NOV 11-20	NOV 21-30	DEC 1-10	DEC 11-20	DEC 21-31
6	4	6	6	3	4	8	12	9	6	6	6	6	6	6	6	6	6	6	6	6	6	6	6	9	15	4	3	8	3	3	6	5	4	6	3

Alpine Swift *(Apus melba)*
Status: Scarce passage migrant.

This species has occurred recently in small numbers every year in Kuwait in spring. The first record was of a single bird seen by S. Howe at Kuwait City/Bay on 6 September 1971. The highest daily count is eight seen at an unstated location by W. A. C. Giles on 31 August 1973. Records are from many coastal and inland sites.

Common Swift *(Apus apus)*
Status: Abundant passage migrant. Rare winter visitor.

This species has been thoroughly confused with Pallid Swift (*A. pallidus*) in Kuwait in the past. The ANHFSG computer list (1975) has 95 sightings of Common Swift, in all months, but only two of Pallid Swift. All of these records are clearly unreliable. The past records of breeding by Common Swift in Kuwait also clearly refer to Pallid Swift. In listing this species, P. R. Haynes (1979) wrote: 'Very common passage migrant and winter visitor. Occasional breeding records but none very recent.' This status is now known to be incorrect.

Common Swift is a passage migrant through Kuwait, with very few autumn records, and there are no reliable summer records. It has never bred in Kuwait. The highest daily count is 200+ seen on several occasions in the past. Many birds resemble the eastern subspecies *A. a. pekinensis*.

Pallid Swift *(Apus pallidus)*
Status: Common passage migrant. Common winter visitor. Breeds.

Pallid Swifts have been largely overlooked in Kuwait in the past as Common Swifts (*A. apus*). Pallid Swift is now known to be a breeding visitor, with many other birds passing through in a pattern of movements that is not understood.

The first record of breeding by this species in Kuwait was by V. Dickson on 2 May 1939. She wrote: ' 'Swift' arrives about the end of Feb. and is now nesting over the city gate and in our stable verandah, in the holes where the beams go into the wall which support the roof. They are browny-grey in colour and are very noisy, screaming as they fly' (V. Dickson, undated). V. A. D. Sales (undated) wrote: 'I suspect breeding (of *pekinensis*) in June 1965 when for 40 mins. I observed a bird(s) continuously entering at the side of an air conditioning unit on 5th storey of a building as if it was feeding young.' Both of these breeding records clearly involved Pallid Swifts.

Other records of confirmed breeding in Kuwait City are by P. A. D. Hollom on 29 April 1963, and by C. W. T. Pilcher on 3 April 1985 and 11 May 1993. In submitting the last record the latter observer wrote: 'For more than 12 years this species has bred in the British Embassy building. I noted in the early 80's that they used to nest in the cavities on top of the air-conditioning units mounted in the walls of the "cloisters". Later these units were removed and the windows bricked up. It seems that the swifts now nest in appropriate spaces in the upper part of the building but I have not personally observed this" (Jennings, undated). He also recorded confirmed breeding at Jahra on 19 April 1985 and at a site in northern Kuwait on 17 April 1986. In April 2004 three nestlings were discovered in a building being demolished in Ahmadi. They were hand-reared and later shown to K. Al-Nasrallah, who photographed them.

In recent years, Pallid Swifts have been seen, during the breeding season, around many of the tall and fairly tall buildings that have been built in Kuwait City, Jahra, Ahmadi and Fahaheel, and, no doubt, they must breed in them. The highest daily count is 200 on several occasions.

JAN 1-10	JAN 11-20	JAN 21-31	FEB 1-10	FEB 11-20	FEB 21-29	MAR 1-10	MAR 11-20	MAR 21-31	APR 1-10	APR 11-20	APR 21-30	MAY 1-10	MAY 11-20	MAY 21-31	JUN 1-10	JUN 11-20	JUN 21-30	JUL 1-10	JUL 11-20	JUL 21-31	AUG 1-10	AUG 11-20	AUG 21-31	SEP 1-10	SEP 11-20	SEP 21-30	OCT 1-10	OCT 11-20	OCT 21-31	NOV 1-10	NOV 11-20	NOV 21-30	DEC 1-10	DEC 11-20	DEC 21-31
8	20	200	30	14	25	10	19	30	15	4	20	10	4	6									1		2	20		7	2	15	4	20			

Little Swift *(Apus affinis)*
Status: Rare disperser in autumn, winter and spring.

The first record of Little Swift in Kuwait was of one seen by P. R. Haynes heading north along the coast at Messilah on 28 March 1978. The only other accessible records are of single birds at Abu Halifa on 1 April 1997, at Jahra Pool Reserve on 5 March 1999 and at Al-Abraq Al-Khabari on 5 September 1999. The observers for these records were S. T. Spencer and C. W. T. Pilcher. There are known to be at least seven other records but details of them are not accessible. Accordingly, the status given above seems the best one.

JAN 1-10	JAN 11-20	JAN 21-31	FEB 1-10	FEB 11-20	FEB 21-29	MAR 1-10	MAR 11-20	MAR 21-31	APR 1-10	APR 11-20	APR 21-30	MAY 1-10	MAY 11-20	MAY 21-31	JUN 1-10	JUN 11-20	JUN 21-30	JUL 1-10	JUL 11-20	JUL 21-31	AUG 1-10	AUG 11-20	AUG 21-31	SEP 1-10	SEP 11-20	SEP 21-30	OCT 1-10	OCT 11-20	OCT 21-31	NOV 1-10	NOV 11-20	NOV 21-30	DEC 1-10	DEC 11-20	DEC 21-31
						1																		1											

White-throated Kingfisher *(Halcyon smyrnensis)*
Status: Uncommon winter visitor. Scarce resident. Breeds.

This species occurs in Kuwait mainly as a winter visitor, arriving mostly from September and staying up to March. Birds have been recorded inland at Ahmadi, Umm Al-Aish, Abdali Farms, Wafra Farms and Jahra Farms, as well as at coastal sites and pools. White-throated Kingfishers eat not only fish, but also invertebrates, small reptiles and small birds.

The first evidence of breeding by this species in Kuwait was in 1999, when J. Gaskell found, at one site at Jahra Farms, two juvenile birds on 20 May, a single unaged bird on 21 May, and an adult and two juveniles on 27 May. What was probably one of these juvenile birds was filmed by K. Al-Nasrallah at a nearby site on 31 August 1999, and another bird may also have been present. The significance of these sightings was not apparent at that time, but became clear later. In 2000 up to four birds remained at

Jahra Farms from January until at least May. On 4 May 2001 G. Gregory observed an adult entering a nest hole, and on 9 May he, P. Robertson, Abdulla Al-Habashi and Ali, a farm worker, saw and photographed two adults and two juveniles together nearby at the Abdulla Al-Habashi Farm. Next day K. Al-Nasrallah and G. Gregory filmed two adults and three juveniles there. Also in 2001 S. T. Spencer confirmed the breeding of a pair in a hole in the sandy bank of a sewage stream at Sulaibikhat Bay.

In 2002 two pairs were found breeding at Jahra Farms, one being in a stone-lined well. Two juveniles were seen nearby in September. An adult flew down into a stone-lined well at a third site, and many old nesting burrows were found at a fourth site. This indicated that this species had bred there years before the first discovery of breeding in 1999. In 2003 two males were heard singing on 27 March, and three active nest holes were observed on 11 April. However, due to restrictions, confirmation of breeding was not obtained that year. At least one bird at remained at Jahra Farms throughout 2004, but again breeding was not confirmed.

Common Kingfisher *(Alcedo atthis)*
Status: Scarce passage migrant. Rare winter visitor.

This species has been recorded only at coastal sites or sewage-water or saline pools, except for one seen inland at Umm Al-Aish by A. B. Caldwell on 2 September 1972. The highest daily count is three seen by B. Settles at Salmiya on 30 September 2004.

Pied Kingfisher *(Ceryle rudis)*
Status: Scarce winter visitor.

This species probably occurs annually in Kuwait. All birds recorded have been at pools or coastal sites, including single birds seen by P. Howe on Failaka Island, on 12 and 21 December 1973, and on 4 and 11 January 1974. They are presumed to originate from the breeding population in Iraq. The highest daily count is two seen on several occasions in the past.

Blue-cheeked Bee-eater *(Merops superciliosus)*
Status: Abundant passage migrant. Rare summer visitor. Has bred.

Migrant Blue-cheeked Bee-eaters, mostly in flocks, are widespread in Kuwait in spring and autumn. The highest count is 'over 1000' seen by V. A. D. Sales at Ahmadi on 2 May 1964 (Sales, undated).

The first breeding of this species in Kuwait, on Maskan Island on 7 May 1942, was described by V. Dickson (1942): 'The Green Bee-eater 'Kadhari' had some 15-20 nests all in burrows. One small white almost spherical egg was picked up at the entrance to one of these tiny burrows. They are dug obliquely into the ground for quite ten feet.' F. E. Warr (undated) considered that they could have been Green Bee-eaters (M. orientalis), but M. C. Jennings (undated) stated that the latter species 'does not nest in colonies or occur in Kuwait', and accepted the breeding record. The only other breeding records involved birds seen by C. W. T. Pilcher, on an unstated date or dates in 1987, entering nest holes at the rubbish dump near Amghara, and the discovery of about 14 old nest holes, which were briefly frequented by adults, at Wafra Farms, on 12 March 2005 by P. Fagel and B. Foster.

JAN 1-10	JAN 11-20	JAN 21-31	FEB 1-10	FEB 11-20	FEB 21-29	MAR 1-10	MAR 11-20	MAR 21-31	APR 1-10	APR 11-20	APR 21-30	MAY 1-10	MAY 11-20	MAY 21-31	JUN 1-10	JUN 11-20	JUN 21-30	JUL 1-10	JUL 11-20	JUL 21-31	AUG 1-10	AUG 11-20	AUG 21-31	SEP 1-10	SEP 11-20	SEP 21-30	OCT 1-10	OCT 11-20	OCT 21-31	NOV 1-10	NOV 11-20	NOV 21-30	DEC 1-10	DEC 11-20	DEC 21-31
1						7	9	32	12	30	11	15	20	15	6	1	3	5			3	8	27	4	30	30	7	35	35	35					

European Bee-eater *(Merops apiaster)*
Status: Abundant passage migrant.

Most birds observed are in migratory flight, in flocks of up to about 60 birds, but singles or small groups are also quite often seen. The highest count is 'over 1000' seen by V. A. D. Sales at Ahmadi in 'April-May' on 25 April 1957 and each day from 12 - 17 April 1963. Records are from almost all areas of Kuwait. European Bee-eaters are not known to have bred in Kuwait, but in 2000 G. Gregory observed a pair lingering around a large old sandpile in Salmiya from 26 April to 12 May. There was no further evidence of breeding, however.

JAN 1-10	JAN 11-20	JAN 21-31	FEB 1-10	FEB 11-20	FEB 21-29	MAR 1-10	MAR 11-20	MAR 21-31	APR 1-10	APR 11-20	APR 21-30	MAY 1-10	MAY 11-20	MAY 21-31	JUN 1-10	JUN 11-20	JUN 21-30	JUL 1-10	JUL 11-20	JUL 21-31	AUG 1-10	AUG 11-20	AUG 21-31	SEP 1-10	SEP 11-20	SEP 21-30	OCT 1-10	OCT 11-20	OCT 21-31	NOV 1-10	NOV 11-20	NOV 21-30	DEC 1-10	DEC 11-20	DEC 21-31
							5	20	57	50	23	39	4	2	1		1			8	7	8	16	120	4	4	8	5							

European Roller *(Coracias garrulus)*
Status: Uncommon passage migrant. Rare summer visitor.

European Rollers are easily seen on spring and summer migration at most sites in Kuwait. The highest daily count is 20 seen by V. A. D. Sales at Ahmadi on 16 April 1964. The only evidence that breeding might have occurred involved birds seen by A.

Al-Sirhan in 2004: an adult in possible breeding habitat at Judailiyat from 9 to at least 25 July, and a newly-fledged juvenile less than ten kilometers away at Sulaibikhat Nature Reserve on 19 July. However, there is some chance that the juvenile hatched outside the state. An isolated record of a bird seen by P. J. Howe on the coast at or near Kuwait City on 16 June 1974 is also interesting.

JAN 1-10	JAN 11-20	JAN 21-31	FEB 1-10	FEB 11-20	FEB 21-29	MAR 1-10	MAR 11-20	MAR 21-31	APR 1-10	APR 11-20	APR 21-30	MAY 1-10	MAY 11-20	MAY 21-31	JUN 1-10	JUN 11-20	JUN 21-30	JUL 1-10	JUL 11-20	JUL 21-31	AUG 1-10	AUG 11-20	AUG 21-31	SEP 1-10	SEP 11-20	SEP 21-30	OCT 1-10	OCT 11-20	OCT 21-31	NOV 1-10	NOV 11-20	NOV 21-30	DEC 1-10	DEC 11-20	DEC 21-31
					3	1	1	1	2		1	3	2	1	2	1		2	1		1	2	5	2	3		1								

Indian Roller *(Coracias benghalensis)*
Status: Scarce disperser in autumn, winter and spring.

Birds of this species seen in Kuwait are presumed to have dispersed from the breeding population in Iraq. The earliest was a single bird seen by J. Hunt at Manageesh on 29 July 1971, and the latest was one also seen by J. Hunt at Manageesh on 17 March 1971. Records are from many sites. The only sign of potential breeding was a 'tumble display' by one bird in the presence of another, observed by G. Gregory at Jahra Farms on 13 December 1996. The highest daily count is two seen on several occasions.

JAN 1-10	JAN 11-20	JAN 21-31	FEB 1-10	FEB 11-20	FEB 21-29	MAR 1-10	MAR 11-20	MAR 21-31	APR 1-10	APR 11-20	APR 21-30	MAY 1-10	MAY 11-20	MAY 21-31	JUN 1-10	JUN 11-20	JUN 21-30	JUL 1-10	JUL 11-20	JUL 21-31	AUG 1-10	AUG 11-20	AUG 21-31	SEP 1-10	SEP 11-20	SEP 21-30	OCT 1-10	OCT 11-20	OCT 21-31	NOV 1-10	NOV 11-20	NOV 21-30	DEC 1-10	DEC 11-20	DEC 21-31
1	1	1	1																							1	1	1	2	2			1	1	

Eurasian Hoopoe *(Upupa epops)*
Status: Common passage migrant.

Eurasian Hoopoes are commonly and easily seen, and, not surprisingly, there are many records of them in Kuwait, in almost all areas. The highest daily count is 57 seen by V. A. D. Sales at Ahmadi on 14 March 1966. Almost all sightings have been in spring and autumn. Despite some summer records in possible breeding habitat in the past, Eurasian Hoopoes have never been known to breed in Kuwait.

JAN 1-10	JAN 11-20	JAN 21-31	FEB 1-10	FEB 11-20	FEB 21-29	MAR 1-10	MAR 11-20	MAR 21-31	APR 1-10	APR 11-20	APR 21-30	MAY 1-10	MAY 11-20	MAY 21-31	JUN 1-10	JUN 11-20	JUN 21-30	JUL 1-10	JUL 11-20	JUL 21-31	AUG 1-10	AUG 11-20	AUG 21-31	SEP 1-10	SEP 11-20	SEP 21-30	OCT 1-10	OCT 11-20	OCT 21-31	NOV 1-10	NOV 11-20	NOV 21-30	DEC 1-10	DEC 11-20	DEC 21-31
1	3	3	4	20	6	8	1	2	1					1		1	5	9	11	18	12	11	2	2	1	1	2								

Eurasian Wryneck *(Jynx torquilla)*
Status: Uncommon passage migrant.

This species is regularly recorded on both spring and autumn migration, almost always at sites where there are trees or bushes. Some, no doubt, have been missed due to their secretive behaviour and cryptic plumage. The highest daily count is nine seen by V. A. D. Sales at Ahmadi on 24 April 1966.

JAN 1-10	JAN 11-20	JAN 21-31	FEB 1-10	FEB 11-20	FEB 21-29	MAR 1-10	MAR 11-20	MAR 21-31	APR 1-10	APR 11-20	APR 21-30	MAY 1-10	MAY 11-20	MAY 21-31	JUN 1-10	JUN 11-20	JUN 21-30	JUL 1-10	JUL 11-20	JUL 21-31	AUG 1-10	AUG 11-20	AUG 21-31	SEP 1-10	SEP 11-20	SEP 21-30	OCT 1-10	OCT 11-20	OCT 21-31	NOV 1-10	NOV 11-20	NOV 21-30	DEC 1-10	DEC 11-20	DEC 21-31
								1	3	2	1	2	1											2	1	1	2	1							

Black-crowned Sparrow-lark *(Eremopterix nigriceps)*
Status: Uncommon resident. Uncommon winter visitor. Breeds.

The first known breeding record of this species in Kuwait involved a young bird seen just west of Ahmadi by an unstated observer on 29 June 1972. In 1996 P. J. Cowan and D. L. Newman confirmed breeding by observing a male feeding a juvenile on 31 May at Sabriya. On 20 April 1997 they found a nest containing two nestlings, and on 15 April 1998 they observed several newly fledged juveniles, in the same area (Cowan and Newman, 1998; Cowan and Pilcher, 2003). Members of BMAPT discovered a small breeding colony at the AbdulFatai Marafie Farm at Wafra on 31 May 2001 and on 31 May 2002. Juvenile birds were also observed by M. O. Chichester at Wafra Oil Field in early May 2002. Fairly large numbers are probably resident there. Family parties of adults with newly-fledged young were seen by G. Gregory at southern Abdali Farms on 14 May and at Sewer Plant Reeds on 8 June 2004. Since October 2003 birds have been resident in the Sabah Al-Ahmed Natural Reserve, with a maximum of 14 seen there on 11 February 2004. Most likely they breed there.

In the summer, after breeding, many birds visit freshwater and sewage pools, such as at Sewer Plant Reeds, and even sprinkled lawns, for example at Ahmadi, presumably in search of water. Five adult specimens, all males, were collected at Hawalli (then an oasis) by V. S. La Personne on 19 June 1923, and were donated to the British Museum (Warr, undated). In winter some fairly large flocks can form, presumably including birds from outside Kuwait. The highest daily count is 140 at Wafra Oil Field seen by M. O. Chichester on 9 January 2002.

JAN 1-10	JAN 11-20	JAN 21-31	FEB 1-10	FEB 11-20	FEB 21-29	MAR 1-10	MAR 11-20	MAR 21-31	APR 1-10	APR 11-20	APR 21-30	MAY 1-10	MAY 11-20	MAY 21-31	JUN 1-10	JUN 11-20	JUN 21-30	JUL 1-10	JUL 11-20	JUL 21-31	AUG 1-10	AUG 11-20	AUG 21-31	SEP 1-10	SEP 11-20	SEP 21-30	OCT 1-10	OCT 11-20	OCT 21-31	NOV 1-10	NOV 11-20	NOV 21-30	DEC 1-10	DEC 11-20	DEC 21-31
140	2	3	1	14		2	12	8	4	6	45	20	12	5	18	35	4	30	30	35	30	30	3	2	3	2	2	1	4	20			2	2	

Dunn's Lark *(Eremalauda dunni)*
Status: Uncommon resident. Has bred.

Dunn's Lark was first recorded in Kuwait by A. Tye at Al-Mazira on 17 March 1987, with a group of four birds observed. The next record was of a single bird seen by C. W. T. Pilcher at an unstated location on 15 December 1989.

In 1999 birds were seen in west and northwest Kuwait by P. Cowan on 14 May (one), 13 August (one), 19 August (three), 26 August (four), 27 August (one), 2 September (eight) and 22 October (three). In the same year, G. Gregory and P. Robertson observed an adult in song flight, and photographed two adults on the ground, at Subiya on 26 May.

Birds were present again in the same areas of north and northwest Kuwait from May to September 2000, with a maximum of five seen on 12 May. A juvenile seen on 1 June indicated possible breeding there (Cowan and Pilcher, 2003). In 2002 there were 12 (the highest daily count) at Ratqa on 7 March, one (singing) at Subiya on 8 March and 14 March, and one at Al-Abraq Al-Khabari on 25 May. From at least May 2003 birds have been resident in the Sabah Al-Ahmed Natural Reserve, and were proven to breed there in 2004, with a newly fledged juvenile seen and photographed there by members of BMAPT. There were two nearby at Bahra on 14 May 2004. It seems likely that other birds are now resident breeders in inaccessible areas near Wadi al-Batin and in various oilfields.

Bar-tailed Lark *(Ammomanes cincturus)*
Status: Uncommon resident. Breeds.

This species used to be quite rare in Kuwait, and the first record apparently involved a single bird seen by L. Corrall on 21 October 1977 near Wadi Al-Batin. There may, however, have previously been some confusion with Desert Lark (***A. deserti***). For about the next twenty years Bar-tailed Lark was only occasionally recorded, mostly in winter.

It was first discovered breeding on 10 May 1996 by P. J. Cowan and D. L. Newman, who saw an adult feeding two juveniles at Sabriya (Cowan and Newman, 1998). In 1997 the former observer found nests containing nestlings in what is now the Sabah Al-Ahmed Natural Reserve on 24 April and 29 May. Breeding was confirmed three times in 2001 and twice in 2002 near Salmi/Wadi Al-Batin (Cowan and Pilcher, 2003), and some birds are probably resident in this area. Since 2003 birds have been resident in the Sabah Al-Ahmed Natural Reserve, and presumably breed there annually. They are also suspected to be resident breeders in the fenced Burgan and Rawdatain Oil Fields, and possibly in Wafra Oil Field. The highest daily count is 48 seen between Salmi and Al-Abraq Al-Khabari on 22 October 1999 by S. T. Spencer.

Desert Lark *(Ammomanes deserti)*
Status: Uncommon resident. Has bred.

Desert Lark is not now as commonly observed as Bar-tailed Lark (***A. cincturus***), and may have decreased in Kuwait, possibly due to overgrazing. Some past records, however, may have involved confusion with this other species.

V. Dickson (undated) wrote: 'On 7-4-39 I found two nests of a small lark called by the Arabs "Hamra" [applies to Desert & Bar-tailed Larks according to Cheesman], close to our camp some 30 miles south of the town. One nest had four eggs, and the other two (the broken shells of probably 2 others were near the nest). Each nest was under a small bush of Arfaj (***Rhanterium epapposum Oliv.***) and had a piece of rag among the grass of the lining of the nest. The eggs were smaller than Bifasciated [Greater Hoopoe Lark (***Alaemon alaudipes***)] and speckled all over. The bird flew off the nest and was reddish brown. Another one was up in the air singing like an English skylark.' It is not certain that these birds were of this species.

The first definite breeding records involved several nests containing 4-5 eggs seen at Ash-Shiggayat and Wadi Al-Batin on 4 April 1974, and a nest with three eggs found at Burgan flint beds as reported in the ANHFSG Newsletters 15 (1975): 4, and 19 (1978): 7. There were many other sightings of this species in the 1970s in many areas of Kuwait, and P. R. Haynes (1979) listed it as a very common resident breeder. The highest daily count is simply 'many' on several occasions.

More recently, breeding was confirmed near Salmi/Wadi Al-Batin once in 1995, twice in 1998, once in 2001 and twice in 2002 (Cowan and Pilcher, 2003). Birds have been regularly seen in that area since. In winter and spring up to five birds (the highest recent daily count) have been recorded in the Sabah Al-Ahmed Natural Reserve. They may possibly breed there, in the fenced Burgan and Rawdatain Oil Fields, and in Wafra Oil Field.

Greater Hoopoe Lark *(Alaemon alaudipes)*
Status: Common resident. Breeds.

This species is quite commonly observed throughout the year, in all areas away from human habitation. The highest daily count is 20 seen by S. Howe at Umm Al-Aish on 28 December 1972.

The first record of breeding was on 4 April 1974 near Wadi Al-Batin, as reported in the ANHFSG *Newsletter* 14 (1974). A nest in the top of a bush was observed to contain three large eggs. Breeding also occurred on Failaka Island in 1993, with C. W. T. Pilcher writing: 'One nest with eggs in late March on Failaka Id. was reported to me and a 2nd pair was also thought to have bred' (Jennings, undated). Surprisingly there are no other breeding records. However, it surely must breed in the Sabah Al-Ahmed Natural Reserve, in Burgan, Rawdatain and Wafra Oil Fields, and in many other areas where there is no disturbance.

Thick-billed Lark *(Ramphocoris clotbey)*
Status: Rare disperser in spring. Has bred.

The first record involved two or three birds seen by P. R. Haynes near Wadi Al-Batin on 20 February, 5 March and 10 March 1978. His description included 'distinct white trailing edges to wings, large, dark markings on face and upper breast/throat. On ground distinct patterning and enormous bill' (Warr, undated). Further records there were single birds on 30 June 1978, 7 July 1978, an unstated day in January 1979 and 20 April 1979. The observers were P. R. Haynes, L. Corrall and W. A. Stuart. The next sighting was by C. W. T. Pilcher there on 1 February 1985. There were no further records until 2002, when five were seen at Ratqa on 4 March by S. Al-Awadi and others, and seven or more, seen by S. T. Spencer, were present near Wadi Al-Batin from 8 March to 4 April. On 29 April a pair of adults was seen there at a nest with four eggs, the first confirmed breeding record for Kuwait. G. Gregory observed a pair near there on 8 March 2005.

JAN 1-10	JAN 11-20	JAN 21-31	FEB 1-10	FEB 11-20	FEB 21-29	MAR 1-10	MAR 11-20	MAR 21-31	APR 1-10	APR 11-20	APR 21-30	MAY 1-10	MAY 11-20	MAY 21-31	JUN 1-10	JUN 11-20	JUN 21-30	JUL 1-10	JUL 11-20	JUL 21-31	AUG 1-10	AUG 11-20	AUG 21-31	SEP 1-10	SEP 11-20	SEP 21-30	OCT 1-10	OCT 11-20	OCT 21-31	NOV 1-10	NOV 11-20	NOV 21-30	DEC 1-10	DEC 11-20	DEC 21-31
						7	7	7	2																										

Calandra Lark *(Melanocorypha calandra)*
Status: Vagrant (one record).
 Two were seen by J. Gaskell at Shaab on 6 November 1998. His description is below:
'Location and Date: a small knoll (covered septic tank) behind the Penguin Café near Green Island on the Gulf Road, 6/11/98.
Duration of Observation: 8.10 - 8.25 a.m. discontinuously at 10 - 15m range through 8 x 40 binoculars. Bright morning sunshine; quite warm after a chilly start.
Summary: Two large larks, at first suspected of having been Bimaculated Larks, were identified as Calandra Larks when they flew revealing diagnostic white trailing edges to wings. Both birds were initially observed on the ground for 10 minutes in the immediate vicinity of a White Wagtail and a Water Pipit which afforded size comparison. Both lark appeared to be so exceedingly worn condition, the feathers having conspicuously frayed edges; one bird appeared to have a shorter tail than the other. On account of a passer-by, both birds eventually took wing, revealing their identity by their upper and under wing patterns viewed laterally.
Description
1. Body: Lower back, mantle and scapulars rich brown with a slightly rufous tint, especially at the edges, uniform and apparently not streaked. Neck and crown concolorous with upper parts, any crown streaking not conspicuous. Under parts, including throat and malar region, to vent white, the breast sides marked with a pair of narrowly tapering black wedges which almost converged in the middle of the breast. The sides of the lower breast below these marks were sparsely marked with widely spaced, short dark streaks. The dark eye was surrounded by a prominent buffish-white ring. A broad line, also buffish-white, reached the eye at the top. Over all the facial pattern was reminiscent of that of Short-toed Lark.
2. Wing: Tertials long, warm beige tinged rufous as upper parts. Very worn. No obvious primary projection, but 3-4 primary tips on one bird clearly visible on left side because wing not fully folded. Primaries greyish-black, those mentioned having misshapen inner webs (reminiscent of pattern on Hawfinch's secondaries), doubtless on account of the poor condition of the birds generally. Secondaries and wing coverts edged light brown appearing uniform with upper parts when birds at rest, but darker in flight. Former, and inner primaries, narrowly but conspicuously tipped white, this pattern being observable on both upper and under wing surfaces. Under wing, viewed obliquely, distinctly dark.
3. Tail: Brown, pale edged, one bird appearing to have whitish tail corners (but not extensive white tip).
4. Soft Parts: Bill, slightly decurved, large, heavy but not disproportionally so relative to the bird's bulk. Pale ochreous, slightly greyer on culmen. This enhanced the 'outsized Short-toed Lark' appearance. Leg, colour not noted.
Call- uttered on ground when birds first alarmed a passer-by, a rolling "prrrp" lacking any euphonious lark-like notes and reminiscent of call of Greater Sand Plover.'

Bimaculated Lark *(Melanocorypha bimaculata)*
Status: Uncommon passage migrant. Uncommon winter visitor. Rare summer visitor. Has bred.
 This species is usually observed, singly or in small groups on flat, vegetated areas, but also has been seen once at Jahra Pool Reserve. Most birds are passage migrants in spring.
 The only breeding record of Bimaculated Lark for Kuwait and, apparently, the Arabian peninsula, was at Umm Al-Aish on 21 April 1978, when W. A. Stuart, L. Corrall and P. R. Haynes found an adult and a fledgling and photographed an empty nest. According to F. E. Warr (undated), 1978 was 'an exceptional year when the desert bloomed after

a wet winter.' The only other indication of possible breeding involved 30 birds, some in pairs, originally found by G. Gregory, K. Al-Nasrallah and M. Shehab, near Al-Abraq Al-Khabari for weeks from 7 March 2002. 30 birds (the equal highest daily count) were also seen by S. T. Spencer at Rawdatain on 22 October 1999.

JAN 1-10	JAN 11-20	JAN 21-31	FEB 1-10	FEB 11-20	FEB 21-29	MAR 1-10	MAR 11-20	MAR 21-31	APR 1-10	APR 11-20	APR 21-30	MAY 1-10	MAY 11-20	MAY 21-31	JUN 1-10	JUN 11-20	JUN 21-30	JUL 1-10	JUL 11-20	JUL 21-31	AUG 1-10	AUG 11-20	AUG 21-31	SEP 1-10	SEP 11-20	SEP 21-30	OCT 1-10	OCT 11-20	OCT 21-31	NOV 1-10	NOV 11-20	NOV 21-30	DEC 1-10	DEC 11-20	DEC 21-31
1	2	10	7			30	30	1		4											2							2							

Greater Short-toed Lark *(Calandrella brachydactyla)*
Status: Abundant passage migrant. Common summer visitor. Common winter visitor. Breeds.

Greater Short-toed Larks are seen, often in flocks, throughout the year, though mostly in spring and autumn. They have been recorded from most areas of Kuwait away from human habitation but with some vegetation. The highest daily count is 3000 seen by G. Gregory and P. Robertson at Manageesh on 10 March 2000.

The first hint that this species might breed in Kuwait involved two pairs, observed by G. Gregory and P. Robertson, holding territory near Subiya for weeks from 26 May 1999. The first record of confirmed breeding involved two newly-fledged juveniles found near Jahra East Outfall by G. Gregory on 28 May 2001. In the same year three birds were singing in what is now the Sabah Al-Ahmed Natural Reserve on 15 February, and breeding was confirmed there on 7 June, with three newly-fledged juveniles observed by K. Al-Nasrallah, M. Shehab and G. Gregory. Also, two birds, seen by M. O. Chichester, were singing at Wafra Oil Field on 6 April. An adult was photographed, by K. Al-Nasrallah, on a nest in the Sabah Al-Ahmed Natural Reserve in May 2004. Breeding seems likely to occur at other locations where grazing is restricted and fresh water is available. These conditions are met in Burgan, Wafra and Rawdatain Oil Fields.

JAN 1-10	JAN 11-20	JAN 21-31	FEB 1-10	FEB 11-20	FEB 21-29	MAR 1-10	MAR 11-20	MAR 21-31	APR 1-10	APR 11-20	APR 21-30	MAY 1-10	MAY 11-20	MAY 21-31	JUN 1-10	JUN 11-20	JUN 21-30	JUL 1-10	JUL 11-20	JUL 21-31	AUG 1-10	AUG 11-20	AUG 21-31	SEP 1-10	SEP 11-20	SEP 21-30	OCT 1-10	OCT 11-20	OCT 21-31	NOV 1-10	NOV 11-20	NOV 21-30	DEC 1-10	DEC 11-20	DEC 21-31
40			35	20	500	50	3000	1300	35	5		1		15	4	4	2		4	14	3			15	1		20	35	30	15			2		

Lesser Short-toed Lark *(Calandrella rufescens)*
Status: Very common winter visitor. Very common passage migrant. Uncommon summer visitor. Breeds.

This species is less commonly observed than the preceding one, but is also found throughout the year, although not many remain in the summer. It also occurs in most areas of Kuwait away from human habitation but with some vegetation. The highest daily count is 550 seen between Ratqa and Al-Abraq Al-Khabari by K. Al-Nasrallah, M. Shehab and G. Gregory on 7 March 2002.

Breeding was first confirmed at Salmi on 22 March 2001 by S. T. Spencer found a nest with three eggs. That same year in what is now the Sabah Al-Ahmed Natural Reserve on 7 June a newly-fledged juvenile was observed by K. Al-Nasrallah, M. Shehab and G. Gregory. In 2002 breeding was also proven at Ratqa on 7 March 2002, with M. Shehab finding an adult on a nest with an egg, which were also seen and photographed by K. Al-Nasrallah and G. Gregory; and at Salmi on 22 March, with S. T. Spencer finding a nest with eggs. Breeding probably occurs at other locations where grazing is restricted and fresh water is available.

JAN 1-10	JAN 11-20	JAN 21-31	FEB 1-10	FEB 11-20	FEB 21-29	MAR 1-10	MAR 11-20	MAR 21-31	APR 1-10	APR 11-20	APR 21-30	MAY 1-10	MAY 11-20	MAY 21-31	JUN 1-10	JUN 11-20	JUN 21-30	JUL 1-10	JUL 11-20	JUL 21-31	AUG 1-10	AUG 11-20	AUG 21-31	SEP 1-10	SEP 11-20	SEP 21-30	OCT 1-10	OCT 11-20	OCT 21-31	NOV 1-10	NOV 11-20	NOV 21-30	DEC 1-10	DEC 11-20	DEC 21-31
150	250	300	60	150	60	550	50	115	10	5			2	3	5		2	50	5	25	25	35	3	15	35	15		4			60	9	75	200	250

Crested Lark *(Galerida cristata)*
Status: Very common resident. Breeds.

Crested Larks are easily seen and are widespread in Kuwait, except near human habitation or where there is little or no vegetation. The highest daily count is ˙p to 1000 seen by V. A. D. Sales near Ahmadi on 3 July 1953. W. A. Stuart noted that numbers were greatly reduced in 1979, a dry year (Warr, undated).

The first record of breeding by this species was by V. Dickson on Maskan Island on 7 June 1942. She wrote: 'The Crested Lark, 'Goba', were nesting. I found one small nest under a 'Hamdh' bush with three eggs. The nest was completely made of dry 'Samaa' grass and very neat. I also found a similar nest under a bush but very small and only about one and a half inches across, but with no eggs. The larks sang each morning and evening' (V. Dickson, 1942).

From 1959 to 1962 V. A. D. Sales filled in British Trust for Ornithology Nest Record Cards on nests that he found at Ahmadi:
Nest 1: 10/4/59: 5 eggs. 14-20/4/59: 5 young. 24/4/59: 4 young. 25/4/59: Nest empty. Nest at base of clump of marram grass on golf course fairway.
Nest 2: 26/3/59: 4 eggs. 1/4/59: 1 egg & 3 young. 2/4/59: 4 young. 9-10/4/59: 2 young. 13/4/59: Nest empty. Nest at base of clump of marram grass on golf course fairway. 9/4/59: Young able to fly away from nest.
Nest 3: 26/2/62: 4 eggs but 2 broken by children, which contained well developed embryos. 27/2/92 - 2/3/62: 1 egg. 1 chick. 9/3/62: 1 egg (addled). Nest on north side of vegetation clump in open desert. 12/3/62: The young bird seen near nest & able to fly a short way.
Nest 4: 9/3/62 - 19/3/62: 4 eggs. 19/3/62: nest deserted with eggs cold. Nest on north side of small patch of vegetation in open desert.
Nest 5: 9/3/62 - 17/3/62: 4 eggs. 18/3/62: 1 egg, 3 chicks. Fourth chick hatched later on 18/3/62. 20/3/62 - 27/3/62: 4 chicks present. Nest on north side of small patch of vegetation in open desert at side of road.

There have been many other breeding records in many other areas of Kuwait by a number of observers.

Wood Lark *(Lullula arborea)*
Status: Rare winter visitor and passage migrant.
 The only accessible records of Wood Lark in Kuwait are: eight (the highest daily count) seen by V. A D. Sales at Ahmadi on 14 October 1953; one seen by V. A. D. Sales at Ahmadi on 14 August 1954; three seen by V. A. D. Sales at Ahmadi most days between 7 December 1967 and 26 February 1968; one seen by S. Howe at Kashma on 19 February 1971; one seen at Qaisat by L. Corrall on 24 November 1978; one seen by L. Corrall and W. A. Stuart at Jal Az-Zor on 26 January 1979; 2 seen by G. Gregory at Al-Abraq Al-Khabari in October 1987 (exact day not accessible); 4 seen by S. T. Spencer and C. W. T. Pilcher at Al-Abraq Al-Khabari on 10 February 1995; 4 seen by unstated observers near Wadi Ar-Rimam on 18 February 1995; and two seen by S. T. Spencer at an unstated location three times in January 2001. There are three more records, according to C. W. T. Pilcher (undated), but the details are not accessible.

Eurasian Skylark *(Alauda arvensis)*
Status: Uncommon winter visitor. Uncommon passage migrant.
 Eurasian Skylarks are occasionally seen, mostly in winter, in open areas with some ground cover, away from human habitation. They have been recorded at many sites in Kuwait. The highest daily count is 65 seen by G. Gregory, C. Moores and W. Müller in the Sabah Al-Ahmed Natural Reserve on 31 January 2005.

JAN 1-10	JAN 11-20	JAN 21-31	FEB 1-10	FEB 11-20	FEB 21-29	MAR 1-10	MAR 11-20	MAR 21-31	APR 1-10	APR 11-20	APR 21-30	MAY 1-10	MAY 11-20	MAY 21-31	JUN 1-10	JUN 11-20	JUN 21-30	JUL 1-10	JUL 11-20	JUL 21-31	AUG 1-10	AUG 11-20	AUG 21-31	SEP 1-10	SEP 11-20	SEP 21-30	OCT 1-10	OCT 11-20	OCT 21-31	NOV 1-10	NOV 11-20	NOV 21-30	DEC 1-10	DEC 11-20	DEC 21-31
9	5	65	4			3	2																			9		7	6	3	4				

Oriental Skylark *(Alauda gulgula)*
Status: Scarce disperser in autumn, winter and spring.
 Oriental Skylarks were first recorded in Kuwait by V. A. D. Sales at Ahmadi on 20 March 1954 and on 18 April 1959. The next sighting was on 11 November 1986 by M. Shehab, G. Gregory and C. W. T. Pilcher at Jahra Pool Reserve. This species had probably been overlooked as Eurasian Skylark (*A. arvensis*) on many other occasions previously. Since then it has probably been present annually in Kuwait, having also been seen at Al-Abraq Al-Khabari, Jahra East Outfall, Subiya, Zour Port, Hujaijah, the Sabah Al-Ahmed Natural Reserve and Sabah Al-Salem. The highest daily count is 2+ seen in the Sabah Al-Ahmed Natural Reserve by G. Gregory, C. Moores and W. Müller on 31 January 2005.

JAN 1-10	JAN 11-20	JAN 21-31	FEB 1-10	FEB 11-20	FEB 21-29	MAR 1-10	MAR 11-20	MAR 21-31	APR 1-10	APR 11-20	APR 21-30	MAY 1-10	MAY 11-20	MAY 21-31	JUN 1-10	JUN 11-20	JUN 21-30	JUL 1-10	JUL 11-20	JUL 21-31	AUG 1-10	AUG 11-20	AUG 21-31	SEP 1-10	SEP 11-20	SEP 21-30	OCT 1-10	OCT 11-20	OCT 21-31	NOV 1-10	NOV 11-20	NOV 21-30	DEC 1-10	DEC 11-20	DEC 21-31
	2								1																1	1				1	1				1

Temminck's Lark *(Eremophila bilophus)*
Status: Uncommon disperser in autumn, winter and spring. Has bred.

The first breeding record of this species involved two adults feeding two chicks, seen by W. A. Stuart near Salmi on 10 March 1978. L. Corrall observed one chick being fed at the same site on 24 March 1978. It was found breeding there again on 30 March 2001, with an adult feeding a juvenile, and on 29 March 2002, with a nest containing eggs seen (Cowan and Pilcher, 2003). It has also been proven to breed in what is now the Sabah Al-Ahmed Natural Reserve on 18 March 2001 and on 31 March 2002, newly-fledged juveniles being seen on both occasions. The observers included K. Al-Nasrallah, A. Al-Suraye'a and M. Shehab.

Outside the breeding season birds can be seen mostly in remote areas with low vegetation. The highest daily count is 22+ in what is now the Sabah Al-Ahmed Natural Reserve on 10 March 2001, seen by O. Schroeder, S. Schroeder and G. Østerø.

JAN 1-10	JAN 11-20	JAN 21-31	FEB 1-10	FEB 11-20	FEB 21-29	MAR 1-10	MAR 11-20	MAR 21-31	APR 1-10	APR 11-20	APR 21-30	MAY 1-10	MAY 11-20	MAY 21-31	JUN 1-10	JUN 11-20	JUN 21-30	JUL 1-10	JUL 11-20	JUL 21-31	AUG 1-10	AUG 11-20	AUG 21-31	SEP 1-10	SEP 11-20	SEP 21-30	OCT 1-10	OCT 11-20	OCT 21-31	NOV 1-10	NOV 11-20	NOV 21-30	DEC 1-10	DEC 11-20	DEC 21-31
3					1	22	12	8							9	2																		4	4

Sand Martin *(Riparia riparia)*
Status: Abundant passage migrant.

Sand Martins are commonly seen in spring and autumn, and have been recorded from almost all areas of Kuwait. The highest daily count is 'several thousand' seen by V. A. D. Sales at Ahmadi on several occasions between 1952 and 1968. A bird ringed in Russia was controlled by V. A. D. Sales at Ahmadi. Both V. Dickson (1942) and V. A. D. Sales (undated) noted heavy mortality in this species during sandstorms in May.

JAN 1-10	JAN 11-20	JAN 21-31	FEB 1-10	FEB 11-20	FEB 21-29	MAR 1-10	MAR 11-20	MAR 21-31	APR 1-10	APR 11-20	APR 21-30	MAY 1-10	MAY 11-20	MAY 21-31	JUN 1-10	JUN 11-20	JUN 21-30	JUL 1-10	JUL 11-20	JUL 21-31	AUG 1-10	AUG 11-20	AUG 21-31	SEP 1-10	SEP 11-20	SEP 21-30	OCT 1-10	OCT 11-20	OCT 21-31	NOV 1-10	NOV 11-20	NOV 21-30	DEC 1-10	DEC 11-20	DEC 21-31
1	5		15	2		50	250	13	100	30	7	100	25	80	20	7	9	8	7		4	3	11	7	25	32	8	10	2	1	2		1		

Eurasian Crag Martin *(Ptyonoprogne rupestris)*
Status: Scarce passage migrant. Rare winter visitor.

Eurasian Crag Martins are probably annually present in Kuwait, and are most often recorded in spring. All records are from near the coast except for single birds seen at Ahmadi by M. Leven on 23 April 1971 and by R. P. Blacker on 27 August 1972. The highest daily count is 30 seen at Shaab by M. Shehab on 14 April 1997.

JAN 1-10	JAN 11-20	JAN 21-31	FEB 1-10	FEB 11-20	FEB 21-29	MAR 1-10	MAR 11-20	MAR 21-31	APR 1-10	APR 11-20	APR 21-30	MAY 1-10	MAY 11-20	MAY 21-31	JUN 1-10	JUN 11-20	JUN 21-30	JUL 1-10	JUL 11-20	JUL 21-31	AUG 1-10	AUG 11-20	AUG 21-31	SEP 1-10	SEP 11-20	SEP 21-30	OCT 1-10	OCT 11-20	OCT 21-31	NOV 1-10	NOV 11-20	NOV 21-30	DEC 1-10	DEC 11-20	DEC 21-31
							1	6		7		1	4																					1	

Rock Martin *(Hirundo fuligula)*
Status: Vagrant (five records).

The first record of this species was of three birds seen by E. Grieve at Kuwait City/Bay on 23 May 1973. Next year a single bird was observed near Jal Az-Zor on 25 February by P. R. Haynes. Two were recorded by H-M. Busch, J. Rathberger-Knan and W. Bindl at Khiran on 4 April 1999. A single bird was seen by S. T. Spencer at an unstated location on 25 December 2001. G. Gregory observed one at Jahra East Outfall on 5 December 2004.

Barn Swallow *(Hirundo rustica)*
Status: Abundant passage migrant. Rare summer visitor.

This species is almost entirely a passage migrant in Kuwait, but birds are present in all months. The highest daily count is simply 'thousands' seen on many occasions. Records are from almost all areas of the state, and even out over the Gulf. V. A. D. Sales noted that mortality in this species during sandstorms was lower than that in Sand Martin (*Riparia riparia*).

Barn Swallows have probably bred in Kuwait. A juvenile with four adults seen by G. Gregory at Sabah Al-Salem on 22 May 2003 was notable. In 2004 a fully-fledged juvenile was seen flying, together with a pair of adults, over Jahra Pool on 11 June by G. Gregory. The juvenile must almost certainly have hatched in Kuwait, but the exact nesting area was uncertain. Additionally, there was an adult male perched at Jahra Farms on the same day. The inaccessible area of Jahra Ponds seemed a possible breeding site. Several juveniles seen with adults by A. Bailey at Jahra East Outfall on 8 July 2005 could also have hatched at the same site.

JAN 1-10	JAN 11-20	JAN 21-31	FEB 1-10	FEB 11-20	FEB 21-29	MAR 1-10	MAR 11-20	MAR 21-31	APR 1-10	APR 11-20	APR 21-30	MAY 1-10	MAY 11-20	MAY 21-31	JUN 1-10	JUN 11-20	JUN 21-30	JUL 1-10	JUL 11-20	JUL 21-31	AUG 1-10	AUG 11-20	AUG 21-31	SEP 1-10	SEP 11-20	SEP 21-30	OCT 1-10	OCT 11-20	OCT 21-31	NOV 1-10	NOV 11-20	NOV 21-30	DEC 1-10	DEC 11-20	DEC 21-31
3	8	13	1000	250	40	100	100	50	120	50	200	1500	100	18	7	3	2	11	7	3	6	9	9	10	10	15	80	45	50	2	4	1	2	3	5

Red-rumped Swallow *(Hirundo daurica)*
Status: Common passage migrant.
 Red-rumped Swallows are regularly seen on spring migration. The highest daily count is 50 seen by V. A. D. Sales at Ahmadi on several occasions in spring between 1952 and 1968. Most records have been from near the coast but there are several from inland locations. There have been no autumn records recently.

JAN 1-10	JAN 11-20	JAN 21-31	FEB 1-10	FEB 11-20	FEB 21-29	MAR 1-10	MAR 11-20	MAR 21-31	APR 1-10	APR 11-20	APR 21-30	MAY 1-10	MAY 11-20	MAY 21-31	JUN 1-10	JUN 11-20	JUN 21-30	JUL 1-10	JUL 11-20	JUL 21-31	AUG 1-10	AUG 11-20	AUG 21-31	SEP 1-10	SEP 11-20	SEP 21-30	OCT 1-10	OCT 11-20	OCT 21-31	NOV 1-10	NOV 11-20	NOV 21-30	DEC 1-10	DEC 11-20	DEC 21-31
				2	18	8	12		7	15	18	5			1	2	2																		

Common House Martin *(Delichon urbica)*
Status: Abundant passage migrant. Rare winter visitor.
 This species has been recorded from most sites in Kuwait in migratory flight, or feeding over pools. The highest daily count is about 100 seen on several occasions.

JAN 1-10	JAN 11-20	JAN 21-31	FEB 1-10	FEB 11-20	FEB 21-29	MAR 1-10	MAR 11-20	MAR 21-31	APR 1-10	APR 11-20	APR 21-30	MAY 1-10	MAY 11-20	MAY 21-31	JUN 1-10	JUN 11-20	JUN 21-30	JUL 1-10	JUL 11-20	JUL 21-31	AUG 1-10	AUG 11-20	AUG 21-31	SEP 1-10	SEP 11-20	SEP 21-30	OCT 1-10	OCT 11-20	OCT 21-31	NOV 1-10	NOV 11-20	NOV 21-30	DEC 1-10	DEC 11-20	DEC 21-31
5	24	20	30	15	10	2	8	15	2	6	1	25	35	15	18	20	3		1		3	1	9	4	2	10	2								

Richard's Pipit *(Anthus richardi)*
Status: Rare passage migrant.
 V. A. D. Sales recorded Richard's Pipits at Ahmadi on 2 and 9 April 1953 (one), 16 and 17 April 1959 (one), 22 May 1960 (one), and 11 (one) and 12 (two) March 1967. A Rare Bird Report form was sent but it is not accessible. G. Nichols gave the following description of up to ten birds that he observed at an unstated location between 7 and 10 May 1975: 'Pale flesh legs, upperparts not so well defined as Red-throated, long legs with upright stance. Wrong time of year for immature Tawny Pipit with which it might be confused I suppose. Called "rr-rripp".' G. Bundy and F. E. Warr regarded all the above records as not accepted. In reviewing them, and considering the more recent occurrence of this species in Kuwait, it seems likely that at least some of the birds were correctly identified.
 One was seen, heard and well described by G. Gregory, M. Shehab and C. W. T. Pilcher at Al-Abraq Al-Khabari on 18 October 1985. G. Gregory photographed one near Jahra Pool Reserve on 23 April 1999. One was seen by J. Gaskell at Sabah Al-Salem on 17 and 22 May 2000. G. Rowlands observed one at Mishref on 17 June 2000. One was photographed by A. Al-Suraye'a at Sulaibikhat Nature Reserve on 13 April 2002. In the circumstances the status given above is probably the best one.

JAN 1-10	JAN 11-20	JAN 21-31	FEB 1-10	FEB 11-20	FEB 21-29	MAR 1-10	MAR 11-20	MAR 21-31	APR 1-10	APR 11-20	APR 21-30	MAY 1-10	MAY 11-20	MAY 21-31	JUN 1-10	JUN 11-20	JUN 21-30	JUL 1-10	JUL 11-20	JUL 21-31	AUG 1-10	AUG 11-20	AUG 21-31	SEP 1-10	SEP 11-20	SEP 21-30	OCT 1-10	OCT 11-20	OCT 21-31	NOV 1-10	NOV 11-20	NOV 21-30	DEC 1-10	DEC 11-20	DEC 21-31
									1			1																							

Blyth's Pipit *(Anthus godlewskii)*
Status: Vagrant (one record).
One was seen by G. Gregory at Jahra East Outfall on 18.4.2003. His description is below:
'At about 10.25 am on 18 April 2003, GG was driving towards the east on the dirt road just to the south of the western part of the reedbed at Jahra East Outfall. He observed a pipit on the ground about 50 metres east of the westernmost reeds and about 2 metres south of the wet area. Stopping the Jeep, he observed the bird from about 20 metres range through Pentax 12x Roof-prism binoculars. It was clearly a large streaky-backed pink-legged pipit. Observing closely for about 10 minutes, he concluded that the bird was a Blyth's Pipit. He reached over the seats for his mirror-lens camera but the bird was disturbed and flew off east. It was not subsequently observed.
Size and shape: Slightly bigger than nearby Water Pipits. Long-legged (with big curved hind claws). Long-tailed. Moderately upright stance at times, but at others body almost horizontal. Bill quite pointed, and looked shorter and less thick than Richard's (from memory of observations of the latter).
Upperparts: Pale lores. Off-white supercilium. Crown moderately streaked dark on browner. Back well streaked dark on browner. Wings fairly dark brownish, most feathers with paler edges. Secondary coverts had dark brown bases and buffish tips, the median coverts' dark bases being quite blunt-ended. Tail had white edges but in flight white triangular corners were observed.
Underparts: Generally pale buffy-white, especially on flanks. Narrow fairly dark brown breast streaks less prominent than Richard's (from memory of observations of the latter).
Exposed parts: Bill horn-coloured with darker at top and tip. Eye appeared dark. Legs pinkish.
Previous experience: Many of the Richard's/Blyth's group in South and East Asia; 5 Richard's Pipits in England, and 2 in Kuwait.
Identification: A combination of features distinguished it from Richard's Pipit - size and shape of bill, shape of dark bases to median coverts, shape of white on tail and prominence of streaking on breast.

Tawny Pipit *(Anthus campestris)*
Status: Very common passage migrant. Uncommon winter visitor.
Tawny Pipits have been recorded from many locations in Kuwait, being commonly seen on passage and less so in winter. The highest daily count is 20 seen on several occasions.

JAN 1-10	JAN 11-20	JAN 21-31	FEB 1-10	FEB 11-20	FEB 21-29	MAR 1-10	MAR 11-20	MAR 21-31	APR 1-10	APR 11-20	APR 21-30	MAY 1-10	MAY 11-20	MAY 21-31	JUN 1-10	JUN 11-20	JUN 21-30	JUL 1-10	JUL 11-20	JUL 21-31	AUG 1-10	AUG 11-20	AUG 21-31	SEP 1-10	SEP 11-20	SEP 21-30	OCT 1-10	OCT 11-20	OCT 21-31	NOV 1-10	NOV 11-20	NOV 21-30	DEC 1-10	DEC 11-20	DEC 21-31
1	2	5	2	6	2	13	20	8	2						1	1									1			2	1	7	3	1		1	2

Olive-backed Pipit *(Anthus hodgsoni)*
Status: Rare winter visitor.

The first record of this species in Kuwait involved four birds found by S. T. Spencer at Jahra Farms on 9 December 1994 and seen also by C. W. T. Pilcher up to 6 January 1995. Up to four were seen, and one photographed, by G. Gregory at Jahra Farms from 8 December 1995 to 19 January 1996. Further records there, seen by many observers, include single birds on 13 December 1996, 29 October 1998, 17 April 1999, 23 April 1999, 18-31 December 2003, 6 December 2004 and 19 February 2005. Additionally, B. Foster and G. Gregory observed one at Al-Abraq Al-Khabari on 3 December 2004.

Tree Pipit *(Anthus trivialis)*
Status: Common passage migrant. Rare winter visitor.

Tree Pipits are regularly observed in spring and autumn. Records have been from all sites with trees and ground vegetation. The highest daily count is 136 seen by V. A. Sales at Ahmadi on 8 April 1966.

Meadow Pipit *(Anthus pratensis)*
Status: Scarce winter visitor.

This species is generally irregular and scarce in Kuwait, although it has been recorded annually recently. Usually, small numbers have been observed. It seems possible that some past records involved confusion with other species. The highest daily count is an exceptional one of about 78 seen by B. Wright near Kuwait City on 12 January 1994. Records have been from many sites, including one seen far inland at Ash-Shiggayat by M. W. Newhouse and P. R. Haynes on 22 November 1974.

Red-throated Pipit *(Anthus cervinus)*
Status: Very common passage migrant. Scarce winter visitor.
Red-throated Pipits are regularly observed, usually in flocks, in spring and autumn, while some remain in winter. The highest daily count is 400, of which some were photographed, by P. Robertson and G. Gregory at Umm Al-Aish on 16 April 1999. Birds in spring vary greatly in colouration on the breast and face.

JAN 1-10	JAN 11-20	JAN 21-31	FEB 1-10	FEB 11-20	FEB 21-29	MAR 1-10	MAR 11-20	MAR 21-31	APR 1-10	APR 11-20	APR 21-30	MAY 1-10	MAY 11-20	MAY 21-31	JUN 1-10	JUN 11-20	JUN 21-30	JUL 1-10	JUL 11-20	JUL 21-31	AUG 1-10	AUG 11-20	AUG 21-31	SEP 1-10	SEP 11-20	SEP 21-30	OCT 1-10	OCT 11-20	OCT 21-31	NOV 1-10	NOV 11-20	NOV 21-30	DEC 1-10	DEC 11-20	DEC 21-31
2	1					2	4	75	75	400	150	15	40	15	1										9	1	5	3	2	3	3				

Water Pipit *(Anthus spinoletta)*
Status: Common winter visitor. Common passage migrant. Rare summer visitor.
This species is often seen in areas with fresh or brackish water in autumn, winter and spring. The highest daily count is 320 at an evening roost at Sewer Plant Reeds seen by M. O. Chichester on 11 December 2002. The same observer recorded an unseasonal bird at Zour Port on 4 July 2003.

JAN 1-10	JAN 11-20	JAN 21-31	FEB 1-10	FEB 11-20	FEB 21-29	MAR 1-10	MAR 11-20	MAR 21-31	APR 1-10	APR 11-20	APR 21-30	MAY 1-10	MAY 11-20	MAY 21-31	JUN 1-10	JUN 11-20	JUN 21-30	JUL 1-10	JUL 11-20	JUL 21-31	AUG 1-10	AUG 11-20	AUG 21-31	SEP 1-10	SEP 11-20	SEP 21-30	OCT 1-10	OCT 11-20	OCT 21-31	NOV 1-10	NOV 11-20	NOV 21-30	DEC 1-10	DEC 11-20	DEC 21-31
35	15	60	28	30	20	4	3	15	6									1									1	8	50	50	50	35	320	12	

Buff-bellied Pipit *(Anthus rubescens)*
Status: Vagrant (one record).
A single bird was seen by A. Bailey, B. Foster and G. Gregory at East Doha on 11 February 2005. The description is below:
'On 11 February 2005, at about 10am, AB, BF and GG were driving back to the main road at East Doha, having observed birds in the area near the reedbeds. After crossing the stream nearest the road, AB noticed a pipit on a flat grassy area near the stream. After turning the vehicle around to view the bird, the observers saw it on the ground in with about six Water Pipits. After prolonged views and comparison with the Water Pipits, they identified the bird as a Buff-bellied Pipit, the first for Kuwait.
Size and shape: About 10% smaller than each nearby Water Pipit, less 'lanky', more 'compact'.
Plumage: Upperparts fairly dark brown, more noticeably browner than the Water Pipits, with fairly distinct darker streaking. Buffish-white supercilium. Outer tail feathers showed white edges. Upperwings fairly dark brown with off-white/pale buff tips to greater and median secondary coverts. Underparts slightly off-white, with buffish wash on sides and fairly dark streaking mostly on breast and flanks. These streaks were clearly more distinct than any on the Water Pipits.

Exposed parts: Bill and eye very dark. Legs dark brown tinged red.
Behaviour: Walked around on short grassy area and on bare ground with Water Pipits. Silent.'

After comparing this bird with nearby Water Pipits (*A. spinoletta*), the observers realised that it had probably been overlooked as this other species before in Kuwait, and that some illustrations in field guides are not entirely accurate.

Yellow Wagtail *(Motacilla flava)*
Status: Very common passage migrant. Rare summer visitor.

Yellow Wagtails are frequently seen on passage, and have been recorded at many locations in Kuwait. In some years birds remain into June, as occurred in 2001 at Jahra East Outfall. Unfortunately, the possibility of breeding was not thought of at that time, but could have occurred. The highest daily count is 800 seen by G. Gregory, A. Bailey and B. Foster at Jahra East Outfall on 25 March 2005.

The most commonly observed subspecies is *M. f. feldegg* (Black-headed Wagtail).

JAN 1-10	JAN 11-20	JAN 21-31	FEB 1-10	FEB 11-20	FEB 21-29	MAR 1-10	MAR 11-20	MAR 21-31	APR 1-10	APR 11-20	APR 21-30	MAY 1-10	MAY 11-20	MAY 21-31	JUN 1-10	JUN 11-20	JUN 21-30	JUL 1-10	JUL 11-20	JUL 21-31	AUG 1-10	AUG 11-20	AUG 21-31	SEP 1-10	SEP 11-20	SEP 21-30	OCT 1-10	OCT 11-20	OCT 21-31	NOV 1-10	NOV 11-20	NOV 21-30	DEC 1-10	DEC 11-20	DEC 21-31
	1	5	1		10	100	100	800	250	60	100	205	26	6	3	3	5	1	5	2	4	25	40	30	50	20	11	20	1	1			1		

Citrine Wagtail *(Motacilla citreola)*
Status: Scarce passage migrant. Rare winter visitor.

This species was listed as an accidental or rare passage migrant by P. R. Haynes (1979). In recent years, however, it has been recorded annually in very small numbers. The highest daily count is three seen by M. O. Chichester, S. T. Spencer and J. Gaskell at Sabah Al-Salem on 7 January 2001. Birds have been seen at Ahmadi, Sabah Al-Salem, Sewer Plant Reeds, Jahra Pool Reserve, Sulaibiya and Sulaibikhat Bay.

JAN 1-10	JAN 11-20	JAN 21-31	FEB 1-10	FEB 11-20	FEB 21-29	MAR 1-10	MAR 11-20	MAR 21-31	APR 1-10	APR 11-20	APR 21-30	MAY 1-10	MAY 11-20	MAY 21-31	JUN 1-10	JUN 11-20	JUN 21-30	JUL 1-10	JUL 11-20	JUL 21-31	AUG 1-10	AUG 11-20	AUG 21-31	SEP 1-10	SEP 11-20	SEP 21-30	OCT 1-10	OCT 11-20	OCT 21-31	NOV 1-10	NOV 11-20	NOV 21-30	DEC 1-10	DEC 11-20	DEC 21-31
3					1	1							2									1	1			1						2	1		

Grey Wagtail *(Motacilla cinerea)*
Status: Uncommon passage migrant. Scarce winter visitor.

Grey Wagtails have been recorded at many coastal and inland locations in Kuwait, mostly on passage, usually in very small numbers. The highest daily count is 20 seen by H-M. Busch, J. Rathberger-Knan, F. Lange and A. Lange at Khiran on 12 March 2000.

JAN 1-10	JAN 11-20	JAN 21-31	FEB 1-10	FEB 11-20	FEB 21-29	MAR 1-10	MAR 11-20	MAR 21-31	APR 1-10	APR 11-20	APR 21-30	MAY 1-10	MAY 11-20	MAY 21-31	JUN 1-10	JUN 11-20	JUN 21-30	JUL 1-10	JUL 11-20	JUL 21-31	AUG 1-10	AUG 11-20	AUG 21-31	SEP 1-10	SEP 11-20	SEP 21-30	OCT 1-10	OCT 11-20	OCT 21-31	NOV 1-10	NOV 11-20	NOV 21-30	DEC 1-10	DEC 11-20	DEC 21-31
1					3		20	3	2	2	1	1															1	1	1		1				1

White Wagtail *(Motacilla alba)*
Status: Abundant winter visitor. Abundant passage migrant.
  This species is seen mostly between October and March, and is widespread in Kuwait. Roosts of 1000+ birds (the highest daily counts) have been observed at a number of sites with trees or reeds.
  Identification of subspecies is not easy. Past records of ***M. a. yarrelli*** clearly involved confusion with other subspecies.
  V. A. D. Sales (undated) noted that: 'Two colour-ringed birds returned to the same garden exactly one year later and in each year remained together in the vicinity for several weeks.'

JAN 1-10	JAN 11-20	JAN 21-31	FEB 1-10	FEB 11-20	FEB 21-29	MAR 1-10	MAR 11-20	MAR 21-31	APR 1-10	APR 11-20	APR 21-30	MAY 1-10	MAY 11-20	MAY 21-31	JUN 1-10	JUN 11-20	JUN 21-30	JUL 1-10	JUL 11-20	JUL 21-31	AUG 1-10	AUG 11-20	AUG 21-31	SEP 1-10	SEP 11-20	SEP 21-30	OCT 1-10	OCT 11-20	OCT 21-31	NOV 1-10	NOV 11-20	NOV 21-30	DEC 1-10	DEC 11-20	DEC 21-31
180	150	30	100	120	50	1000	80	250	20	2		2		4										5	1	1	30	200	200	1000	400	20	40	35

White-eared Bulbul *(Pycnonotus leucogenys)*
Status: Very common resident. Breeds.
  R. Meinertzhagen (1954) noted that this species was absent from Kuwait. The first record from the state was that of a single bird seen at Ahmadi by V. A. D. Sales on an unstated date in 1957 (Sales, undated). It then gradually increased in numbers and is now commonly seen at Abdali Farms, Kuwait City and suburbs, Jahra, Ahmadi and Wafra Farms. Smaller numbers are resident at Zour Port, Bahra and Qaisat, and one bird was seen by G. Gregory and A. Al-Fadhel at Al-Abraq Al-Khabari on 19 December 2004. The highest daily count is 35 seen at Zour Port by M. O. Chichester on 20 and 27 September 2002.
  Breeding was first recorded at Sulaibikhat, according to the ANHFSG Newsletter 11 (1972). It has since been proven at Kuwait City, Jahra, Ahmadi, Abdali Farms, Bahra, Zour Port and Wafra Farms.

Red-vented Bulbul *(Pycnonotus cafer)*
Status: Common resident. Breeds.
  The first record of Red-vented Bulbul in Kuwait involved a bird seen by C. W. T. Pilcher in the grounds of Ahmadi Hospital in spring 1981. The same observer wrote: 'The first confirmed breeding came from a private agricultural garden/plot in Messilah, some 30 km north of Ahmadi. ... At the end of January 1986 I noted that a pair of bulbuls appeared to have a nest site in a group of Tamarix and by 20 February they were

feeding young. In the following year three pairs of birds were established in or within 300 metres of this same garden and young were being fed through early March. I also received a report that Red-vented Bulbuls were breeding at that time in a large private garden about 3 km to the south-west of the Messilah site' (Pilcher, 1988a).

Since then this species has spread and increased in numbers, being present at Zour Port, Ahmadi, Messilah, Salwa, Rumaithiya, Salmiya, Shaab, Dai'ya, Shuwaikh and Jahra. The only other breeding record was by G. Gregory and S. Al-Ahmadi, who observed recently-fledged young with adults at Jahra Farms on 19 May 2000.

This species prefers broad-leaved trees, which, in Kuwait, are most often in large, fenced, private gardens to which entrance is difficult. However, with searching, it can be seen most times. The resident breeding population is estimated at about 100 pairs. The highest daily count is six seen on several occasions.

In January 2005 a hybrid Red-vented Bulbul x White-eared Bulbul (*P. leucogenys*) was seen several times at Jahra Farms. It had the crest and breast marking of a Red-vented Bulbul, a semi-distinct cheek patch and an orange vent.

Grey Hypocolius *(Hypocolius ampelinus)*
Status: Uncommon winter visitor. Uncommon passage migrant.

Grey Hypocolius is recorded every year in Kuwait but it is usually very unpredictable in its occurrence. It has been seen at Al-Abraq Al-Khabari, Umm Al-Aish, the Sabah al-Ahmed Natural Reserve, Qaisat, Jal Az-Zor, Jahra Pool Reserve, Jahra Farms, Jahra East Outfall, Shaab, Salwa, Sabah Al-Salem, Zour and Wafra Oil Field. It is mostly observed towards the tops of palms and trees, but on several occasions groups have been seen in reedbeds at Jahra Pool Reserve and Jahra East Outfall. The highest daily count is 46 seen by P. Robertson and G. Gregory at Jahra East Outfall on 31 March 2000. A bird was in sub-song at Salwa during March 1996, but breeding has never been recorded in Kuwait. This species is sometimes on sale in the main bird market and is kept in several private collections.

JAN 1-10	JAN 11-20	JAN 21-31	FEB 1-10	FEB 11-20	FEB 21-29	MAR 1-10	MAR 11-20	MAR 21-31	APR 1-10	APR 11-20	APR 21-30	MAY 1-10	MAY 11-20	MAY 21-31	JUN 1-10	JUN 11-20	JUN 21-30	JUL 1-10	JUL 11-20	JUL 21-31	AUG 1-10	AUG 11-20	AUG 21-31	SEP 1-10	SEP 11-20	SEP 21-30	OCT 1-10	OCT 11-20	OCT 21-31	NOV 1-10	NOV 11-20	NOV 21-30	DEC 1-10	DEC 11-20	DEC 21-31
1	10	1	2			46	22	18																1						25	25	20	1	3	

Winter Wren *(Troglodytes troglodytes)*
Status: Vagrant (two records).

A first-year bird was ringed and photographed by N. Cleere and D. Kelly, and also seen by M. Shehab, at Jahra Pool Reserve on 23 November 1995. Their description is below:

'**Size and structure:** Rather small, with a very short tail and thin bill.
Head: Forehead and crown brownish. Broad off-white supercilium. Lores and ears-coverts dusky brown.
Upperparts: Nape, mantle and back brownish. Rump and uppertail-coverts chestnut-brown. Wing-coverts chestnut-brown, barred dark brown. Primaries brown, barred buffish.
Underparts: Chin, throat, breast and belly buffish white. Flanks buffish.

Bare Parts: Bill dark brown, iris brown, legs and feet brownish.
Age: Immature (EURING code 3) based on contrast in colouration of the greater coverts, the inner, moulted feathers being browner and paler than more rufous-brown, unmoulted outer feathers.
Biometrics: Wing length 49.5 mm tail length 32 mm, bill to skull 13.2 mm, and weight 7.9 g.'
One was seen by G. Gregory at Sabah Al-Salem on 24 January 2002. His description is below:
'At about 4.00pm GG was checking the reeds at Sabah Al-Salem, about 60m to the west of the dividing road, in the northward facing tangle of reeds mixed with some dwarf tamarisk bushes. A tiny bird, immediately identified as a Wren flew from about half a metre up in the reeds, across an open area of about 5 metres across, and disappeared into more reeds the other side.
Size and Shape: A tiny bird, smaller and shorter than nearby Chiffchaffs; wings appeared rounded in flight. Quite round body basically, with a shortish square tail, cocked straight up.
Plumage: Upper parts were all chestnutty-brown, with dark and paler barring all over the back and wings. Under parts were paler off-brownish. A pale supercilium, quite long, was briefly glimpsed.
Exposed Parts: Bill appeared thin and dark. Eye not observed. Legs not observed.
Range: About 2 metres. Observed with unaided eye for c.5 seconds.
Previous Experiences: Many in Europe, including up to 50 ringed every recent year in Britain.'

Dunnock *(Prunella modularis)*
Status: Vagrant (four records).
The first Kuwait record involved a juvenile ringed and photographed by M. Reed and T. Cross at Sabah Al-Salem on 11-21 November 1991. Their description follows:
'In the early morning of 11 November 1991, while MR and TC were carrying out wader and passerine ringing activities over and adjacent to shallow pools at Messila, on the southern outskirts of Kuwait City, amongst the passerines trapped was a juvenile Dunnock Prunella modularis. TC had previously heard a call, which he had recognized as that of Dunnock, but Mahmoud Shehab had said that Dunnock did not occur in Kuwait; an opinion confirmed by the literature available to MR and TC at that time. The bird was processed and, before release and flying off into nearby cover, the below brief description and a series of photographs was taken. When subsequently released the bird flew a short distance into a small clump of tall vegetation close to the ringing station.
Description: The archetypal, insignificant small brown bird. Slim build with dark grey-brown plumage, streaked brown-black on upper-parts. The head, neck and under-parts slate blue-grey with brownish crown and ear-coverts. Thin, pointed dark bill. Biometrics taken during processing, by TC at 0700 local time, were wing length (flattened and straightened chord) 67 millimetres and weight 16.3 grams. The bird was aged as first-year by eye colour, a dull muddy brown.
After release the bird was not seen again that day, although on a later visit to the Messila Pools, on the morning of 21 November 1991, the bird was re-located in the same clump of vegetation into which it had previously been released.'
M. Shehab has a record of this species in the same place on 8 or 18 November 1991. This clearly refers to the same bird.
The second and third records of this species in Kuwait were made during mist-netting

operations by Nigel Cleere and David Kelly at Jahra Pools, 28 kilometres west of Kuwait City, during October-December 1995 (Sandgrouse 18 (1): 79 and Birding World 8 (12): 451).
One was seen by P. Robertson and G. Gregory at Sulaibiya on 1 February 2001.

Black-throated Accentor *(Prunella atrogularis)*
Status: Vagrant (one record).
One, age undetermined, was ringed and photographed by N. Cleere and D. Kelly at Jahra Pool Reserve on 28 November 1995. Their description reads:
'Size and structure: Similar to Dunnock Prunella modularis.
Head: Forehead and crown greyish, heavily blotched brown, crown-sides dark brown. Broad greyish-white supercilium, becoming narrower in front of eye and extending to bill, tinged buffish behind eye. Incomplete whitish eye-ring. Lores and ear-coverts dusky brown. Greyish-white submoustachial stripe.
Upper Parts: Nape greyish, heavily blotched brown. Mantle and back brown, heavily streaked dark brown. Rump olive-brown tinged greyish, lightly streaked brown. Upper tails-coverts olive-brown, faintly streaked brown. Lesser coverts chestnut-brown, streaked dark drown. Greater coverts brown, broadly streaked dark brown, the innermost with buffish-white tips to outer webs, the four outermost with whitish tips.
Under Parts: Chin and throat dusky grey, faintly speckled whitish. Lower throat edged whitish, forming distinct band between dark throat and brighter breast. Prominent orange-brown band across lower throat and upper breast. Breast and belly greyish white, faintly blotched grey. Flanks buffish brown streaked brown.
Bare Parts: Bill (both mandibles) pale pinkish on proximal third, dark grey-brown on distal two thirds. Iris brown with a richer, brighter outer ring and a duller, inner ring. Tarsus and feet pale orange-flesh.'

Rufous-tailed Scrub Robin *(Cercotrichas galactotes)*
Status: Common passage migrant. Uncommon summer visitor. Breeds.
Rufous-tailed Scrub Robins are commonly seen on spring and autumn passage, and some birds have long been recorded as being present all summer. This species has been seen at all locations with trees or bushes.
J. Gaskell first discovered proof of breeding at Abu Halifa on 2 June 2000, with adults carrying food to a nest. Members of BMAPT found 18+ birds, including two fledglings, at the Mohammed Al-Ajmi Farm at Abdali on 17 May 2001. Up to 15 pairs (the highest daily count) have been recorded breeding there in every subsequent year. In 2004 breeding was confirmed at Sabriya Farm on 10 June and at Jahra Pool Reserve on 11 June. On the latter occasion adults and juveniles were together in reeds. In 2005 breeding was confirmed at South Doha Nature Reserve, with two newly-fledged young observed with adults on 23 June 2005. This species probably breeds quite widely in Kuwait, with additional summer records being from Shuwaikh and Ahmadi.

JAN 1-10	JAN 11-20	JAN 21-31	FEB 1-10	FEB 11-20	FEB 21-29	MAR 1-10	MAR 11-20	MAR 21-31	APR 1-10	APR 11-20	APR 21-30	MAY 1-10	MAY 11-20	MAY 21-31	JUN 1-10	JUN 11-20	JUN 21-30	JUL 1-10	JUL 11-20	JUL 21-31	AUG 1-10	AUG 11-20	AUG 21-31	SEP 1-10	SEP 11-20	SEP 21-30	OCT 1-10	OCT 11-20	OCT 21-31	NOV 1-10	NOV 11-20	NOV 21-30	DEC 1-10	DEC 11-20	DEC 21-31
1	1					2	2	4	18	4	20	18	24	4	5	6	1	2	1	2	5	2	2	4	2			1							

Black Scrub Robin *(Cercotrichas podobe)*
Status: Vagrant (one record).

On an unrecorded day in April 1998 hunters at Al-Abraq Al-Khabari shot an unfamiliar bird. Shaikh Sabah Al-Sabah examined it and, using a field guide, identified it as a Black Scrub Robin. Unfortunately, the specimen was not preserved or photographed. However, it was described convincingly to M. Shehab and G. Gregory. The salient features were: size smaller than a thrush, all black plumage, except for white tips to outer feathers on a wedge-shaped tail, and some white around the vent area. Beyond all reasonable doubt the identification was correct. This species has been spreading north in Arabia and its occurrence in Kuwait was predictable.

European Robin *(Erithacus rubecula)*
Status: Uncommon winter visitor.

This species occurs in small numbers in winter at most sites with trees or bushes. Sometimes winter song can be heard. The highest daily count is six on several occasions in the past.

JAN 1-10	JAN 11-20	JAN 21-31	FEB 1-10	FEB 11-20	FEB 21-29	MAR 1-10	MAR 11-20	MAR 21-31	APR 1-10	APR 11-20	APR 21-30	MAY 1-10	MAY 11-20	MAY 21-31	JUN 1-10	JUN 11-20	JUN 21-30	JUL 1-10	JUL 11-20	JUL 21-31	AUG 1-10	AUG 11-20	AUG 21-31	SEP 1-10	SEP 11-20	SEP 21-30	OCT 1-10	OCT 11-20	OCT 21-31	NOV 1-10	NOV 11-20	NOV 21-30	DEC 1-10	DEC 11-20	DEC 21-31
2	2	2	2	1	2	1	1																				1	1	4	1	2	4	1	2		

Thrush Nightingale *(Luscinia luscinia)*
Status: Uncommon passage migrant.

Thrush Nightingale is regularly observed on spring and autumn migration through Kuwait. It is a skulking species and is no doubt under-recorded. It has been seen at all sites with bushes or trees. Fairly large concentrations are occasionally encountered, and the highest daily count is an exceptional 99 seen by V. A. D. Sales at Ahmadi on 25 April 1968.

JAN 1-10	JAN 11-20	JAN 21-31	FEB 1-10	FEB 11-20	FEB 21-29	MAR 1-10	MAR 11-20	MAR 21-31	APR 1-10	APR 11-20	APR 21-30	MAY 1-10	MAY 11-20	MAY 21-31	JUN 1-10	JUN 11-20	JUN 21-30	JUL 1-10	JUL 11-20	JUL 21-31	AUG 1-10	AUG 11-20	AUG 21-31	SEP 1-10	SEP 11-20	SEP 21-30	OCT 1-10	OCT 11-20	OCT 21-31	NOV 1-10	NOV 11-20	NOV 21-30	DEC 1-10	DEC 11-20	DEC 21-31
									1	2	1	1												1	1	1	2	1							

Common Nightingale *(Luscinia megarhynchos)*
Status: Uncommon passage migrant.

This species is usually not as common as the preceding one, but is also seen on spring and autumn passage. Likewise, all records are from locations with bushes or trees. It is also a skulking species and is no doubt under-recorded. The highest daily count is 20 seen at Ahmadi by V. A. D. Sales on 23 April 1966.

JAN 1-10	JAN 11-20	JAN 21-31	FEB 1-10	FEB 11-20	FEB 21-29	MAR 1-10	MAR 11-20	MAR 21-31	APR 1-10	APR 11-20	APR 21-30	MAY 1-10	MAY 11-20	MAY 21-31	JUN 1-10	JUN 11-20	JUN 21-30	JUL 1-10	JUL 11-20	JUL 21-31	AUG 1-10	AUG 11-20	AUG 21-31	SEP 1-10	SEP 11-20	SEP 21-30	OCT 1-10	OCT 11-20	OCT 21-31	NOV 1-10	NOV 11-20	NOV 21-30	DEC 1-10	DEC 11-20	DEC 21-31
						1			1	8	1													1											

Bluethroat *(Luscinia svecica)*

Status: Common passage migrant. Common winter visitor.

Bluethroats are regularly seen at mostly wet locations from August to April. The highest daily count is 30 at Sabah Al-Salem on 16 March 2002 and at South Doha Nature Reserve on 20 March 2002, seen by several observers. In spring this species sometimes sings, but breeding has never been recorded in Kuwait.

Subspecific identification, even of males, is often very difficult or impossible. Birds with white spots are occasionally seen in autumn, winter and spring, but the subspecies is uncertain. W. A. C. Giles stated that from his observations in Bahrain there was a form with a 'white spot in autumn which becomes progressively white with red centre in spring' (Warr, undated). Other birds have red spots or curved bars, or no spots at all. Large measured birds are certainly *L. s. magna*. It seems safer not to attempt further precision, especially since intergrades are known to exist.

JAN 1-10	JAN 11-20	JAN 21-31	FEB 1-10	FEB 11-20	FEB 21-29	MAR 1-10	MAR 11-20	MAR 21-31	APR 1-10	APR 11-20	APR 21-30	MAY 1-10	MAY 11-20	MAY 21-31	JUN 1-10	JUN 11-20	JUN 21-30	JUL 1-10	JUL 11-20	JUL 21-31	AUG 1-10	AUG 11-20	AUG 21-31	SEP 1-10	SEP 11-20	SEP 21-30	OCT 1-10	OCT 11-20	OCT 21-31	NOV 1-10	NOV 11-20	NOV 21-30	DEC 1-10	DEC 11-20	DEC 21-31
3	3	6	3	4	5	4	30	5	3	1		1									1	1	2	1		2	1		1	2	1	12	7	3	5

White-throated Robin *(Irania gutturalis)*

Status: Uncommon passage migrant.

This species is a migrant through Kuwait in spring and autumn, and has been recorded in most areas with trees or bushes. Males in spring have quite variable throat markings. The highest daily count is 16 seen by V. A. D. Sales at Ahmadi on 11 April 1963 and 8 April 1966.

JAN 1-10	JAN 11-20	JAN 21-31	FEB 1-10	FEB 11-20	FEB 21-29	MAR 1-10	MAR 11-20	MAR 21-31	APR 1-10	APR 11-20	APR 21-30	MAY 1-10	MAY 11-20	MAY 21-31	JUN 1-10	JUN 11-20	JUN 21-30	JUL 1-10	JUL 11-20	JUL 21-31	AUG 1-10	AUG 11-20	AUG 21-31	SEP 1-10	SEP 11-20	SEP 21-30	OCT 1-10	OCT 11-20	OCT 21-31	NOV 1-10	NOV 11-20	NOV 21-30	DEC 1-10	DEC 11-20	DEC 21-31
						1	4	5	1	6	1	1									1	1			1					1	1				

Eversmann's Redstart *(Phoenicurus erythronotus)*
Status: Vagrant (five records).
S. Howe and N. Montford observed a male at Burgan Oil Field on 12 December 1970. The former observer took 'copious notes' as reported in the ANHFSG Newsletter 3 (1971). C. W. T. Pilcher, M. Shehab and G. Gregory saw a male in winter plumage at Al-Abraq Al-Khabari on 4 December 1987. A male was seen and thoroughly described by C. W. T. Pilcher and S. T. Spencer at Wadi Ar-Rimam Farm on 21 February 1997. G. Gregory observed a female at Mishref on 16 February 2001 and a male at Sabriya Farm on 23 January 2004.

Males in winter have a plumage that is remarkably reminiscent of that of male Chaffinch (*Fringilla coelebs*).

Black Redstart *(Phoenicurus ochruros)*
Status: Uncommon winter visitor. Uncommon passage migrant.
Black Redstarts have been seen in very small numbers at many sites in Kuwait with trees, bushes or stonework. They occur mostly from November to March, but some have been recorded as early as September and as late as May. The highest daily count is 4 seen by G. Gregory at Jahra Farms on 25 May 2001.

JAN 1-10	JAN 11-20	JAN 21-31	FEB 1-10	FEB 11-20	FEB 21-29	MAR 1-10	MAR 11-20	MAR 21-31	APR 1-10	APR 11-20	APR 21-30	MAY 1-10	MAY 11-20	MAY 21-31	JUN 1-10	JUN 11-20	JUN 21-30	JUL 1-10	JUL 11-20	JUL 21-31	AUG 1-10	AUG 11-20	AUG 21-31	SEP 1-10	SEP 11-20	SEP 21-30	OCT 1-10	OCT 11-20	OCT 21-31	NOV 1-10	NOV 11-20	NOV 21-30	DEC 1-10	DEC 11-20	DEC 21-31
1	1	1		2	1		1	1	1					4														2	2				1	1	1

Common Redstart *(Phoenicurus phoenicurus)*
Status: Very common passage migrant. Rare winter visitor.
Redstarts are commonly seen in spring and autumn at sites with trees or bushes. The highest daily count is 100 seen on several occasions. There are a few winter records, but some or all of them may involve confusion with various subspecies of Black Redstart (*P. ochruros*). About one male in three is of the subspecies *P. p. samamisicus*, the others being of the nominate subspecies.

JAN 1-10	JAN 11-20	JAN 21-31	FEB 1-10	FEB 11-20	FEB 21-29	MAR 1-10	MAR 11-20	MAR 21-31	APR 1-10	APR 11-20	APR 21-30	MAY 1-10	MAY 11-20	MAY 21-31	JUN 1-10	JUN 11-20	JUN 21-30	JUL 1-10	JUL 11-20	JUL 21-31	AUG 1-10	AUG 11-20	AUG 21-31	SEP 1-10	SEP 11-20	SEP 21-30	OCT 1-10	OCT 11-20	OCT 21-31	NOV 1-10	NOV 11-20	NOV 21-30	DEC 1-10	DEC 11-20	DEC 21-31
1			1	4	8	10	30	30	50	10	4	2			1									2	1	2	3	2	7	1	1	1	1		1

Whinchat *(Saxicola rubetra)*
Status: Uncommon passage migrant. Rare winter visitor.
This species is occasionally observed on passage through Kuwait, with records from most locations. There are a few past winter records, but some or all of these may

involve confusion with female Common Stonechats (*S. torquatus*). The highest daily count is 14 seen by V. A. D. Sales at Ahmadi on 25 April 1964.

JAN 1-10	JAN 11-20	JAN 21-31	FEB 1-10	FEB 11-20	FEB 21-29	MAR 1-10	MAR 11-20	MAR 21-31	APR 1-10	APR 11-20	APR 21-30	MAY 1-10	MAY 11-20	MAY 21-31	JUN 1-10	JUN 11-20	JUN 21-30	JUL 1-10	JUL 11-20	JUL 21-31	AUG 1-10	AUG 11-20	AUG 21-31	SEP 1-10	SEP 11-20	SEP 21-30	OCT 1-10	OCT 11-20	OCT 21-31	NOV 1-10	NOV 11-20	NOV 21-30	DEC 1-10	DEC 11-20	DEC 21-31
						1	2	1	2	1	1	3	2	1	1									1	1	1			1			1	1		

Common Stonechat *(Saxicola torquatus)*
Status: Uncommon winter visitor. Uncommon passage migrant.

Stonechats are easily seen, though usually in small numbers, at many sites in winter or on passage. The highest daily count is 22 seen by H-M. Busch, J. Rathberger-Knan, F. Lange and A. Lange at Doha on 7 March 2000.
The subspecies *S. t. variegatus* is the most frequently recorded. *S. t. armenicus* and *S. t. maurus* are rare in winter and on passage. V. A. D. Sales noted mostly *S. t. rubicola* from 1952 to 1968. However, these records are considered to be erroneous, since no birds of this subspecies have been reliably recorded in Kuwait since then.

JAN 1-10	JAN 11-20	JAN 21-31	FEB 1-10	FEB 11-20	FEB 21-29	MAR 1-10	MAR 11-20	MAR 21-31	APR 1-10	APR 11-20	APR 21-30	MAY 1-10	MAY 11-20	MAY 21-31	JUN 1-10	JUN 11-20	JUN 21-30	JUL 1-10	JUL 11-20	JUL 21-31	AUG 1-10	AUG 11-20	AUG 21-31	SEP 1-10	SEP 11-20	SEP 21-30	OCT 1-10	OCT 11-20	OCT 21-31	NOV 1-10	NOV 11-20	NOV 21-30	DEC 1-10	DEC 11-20	DEC 21-31
5	2	3	6	2	20	22	20	4	2	1								1			1			1	2	2	2	4	2	2

Isabelline Wheatear *(Oenanthe isabellina)*
Status: Very common passage migrant. Very common winter visitor.

This species is very frequently observed in almost all areas of Kuwait on passage or in winter. The highest daily count is 50 recorded by H-M. Busch, J. Rathberger-Knan, F. Lange and A. Lange at Khiran on 12 March 2000.

JAN 1-10	JAN 11-20	JAN 21-31	FEB 1-10	FEB 11-20	FEB 21-29	MAR 1-10	MAR 11-20	MAR 21-31	APR 1-10	APR 11-20	APR 21-30	MAY 1-10	MAY 11-20	MAY 21-31	JUN 1-10	JUN 11-20	JUN 21-30	JUL 1-10	JUL 11-20	JUL 21-31	AUG 1-10	AUG 11-20	AUG 21-31	SEP 1-10	SEP 11-20	SEP 21-30	OCT 1-10	OCT 11-20	OCT 21-31	NOV 1-10	NOV 11-20	NOV 21-30	DEC 1-10	DEC 11-20	DEC 21-31
5	3	5	2	5	6	20	50	11	5	3	4	4	1	1					2	2	3	5	20	4	5	2	5	2	4	5	3	4	6	4

Northern Wheatear *(Oenanthe oenanthe)*
Status: Common passage migrant.

Northern Wheatears are quite commonly seen on migration at most locations. The highest daily count is 50 seen by H-M. Busch, J. Rathberger-Knan, F. Lange and A. Lange between Kuwait City and Jahra on 11 March 2000.

JAN 1-10	JAN 11-20	JAN 21-31	FEB 1-10	FEB 11-20	FEB 21-29	MAR 1-10	MAR 11-20	MAR 21-31	APR 1-10	APR 11-20	APR 21-30	MAY 1-10	MAY 11-20	MAY 21-31	JUN 1-10	JUN 11-20	JUN 21-30	JUL 1-10	JUL 11-20	JUL 21-31	AUG 1-10	AUG 11-20	AUG 21-31	SEP 1-10	SEP 11-20	SEP 21-30	OCT 1-10	OCT 11-20	OCT 21-31	NOV 1-10	NOV 11-20	NOV 21-30	DEC 1-10	DEC 11-20	DEC 21-31
1		1			7	50	8	21	1	1	1	1	1											1	3	2	2	4	1		2				

Pied Wheatear *(Oenanthe pleschanka)*

Status: Very common passage migrant. Rare winter visitor.

This species is commonly observed at all sites in spring and autumn, and there are some winter records. The highest daily count is 40 seen at Al-Abraq Al-Khabari by H-M. Busch, J. Rathberger-Knan, F. Lange and A. Lange on 14 March 2000. Some males show fair amounts of dark on the cap. The *vittata* variant is recorded every few years.

JAN 1-10	JAN 11-20	JAN 21-31	FEB 1-10	FEB 11-20	FEB 21-29	MAR 1-10	MAR 11-20	MAR 21-31	APR 1-10	APR 11-20	APR 21-30	MAY 1-10	MAY 11-20	MAY 21-31	JUN 1-10	JUN 11-20	JUN 21-30	JUL 1-10	JUL 11-20	JUL 21-31	AUG 1-10	AUG 11-20	AUG 21-31	SEP 1-10	SEP 11-20	SEP 21-30	OCT 1-10	OCT 11-20	OCT 21-31	NOV 1-10	NOV 11-20	NOV 21-30	DEC 1-10	DEC 11-20	DEC 21-31
1						3	25	40	30	15	2	3	1	4	1									2	2	2	3	3	2			1			

Black-eared Wheatear *(Oenanthe hispanica)*

Status: Uncommon passage migrant.

Black-eared Wheatears are occasionally recorded on migration through Kuwait, and have been sighted at many locations. The highest daily count is 10 seen at Al-Abraq Al-Khabari by H-M. Busch, J. Rathberger-Knan, F. Lange and A. Lange on 14 March 2000. Past winter records probably involved confusion with Finsch's Wheatear (*O. finschii*).

JAN 1-10	JAN 11-20	JAN 21-31	FEB 1-10	FEB 11-20	FEB 21-29	MAR 1-10	MAR 11-20	MAR 21-31	APR 1-10	APR 11-20	APR 21-30	MAY 1-10	MAY 11-20	MAY 21-31	JUN 1-10	JUN 11-20	JUN 21-30	JUL 1-10	JUL 11-20	JUL 21-31	AUG 1-10	AUG 11-20	AUG 21-31	SEP 1-10	SEP 11-20	SEP 21-30	OCT 1-10	OCT 11-20	OCT 21-31	NOV 1-10	NOV 11-20	NOV 21-30	DEC 1-10	DEC 11-20	DEC 21-31
						1	3	10	4	7														3		1	1								

Desert Wheatear *(Oenanthe deserti)*

Status: Very common passage migrant. Common winter visitor.

This species is very commonly observed at almost all sites in Kuwait during most of the year. The highest daily count is about 20 seen on several occasions. The only indication of possible breeding involved a male, seen by many observers, repeatedly chasing a female, while flicking its wings, at Bahra on 14 March 2002.

Finsch's Wheatear *(Oenanthe finschii)*
Status: Scarce winter visitor and passage migrant.

Finsch's Wheatear has been recorded from many sites in Kuwait away from the urban areas, but usually in very low numbers. The highest daily count is six seen at 'Northeast Kuwait' by M. O. Chichester, J. Gaskell and S. T. Spencer on 7 January 2000.

Mourning Wheatear *(Oenanthe lugens)*
Status: Uncommon winter visitor.

This species occurs regularly in winter along the Jal Az-Zor escarpment and at Wadi Ar-Rimam. It is sometimes seen at other sites, but only in small numbers. The highest daily count is 6 seen on several occasions.

Kurdish Wheatear *(Oenanthe xanthoprymna)*
Status: Scarce winter visitor.

Many past records did not distinguish between this species and the next one. Only single birds have been recorded recently, from several sites, in winter. Some birds have been seen in reedbeds.

Red-tailed Wheatear *(Oenanthe chrysopygia)*
Status: Scarce winter visitor.
Red-tailed Wheatear is more commonly observed than the preceding species. Many past records did not distinguish between the two. The highest daily count is two seen on several occasions in winter.

Hooded Wheatear *(Oenanthe monacha)*
Status: Vagrant (seven records).
The first Hooded Wheatear recorded in Kuwait was seen by V. A. D. Sales at northwest Ahmadi on 16 March 1958. His description reads:
'Wheatear seen very similar to Pied but with chin and whole of the upper breast black - far greater than I have seen in any wheatear. Crown white, undpts white, wings black, tail except for black central feathers white.'
One was seen by J. Webb at Sulaibikhat on 26 March 1971. C. W. T. Pilcher recorded one in 1984 but the details are not accessible. M. O. Chichester and other observers saw one at Jal Az-Zor from 31 December 1998 to 1 January 1999. One was seen in what is now the Sabah Al-Ahmed Natural Reserve by O. Schroeder, S. Schroeder and G. Østerø on 10 and 13 March 2001. A. Al-Sirhan observed and photographed a male singing and displaying to a female in the Sabah Al-Ahmed Natural Reserve on 4 April 2002. Several observers recorded one at Jahra Pool Reserve on 1 October 2002.

Hume's Wheatear *(Oenanthe alboniger)*
Status: Vagrant (about six records).
V. A. D. Sales observed and took notes on a single bird in 'North Kuwait' on 12 December 1963. According to the ANHFSG *Newsletter* 3 (1971) one was seen in 1970, but no details are accessible. The observer may have been N. Montford, since his initials appear on a record with no other details on the computer list of the ANHFSG (1975). Two birds were well observed by P. R. Haynes, L. Corrall and W. A. Stuart at Jal Az-Zor on 30 September 1977. One was seen by W. A. Stuart, apparently at Wadi Al-Batin, in autumn 1978, and another by C. W. T. Pilcher in 1983 at an unknown site. However, further details of these two records are not accessible. A single bird was well observed by A. Bailey, B. Foster and G. Gregory in the Sabah Al-Ahmed Natural Reserve on 11 February 2005. They noted black head, throat, upper back, wings and tail 'tee', with rest of plumage white, which extended far up the back.

White-crowned Wheatear *(Oenanthe leucopyga)*
Status: Rare disperser in autumn, winter and spring.
The first White-crowned Wheatear for Kuwait was seen by V. A. D. Sales at Ahmadi on 19 September 1954. He originally listed it as a Black Wheatear (*O. leucura*), so it was clearly a first-year bird, but later corrected his identification. Further records were on an unstated date in 1970, 28 February 1971, 17 March 1971, 24 March 1972, an

unstated date in 1980, 7 March 1987, 1 April 1989, 26 March 1995, 31 December 1998, 28 March 1999, 6 January 2000, 26-27 March 2003 and 8 March 2005. Known sites for these records are Ahmadi, Mina, Jal Az-Zor, Qaisat, Wafra-Nuwaisib Road, Wadi Al-Batin Area, Sulaibikhat Nature Reserve and Sulaibikhat Bay.

Rufous-tailed Rock Thrush *(Monticola saxatilis)*
Status: Uncommon passage migrant.

This species is occasionally recorded on passage. It has been sighted mostly where there are trees of bushes. The highest daily count is 10 seen at Ahmadi by V. A. D. Sales on 2 May 1967.

Blue Rock Thrush *(Monticola solitarius)*
Status: Uncommon passage migrant. Scarce winter visitor.

Most Blue Rock Thrushes observed are migrants stopping in locations with trees and bushes. In winter small numbers are present along the Jal Az-Zor escarpment. The highest daily count is 6 seen on several occasions.

Ring Ouzel *(Turdus torquatus)*
Status: Vagrant (five records).

The first record was of a bird seen at Rawdatain by S. Howe and R. Stafford on 20 November 1971. Two birds were seen by G. Gregory, C. W. T. Pilcher and M. Shehab at Al-Abraq Al-Khabari in February 1989. One bird was an adult male with a prominent chest crescent, the other an adult female or second-year male. A quite dull bird was seen and described by G. Gregory at Jahra Farms in November 1995. The exact dates for these last two records are inaccessible. One, observed and described at Wafra Oil Field by M. O. Chichester on 15 November 1998, was not an adult male. One was seen at Jahra Pool Reserve by members of BMAPT in mid February 2005.

Common Blackbird *(Turdus merula)*

Status: Scarce winter visitor.

Common Blackbirds are observed every year in winter, but always in very small numbers. The highest daily count is three seen on several occasions. Records have been from Ahmadi, Khadima, Umm Al-Aish, Jahra Farms, Sabah Al-Salem, Abdali Farms and Al-Abraq Al-Khabari.

JAN 1-10	JAN 11-20	JAN 21-31	FEB 1-10	FEB 11-20	FEB 21-29	MAR 1-10	MAR 11-20	MAR 21-31	APR 1-10	APR 11-20	APR 21-30	MAY 1-10	MAY 11-20	MAY 21-31	JUN 1-10	JUN 11-20	JUN 21-30	JUL 1-10	JUL 11-20	JUL 21-31	AUG 1-10	AUG 11-20	AUG 21-31	SEP 1-10	SEP 11-20	SEP 21-30	OCT 1-10	OCT 11-20	OCT 21-31	NOV 1-10	NOV 11-20	NOV 21-30	DEC 1-10	DEC 11-20	DEC 21-31
1	3	1	2	1		1																					1			1	1		1	1	

Dusky Thrush *(Turdus naumanni)*

Status: Vagrant (one record).

One was seen, photographed and described by C. W. T. Pilcher, G. Gregory and M. Shehab at Al-Abraq Al-Khabari from 16 January to 13 February 1987. The description is below:

'On 16 January 1987 CWTP discovered a thrush foraging in a furrow on one of the small agricultural plot on a farm at Al-Abraq Al-Khabari. During two brief views a large white supercilium and half-collar were visible on the head and a conspicuous double black breast-band on white underparts was noted. The back was dark brown and tail blackish. The bird was not seen again that day but was tentatively identified as a Dusky Thrush. Two weeks later, what was probably the same individual was seen in the same locality by MSA, GG, and CWTP, when it was viewed clearly on the ground at about 30 m. During the next four hours it was observed intermittently and photographed. It was last seen on 13 February.

Size and Shape: Typical thrush shape with a rather square tail; somewhat sturdier than nearby Song Thrushes *T. philomelos*.

Head: Crown dark brown. Supercilium bright white, starting at forehead and becoming very wide above and behind eye. Eye-stripe, cheek, and ear-coverts formed a fairly well defined dark brown patch, becoming blackish towards tips of ear-coverts. Chin and throat white; white half-collar; thin blackish malar stripe extended to meet dark upper breast-band.

Upper Parts: Back and scapulars dark brown, with indistinct darker streaking/scalloping. Rump and upper tail-coverts dark brown with slight rufous tint observed in flight. Upper wing-feathers edged pale, warm brown, giving folded wing a pale appearance.

Tail: Blackish, contrasting with upper tail-coverts.

Under Parts: Prominent blackish double breast-band, the upper one unbroken, broad and separated by a narrow white strip from the more diffuse lower one, which extended along the flanks in the form of a crescent-shaped spots. Belly, vent, and thighs white.

Under tail-coverts blackish. Underwing orange-rufous in centre.
Bare Parts: Bill dark with pale base and cutting edges. Eye dark. Legs blue-grey.
Voice: When flushed, a double or triple 'chk' note rather like a Blackbird *T. merula* or Fieldfare *T. pilaris*. On alighting in a tree, it gave a single 'chk'.
Behaviour: When on the ground, it fed, hopped, and walked in a typical thrush manner, sometimes holding its wings below body level. It was very shy and difficult to approach and preferred shady areas under trees.'

Dark-throated Thrush *(Turdus ruficollis)*
Status: Rare winter visitor.
 Small numbers of Dark-throated Thrushes are seen almost every winter. This species has been recorded at Ahmadi, Jahra Pool Reserve, Jahra Farms and Abdali Farms. The highest daily count is 24 seen by C. W. T. Pilcher and M. Shehab at Al-Abraq Al-Khabari on 18 January 1985. All birds seen have been of the subspecies *T. r. atrogularis* (Black-throated Thrush).

JAN 1-10	JAN 11-20	JAN 21-31	FEB 1-10	FEB 11-20	FEB 21-29	MAR 1-10	MAR 11-20	MAR 21-31	APR 1-10	APR 11-20	APR 21-30	MAY 1-10	MAY 11-20	MAY 21-31	JUN 1-10	JUN 11-20	JUN 21-30	JUL 1-10	JUL 11-20	JUL 21-31	AUG 1-10	AUG 11-20	AUG 21-31	SEP 1-10	SEP 11-20	SEP 21-30	OCT 1-10	OCT 11-20	OCT 21-31	NOV 1-10	NOV 11-20	NOV 21-30	DEC 1-10	DEC 11-20	DEC 21-31
3	2	7																												1			1		

Fieldfare *(Turdus pilaris)*
Status: Rare winter visitor.
 The first record for Kuwait was by V. A. D. Sales at Ahmadi on 16-26 November 1958. Further sightings there by the same observer were on 7-11 November 1959 (one), 27 November 1959 (six), 28 November 1959 (one), 13 January 1961 (one), 19-26 December 1963 (one), 21 November 1965 (eight, the highest daily count), late January 1966 (3 or 4), 4 December 1966 (five), and 30 November to 16 December 1967 (1 or 2).
 J. Webb saw one bird at Ash-Shiggayat on 16 November 1971. M. Shehab, C. W. T. Pilcher observed one at Al-Abraq Al-Khabari on 2 December 1988, and a very noisy bird was seen by G. Gregory near Jahra Pool Reserve on 2 December 1994. There have been no known records since then.

Song Thrush *(Turdus philomelos)*
Status: Common winter visitor. Uncommon passage migrant.
 Song Thrushes are regularly seen in winter and on passage. Records have been from all locations with trees and bushes. The highest daily count is 55 at Ahmadi seen by V. A. D. Sales on 17 February 1967.

JAN 1-10	JAN 11-20	JAN 21-31	FEB 1-10	FEB 11-20	FEB 21-29	MAR 1-10	MAR 11-20	MAR 21-31	APR 1-10	APR 11-20	APR 21-30	MAY 1-10	MAY 11-20	MAY 21-31	JUN 1-10	JUN 11-20	JUN 21-30	JUL 1-10	JUL 11-20	JUL 21-31	AUG 1-10	AUG 11-20	AUG 21-31	SEP 1-10	SEP 11-20	SEP 21-30	OCT 1-10	OCT 11-20	OCT 21-31	NOV 1-10	NOV 11-20	NOV 21-30	DEC 1-10	DEC 11-20	DEC 21-31
20	12	20	15	7	7	9	5	5	2		2												1				1	2	3	20	30	6	10	8	

Redwing *(Turdus iliacus)*
Status: Rare winter visitor.
The first record of this species in Kuwait was by V. A. D. Sales at Ahmadi on 15-16 November 1953. He saw further single birds there on 1-3 December 1961 and 10-11 November 1966. Another one was recorded there by M. Blacker on 27 January 1971. J. Webb saw one at Subiya on 11 November 1971. P. R. Haynes sighted one at an unstated location on 22 November 1977.

More recent records are of single birds seen at Al-Abraq Al-Khabari in November 1988 (exact day not accessible), on 9 December 1994 (location not accessible), and at Jahra Farms in December 1995 (exact day not accessible) and on 2 January 2002. The observers for these records include M. Shehab, C. W. T. Pilcher, S. T. Spencer and G. Gregory.

JAN 1-10	JAN 11-20	JAN 21-31	FEB 1-10	FEB 11-20	FEB 21-29	MAR 1-10	MAR 11-20	MAR 21-31	APR 1-10	APR 11-20	APR 21-30	MAY 1-10	MAY 11-20	MAY 21-31	JUN 1-10	JUN 11-20	JUN 21-30	JUL 1-10	JUL 11-20	JUL 21-31	AUG 1-10	AUG 11-20	AUG 21-31	SEP 1-10	SEP 11-20	SEP 21-30	OCT 1-10	OCT 11-20	OCT 21-31	NOV 1-10	NOV 11-20	NOV 21-30	DEC 1-10	DEC 11-20	DEC 21-31
1																																			

Mistle Thrush *(Turdus viscivorus)*
Status: Rare winter visitor.
Mistle Thrushes were much more commonly observed in Kuwait in the past. The first record was of up to three birds seen by S. Howe at Ahmadi from 29 November to 27 December 1961. Other sightings up to 1974 were on 30 December 1965 (one), 21 November 1965 to 20 January 1966 (up to three), 3 December 1966 (one), 30 November to 16 December 1967 (up to two), 18 February 1968 (one), 11 March 1968 (one), 4 March 1969 (one), 12 March 1970 (one), 1 November 1970 (one), 27 November 1970 (one), 19 February 1971 (one), 4 March 1971 (one), 20 November 1971 (one), 4 January 1974 (one), 30 November to 31 December 1974 (one), 22 and 31 December 1974 (one) and 30 December 1974 (one). The locations for these other records included Ahmadi, Kuwait Bay, Umm Al-Aish and Abraq Khaitan, and the observers included S. Howe, M. Blacker, R. Stafford, R. D. Younger.

The only subsequent known records are of single birds seen in 1986, at Umm Al-Aish on 14 November, and at Al-Abraq Al-Khabari on 5 December, by M. Shehab, G. Gregory and C. W. T. Pilcher. Like Fieldfare (*T. pilaris*), this species of thrush has, for unknown reasons, become much rarer in Kuwait.

Cetti's Warbler *(Cettia cetti)*
Status: Uncommon passage migrant and winter visitor.
One, the first recorded in Kuwait, was trapped and ringed at Ahmadi by V. A. D. Sales on 18 March 1966. He recorded seven more there in spring and one in autumn of that same year. In 1967 the same observer saw there three in spring and four in autumn.

This species is very skulking and is clearly seriously under-recorded in Kuwait. It has most often been seen by being netted during ringing operations, or when singing in spring. Two were netted at Umm Al-Aish by G. Gregory, C. W. T. Pilcher and M. Shehab on 27 March and 3 April 1987. During one ringing operation between 3 and 24 November 1991, M. Reed and T. Cross trapped six birds and saw one other. They

wrote that 'given our small scale coverage of this extensive reedbed system, the number present may well be in excess of 50 birds.' (Reed and Cross, 1991).
In 2002 a single bird sang from the reedbed at Sabah Al-Salem from 7 February to 16 March. In 2003 single birds were occasionally heard singing at Jahra East Outfall and at Sabah Al-Salem from March onwards. These birds could have just been singing on spring migration. There was no further evidence of breeding. In 2005 one was heard singing at South Doha Nature Reserve by P. Fagel and B. Foster on 17 March 2005.

JAN 1-10	JAN 11-20	JAN 21-31	FEB 1-10	FEB 11-20	FEB 21-29	MAR 1-10	MAR 11-20	MAR 21-31	APR 1-10	APR 11-20	APR 21-30	MAY 1-10	MAY 11-20	MAY 21-31	JUN 1-10	JUN 11-20	JUN 21-30	JUL 1-10	JUL 11-20	JUL 21-31	AUG 1-10	AUG 11-20	AUG 21-31	SEP 1-10	SEP 11-20	SEP 21-30	OCT 1-10	OCT 11-20	OCT 21-31	NOV 1-10	NOV 11-20	NOV 21-30	DEC 1-10	DEC 11-20	DEC 21-31
1			1			1																													2	1

Zitting Cisticola *(Cisticola juncidis)*
Status: Vagrant (four records).
A record of up to two seen, heard and photographed by L. Corrall and W. Stuart at Jahra Pool Reserve from 19 January to 9 March 1979 was submitted on a Rare Bird Report form and was accepted by the referees. The description noted small size, heavy streaking on back, head and tail, 'black and white' on tail, and continuous 'chip-chip-chip' song. A single bird was seen at Jahra Pool Reserve by W. A. Stuart and M. Shehab on 1 and 18 January 1980. Single birds were trapped and photographed at Al-Abraq Al-Khabari in March 1988 and at Umm Al-Aish in March 1989 (exact dates not accessible). The observers included G. Gregory, C. W. T. Pilcher and M. Shehab.

Graceful Prinia *(Prinia gracilis)*
Status: Common resident. Breeds.
This species was probably present since at least the late 1970s at Abdali Farms. A record of a Scrub Warbler (*Scotocerca inquieta*) seen there by W. Stuart and L. Corrall from 9-10 February 1979 was submitted on a Rare Bird Report form but was rejected by the panel, with a comment that it could have been a Graceful Prinia. B. Wright (1995) wrote of this species: 'One small party of either this [Scrub Warbler] or the preceding species [Graceful Prinia] recorded in April 1985.' The first definite sight and breeding record for Kuwait was at Abdali Farms on 27 April 1990, when W. A. Stuart and C. W. T. Pilcher found a pair with at least one juvenile. By 1996 this species had spread to Jahra Pool Reserve, and was proven to breed there in 1997 (Pilcher, Stuart and Spencer, 1997).
Since then Graceful Prinias have spread along the southern shore of Kuwait Bay to Sulaibikhat Nature Reserve, to Failaka Island, and to Sabah Al-Salem and Sewer Plant Reeds in the south. They are known or suspected to breed at all these sites. The highest daily count is 15 seen by K. Al-Nasrallah and G. Gregory at South Doha Nature Reserve on 3 May 2001.

Common Grasshopper Warbler *(Locustella naevia)*
Status: Scarce passage migrant.
This skulking species is no doubt thoroughly under-recorded in Kuwait. It is, almost entirely, only observed when caught during ringing operations in spring and autumn.

The highest daily count is three seen on several occasions. Other records have been from Jahra Pool Reserve, Sabah Al-Salem, Umm Al-Aish, Sulaibikhat Nature Reserve and Al-Abraq Al-Khabari. On 11 April 2005 a bird was heard singing at Sabah Al-Salem by B. Foster, but there was no further evidence of breeding.

JAN 1-10	JAN 11-20	JAN 21-31	FEB 1-10	FEB 11-20	FEB 21-29	MAR 1-10	MAR 11-20	MAR 21-31	APR 1-10	APR 11-20	APR 21-30	MAY 1-10	MAY 11-20	MAY 21-31	JUN 1-10	JUN 11-20	JUN 21-30	JUL 1-10	JUL 11-20	JUL 21-31	AUG 1-10	AUG 11-20	AUG 21-31	SEP 1-10	SEP 11-20	SEP 21-30	OCT 1-10	OCT 11-20	OCT 21-31	NOV 1-10	NOV 11-20	NOV 21-30	DEC 1-10	DEC 11-20	DEC 21-31
						3	1	1															1												

River Warbler *(Locustella fluviatilis)*

Status: Scarce passage migrant.

River Warbler is another skulking species that is clearly greatly under-recorded in Kuwait, being recorded mostly when mist-netted. V. A. D. Sales ringed nine birds and observed others of this species in spring and autumn at Ahmadi between 1952 and 1968, with the highest daily count being five seen there on 12 May 1966. Some of the sight records may have involved confusion with the eastern subspecies *L. luscinioides fusca* of Savi's Warbler, but the majority, at least, were, beyond reasonable doubt, correctly identified. This species has subsequently been trapped and photographed several times during several ringing programmes from the mid 1980s onwards. Besides at Ahmadi, birds have been netted or seen at Al-Abraq Al-Khabari, Umm Al-Aish, Jahra Farms and Jahra Pool Reserve.

JAN 1-10	JAN 11-20	JAN 21-31	FEB 1-10	FEB 11-20	FEB 21-29	MAR 1-10	MAR 11-20	MAR 21-31	APR 1-10	APR 11-20	APR 21-30	MAY 1-10	MAY 11-20	MAY 21-31	JUN 1-10	JUN 11-20	JUN 21-30	JUL 1-10	JUL 11-20	JUL 21-31	AUG 1-10	AUG 11-20	AUG 21-31	SEP 1-10	SEP 11-20	SEP 21-30	OCT 1-10	OCT 11-20	OCT 21-31	NOV 1-10	NOV 11-20	NOV 21-30	DEC 1-10	DEC 11-20	DEC 21-31
												1																							

Savi's Warbler *(Locustella luscinioides)*

Status: Uncommon passage migrant. Scarce summer visitor.

This species is, no doubt, heavily under-recorded in Kuwait. It has been netted on many days during ringing operations in spring and autumn. The highest daily count is seven seen or trapped by V. A. D. Sales at Ahmadi on 31 March 1966. Almost all birds are passage migrants, but B. Wright (1995) recorded one wintering in 1984/1985. Away from reedbeds, birds have been seen at Manageesh, Jebel Benayeh, Umm Al-Aish and Jahra Farms.

Savi's Warbler has probably bred in Kuwait. Three birds, originally found by S. T. Spencer, sang at Jahra East Outfall for months from at least 5 April 2002. In 2003 a single bird sang there for months from 14 March. In 2005 birds sang at East Doha and Sabah Al-Salem from March onwards. However, no further evidence of breeding has been obtained.

Moustached Warbler *(Acrocephalus melanopogon)*
Status: Uncommon passage migrant. Uncommon resident. Breeds.

Moustached Warbler is no doubt under-recorded in Kuwait, but is present throughout the year. The highest daily count is 40+ birds seen at Jahra Pool Reserve by C. W. T. Pilcher on many days in February 1985-1988. Most birds pass through in spring and autumn, with birds seen at many locations with bushes or trees, but some are resident.

Birds have for many years sung and held territory from February onwards in reedbeds at Jahra Pool Reserve, South Doha Nature Reserve and Jahra East Outfall. Breeding was first confirmed by G. Gregory at Sabah Al-Salem on 13 May 2002, with a not-fully-grown juvenile being fed by an adult. It was proven again there in 2003.

Sedge Warbler *(Acrocephalus schoenobaenus)*
Status: Common passage migrant.

This species is a passage migrant through Kuwait, and has been recorded at many locations with reeds, bushes or trees. The highest daily count is 50 seen by V. A. D. Sales at Ahmadi on 12 May 1966. Most recent records have been in spring. Some past winter and summer records may involve confusion with Moustached Warbler (*A. melanopogon*).

European Reed Warbler *(Acrocephalus scirpaceus)*
Status: Very common passage migrant. Uncommon summer visitor. Breeds.

European Reed Warblers are commonly seen in spring and autumn at many sites in Kuwait. The highest daily count is 100+ seen on many occasions.

This species was first proven to breed in Kuwait by M. Reed and J. Middleton at Jahra Pool Reserve in May 1995, when newly-fledged juveniles and females with brood patches were trapped. It was confirmed at Jahra East Outfall on 12 June 2000, with about 15 adults and fledglings observed, at Sabah Al-Salem on 9 June 2003, with a pair feeding young, at Sewer Plant Reeds on 14 June 2004, with six newly-fledged juveniles observed, and at South Doha Nature Reserve on 23 June 2005, with two newly-fledged juveniles observed. Birds have repeatedly sung for months, from late February, at East Doha. Without much doubt, they breed at this site also. With the recovery of the reeds at Jahra Pool Reserve, breeding of this, and other reedbed species, could occur in future.

All breeding birds and most of the migrants are of the subspecies *A. s. fuscus*. However, other migrants appear to be *A. s. scirpaceus* or are indeterminate.

Marsh Warbler *(Acrocephalus palustris)*

Status: Common passage migrant.

Marsh Warbler is reasonably common on spring and autumn passage, with birds seen at many locations, even some without reeds. A bird found dead at Salmi on 5 May 2001 had been ringed with a Swedish ring, Riksmuseum Stockholm BN51960, at Ngulia, Tsavo National Park, Kenya (3°00' S, 38°13'). The highest daily count is 25+ seen by V. A. D. Sales at Ahmadi on 12 April 1960.

Blyth's Reed Warbler *(Acrocephalus dumetorum)*

Status: Vagrant (two records).

Many records of this species in Kuwait in the past probably involved confusion with European Reed Warbler (*A. scirpaceus*) or with Marsh Warbler (*A. palustris*). V. A. D. Sales found a dead bird on 12 May 1963, and trapped and ringed 36 other birds there from 1964 to 1968, identifying them as this species. This total appears to be much too high. C. W. T. Pilcher (undated) mentions four records from about 1965 to 1985, but supplies no details. B. Wright (1995) wrote: 'A single bird in May 1994 was later found shot, while in September 1984 an individual was exceptionally tame and confiding.' However, no measurements or descriptions are provided.

In considering all records of Blyth's Reed Warbler in Kuwait, it is probably best to accept only those of birds measured in the hand during netting operations since the publication of *Identification of European Passerines* by L. Svensson (1970). Accordingly, all the above records cannot be accepted, even though it is possible that some of them were of this species. The only records that can be allowed onto the Kuwait bird list involve single birds netted and measured by S. Howe at Ahmadi on 15 July and on 19 August 1971.

Basra Reed Warbler *(Acrocephalus griseldis)*
Status: Common passage migrant. Uncommon summer visitor.

Basra Reed Warbler passes through Kuwait in spring and autumn. Records have been from many sites, including those without reeds. The highest daily count is 13 seen by V. A. D. Sales at Ahmadi on 20 April 1966.

This species probably breeds in Kuwait, but, despite great efforts, it has not been possible to obtain proof. C. W. T. Pilcher (undated) reported, at second hand, 'one with egg in oviduct and visible through abdominal skin' in spring 1995. However, the ringers who handled the bird, M. Reed and J. Middleton, in a personal communication to G. Gregory, stated that this was incorrect. From March to May 1995 they ringed 105 birds of this species and they only once caught a bird with a brood patch.

Three pairs sang and held territory at Jahra East Outfall from 25 May 1999. There were two unpaired birds there after a massive fire on 12 June 2000. In 2001, two singing at South Doha Nature Reserve on 9 March, one there on 3 May and one carrying food at Jahra East Outfall on 25 May were possibly breeding. Birds were repeatedly heard singing at Jahra East Outfall, South Doha Nature Reserve, Sabah Al-Salem and Sewer Plant Reeds for months in 2002. In 2003 three were singing at Jahra East Outfall on 14 March, and at least one was still present in reeds at Sabah Al-Salem on 13 June. One was singing at a new site, Sewer Plant Reeds, on 8 June 2004, and again at South Doha Nature Reserve on 20 May 2005.

Great Reed Warbler *(Acrocephalus arundinaceus)*
Status: Common passage migrant. Uncommon summer visitor. Has bred.

This species is widespread in Kuwait on migration. The highest daily count is 40+ seen on several days in May 1961 by V. A. D. Sales at Ahmadi. Some past winter records may involve confusion with Clamorous Reed Warbler (*A. stentoreus*).

Great Reed Warbler probably breeds annually at all the main reedbed sites, but confirmation has only been obtained twice. On 12 June 2000 two adults were seen, by G. Gregory and P. Robertson, feeding three very short-tailed fledglings on the ashy ground of a burnt-out reedbed at Jahra East Outfall. Every year since, birds have been heard singing for months at Jahra East Outfall, South Doha Nature Reserve, Sabah Al-Salem and Sewer Plant Reeds. On 23 June 2005 B. Foster observed an adult feeding young at South Doha Nature Reserve.

Oriental Reed Warbler *(Acrocephalus orientalis)*
Status: Vagrant (one record).

A large *Acrocephalus* was photographed by A. Al-Sirhan in the Sabah Al-Ahmed Natural Reserve on 20 April 2004. His description is below:
'On the 20th April 2004 AbdulRahman Al-Sirhan was photographing birds in Sabah Al-Ahmed Nature Reserve at a small pool in Tulha (29° 35' N, 47°46' E). A bird came to the pool, stayed only one minute, drank water and left, never being seen again. I managed to take only five photographs of the bird. Since that time nobody was allowed entrance to the Reserve so the bird was never seen thereafter.
The photographed bird shows the following features: dark grey-brownish head contrasting with the off-white supercilium, not well defined black lores, a gorget of greyish streaks on the lower throat/upper breast, white tips to tail feathers, bill all black with pale base of lower mandible, bill appearing triangular in shape (which is much different from Great Reed Warbler bill), and pinkish legs with pale grey toes.'

Clamorous Reed Warbler *(Acrocephalus stentoreus)*
Status: Uncommon passage migrant. Scarce resident.

Most Clamorous Reed Warblers recorded in Kuwait are passage migrants. Relatively small numbers are present in winter and summer, and these birds are probably residents. The highest daily count is six seen on several occasions. Records are from many locations, not just those with reeds.
This species probably breeds regularly in Kuwait, but this has never been proven. Singing birds are heard for months every year at Jahra East Outfall, South Doha Nature Reserve, Sabah Al-Salem and Sewer Plant Reeds. From February 2005 song was heard at a new reedbed at East Doha.

Eastern Olivaceous Warbler *(Hippolais pallida)*
Status: Common passage migrant. Uncommon summer visitor. Breeds.

This species is mostly a passage migrant in Kuwait, with records from most locations with trees and bushes. The highest daily count outside of the breeding season is 11 or 12 seen by V. A. D. Sales at Ahmadi 10 May 1955.
Evidence of breeding by this species in Kuwait has only recently been obtained. A singing male was heard on two occasions from 14 May 1999 in the same tree at

Salwa. One of a pair approached the observer, perched up in front of him and gave agitated calls from 18 May 2000 in Salmiya. On 17 May 2001 there were a maximum of eight birds, including three pairs visiting possible nest sites and one singing, at the Mohammed Al-Ajmi Farm in Abdali. In 2002 breeding was confirmed by G. Gregory, K. Al-Nasrallah and M. O. Chichester at Abdali Farms on 10 May 2002, with a not fully-grown juvenile being fed by an adult, and by A. Bailey in Kuwait City with a nest being found in the hollow of the roof of a low building. Nine pairs were on territory at the Mohammed Al-Ajmi Farm at Abdali on 31 May 2003. There was a maximum of 12 birds there on 30 April, with song heard there from 12 April, in 2004. In the same year there was confirmed breeding at Sabriya Farm on 10 June. It is suspected that Eastern Olivaceous Warblers now breed widely in Kuwait.

Booted Warbler *(Hippolais caligata)*
Status: Vagrant (at least one record).

Some records of the old Booted Warbler in Kuwait probably referred to the modern Booted Warbler, but there is no reliable practical method of determining which ones.

There is only one definite record of Booted Warbler in Kuwait, that of a bird seen by A. Bailey and B. Foster in the Sabah Al-Ahmed Natural Reserve on 22 April 2005. A. Bailey noted that it was 'too warm and buffy for Syke's' and was 'unlike the washed-out-looking greyish Syke's (with pale tertial fringes) we saw later in the season.'

Syke's Warbler *(Hippolais rama)*
Status: Scarce passage migrant.

Syke's Warbler has recently been split off from Booted Warbler (*H. caligata*). Until a few years ago all sightings of Syke's Warbler in the state were recorded as Booted Warblers. Most or all of these past records cannot be safely allocated to either Syke's Warbler or to the modern Booted Warbler. Syke's Warbler occurs in very small numbers mostly in spring and autumn in Kuwait. Records have been from many locations. The highest daily count is three on several occasions.

This species has not been proven to breed in the state. However, in 2002 a bird sang at Sabah Al-Salem from 22 March to 3 May. In 2004 there were single birds in possible breeding habitat at the Mohammed Al-Ajmi Farm at Abdali on 8 May and 3 June, and at Qaisat on 8 May. On this last date there was a bird seemingly intermediate between Syke's Warbler and Olivaceous Warbler (*H. pallida*) at the Mohammed Al-Ajmi Farm at Abdali.

Upcher's Warbler *(Hippolais languida)*
Status: Uncommon passage migrant.
This species is quite commonly observed on passage through Kuwait, Records have been from all main sites with trees or bushes. The highest daily count is 5 seen on many occasions.

JAN 1-10	JAN 11-20	JAN 21-31	FEB 1-10	FEB 11-20	FEB 21-29	MAR 1-10	MAR 11-20	MAR 21-31	APR 1-10	APR 11-20	APR 21-30	MAY 1-10	MAY 11-20	MAY 21-31	JUN 1-10	JUN 11-20	JUN 21-30	JUL 1-10	JUL 11-20	JUL 21-31	AUG 1-10	AUG 11-20	AUG 21-31	SEP 1-10	SEP 11-20	SEP 21-30	OCT 1-10	OCT 11-20	OCT 21-31	NOV 1-10	NOV 11-20	NOV 21-30	DEC 1-10	DEC 11-20	DEC 21-31
						1		1	1	1	2	3	5	1							2	1	2	3	1	1		1							

Olive-tree Warbler *(Hippolais olivetorum)*
Status: Vagrant (one record).
There are many past Kuwait records of Olive-tree Warbler which were not of birds measured in the hand. These include: at Ahmadi on 6 May 1955 (three), 15 April (or June) 1959 (one), 30 March 1966 (one), 11-14 May 1966 (one), 25 April 1968 (two), 2 September 1971 (two) and 27 September 1974 (one); at Umm Al-Aish on 24 September 1972 (one), 9 May 1974 (one) and 10 April 1981 (one); and at Al-Abraq Al-Khabari on an inaccessible date between 1985 and 1989 (two). Although it is possible that one or more of these birds were correctly identified, it is probably best to disregard all of them, due to the distinct possibility of confusion with Upcher's Warbler (*H. languida*) or even with Barred Warbler (***Sylvia nisoria***).

The only acceptable Kuwait record of this species was of a bird found dead, measured and photographed by S. Howe at Umm Al-Aish on 14 September 1972. His measurements, written on a Rare Bird Report form, are below:
Length 165. Wing 84. Tail 68. Culmen 19. Tarsus 25. Tarsus was observed to be 'booted'.

The panel, who did not see the photograph, rejected this record, on the grounds of inadequate description and possible confusion with other species. In reconsidering it, the measurements of wing and culmen eliminate all other confusion species. The photograph, in black-and-white, shows a large-billed Hippolais with slightly darker suffusion on the sides of the breast and flanks, and paler edgings to some upper wing feathers. Beyond all reasonable doubt this bird was an Olive-tree Warbler.

Icterine Warbler *(Hippolais icterina)*
Status: Scarce passage migrant.
The species probably occurs annually in Kuwait, but it is no doubt under-recorded. The highest daily count is five seen at Ahmadi on 5 May 1961 by V. A. D. Sales. Other records have been from Khaitan, Mina, Umm Al-Aish, Jahra Farms, Al-Abraq Al-Khabari and the Sabah Al-Ahmed Natural Reserve. All recent records have been in spring.

JAN 1-10	JAN 11-20	JAN 21-31	FEB 1-10	FEB 11-20	FEB 21-29	MAR 1-10	MAR 11-20	MAR 21-31	APR 1-10	APR 11-20	APR 21-30	MAY 1-10	MAY 11-20	MAY 21-31	JUN 1-10	JUN 11-20	JUN 21-30	JUL 1-10	JUL 11-20	JUL 21-31	AUG 1-10	AUG 11-20	AUG 21-31	SEP 1-10	SEP 11-20	SEP 21-30	OCT 1-10	OCT 11-20	OCT 21-31	NOV 1-10	NOV 11-20	NOV 21-30	DEC 1-10	DEC 11-20	DEC 21-31
									2			1	1																						

Blackcap *(Sylvia atricapilla)*
Status: Very common passage migrant.

Blackcaps are commonly seen in spring and autumn, and have been recorded from al most all sites in Kuwait. The highest daily count is about 100 seen at Ahmadi by V. A. D. Sales on several days in spring 1956.

Garden Warbler *(Sylvia borin)*
Status: Uncommon passage migrant.

This species passes through Kuwait, generally in small numbers, in spring and autumn. Records have been from most sites with trees or bushes. The highest daily count is over 1000 birds seen by V. A. D. Sales at Ahmadi on 12 and 13 May 1966. Such an extraordinarily large fall of birds has not been observed in the state since.

Barred Warbler *(Sylvia nisoria)*
Status: Uncommon passage migrant.

Barred Warblers are often seen in small numbers in spring and autumn, at most locations with trees and bushes. The highest daily count is 12 seen on 12 May 1966 by V. A. D. Sales at Ahmadi. This species is regarded as a delicacy by many Kuwaitis, who say that it cooks well because of its stored fat.

Lesser Whitethroat *(Sylvia curruca)*
Status: Common passage migrant. Scarce winter visitor.

This species is mostly a passage migrant through Kuwait, and has been recorded at all locations with some cover. A few are seen in winter. The highest daily count is 30 seen on several occasions.

It is often very difficult to identify the subspecies of many Lesser Whitethroats in the field, and some subspecies may be only statistically distinguishable in the hand. Accordingly, no attempt is made here to list them.

JAN 1-10	JAN 11-20	JAN 21-31	FEB 1-10	FEB 11-20	FEB 21-29	MAR 1-10	MAR 11-20	MAR 21-31	APR 1-10	APR 11-20	APR 21-30	MAY 1-10	MAY 11-20	MAY 21-31	JUN 1-10	JUN 11-20	JUN 21-30	JUL 1-10	JUL 11-20	JUL 21-31	AUG 1-10	AUG 11-20	AUG 21-31	SEP 1-10	SEP 11-20	SEP 21-30	OCT 1-10	OCT 11-20	OCT 21-31	NOV 1-10	NOV 11-20	NOV 21-30	DEC 1-10	DEC 11-20	DEC 21-31
1			1	1	1	1	1	2	30	14	10	6	3	3							2		2	2	1	3	1		2					1	1

Eastern Orphean Warbler *(Sylvia crassirostris)*
Status: Uncommon passage migrant.

Eastern Orphean Warblers occur in small numbers in spring and autumn at sites with trees and bushes, but are no doubt overlooked and under-recorded. The highest daily count is 11 seen at Ahmadi by V. A. D. Sales on 3 March 1957.

JAN 1-10	JAN 11-20	JAN 21-31	FEB 1-10	FEB 11-20	FEB 21-29	MAR 1-10	MAR 11-20	MAR 21-31	APR 1-10	APR 11-20	APR 21-30	MAY 1-10	MAY 11-20	MAY 21-31	JUN 1-10	JUN 11-20	JUN 21-30	JUL 1-10	JUL 11-20	JUL 21-31	AUG 1-10	AUG 11-20	AUG 21-31	SEP 1-10	SEP 11-20	SEP 21-30	OCT 1-10	OCT 11-20	OCT 21-31	NOV 1-10	NOV 11-20	NOV 21-30	DEC 1-10	DEC 11-20	DEC 21-31
					3	1		2	1	1		1										1	1						1						1

Common Whitethroat *(Sylvia communis)*
Status: Very common passage migrant.

This species is commonly observed on passage at all sites with some cover. The highest daily count is 'thousands' seen by V. A. D. Sales at Ahmadi on 12-14 May 1966. Identifying subspecies is very difficult, but many birds seen are much greyer than the nominate subspecies.

JAN 1-10	JAN 11-20	JAN 21-31	FEB 1-10	FEB 11-20	FEB 21-29	MAR 1-10	MAR 11-20	MAR 21-31	APR 1-10	APR 11-20	APR 21-30	MAY 1-10	MAY 11-20	MAY 21-31	JUN 1-10	JUN 11-20	JUN 21-30	JUL 1-10	JUL 11-20	JUL 21-31	AUG 1-10	AUG 11-20	AUG 21-31	SEP 1-10	SEP 11-20	SEP 21-30	OCT 1-10	OCT 11-20	OCT 21-31	NOV 1-10	NOV 11-20	NOV 21-30	DEC 1-10	DEC 11-20	DEC 21-31
						1	9	1	1	29	11	10	5	2							3	2	11	4	3	4	5	1	2						

Asian Desert Warbler *(Sylvia nana)*
Status: Common winter visitor. Common passage migrant.

Asian Desert Warbler are seen in small numbers on passage and in winter, in all locations with bushes. The highest daily count is 10 seen on several occasions. From February onwards birds often sing and appear to form pairs. However, there has been no further evidence of breeding.

JAN 1-10	JAN 11-20	JAN 21-31	FEB 1-10	FEB 11-20	FEB 21-29	MAR 1-10	MAR 11-20	MAR 21-31	APR 1-10	APR 11-20	APR 21-30	MAY 1-10	MAY 11-20	MAY 21-31	JUN 1-10	JUN 11-20	JUN 21-30	JUL 1-10	JUL 11-20	JUL 21-31	AUG 1-10	AUG 11-20	AUG 21-31	SEP 1-10	SEP 11-20	SEP 21-30	OCT 1-10	OCT 11-20	OCT 21-31	NOV 1-10	NOV 11-20	NOV 21-30	DEC 1-10	DEC 11-20	DEC 21-31
3	1	1	2	1	10	3	1	1																2	1	4	2	4		2	4	1			

Ménétries's Warbler *(Sylvia mystacea)*
Status: Common passage migrant. Scarce winter visitor.

This species is mostly seen in spring and autumn, but some individuals winter at a number of sites with trees and bushes. The highest daily count is five seen on many occasions. Males often do not develop the pinkish on the underparts until quite late in spring, and can until then be confused with other species of *Sylvia*.

JAN 1-10	JAN 11-20	JAN 21-31	FEB 1-10	FEB 11-20	FEB 21-29	MAR 1-10	MAR 11-20	MAR 21-31	APR 1-10	APR 11-20	APR 21-30	MAY 1-10	MAY 11-20	MAY 21-31	JUN 1-10	JUN 11-20	JUN 21-30	JUL 1-10	JUL 11-20	JUL 21-31	AUG 1-10	AUG 11-20	AUG 21-31	SEP 1-10	SEP 11-20	SEP 21-30	OCT 1-10	OCT 11-20	OCT 21-31	NOV 1-10	NOV 11-20	NOV 21-30	DEC 1-10	DEC 11-20	DEC 21-31
1	4	1		1	2	3	4	5	2	1	2	2	1											1	2	1	1		1				1	2	1

Greenish Warbler *(Phylloscopus trochiloides)*
Status: Rare passage migrant.

Greenish Warbler is no doubt under-recorded in Kuwait. V. A. D. Sales wrote descriptions of two birds that he saw at Ahmadi on 2 February 1953 and of one he saw there on 6 June 1953, on a Rare Bird Report form, but the panel rejected these records, with comments that other species were not eliminated. During ringing operations at Wadi Ar-Rimam Farm in just one year, 1997, N. Cleere and D. Kelly caught birds on 30 April (two), 23 May (one) and 27 May (one). This gives an indication of how many may pass through undetected. One was seen and described by J. Gaskell and M. O. Chichester at Wafra Oil Field on 5 October 1998. G. Gregory observed a bird at Subiya on 29 April 2004. There are known to be at least several other sight records, with at least one photograph taken, at Umm Al-Aish and Al-Abraq Al-Khabari by several Kuwaiti photographers, but the exact dates are not accessible. Accordingly, the status given above is probably the best one.

All birds subspecifically identified have been *P. t. nitidus* (Green Warbler).

Yellow-browed Warbler *(Phylloscopus inornatus)*
Status: Rare passage migrant and winter visitor.

The only available records of this species in Kuwait are at Ahmadi on 9 November 1953 (one), at Ahmadi on 12 December 1968 (one), at Al-Abraq Al-Khabari on 18 October 1985 (one), at Umm Al-Aish in early 1986 (one), at Al-Abraq Al-Khabari in October 1986 (two), at Al-Abraq Al-Khabari in October 1987 (one), at an unstated location on 26 January 2001 (one) and at Jahra on 20 December 2002 (one). The observers included V. A. D. Sales, S. Howe, G. Gregory, C. W. T. Pilcher, M. Shehab and S. T. Spencer. There are known to be at least three other records, but details are not accessible. Some of these records may refer to Hume's Leaf Warbler (*P. humei*).

Hume's Leaf Warbler *(Phylloscopus humei)*
Status: Vagrant (one record).

A written description of a very dull bird seen at Jahra Farms by G. Gregory from 8 December 1995 to 23 January 1996 was accepted by KORC. The description reads: 'On 8th December, GG was checking through trees and bushes in the enclosed part of Jahra Gardens for small passerines. At about 10.25 a.m. in one bush he found several House Sparrows, two Chiffchaffs and a smaller *Phylloscopus sp.* with wing bars. This bird was viewed for about 10 seconds, and then it flew off into a palm tree about 30 metres away. Despite considerable searching it could not be relocated that day. It was seen again on 12 January and 23 February, for brief periods.

Size and Shape:
Somewhat smaller than nearby Chiffchaffs. Typical *Phylloscopus* shape from side, but appeared Goldcrest-like in shape from behind.

Upper Parts: Long off-white supercilium, above a darkish eye-stripe. Rest of head and upper mantle dull greenish-grey or greyish-green, much drabber than nearby Chiffchaffs. Rest of body and tail greenish-brown. Wings basically greenish-brown with a fairly prominent off-white wing-bar on tips of greater coverts, a much less prominent off-white wing-bar on tips of median coverts, and pale edges/tips to tertials.

Under Parts: Off-white generally.

Exposed Parts: Bill and eye appeared dark. Legs not well seen, but appeared quite dark.

Behaviour: Moved along branch of bush, then hopped/flew to another, then flew off

into palm tree, perching high up. Silent.'
Some records of Yellow-browed Warbler (*P. inornatus*) may refer to this species.

Wood Warbler *(Phylloscopus sibilitrax)*
Status: Scarce passage migrant.
Wood Warbler probably occurs annually in small numbers, but is under-recorded. Records have been from many locations with trees and bushes. The highest daily count is three seen on several occasions.

JAN 1-10	JAN 11-20	JAN 21-31	FEB 1-10	FEB 11-20	FEB 21-29	MAR 1-10	MAR 11-20	MAR 21-31	APR 1-10	APR 11-20	APR 21-30	MAY 1-10	MAY 11-20	MAY 21-31	JUN 1-10	JUN 11-20	JUN 21-30	JUL 1-10	JUL 11-20	JUL 21-31	AUG 1-10	AUG 11-20	AUG 21-31	SEP 1-10	SEP 11-20	SEP 21-30	OCT 1-10	OCT 11-20	OCT 21-31	NOV 1-10	NOV 11-20	NOV 21-30	DEC 1-10	DEC 11-20	DEC 21-31
								3																											

Mountain Chiffchaff *(Phylloscopus sindianus)*
Status: Rare passage migrant and winter visitor.
This species was first noticed in Kuwait on 15 February 1939 (V. Dickson, undated). From 1985-1989 in every winter a few very 'brown-and-white' *Phylloscopus* were seen and a few were trapped, at Umm Al-Aish and Al-Abraq Al-Khabari, by G. Gregory, M. Shehab and C. W. T. Pilcher. In retrospect these birds were clearly Mountain Chiffchaffs. B. Wright (1995) wrote: 'Birds showing the characters of *P. s. lorenzii* were observed during February/March 1994. One individual was ringed.' One was ringed by N. Cleere and D. Kelly, and also seen by C. W. T. Pilcher and S.T. Spencer, at Jahra Pool Reserve on 28 March 1997. Another was ringed by D. Kelly and N. Cleere at the same place on 12 April 1997. Birds showing the characteristics of this species were seen at Jahra Farms on 23 November 2001 (one), at Sabah Al-Salem from 31 January to 16 March 2002 (one) and at Al-Abraq Al-Khabari on 11 March 2005 (two). In addition, there are a number of sight records by Kuwaiti photographers, but the exact dates are not accessible.

JAN 1-10	JAN 11-20	JAN 21-31	FEB 1-10	FEB 11-20	FEB 21-29	MAR 1-10	MAR 11-20	MAR 21-31	APR 1-10	APR 11-20	APR 21-30	MAY 1-10	MAY 11-20	MAY 21-31	JUN 1-10	JUN 11-20	JUN 21-30	JUL 1-10	JUL 11-20	JUL 21-31	AUG 1-10	AUG 11-20	AUG 21-31	SEP 1-10	SEP 11-20	SEP 21-30	OCT 1-10	OCT 11-20	OCT 21-31	NOV 1-10	NOV 11-20	NOV 21-30	DEC 1-10	DEC 11-20	DEC 21-31
1	1	1	1	1	2																									1					

Common Chiffchaff *(Phylloscopus collybita)*
Status: Abundant passage migrant. Abundant winter visitor.
Common Chiffchaffs are widespread in Kuwait on passage and in winter. The highest daily count is 'over 500' seen on several occasions by V. A. D. Sales at Ahmadi between 1952 and 1968. A bird ringed by this observer at Ahmadi on 24 April 1966 was recovered at Ras Baalbek, Lebanon on 5 November 1967.

Identifying subspecies is not easy, but many birds give *P. c. tristis*-like calls. Other birds give a more drawn-out call, and some of these are probably *P. c. abietanus*. From February onwards some birds sing, but there is no further evidence of breeding.

JAN 1-10	JAN 11-20	JAN 21-31	FEB 1-10	FEB 11-20	FEB 21-29	MAR 1-10	MAR 11-20	MAR 21-31	APR 1-10	APR 11-20	APR 21-30	MAY 1-10	MAY 11-20	MAY 21-31	JUN 1-10	JUN 11-20	JUN 21-30	JUL 1-10	JUL 11-20	JUL 21-31	AUG 1-10	AUG 11-20	AUG 21-31	SEP 1-10	SEP 11-20	SEP 21-30	OCT 1-10	OCT 11-20	OCT 21-31	NOV 1-10	NOV 11-20	NOV 21-30	DEC 1-10	DEC 11-20	DEC 21-31
6	15	12	20	200	15	20	200	350	50	8	10	5	6	4										2	1	1	6	2	6	6	4	5	15	6	

Willow Warbler *(Phylloscopus trochilus)*
Status: Abundant passage migrant. Rare winter visitor.
This species is widespread in Kuwait in spring and autumn. The highest daily count is about 150 seen at Abu Halifa by B. Wright in April 1993. One recorded by G. Gregory at the Mohammed Al-Ajmi Farm at Abdali on 23 January 2004 was apparently wintering.

JAN 1-10	JAN 11-20	JAN 21-31	FEB 1-10	FEB 11-20	FEB 21-29	MAR 1-10	MAR 11-20	MAR 21-31	APR 1-10	APR 11-20	APR 21-30	MAY 1-10	MAY 11-20	MAY 21-31	JUN 1-10	JUN 11-20	JUN 21-30	JUL 1-10	JUL 11-20	JUL 21-31	AUG 1-10	AUG 11-20	AUG 21-31	SEP 1-10	SEP 11-20	SEP 21-30	OCT 1-10	OCT 11-20	OCT 21-31	NOV 1-10	NOV 11-20	NOV 21-30	DEC 1-10	DEC 11-20	DEC 21-31
1			1	2	3	3	4	50	24	26	25	25	4	1							1	4	2	5	18	2	4								

Spotted Flycatcher *(Muscicapa striata)*
Status: Very common passage migrant.
Spotted Flycatchers are easily seen on passage through Kuwait. The highest daily count is 75 seen by V. A. D. Sales at Ahmadi on 27 April 1968. Records have been from all areas with trees and bushes.

JAN 1-10	JAN 11-20	JAN 21-31	FEB 1-10	FEB 11-20	FEB 21-29	MAR 1-10	MAR 11-20	MAR 21-31	APR 1-10	APR 11-20	APR 21-30	MAY 1-10	MAY 11-20	MAY 21-31	JUN 1-10	JUN 11-20	JUN 21-30	JUL 1-10	JUL 11-20	JUL 21-31	AUG 1-10	AUG 11-20	AUG 21-31	SEP 1-10	SEP 11-20	SEP 21-30	OCT 1-10	OCT 11-20	OCT 21-31	NOV 1-10	NOV 11-20	NOV 21-30	DEC 1-10	DEC 11-20	DEC 21-31
								1	5	20	12	10	8	3	2					1	1	4	2	3	3	3	3	1	1						

Red-breasted Flycatcher *(Ficedula parva)*
Status: Scarce passage migrant.
This species is annually recorded in small numbers, with records from many sites. Most birds are observed in autumn. One seen by M. O. Chichester at Wafra Oil Field on 27 March 2000 was an unusual spring record. The highest daily count is five seen at Al-Abraq Al-Khabari by B. Foster and G. Gregory on 22 October 2004.

Semi-collared Flycatcher *(Ficedula semitorquata)*
Status: Uncommon passage migrant.
Semi-collared Flycatchers are recorded in small numbers in spring from sites with trees and bushes. There are no recent autumn records. The highest daily count is seven seen by B. Foster at Sabah Al-Salem on 26 March 2005.

Common Babbler *(Turdoides caudatus)*
Status: Vagrant (three records).
Up to four, discovered by M. O. Chichester, were present at Zour Port from 14 August 1998 to 7 December 2001. His description follows:
'Size and Shape:
The bird is about 9" long and over half of this length is its tail. The bird reminds me a lot of a California Thrasher (*Toxostoma redivium*). Its most prominent features is its long, floppy (loosely articulated?), ragged looking tail. It has short, rounded wings, a large head with a strong decurved bill, and long, strong legs and feet. The tail is often cocked or wagged. Graduated tail feathers.
Head:
The head is large and flat-crowned. The overall colour of the head is greyish-brown. Fine, dark (blackish or darker brown) streaks cover the crown and nape. The loral area and just behind the eyes are grey and free of any streaking. The auricular and malar are brownish than grey.
Upper Parts:
The back is streaked with heavier, wider streaks than crown and nape with the same blackish-brown. I haven't observed the rump well enough to determine if the streaking extends that far. The wings are grey-brown. The tail is grey-brown with central feathers a bit lighter when the tail is spread on landing.
Under Parts:
The throat is unmarked paler grey brown. Fine streaks are on the side of the neck and cover the corner of the side of the breast in front of the bend of the wing and form a faint necklace, bib, or gorget on the breast. The streaks don't extend down the flanks. The balance of the under parts are light-brown like milky tea and lightest on the lower belly. Under tail coverts are the same grey-brown as the flanks and breast.

Bare Parts:
Legs - dull yellow. Eye - golden-yellow with a black pupil. Bill - decurved, dark grey and yellowish on base of lower mandible. The base of the gape appears slightly yellowish and swollen. Its length is about two-thirds the length of the head. When observed panting, the inside of the mouth is pink and the interior of the horny parts of the bill appears yellowish.

Vocalizations:
Note - loud barking note. Longer in duration and hollower than House Sparrow song - a wheezy "weez weez", descending (4-5 notes) into a clearer, whistled peeew, peeew, peeew on the same pitch, then slower at the last few notes as though getting tired. The entire song is 7-10 seconds. Given from prominent perch in a treetop or building corner. The song does not seem to be seasonal (January, February, May, June August, September, November, December). Sometimes individual or paired "weez" notes are given.

One odd vocalization was noted on July '00. It gave a squeaky, "creeee" immediately followed by a robust whistle. It was given from a tree repeatedly and then it stopped when then it stopped when the bird dropped to the ground. It returned to the same call upon flying back into a tree.

A muted, duet vocalization song was heard on one occasion being performed by two birds (14 Jan '99) Two birds were not seen, but the vocals seemed to come from two places simultaneously.

Behaviour:
The bird's on-ground foraging style is to hop rather than walk. It seems to spend time foraging in grass and grass and bare dirt areas. It uses its feet to disturb the shallow soil and to search for food items. It also users its bill in a side-to-side thrashing motion, presumably to forage (as do the thrashers of the New World). It has been observed in the trees foraging on small, ripe figs (9 Oct '98). A bird was observed feeding on a caterpillar on 22 Feb '00. Observations of its interactions with other species are limited to House Sparrows. At times the Babbler is indifferent to HOSP [House Sparrow (Passer domesticus)] allowing them to be quite close in the same tree. On one occasion, it was pugnacious and aggressive, driving several HOSP entirely out of a tree in which it was singing (25 Feb '00). As mentioned above, the bird has been observed performing territorial singing on many occasions and even carrying nesting material (29 April '00). Nuptial optimism rather than an actual nesting attempt probably trigger this behaviour. Preening was observed on 20 Nov '98 and a couple of body feathers dropped from the bird, indicating a body moult at this time.'

In early 1999 a number of observers saw and photographed one at Jahra Pool Reserve. S. T. Spencer and J. Gaskell wrote a description of it on 25 February.

David Sherrelll observed a single bird at Zour Port between 10 and 29 April 2004. This was originally thought to be the previously long-staying bird reappearing, but, on the balance of probabilities, was a new bird.

A group of at least four, including one singing bird, was seen by G. Gregory and B. Foster at the Mohammed Al-Ajmi Farm at Abdali on 10 September 2004.

[Two *Turdoides*, probably of this species, were briefly seen at Jahra Pool Reserve by G. Gregory in October 1994, but flew off before specific identification could be determined.]

Eurasian Penduline Tit *(Remiz pendulinus)*
Status: Uncommon winter visitor.
Penduline Tits occur annually, usually in small numbers. Records have been from many areas with reeds, trees and bushes. The highest daily count is 28 seen by G. Gregory at Rawdatain on 29 March 2005.

JAN 1-10	JAN 11-20	JAN 21-31	FEB 1-10	FEB 11-20	FEB 21-29	MAR 1-10	MAR 11-20	MAR 21-31	APR 1-10	APR 11-20	APR 21-30	MAY 1-10	MAY 11-20	MAY 21-31	JUN 1-10	JUN 11-20	JUN 21-30	JUL 1-10	JUL 11-20	JUL 21-31	AUG 1-10	AUG 11-20	AUG 21-31	SEP 1-10	SEP 11-20	SEP 21-30	OCT 1-10	OCT 11-20	OCT 21-31	NOV 1-10	NOV 11-20	NOV 21-30	DEC 1-10	DEC 11-20	DEC 21-31
4	1				1		4	28	3				12															5			25	1	5		

Eurasian Golden Oriole *(Oriolus oriolus)*
Status: Common passage migrant. Rare summer visitor. Has bred.
This species is quite commonly observed on spring and summer migration. The highest daily count is 20 seen at Ahmadi on several occasions by V. A. D. Sales between 1952 and 1968. Records have been from all areas with trees and bushes. According to the ANHFSG Newsletter 3 (1971) Eurasian Golden Orioles are traditionally the last migrant north and the first one south.
This species appears to be a secretive breeder and could well have bred undiscovered many times in Kuwait. Breeding was first proven in 2004 at the Abdulla Al-Habashi Farm at Jahra. A pair was first seen by G. Gregory there on 21 May, then two not-fully-grown juveniles on 6 June, and an adult female and one juvenile on 11 June. Also in 2004, six adults were present at Sabriya Farm on 8 May, with a pair remaining until at least 27 May and an adult female until at least 10 June. M. C. Jennings, in a personal communication to G. Gregory, stated that *Eucalyptus* is a favoured nesting tree species for this species. Ahmadi has very many such trees, and evidence of breeding should be sought there in future.

JAN 1-10	JAN 11-20	JAN 21-31	FEB 1-10	FEB 11-20	FEB 21-29	MAR 1-10	MAR 11-20	MAR 21-31	APR 1-10	APR 11-20	APR 21-30	MAY 1-10	MAY 11-20	MAY 21-31	JUN 1-10	JUN 11-20	JUN 21-30	JUL 1-10	JUL 11-20	JUL 21-31	AUG 1-10	AUG 11-20	AUG 21-31	SEP 1-10	SEP 11-20	SEP 21-30	OCT 1-10	OCT 11-20	OCT 21-31	NOV 1-10	NOV 11-20	NOV 21-30	DEC 1-10	DEC 11-20	DEC 21-31
						1	1	2	6	9	16	2	2					1					1	1	1	1		1							

Isabelline Shrike *(Lanius isabellinus)*
Status: Common passage migrant. Uncommon winter visitor.
Isabelline Shrikes are widespread in Kuwait in autumn, winter and spring. The highest daily count is 40 seen on several occasions.
Many females, juveniles and even sometimes males are very difficult to subspecifically identify, and some birds are probably intergrades. Male hybrid Isabelline Shrikes x Red-backed Shrikes (*L. collurio*) are sometimes observed.

JAN 1-10	JAN 11-20	JAN 21-31	FEB 1-10	FEB 11-20	FEB 21-29	MAR 1-10	MAR 11-20	MAR 21-31	APR 1-10	APR 11-20	APR 21-30	MAY 1-10	MAY 11-20	MAY 21-31	JUN 1-10	JUN 11-20	JUN 21-30	JUL 1-10	JUL 11-20	JUL 21-31	AUG 1-10	AUG 11-20	AUG 21-31	SEP 1-10	SEP 11-20	SEP 21-30	OCT 1-10	OCT 11-20	OCT 21-31	NOV 1-10	NOV 11-20	NOV 21-30	DEC 1-10	DEC 11-20	DEC 21-31
3	2	6	3	4	2	6	15	40	22	7	10	7	4			1	1						1	4	2	4	2	3	3	14	4	4	4	4	3

Red-backed Shrike *(Lanius collurio)*

Status: Very common passage migrant. Rare winter visitor.

This species is commonly observed in spring and autumn at all sites with bushes or trees. The highest daily count is 1000 - 2000 seen by V. A. D. Sales at Ahmadi on each day from 12 - 18 May 1966. Certainly large falls occur: the KISR Bird Team observed 120 in one fairly small area on Bubiyan Island on 7 May 2004. Wintering birds are occasionally seen.

A hybrid shrike was photographed in June 2003. It had a pale grey head, white supercilium, fairly wide black face stripe extending over bill, rufous-brown back, dark brown wings with fine paler feather edges, dark brown tail with rufous at top corners and on outer webs of outer feathers, and white underparts with a rufous wash on flanks. One parent was clearly a Red-backed Shrike; the other was uncertain.

JAN 1-10	JAN 11-20	JAN 21-31	FEB 1-10	FEB 11-20	FEB 21-29	MAR 1-10	MAR 11-20	MAR 21-31	APR 1-10	APR 11-20	APR 21-30	MAY 1-10	MAY 11-20	MAY 21-31	JUN 1-10	JUN 11-20	JUN 21-30	JUL 1-10	JUL 11-20	JUL 21-31	AUG 1-10	AUG 11-20	AUG 21-31	SEP 1-10	SEP 11-20	SEP 21-30	OCT 1-10	OCT 11-20	OCT 21-31	NOV 1-10	NOV 11-20	NOV 21-30	DEC 1-10	DEC 11-20	DEC 21-31
1						5	3	1	20	4	120	30	8	2	3	1					1	2	2	2	4	2		4	2			1			1

Lesser Grey Shrike *(Lanius minor)*

Status: Uncommon passage migrant.

Lesser Grey Shrikes are seen at many locations with trees and bushes on passage through Kuwait, but usually in small numbers. The highest daily count is 16 seen by V. A. D. Sales at Ahmadi on 2 May 1965.

JAN 1-10	JAN 11-20	JAN 21-31	FEB 1-10	FEB 11-20	FEB 21-29	MAR 1-10	MAR 11-20	MAR 21-31	APR 1-10	APR 11-20	APR 21-30	MAY 1-10	MAY 11-20	MAY 21-31	JUN 1-10	JUN 11-20	JUN 21-30	JUL 1-10	JUL 11-20	JUL 21-31	AUG 1-10	AUG 11-20	AUG 21-31	SEP 1-10	SEP 11-20	SEP 21-30	OCT 1-10	OCT 11-20	OCT 21-31	NOV 1-10	NOV 11-20	NOV 21-30	DEC 1-10	DEC 11-20	DEC 21-31
		2				1	1	1		2	9	5	2	1							1	2	2	1											

Southern Grey Shrike *(Lanius meridionalis)*

Status: Uncommon passage migrant. Uncommon winter visitor.

This species is observed almost every day in autumn, winter and spring in all areas away from human habitation. The highest daily count is 15+ seen by G. Rowlands at

Kabd on 24 March 2000.
L. m. pallidirostris (Steppe Grey Shrike) is an uncommon passage migrant and winter visitor. *L. m. aucheri* is a scarce passage migrant and winter visitor.

JAN 1-10	JAN 11-20	JAN 21-31	FEB 1-10	FEB 11-20	FEB 21-29	MAR 1-10	MAR 11-20	MAR 21-31	APR 1-10	APR 11-20	APR 21-30	MAY 1-10	MAY 11-20	MAY 21-31	JUN 1-10	JUN 11-20	JUN 21-30	JUL 1-10	JUL 11-20	JUL 21-31	AUG 1-10	AUG 11-20	AUG 21-31	SEP 1-10	SEP 11-20	SEP 21-30	OCT 1-10	OCT 11-20	OCT 21-31	NOV 1-10	NOV 11-20	NOV 21-30	DEC 1-10	DEC 11-20	DEC 21-31
4			1			1	4	1	5	4	15	4	1	1	1	2	1				1	1	5	2	4	2	2	1	1	1	1	1	1	1	

Woodchat Shrike *(Lanius senator)*
Status: Uncommon passage migrant. Has bred.

Woodchat Shrikes are usually seen on spring and autumn migration in small numbers at all sites with trees and bushes. One or two, recorded by V. A. D. Sales, overwintered at Ahmadi from 21 December 1965 to late February 1966. The highest daily count is 20 seen at Al-Abraq Al-Khabari on 15 March 2000 by H-M. Busch, J. Rathberger-Knan, F. Lange and A. Lange.

This species has bred once in Kuwait (and the Arabian peninsula), in 2004 at Tulha in the Sabah Al-Ahmed Natural Reserve. On 25 March K. Al-Nasrallah found a nest in an *Acacia* there, which had two eggs on 29 March, four eggs on 1 April and six eggs on 5 April, when the nest was found blown down by strong winds. Only the female was seen incubating the eggs, while the male sang and brought food to the female (Al-Nasrallah, 2005).

JAN 1-10	JAN 11-20	JAN 21-31	FEB 1-10	FEB 11-20	FEB 21-29	MAR 1-10	MAR 11-20	MAR 21-31	APR 1-10	APR 11-20	APR 21-30	MAY 1-10	MAY 11-20	MAY 21-31	JUN 1-10	JUN 11-20	JUN 21-30	JUL 1-10	JUL 11-20	JUL 21-31	AUG 1-10	AUG 11-20	AUG 21-31	SEP 1-10	SEP 11-20	SEP 21-30	OCT 1-10	OCT 11-20	OCT 21-31	NOV 1-10	NOV 11-20	NOV 21-30	DEC 1-10	DEC 11-20	DEC 21-31
			1	1		4	20	5	6	2	2	2	1	1							2	2	1	1	2	1									

Masked Shrike *(Lanius nubicus)*
Status: Common passage migrant. Rare winter visitor.

This species is usually seen in small numbers in spring and autumn at locations with trees and bushes. The highest daily count is 16 seen by V. A. D. Sales at Ahmadi on 6 June 1956. Single birds wintered at Jahra Farms in 2001-2002 and 2002-2003.

JAN 1-10	JAN 11-20	JAN 21-31	FEB 1-10	FEB 11-20	FEB 21-29	MAR 1-10	MAR 11-20	MAR 21-31	APR 1-10	APR 11-20	APR 21-30	MAY 1-10	MAY 11-20	MAY 21-31	JUN 1-10	JUN 11-20	JUN 21-30	JUL 1-10	JUL 11-20	JUL 21-31	AUG 1-10	AUG 11-20	AUG 21-31	SEP 1-10	SEP 11-20	SEP 21-30	OCT 1-10	OCT 11-20	OCT 21-31	NOV 1-10	NOV 11-20	NOV 21-30	DEC 1-10	DEC 11-20	DEC 21-31
1	1	1	1	1	1				6	1	2	2	1								2	2	3	1						1			1	1	

House Crow *(Corvus splendens)*
Status: Uncommon resident. Scarce disperser in all seasons. Breeds.

House Crow is an exotic species from south Asia which has been ship-borne to many ports and other coastal sites around the world, where it sometimes becomes established. It is a notorious nest-robber and can be a major threat to native species.

Rejected records of Hooded Crows (*C. corone capellanus* or *C. corone sharpii*) at Ahmadi from 23 January to 23 April 1957 (up to two), at Shuaiba on 24 October 1958 (one) and at Mina on 8 December 1972 (one) probably referred to House Crows. The first definite record of this species in Kuwait involved a juvenile brought to S. Howe at Ahmadi on 5 May 1972. This bird may have hatched locally. Five birds were present on the Kuwait University campus at Shuwaikh in 1979, and up to 10 birds have been seen there in almost all subsequent years.

The first confirmed breeding record was at Shuwaikh in mid-May 1983, when nest-building was observed; later parents were seen carrying food to the nest in a tall tamarisk tree (Pilcher, 1986; 1989b). Breeding has subsequently been proven again there on many occasions. The only other definite breeding record involved a pair found nesting on the communication tower on Kubbar Island by members of BMAPT on 10 May 2003. This was clearly a threat to the breeding terns on the island, and G. Kirwan, in a personal communication to G. Gregory, recommended control measures. Breeding is suspected to occur at several other sites, including port facilities, to which access by ornithologists is not possible.

Outside of the breeding season some of the birds at Shuwaikh, and also presumably others from elsewhere, often disperse around the coastline and urban areas. Others remain around the Shuwaikh area. Maximum counts at other sites include four at Salwa on 13 January 1999, 13 at Ahmadi on 2 November 2000 and one at Zour Port on several dates. The population in Kuwait is estimated as up to 30 birds. C. W. T. Pilcher (1986) wrote that this species was absent from the state at certain times of year, but it is more likely that the birds are scattered around uncovered sites.

JAN 1-10	JAN 11-20	JAN 21-31	FEB 1-10	FEB 11-20	FEB 21-29	MAR 1-10	MAR 11-20	MAR 21-31	APR 1-10	APR 11-20	APR 21-30	MAY 1-10	MAY 11-20	MAY 21-31	JUN 1-10	JUN 11-20	JUN 21-30	JUL 1-10	JUL 11-20	JUL 21-31	AUG 1-10	AUG 11-20	AUG 21-31	SEP 1-10	SEP 11-20	SEP 21-30	OCT 1-10	OCT 11-20	OCT 21-31	NOV 1-10	NOV 11-20	NOV 21-30	DEC 1-10	DEC 11-20	DEC 21-31
4	10	15	1	1	1						1	10	2	1					2				8		1			13				2			

Rook *(Corvus frugilegus)*
Status: Vagrant (two records).

A description of one seen by V. A. D. Sales at Ahmadi on 30 March 1955 was submitted on a Rare Bird Report form and was accepted by the panel. The description is below:

'30.3.56 Rook like bird seen for a few minutes when it flew directly overhead and then out of view over the house.

Black with a bluish and greenish blue gloss with a suspicion of grey at the base of the bill.

The left leg was hanging apparently useless below the body.

A few minutes later it was seen again observed when the greyish area of the face was confirmed as it was rapidly drifting downward and before it was out of view.

N.B. My wife had reported seeing this bird on the 28th. It was again reported mentally [sic] to me on the 30th.'

On the same Rare Bird Report form the same observer described a dead and decomposing bird that he found on the beach at Kuwait Bay on 25 May 1963.

Brown-necked Raven *(Corvus ruficollis)*
Status: Scarce disperser in spring. Has bred.

According to the AHNFSG Newsletter 14 (1974) 'In 1969 N. Montford found a deserted nest in a wadi in the Zor Hills north of Kuwait Bay, which he tentatively identified as being a raven's nest ...'. The first definite record of this species, however, was of a pair seen by S. Howe at Jal Az-Zor on 10 March 1972. On 17 March of that year J. Webb and B. Brown found them breeding, with two young in a nest. Birds have subsequently nested there in 1974, 1978, 1991, 1999, 2000 and probably in other years. Brown-necked Ravens are best described as an irregular breeder in Kuwait.

After breeding the birds disperse away from the Jal Az-Zor area, and return in spring, having been seen at Ras Al-Ardh, Umm Ar-Rimam, East Doha, Jahra Farms, Fahaheel, Ras Subiya and near Wafra. For much of the year they are absent from the state, and are probably in Saudi Arabia or Iraq. Brown-necked Ravens are imported to be used as live bait in raptor traps. Some records may refer to escaped such birds.

JAN 1-10	JAN 11-20	JAN 21-31	FEB 1-10	FEB 11-20	FEB 21-29	MAR 1-10	MAR 11-20	MAR 21-31	APR 1-10	APR 11-20	APR 21-30	MAY 1-10	MAY 11-20	MAY 21-31	JUN 1-10	JUN 11-20	JUN 21-30	JUL 1-10	JUL 11-20	JUL 21-31	AUG 1-10	AUG 11-20	AUG 21-31	SEP 1-10	SEP 11-20	SEP 21-30	OCT 1-10	OCT 11-20	OCT 21-31	NOV 1-10	NOV 11-20	NOV 21-30	DEC 1-10	DEC 11-20	DEC 21-31
1	2		2	2	2	1																													

Common Starling *(Sturnus vulgaris)*
Status: Very common winter visitor. Common passage migrant.

Common Starlings are seen, sometimes in big flocks, at many sites, in winter or on passage. The highest daily count is 1000+ seen on many occasions, including 'A roost of 1-2000 at the Police Station in Fahad Al-Salem Street, Kuwait City on 24th November 1979' (Warr, undated). For many years the biggest flock was at the old camel market at Al-Atraf, but this has since been removed. Now, the largest flocks are seen in reedbeds at Jahra East Outfall.

JAN 1-10	JAN 11-20	JAN 21-31	FEB 1-10	FEB 11-20	FEB 21-29	MAR 1-10	MAR 11-20	MAR 21-31	APR 1-10	APR 11-20	APR 21-30	MAY 1-10	MAY 11-20	MAY 21-31	JUN 1-10	JUN 11-20	JUN 21-30	JUL 1-10	JUL 11-20	JUL 21-31	AUG 1-10	AUG 11-20	AUG 21-31	SEP 1-10	SEP 11-20	SEP 21-30	OCT 1-10	OCT 11-20	OCT 21-31	NOV 1-10	NOV 11-20	NOV 21-30	DEC 1-10	DEC 11-20	DEC 21-31
1000	500	50	300	8	2	11	3	1																			1			35	90		35		

Rosy Starling *(Sturnus roseus)*
Status: Scarce passage migrant. Rare summer visitor. Rare winter visitor.

This species is observed annually on passage through Kuwait. Records have been from Al-Abraq Al-Khabari, Wafra Oil Field, Zour Port, Sulaibiya and Kuwait City. The highest daily count is 28 seen by V. A. D. Sales at Ahmadi on 28 November 1964.

In 2001 a male and a female were seen by M. Shehab at Al-Abraq Al-Khabari on 31 May and 26 June. It is possible that these birds bred there.

JAN 1-10	JAN 11-20	JAN 21-31	FEB 1-10	FEB 11-20	FEB 21-29	MAR 1-10	MAR 11-20	MAR 21-31	APR 1-10	APR 11-20	APR 21-30	MAY 1-10	MAY 11-20	MAY 21-31	JUN 1-10	JUN 11-20	JUN 21-30	JUL 1-10	JUL 11-20	JUL 21-31	AUG 1-10	AUG 11-20	AUG 21-31	SEP 1-10	SEP 11-20	SEP 21-30	OCT 1-10	OCT 11-20	OCT 21-31	NOV 1-10	NOV 11-20	NOV 21-30	DEC 1-10	DEC 11-20	DEC 21-31
1												1	2	1							2	1	7	3	1										

Common Myna *(Acridotheres tristis)*
Status: Very common resident. Breeds.

This species has long been on sale in the main bird market at Al-Rai and in smaller markets. P. R. Haynes (1979) stated that occasional escapes were observed. W. A. Stuart wrote that on an unstated date, probably in the 1970s, 'One built a nest in a lamp standard in the middle of a busy main road alongside Kuwait Bay', but added 'As far as I know the nest came to nothing and the bird disappeared' (Warr, undated). J. N. B. Brown mentioned a 'Report of a group of Mynahs travelling on a ship from Abu Dhabi which flew off when it reached Kuwait' (Warr, undated).

The first record of breeding was by C. W. T. Pilcher in Kuwait City on 14 March 1981. Common Mynas have since spread and are now established breeding residents from Jahra Farms throughout Kuwait City down to Fahaheel and Ahmadi. The most common nest site is in tall lamp standards, but nests are sometimes made in spaces in buildings. The highest daily count is 'hundreds' on several occasions.

Bank Myna *(Acridotheres ginginianus)*
Status: Uncommon resident. Breeds.

Imported Bank Mynas have long been on sale in the main bird market at Al-Rai and in smaller markets. Unrecorded presumed escapes were probably observed on several occasions prior to the first recorded one seen by W. A. Stuart and C. W. T. Pilcher at an unstated location on 7-8 March 1980. From 1985 until at least 1989 up to ten were present in the grounds of the Orthopedic Hospital at Shuwaikh/Sulaibikhat. Other birds were recorded in Khaldiya, Jabriya, Rumaithiya, Salmiya, Sabah Al-Salem and what is now the Sabah Al-Ahmed Natural Reserve. From about 1991 to 2003 pairs nested in wells at the Abdulla Al-Habashi Farm in Jahra, peaking at about 100 pairs, which raised about 300 young, in 2001 (Gregory and Al-Nasrallah, 2001). The highest daily count is, therefore, about 500 on various dates in 2001 at or near the Abdulla Al-Habashi Farm in Jahra. In 2004, the main Jahra breeding colony appeared to have moved elsewhere, possibly to the inaccessible area at Jahra Ponds. Up to 15 birds have been recorded thereafter at Jahra Farms, Sabah Al-Salem and Kuwait City. In early March 2005 six birds started re-excavating nest holes in a well at the Abdullah Al-Habashi Farm at Jahra and the colony was clearly re-establishing itself there. Numbers of breeding birds clearly fluctuate in Kuwait.

House Sparrow *(Passer domesticus)*
Status: Abundant resident. Breeds.
This species has long been an established resident in Kuwait. It occurs and breeds everywhere where there are buildings, trees or bushes. The highest daily count is simply 'thousands' on many occasions.

Spanish Sparrow *(Passer hispaniolensis)*
Status: Very common winter visitor. Common resident. Breeds.
Spanish Sparrow is mostly a winter visitor to most sites with trees, bushes or reeds. The highest daily count is about 1500 seen by G. Gregory at Jahra Farms on 11 January 2002.

Colonies sometimes build nests and then abandon them without breeding. This behaviour was first observed in 1955, when V. A. D. Sales observed over 100 Spanish Sparrows, of which 24 pairs built nests from 6 February. Display and copulation were observed, but by 28 February the colony had deserted and had left the area. It was observed again in March 2004, when a small colony built nests, but then abandoned them, at the Sabah Al-Ahmed Natural Reserve.

On 1 May 1987 a hybrid male, paired with a House Sparrow (*P. domesticus*), entered the same nest at Umm Al-Aish, but there was no further evidence of breeding. The first confirmed breeding in Kuwait occurred in 2001 in what is now the Sabah Al-Ahmed Natural Reserve. A colony of c60 pure pairs commenced nest-building in February and the breeding cycle finished in April, with about 200 young fledging. Also about 10 hybrid Spanish x House Sparrow pairs bred nearby, producing c30 juveniles (Al-Jeriwi and Al-Mansoori, 2001). Other records in late spring of 2001 included five juveniles and an adult male at Abdali Farms on 17 May and one at Wafra Oil Field on 11 June. In 2002 about 50 pairs were seen entering domed nests at the Mohammed Al-Ajmi Farm at Abdali, and this species has been observed breeding there every year since. In 2004 breeding was confirmed at Jahra Farms, with a newly-fledged juvenile seen there on 13 May, and at Sabriya Farm, with three newly-fledged juveniles observed on 10 June.

JAN 1-10	JAN 11-20	JAN 21-31	FEB 1-10	FEB 11-20	FEB 21-29	MAR 1-10	MAR 11-20	MAR 21-31	APR 1-10	APR 11-20	APR 21-30	MAY 1-10	MAY 11-20	MAY 21-31	JUN 1-10	JUN 11-20	JUN 21-30	JUL 1-10	JUL 11-20	JUL 21-31	AUG 1-10	AUG 11-20	AUG 21-31	SEP 1-10	SEP 11-20	SEP 21-30	OCT 1-10	OCT 11-20	OCT 21-31	NOV 1-10	NOV 11-20	NOV 21-30	DEC 1-10	DEC 11-20	DEC 21-31
250	1500	500	100	100	10	35	300	100	275	8	10	100	50	6	3	2								1			200	50	25	100	500	60	500	400	

Dead Sea Sparrow *(Passer moabiticus)*
Status: Vagrant (three records).
Seven were seen and photographed at Jahra Pool Reserve by G. Gregory, C. W. T. Pilcher and S. T. Spencer on 1 November 1996. The description is below:

'At 9.45 a.m. GG observed a flock of 7 small passerines flying in towards the reed bed from the NW, while he, TS and CP were standing by the main area of open water at Jahra Pool. They appeared pale, and had an undulating flight, though not marked. One had a prominent white patch around the area of the greater secondary coverts on the right wing. In size they appeared smaller than, say, House or Spanish Sparrow. They landed in the reeds around the end of the old covered channel. After walking together down to this are, TS refound the birds, and GG quickly identified them as Dead Sea Sparrows, stating several features, including small black bib, which CP stated was pointed. GG then wrote a description, and took photographs, while TS ran back for his telescope. However, the birds had flown off before TS returned. The birds were repeatedly refound by GG, from call, in various places around the covered channel. 1 bright male, 2 other males, 4 females. Small, dumpy. Generally pale underneath; pale buffish brown above. Bills unremarkable brownish & visible legs no different. Males had small pointed black bib, pale buff/yellow on supercilium and in front of eye, dark brown streaks on back, whiteish tips to greater and median coverts and pale chestnut inbetween. Females had pale buff on supercilium and in front of eye, and off white tips to greater and median coverts. The prominent white patch observed in flight was unexplained, but could have represented feather loss, revealing white feathers below.'

A flock of 23 was seen and described by G. Gregory at Jahra Pool Reserve on 6 November 1998.

Two were photographed by K. Al-Ghanim at Jahra Pool Reserve on 6 October 2003.

Pale Rockfinch *(Petronia brachydactyla)*
Status: Uncommon passage migrant. Rare summer visitor. Has bred.

Pale Rockfinch has probably been seriously under-recorded in Kuwait. According to C. W. T. Pilcher (undated) there were only six records up to about 1995, although details are not accessible. Since then it has been recorded every year in small numbers on passage. Sightings have been at Bahra, Wafra Oil Field, Zour Port, Jahra Farms, Subiya, Sulaibikhat Nature Reserve and the Sabah Al-Ahmed Natural Reserve. The highest daily count outside the breeding season is eight seen by S. Holliday south of Sabah Al-Salem on 22 March 2000.

The first record of confirmed breeding was by S. T. Spencer and C. W. T. Pilcher at Bahra on 17 May 1996. Breeding was proven in that area at least seven more times up to 1 May 1998. However, it has not been confirmed since then in the state.

JAN 1-10	JAN 11-20	JAN 21-31	FEB 1-10	FEB 11-20	FEB 21-29	MAR 1-10	MAR 11-20	MAR 21-31	APR 1-10	APR 11-20	APR 21-30	MAY 1-10	MAY 11-20	MAY 21-31	JUN 1-10	JUN 11-20	JUN 21-30	JUL 1-10	JUL 11-20	JUL 21-31	AUG 1-10	AUG 11-20	AUG 21-31	SEP 1-10	SEP 11-20	SEP 21-30	OCT 1-10	OCT 11-20	OCT 21-31	NOV 1-10	NOV 11-20	NOV 21-30	DEC 1-10	DEC 11-20	DEC 21-31
					1	3	8		1						1									1	3									2	

Chestnut-shouldered Sparrow *(Petronia xanthocollis)*
Status: Uncommon passage migrant. Scarce summer visitor. Breeds.

The first record of Chestnut-shouldered Sparrow in Kuwait involved up to 16 birds seen at Ahmadi between 5 and 13 May 1966 by V. A. D. Sales. For many years there were only occasional sightings and P. R. Haynes (1979) listed this species as an accidental. With increased coverage recently it has been shown to be mostly an uncommon passage migrant, with a highest daily count of 48 seen by M. O. Chichester at Zour Port on 10 August 2000. Birds have been recorded at most sites with trees and bushes.

On 24 March and 28 April 2000 G. Gregory saw a male singing to a female in a huge old Tamarisk tree at Jahra Farms, but they were not seen subsequently. Breeding was first confirmed at Zour Port on 1 June 2000 by M. O. Chichester, who found a nest in a tall light tower (Chichester and Gregory, 2000). Fledglings were later seen and photographed. At least one pair has bred there in every subsequent year. Breeding has also been confirmed at Jahra Farms on 25 May 2001 and at the Sabah Al-Ahmed Natural Reserve in May 2004. Birds have also been seen in possible breeding habitat at Abdali Farms and at Sabriya Farm. It is possible that this species breeds undetected at other sites.

JAN 1-10	JAN 11-20	JAN 21-31	FEB 1-10	FEB 11-20	FEB 21-29	MAR 1-10	MAR 11-20	MAR 21-31	APR 1-10	APR 11-20	APR 21-30	MAY 1-10	MAY 11-20	MAY 21-31	JUN 1-10	JUN 11-20	JUN 21-30	JUL 1-10	JUL 11-20	JUL 21-31	AUG 1-10	AUG 11-20	AUG 21-31	SEP 1-10	SEP 11-20	SEP 21-30	OCT 1-10	OCT 11-20	OCT 21-31	NOV 1-10	NOV 11-20	NOV 21-30	DEC 1-10	DEC 11-20	DEC 21-31
							2	2	8	10	2	2	4	4	2	5	2	1			48	30	9	5											

Indian Silverbill *(Euodice malabarica)*
Status: Uncommon resident. Has bred.

This species is indigenous to eastern Arabia and has been extending its range along the Gulf coast towards Kuwait (Jennings, 1995). It is frequently on sale in bird markets in Kuwait, and the small population in the state probably derives mostly from escaped birds. Records have been from Ras Al-Ardh, Zour Port, Sabah Al-Salem, Doha, Al-Rai, Jahra Farms and the Sabah Al-Ahmed Natural Reserve. The highest daily count is 25 seen at Al-Rai by G. Gregory on 22 January 2004.

Breeding was first confirmed at Sabah Al-Salem on 11 June 2004 when G. Gregory observed two not-fully-grown juveniles accompanied by two adults. Breeding probably occurs at Doha, where up to 20 have been recorded repeatedly, and at several other sites, where birds have been seen carrying nesting materials.

Common Chaffinch *(Fringilla coelebs)*
Status: Rare winter visitor.

Common Chaffinch occurs about every other winter in Kuwait. Records have been from Ahmadi, Umm Al-Aish, Al-Abraq Al-Khabari, Jahra Farms and Wafra Farms. The highest daily count is nine seen by V. A. D. Sales at Ahmadi on 16 December 1958.

JAN 1-10	JAN 11-20	JAN 21-31	FEB 1-10	FEB 11-20	FEB 21-29	MAR 1-10	MAR 11-20	MAR 21-31	APR 1-10	APR 11-20	APR 21-30	MAY 1-10	MAY 11-20	MAY 21-31	JUN 1-10	JUN 11-20	JUN 21-30	JUL 1-10	JUL 11-20	JUL 21-31	AUG 1-10	AUG 11-20	AUG 21-31	SEP 1-10	SEP 11-20	SEP 21-30	OCT 1-10	OCT 11-20	OCT 21-31	NOV 1-10	NOV 11-20	NOV 21-30	DEC 1-10	DEC 11-20	DEC 21-31
1					1																											6			

Brambling *(Fringilla montifringilla)*
Status: Rare winter visitor.

Brambling was first recorded in Kuwait by V. A. D. Sales, who observed one at Ahmadi from 9 December 1953 to 18 February 1954. This observer had further records there from 17 to 28 November 1955 (one or two), 23 January 1957 (one), 7

February 1957 (one), 12 December 1957 to 26 February 1958 (one or two) and 23 November 1961 (one). P. R. Haynes saw one there on 22 November 1977. In most years from 1985 to 1995 there were small flocks of up to 15 birds (the highest daily count), from mid-November to mid-March, seen by C. W. T. Pilcher, M. Shehab, G. Gregory and S. T. Spencer at Al-Abraq Al-Khabari, Umm Al-Aish and Jahra Farms (Pilcher, undated). The last known record is of a bird seen at Jahra Farms by G. Gregory on 5 January 1996. This species is clearly of irregular occurrence in Kuwait.

European Goldfinch *(Carduelis carduelis)*
Status: Rare winter visitor and passage migrant.

The only accessible records of European Goldfinch in Kuwait are: at Ahmadi on 9 February 1962 (one), at Ahmadi from 30 December 1964 to 4 January 1964 (up to five), at Ahmadi on 16 December 1966 (one), at Ahmadi (photographed) in April 1970 or 1971 (one), at Ahmadi on 22 November 1978 (one), at Kuwait City on 12 March 1983, at Al-Abraq Al-Khabari on 30 November 1984, at Salwa on 27 October 1998 (one), at Jahra Farms on 23 November 2001 (one) and at the Sabah Al-Ahmed Natural Reserve on 20 May 2004. The observers included V. A. D. Sales, A. Caldwell, S. Howe, C. W. T. Pilcher, M. Shehab, G. Gregory, H. Al-Qallaf and K. Al-Nasrallah. There are known to be at least three other records, but details are not accessible.

JAN 1-10	JAN 11-20	JAN 21-31	FEB 1-10	FEB 11-20	FEB 21-29	MAR 1-10	MAR 11-20	MAR 21-31	APR 1-10	APR 11-20	APR 21-30	MAY 1-10	MAY 11-20	MAY 21-31	JUN 1-10	JUN 11-20	JUN 21-30	JUL 1-10	JUL 11-20	JUL 21-31	AUG 1-10	AUG 11-20	AUG 21-31	SEP 1-10	SEP 11-20	SEP 21-30	OCT 1-10	OCT 11-20	OCT 21-31	NOV 1-10	NOV 11-20	NOV 21-30	DEC 1-10	DEC 11-20	DEC 21-31
											1																	1		1					

European Siskin *(Carduelis spinus)*
Status: Rare winter visitor.

This species occurs almost every winter in Kuwait, with records from Ahmadi, Al-Abraq Al-Khabari, Kuwait City/Bay, Jahra Pool Reserve, Fahaheel Park and Jahra Farms. The highest daily count is 19 seen by G. Gregory and A. Al-Fadhel at Al-Abraq Al-Khabari on 19 December 2004.

JAN 1-10	JAN 11-20	JAN 21-31	FEB 1-10	FEB 11-20	FEB 21-29	MAR 1-10	MAR 11-20	MAR 21-31	APR 1-10	APR 11-20	APR 21-30	MAY 1-10	MAY 11-20	MAY 21-31	JUN 1-10	JUN 11-20	JUN 21-30	JUL 1-10	JUL 11-20	JUL 21-31	AUG 1-10	AUG 11-20	AUG 21-31	SEP 1-10	SEP 11-20	SEP 21-30	OCT 1-10	OCT 11-20	OCT 21-31	NOV 1-10	NOV 11-20	NOV 21-30	DEC 1-10	DEC 11-20	DEC 21-31
	5	2				1																					2	19			9	3			

Common Linnet *(Carduelis cannabina)*
Status: Rare winter visitor.

The first record of Common Linnet in Kuwait was of up to four males and two females seen by V. A. D. Sales at Ahmadi between 1 and 24 January 1965. P. R. Haynes recorded one at an unstated site on 11 December 1977. C. W. T. Pilcher (undated) mentioned a total of nine records up to about 1995, but details of the other seven are not accessible. M. Shehab saw one on 10 April 1987 (location not accessible). The KISR Bird Team observed one on Warba Island on 30 December 2003. Accordingly, the status given above is probably the best one.

JAN 1-10	JAN 11-20	JAN 21-31	FEB 1-10	FEB 11-20	FEB 21-29	MAR 1-10	MAR 11-20	MAR 21-31	APR 1-10	APR 11-20	APR 21-30	MAY 1-10	MAY 11-20	MAY 21-31	JUN 1-10	JUN 11-20	JUN 21-30	JUL 1-10	JUL 11-20	JUL 21-31	AUG 1-10	AUG 11-20	AUG 21-31	SEP 1-10	SEP 11-20	SEP 21-30	OCT 1-10	OCT 11-20	OCT 21-31	NOV 1-10	NOV 11-20	NOV 21-30	DEC 1-10	DEC 11-20	DEC 21-31
																																			1

Desert Finch *(Rhodospiza obsoleta)*
Status: Vagrant (four records).

One was seen by S. T. Spencer and C. W. T. Pilcher in the period between 1998 and 2002, but details are not accessible. Members of BMAPT photographed an adult female and a juvenile moulting into first-winter plumage in the Sabah Al-Ahmed Natural Reserve on 20 May 2004. G. Gregory observed a juvenile moulting into first-winter plumage at Jahra Farms on 11 June 2004. Both of these records indicated probable breeding in Kuwait, but the exact nesting site remained unknown. G. Gregory saw one at Al-Abraq Al-Khabari on 15 November 2004.

This species has been spreading in Arabia, and the colonisation of Kuwait seems imminent.

Trumpeter Finch *(Bucanetes githagineus)*
Status: Uncommon resident.

The first record of Trumpeter Finch in Kuwait involved two birds seen by V. A. D. Sales at Ahmadi on 15 November 1957. Birds have since been observed at many other sites, including Salmi/Wadi Al-Batin, near Umm Al-Aish, Manageesh, Zour Port, Wafra Oil Field, Kabd, Jal Az-Zor and the Sabah Al-Ahmed Natural Reserve. The highest daily count is ten seen by V. A. D. Sales at Ahmadi on 29 January 1958.

In recent years almost all records have been from two sites. The first is the Salmi/Wadi Al-Batin area. Two birds were seen there in 1999, two in 2001 and four in 2002. Breeding was reported as confirmed there on 16 February and 16 March 2001, and on 22 March 2002, with adult males feeding apparent juveniles. However, these reports were retracted later, as they were considered to have probably involved courtship feeding of adult females (Cowan, Pilcher and Spencer, 2004). Access there is now very difficult, but the habitat seems ideal for breeding by this species.

The second area is in the Sabah Al-Ahmed Natural Reserve. The provision of a drinking pool and the regeneration of vegetation have created ideal habitat for this species. Up to nine birds have repeatedly been seen along the part of the Jal Az-Zor escarpment inside the reserve, and this species is now considered to be resident there. Breeding probably occurs there, but has not yet been proven.

Common Rosefinch *(Carpodacus erythrinus)*
Status: Scarce passage migrant.

This species probably occurs annually in small numbers but is no doubt under-recorded. All sightings have been from areas with trees and bushes. The first record was of a single bird seen by N. Montfort and S. Howe at Jal Az-Zor on 15 March 1971. The highest daily count is four seen by M. O. Chichester and J. Gaskell at Jahra Farms on 23 September 2001.

JAN 1-10	JAN 11-20	JAN 21-31	FEB 1-10	FEB 11-20	FEB 21-29	MAR 1-10	MAR 11-20	MAR 21-31	APR 1-10	APR 11-20	APR 21-30	MAY 1-10	MAY 11-20	MAY 21-31	JUN 1-10	JUN 11-20	JUN 21-30	JUL 1-10	JUL 11-20	JUL 21-31	AUG 1-10	AUG 11-20	AUG 21-31	SEP 1-10	SEP 11-20	SEP 21-30	OCT 1-10	OCT 11-20	OCT 21-31	NOV 1-10	NOV 11-20	NOV 21-30	DEC 1-10	DEC 11-20	DEC 21-31
									1														1			4	2								

Yellowhammer *(Emberiza citrinella)*
Status: Vagrant (one record).

A female was seen and photographed by Musaad Al-Saleh at Heraijah on 14.3.2002 (1st Kuwait record). The description is below:
'On 14 March MS was photographing birds at Heraijah, northern Kuwait. He took two photographs of an *Emberiza*-type bunting. After G. Gregory and others observed the photographs, the bird was identified as a second-year Yellowhammer.
Size and Shape: No direct comparison, but appears as a medium-size bunting, with typical Emberiza shape.
Upper parts: Forehead and crown streaked pale and medium brown. Lores pale buffish-brown. Long wide pale yellowish buff supercilium extending to just above neck. Yellowish-buff eye-ring. Fairly wide medium brownish eye-stripe extending to back of ear coverts. Cheeks and ear coverts medium-pale greyish-brown, adjoining slightly darker moustachial stripe which extended below ear-coverts as a wider darker patch. Semi-prominent yellowish-buff patch at rear of ear-coverts. Back of neck olive-brown with fairly narrow darker streaks. Mantle and scapulars buffish-brown widely streaked darker brownish, and with suggestion of paler 'braces'. Rump not visible. Most of upper tail coverts not visible, but bases appear brownish with possible rufous tint. Lesser secondary coverts olive brown with paler tips and edges. Median secondary coverts with very dark brown spade-shaped centres, edged and tipped pale yellowish buff. Greater secondary coverts centrally slightly dark brown, edged buffish, tipped buffish-white. Alula dark brown edged paler. Primary coverts medium brownish, edged paler. Primaries and secondaries medium brownish thinly edged and tipped pale. Tertials medium/dark brownish, tipped and edged buffish-brown. Tail dark brownish, with buffish-brown tips and edges, except for some white in outer webs of outer tail feathers.
Under parts: Chin and throat pale yellowish-white with dark brown malar streaks and slight 'gorget'. Breast pale yellowish white with numerous medium width, olive-brown streaks thinning on lower breast. Belly pale yellowish-white. Flanks and thighs pale yellowish-white with some olive-brown streaks. Undertail coverts pale yellowish white. Under wing and undertail not visible.
Exposed parts: Bill greyish, paler around cutting edge of base. Eye dark. Legs pinkish-brown, with apparently darker, more greyish feet and dark curved claws.'
There have been previous records of this species: in September 1978, 16 April 1977 and 15 December 1978. However, no thorough descriptions were written, and there is the possibility of confusion with other species, including Cinereous Bunting (*E. cineracea*) and Pine Bunting (*E. leucocephalos*).

Rock Bunting *(Emberiza cia)*
Status: Vagrant (two records).
A description of one seen by V. A. D. Sales at Ahmadi on 24-26 March 1966 was submitted on a Rare Bird Report form and was accepted by the panel. The description is below:
'24.3.66 Bunting seen briefly with white and black head.
26.3.66 Bunting seen again. White and black striped head most conspicuous but at a distance appeared greyish. Mantle black brownish/chestnut ?streaked, lower back and rump lighter. Under parts: chin, throat, upper breast greyish, remainder buffish, pale chestnut. Tail dark brown, white on outer pair. Wings dark brown with lighter fringes, colour not readily discernible, narrow lightish wing bar.
Bird actively feeding in the grass and only occasionally perched on grass tops before returning to the ground and some stones.
Head never the less distinctive.'
V. A. D. Sales also saw one bird at Ahmadi on 1 March 1967. This record was accepted by F. E. Warr (undated).

Cinereous Bunting *(Emberiza cineracea)*
Status: Scarce passage migrant.
Cinereous Buntings probably occur annually in Kuwait on passage. Most sightings have been in spring. The first record, and highest daily count, was of a maximum of four males and three females seen at Ahmadi by V. A. D. Sales from 27 March to 14 April 1968. Other records are: at Kashman from 27 March to 26 April 1973 (2-3), Araifjan on 25 May 1973, Umm Al-Aish on 10 April 1981 (one), Sabah Al-Salem on unknown dates in 1994 (one female) and 1996 (one male), Wafra Oil Field on 31 August 1998 (one), Subiya on 5 April 1999 (one), Tulha on 23 April 1999 (one female), Jahra Bay on 18 March 2000 (one male) and on 20 September (year not accessible), Sabah Al-Salem on 29-30 March 2000 (three males), Zour Port on 30 March 2000 (1 or 2), Wadi Ar-Rimam on 31 March 2000 (two), Qaisat on 23 September 2000 (one), Jal Az-Zor on 28 March 2001 (one), Abu Halifa on 31 March 2002 (one male) and the Sabah Al-Ahmed Natural Reserve on 3 March 2005 and from 19 to at least 26 March 2004 (up to three). The observers included V. A. D. Sales, M. Leven, E. Grieve, S. T. Spencer, M. Shehab, S. Holliday, G. Gregory, P. Robertson, H. Al-Qallaf and K. Al-Nasrallah.

JAN 1-10	JAN 11-20	JAN 21-31	FEB 1-10	FEB 11-20	FEB 21-29	MAR 1-10	MAR 11-20	MAR 21-31	APR 1-10	APR 11-20	APR 21-30	MAY 1-10	MAY 11-20	MAY 21-31	JUN 1-10	JUN 11-20	JUN 21-30	JUL 1-10	JUL 11-20	JUL 21-31	AUG 1-10	AUG 11-20	AUG 21-31	SEP 1-10	SEP 11-20	SEP 21-30	OCT 1-10	OCT 11-20	OCT 21-31	NOV 1-10	NOV 11-20	NOV 21-30	DEC 1-10	DEC 11-20	DEC 21-31
						1	3	3	1		1														1	1									

Ortolan Bunting *(Emberiza hortulana)*
Status: Common passage migrant.
This species is commonly seen in spring and autumn at most sites. The highest daily count is an exceptional 400+ seen at Ahmadi by V. A. D. Sales on 18 April 1959. C. W. T. Pilcher and others have noted that Ortolan Buntings have very variable plumage, and that some are rather like Grey-necked Bunting (*Emberiza buchanani*) and Cretzschmar's Bunting (*Emberiza caesia*) (Warr, undated).

Rustic Bunting *(Emberiza rustica)*

Status: Vagrant (one record).

A description of two males seen by V. A. D. Sales at Ahmadi on 9 May 1953 was submitted on a Rare Bird Report form and was accepted by the referees. The description is below:

'**Plumage:** Bunting - quite striking with black and white head the same size as H. Sparrow. Crown and nape black with a suspicion at crest. Side of Head - lores black, distinct white stripe behind eye and over ear coverts. Ear coverts sooty black. Chin and sides of neck white. Mantle and rump chestnut brown ? slightly streaked. Tail - blackish with outer web of outer pair white. Under parts off-white with rusty chestnut breast band. Wing - primaries blackish with lighter edges, secondaries with broader buff edges and tips. Greater wing coverts with lighter tips forming narrow wing bar. Lesser coverts similar but wing bar less distinct buffish. Some chestnut flecks on sides of breast.

Legs - dull, reddish. Bill - dark horn, smaller and not so stout as sparrow. Iris - dark brown.

A second bird also present but not quite so distinctly marked.'

Little Bunting *(Emberiza pusilla)*

Status: Rare winter visitor and passage migrant.

Little Buntings probably occur in most years in Kuwait, but are under-recorded. The first record was of a single bird seen at Jal Az-Zor by M. Shehab on 30 October 1984. Further records included single birds at Al-Abraq Al-Khabari between 1985 and 1987, Umm Al-Aish on 3 October 1986, Qaisat in November 1986, Jabriya in November 1987, Sabah Al-Salem on 11 October 2001, Zour Port on 7 December 2001, Sabah Al-Salem on 15 January 2002, and two birds seen and photographed by E. Ramadan in the Sabah Al-Ahmed Natural Reserve on 20 May 2004. Exact dates are not accessible for some of these records. There are known to be at least four other records, but the details are not accessible. Accordingly, the status given above is probably the best one.

Common Reed Bunting *(Emberiza schoeniclus)*
Status: Rare winter visitor.
Most of the data for this species are not accessible. M. Shehab saw one at Jal Az-Zor on 16 October 1994. C. W. T. Pilcher (undated) stated that there eight records up to about 1995. At least two of these records involved single birds seen at Jahra Pool Reserve by M. Shehab, C. W. T. Pilcher and G. Gregory between 1985 and 1989. One female/juvenile was observed by A. Bailey and G. Gregory at Jahra East Outfall on 19 October 2001. A single bird was seen and photographed by K. Al-Ghanim and others at Jahra Pool Reserve in mid February 2005. Accordingly, the status given above is probably the best one.

Red-headed Bunting *(Emberiza bruniceps)*
Status: Rare passage migrant and winter visitor.
The first record of this species in Kuwait involved a single bird seen by C. W. T. Pilcher and M. Shehab at an unstated location on 3 September 1982. One was observed and described by M. O. Chichester and J. Gaskell at Wafra Oil Field on 31 August 1998. One was seen by S. T. Spencer and C. W. T. Pilcher at an unstated location on 13 January 2001. A first-year bird was seen and photographed by K. Al-Ghanim at Jahra Pool Reserve on 6 October 2003. A male was seen by P. Fagel in the Sabah Al-Ahmed Natural Reserve on 13 May 2005. There are known to be at least seven more records, some supported by photographs, but the dates are not accessible. In the circumstances, the status given above is probably the best one.

Black-headed Bunting *(Emberiza melanocephala)*
Status: Scarce passage migrant. Rare winter visitor.
Black-headed Buntings are probably present every year in Kuwait. All birds have been in spring or autumn, except for a female seen at Ahmadi on 31 January 1956 by V. A. D. Sales. The first record was of up to two seen at Ahmadi by V. A. D. Sales from 15-29 August 1953. The highest daily count is 20+ seen by members of BMAPT at Tulha in the Sabah Al-Ahmed Natural Reserve in late August 2005. Other records have been from Al-Abraq Al-Khabari, the Sabah Al-Ahmed Natural Reserve, Zour Port, Jahra Pool Reserve and Jahra Farms. There have been a number of photographs of this species

taken in the last five years, but not all dates are accessible. A specimen of an old female found dead in what is now the Sabah Al-Ahmed Natural Reserve by G. Gregory and P. Robertson is now in the British Museum.

JAN 1-10	JAN 11-20	JAN 21-31	FEB 1-10	FEB 11-20	FEB 21-29	MAR 1-10	MAR 11-20	MAR 21-31	APR 1-10	APR 11-20	APR 21-30	MAY 1-10	MAY 11-20	MAY 21-31	JUN 1-10	JUN 11-20	JUN 21-30	JUL 1-10	JUL 11-20	JUL 21-31	AUG 1-10	AUG 11-20	AUG 21-31	SEP 1-10	SEP 11-20	SEP 21-30	OCT 1-10	OCT 11-20	OCT 21-31	NOV 1-10	NOV 11-20	NOV 21-30	DEC 1-10	DEC 11-20	DEC 21-31
							2			1												2	1	1											

Corn Bunting *(Miliaria calandra)*

Status: Common winter visitor. Uncommon passage migrant.

This species is a regularly observed, usually in flocks, in winter and on passage at many sites, which have included Ahmadi, Qaisat, Sulaibiya, Chedadiah, Abdali, Al-Abraq Al-Khabari, Umm Al-Aish, Sabah Al-Salem, East Doha and Jahra Farms. The highest daily count is 184 seen by S. T. Spencer and C. W. T. Pilcher at Jahra Pool Reserve on 4 January 2002.

JAN 1-10	JAN 11-20	JAN 21-31	FEB 1-10	FEB 11-20	FEB 21-29	MAR 1-10	MAR 11-20	MAR 21-31	APR 1-10	APR 11-20	APR 21-30	MAY 1-10	MAY 11-20	MAY 21-31	JUN 1-10	JUN 11-20	JUN 21-30	JUL 1-10	JUL 11-20	JUL 21-31	AUG 1-10	AUG 11-20	AUG 21-31	SEP 1-10	SEP 11-20	SEP 21-30	OCT 1-10	OCT 11-20	OCT 21-31	NOV 1-10	NOV 11-20	NOV 21-30	DEC 1-10	DEC 11-20	DEC 21-31
184			6	2	3	40	7	2		2	1																1		1			1			18

(b) THE SPECIES OF BIRDS OF CAPTIVE ORIGIN

The Species of Birds of Captive Origin are those species whose occurrence is judged to involve, either certainly or probably, only deliberately released or escaped individuals of species which have bred or been recorded in the wild elsewhere in the OSME region, but which are not established breeders in Kuwait.

Chukar *(Alectoris chukar)*

Single birds were observed by V. A. D. Sales at Ahmadi on 29 January 1959 and on 22 March 1967 (Sales, undated). This species has been on sale in the main bird market at Al-Rai, and some birds are kept in private collections. The nearest breeding populations are in the highlands of Iran, Oman, the United Arab Emirates and northeast Saudi Arabia. It is a resident that performs only local movements. The records above clearly involved escapes.

See-see Partridge *(Ammoperdix griseogularis)*

A female with damaged plumage was captured by two labourers at Kabd on 8 July 1999, and was later seen by P. Cowan (Cowan, 2000a). This species has been on sale in the main bird market. The nearest breeding populations are in the highlands of Iraq and Iran, and only limited winter dispersal is known. The Kabd bird was, beyond any reasonable doubt, an escape.

Black Francolin *(Francolinus francolinus)*

A male was seen in the coastal section of what is now the Sabah Al-Ahmed Natural Reserve by O. Schroeder, S. Schroeder and G. Østerø on 14 March 2001. Their description reads as follows:

'OS, SS and GØ were crossing the area of scrub in the dunes of the coastal section of the National Park on 14 March 2001, when they disturbed a bird with the car. It was seen on the ground 3m from the car, flew away very low and then ran into the scrub again 35m away from the observers, who waited half an hour, but never saw the bird again.

Size and Shape: A large, stump-tailed partridge.
Plumage: Mostly black or blackish with a rufous neck-ring and a distinct white spot behind the eye.
Exposed Parts: Not clearly seen.
Range: From 3m to 35m.
Time of Observation: About 20 seconds at most.
Previous Experience: The observers have never seen this species before, but used Birds of the Middle East to identify the bird.'

This was possibly a wild bird since this species occurs in the lowlands of southeast Iraq, and there are two or three records from the Eastern Province of Saudi Arabia, probably of naturally occurring wild birds (Bundy, Connor and Harrison, 1989). However, it has been on sale in the main bird market, and there is some possibility of captive origin.

Grey Crowned Crane *(Balearica regulorum)*

An individual of this African species was shot and captured at Zour in early September 2001, and later was seen and photographed by G. Gregory, K. Al-Nasrallah and M. O. Chichester. Another was shot and captured in northern Kuwait in 2004, and was then kept at Sulaibikhat Nature Reserve. Both presumably originated from the feral colony on Sir Bani Yas Island in the United Arab Emirates, or possibly from a private collection or zoo elsewhere.

Bruce's Green Pigeon *(Treron waalia)*

In spring 2001 two unfamiliar pigeons were seen by Kuwaiti hunters at Al-Abraq Al-Khabari. One escaped but the other was shot. It was later shown to M. Shehab, who identified it as a Bruce's Green Pigeon, and photographed it.

This species is resident in south and south-west Arabia, with numbers augmented by summer migrants from Africa, which could possibly overshoot and reach Kuwait. It has not been seen on sale in the bird markets in Kuwait. Al-Abraq Al-Khabari is a remote and isolated oasis in the west of Kuwait. Both these considerations indicate a wild origin for these birds. However, there is some possibility that they were escapes.

Alexandrine Parakeet *(Psittacula eupatria)*

This exotic species has been seen on several occasions in Kuwait, but the only accessible record is of a bird seen and described by A. Bailey at Shaab on 20 September 2001. It may breed in various parts of Arabia (Jennings, 1992). However, it has been on sale in the main bird market, and all Kuwait records are considered to involve local escapes.

Budgerigar *(Melopsittacus undulatus)*

Budgerigars, of various colours, are occasionally seen flying around Kuwait City and other areas. This exotic species has bred occasionally in other parts of Arabia (Jennings, 1986a). However, it is often on sale in bird markets, and is widely kept as a pet. All records in Kuwait clearly involve local escapes.

Yellow-vented Bulbul *(Pycnonotus xanthopygos)*

Two birds were seen on 6 April 1989, but the location and observers were unstated (Pilcher, undated).

One was seen by J. Gaskell and M. O. Chichester at Green Island on 23 and 24 September 1998. The latter observer's description is below:

'Size and Shape: Similar in size and build to the ubiquitous White-cheeked Bulbul [White-eared Bulbul *(Pycnonotus leucogenys)*]. Fairly long, unmarked tail. Its crown and nape was puffy and scruffy when the bird was agitated as though it was trying to raise a non-existent crest. WCBU [White-eared Bulbuls] often have this same look.
Head: Blackish about the face with a whitish eye ring. The head faded to a sooty brown on the crown and nape.
Upper Parts: Sooty brown including the wings. The wings were unmarked with no discernible pale edges or other distinctive markings.
Under Parts: Grey-brown. The area of the under tail coverts behind the legs was lemon yellow.
Bare Parts: Bill - black (curved culmen - slightly decurved bill shape). Eyes - black. Legs - black.
Vocalizations: Silent.
Behaviour: Active feeding and foraging on the ground, in a small hedge and in a dense tree.'

This species is resident in many parts of Arabia, but not in Kuwait. It has been recorded as a vagrant in Iraq, perhaps breeding, and could possibly colonise Kuwait in the future. It has been on sale in the main bird market, and captive origin for the Kuwait records is likely.

Bearded Reedling *(Panurus biarmicus)*

A pair was seen by B. Wright at Jahra Pool Reserve on 11 February 1994 (Wright, 1994), and by M. Shehab there the same day and on 11 March 1994. S. T. Spencer recorded single birds there on 28 August 1999 and at Sabah Al-Salem on 20 April 2002.

This species breeds in Turkey and Syria (Tavares, Sá Pessoa and Brito Y Abreu, 2000), and is a rare or irregular winter visitor to Iran, Cyprus and Israel. It is occasionally on sale in batches of up to 100 birds in the main bird market in Kuwait, and is kept in private collections. The above Kuwait records could have involved wild birds, but there is a distinct possibility that they involved escapes.

Black Drongo *(Dicrurus macrocercus)*

A single bird was seen and photographed on 24 December 1992, but the location and observers were unstated (Pilcher, undated).

Black Drongos formerly bred in southeast Iran, and they are rare in the United Arab Emirates and accidental in Oman. They have been on sale in the main bird market, and the record above probables involved a local escape.

Common Magpie *(Pica pica)*

A single bird, originally found by an American horticulturalist, was present in various parks in Kuwait City from 5 November 1998 to 26 November 1989.
This species breeds in the highlands of northern Iraq and Iran, and disperses in winter to southern Iraq. The above bird was perhaps wild but could have been an escape, despite it not having been seen on sale in the bird markets.

Wattled Starling *(Creatophora cineracea)*

One was photographed by K. Al-Ghanim at Jahra Pool Reserve in April 2001.
Wattled Starling is an African species that occurs occasionally in southwestern Arabia, Dhofar and Masirah Island. It is sometimes on sale in the main bird market and is kept in several private collections in Kuwait. The above record, beyond all reasonable doubt, involved a local escape.

Brahminy Myna *(Sturnus pagodarum)*

Single birds were seen by G. Gregory at Jahra Farms on 5 February 1999, and by G. Gregory and P. Robertson at Hujaijah on 10 May 1999.
This exotic species has bred in Dubai (Jennings, 1994). It has not been seen on sale in the bird markets, but the Kuwait records clearly involved local escapes.

Streaked Weaver *(Ploceus manyar)*

S. T. Spencer recorded this species singing at Sabah Al-Salem several times in 1998. In 2002 a male, seen by many observers, sang there for months from 16 March, and a male and a female were seen there on 27 September. In 2003 a male sang there for months from April onwards. No other evidence of breeding was obtained.
In Arabia this species is a scarce but widespread exotic, which has bred at Riyadh and probably in the United Arab Emirates (Jennings, 1995). It has been on sale in the main bird market in Kuwait. The birds at Sabah Al-Salem could have arrived from outside Kuwait, but also could have been local escapes

Red Avadavat *(Amandava amandava)*

A male flew over Sabah Al-Salem on 13 May 2002, a pair flew over Pipeline Beach on 25 April 2003, a male was in reeds at Sabah Al-Salem on 13 June 2004, and one was at South Doha Nature Reserve on 2 May 2005. The observers were G. Gregory, B. Settles, S. Carter-Brown and P. Fagel.
This species is a widespread but not often recorded exotic which has bred at Riyadh and probably in Bahrain and Sharjah (Jennings, 1995). It is often on sale in the bird markets and the Kuwait records probably involved local escapes.

Zebra Waxbill *(Amandava subflava)*

A tame female (or possibly immature male) was seen by G. Gregory at Salwa on 24 May 1999.
This species breeds in Yemen, where it was possibly introduced. It has been on sale in the main bird market in Kuwait, and the Salwa bird was obviously an escape.

(c) THE SPECIES OF BIRDS REQUIRING CONFIRMATION

The Species of Birds Requiring Confirmation are those species which have been published or stated as occurring in Kuwait, but about whose records there is at least some justifiable doubt.

Ostrich *(Struthio camelus)*

The Arabian subspecies of Ostrich (*S. c. syriacus*) has long been extinct, no doubt due to the advent of four-wheel-drive vehicles used for hunting. However, fragments of Ostrich eggs have been discovered in Kuwait at least since about 1970. J. N. B. Brown and J. Webb found a 'piece of a possible fossil egg shell' at Mufattah, and W. A. Stuart observed 'an almost complete egg in the [ANHFSG] work room' and recorded that he found 'many fragments of shell within half a mile of Ahmadi and those should be in the work room' (Warr, undated). However, M. C. Jennings (1986d; personal communications to G. Gregory) has advised that presence of fragments of eggs or even entire eggs is not definite evidence of past breeding, and that the almost complete egg in the work room originated in Saudi Arabia. In Kuwait at present there are four Ostrich farms and several private collections of Ostriches, called locally 'red-necked' and 'black-necked' birds. However, there is no reintroduction scheme in the state.

Lesser White-fronted Goose *(Anser erythropus)*

C. W. T. Pilcher (undated) lists the only record as being 'Two birds in January or February 1982'. However, no description of these birds was written or is available, and the date is vague. Confusion with White-fronted Goose (*A. albifrons*), more likely to occur, is possible.

Fulvous Whistling Duck *(Dendrocygna bicolor)*

A record of a single bird seen at Doha Port on 6 April 1999 by H-M. Busch, J. Rathberger-Knan and W. Bindl was not accompanied by a description and would, in any case, most likely have involved an escaped bird.

Long-tailed Duck *(Clangula hyemalis)*

The only record, which appeared in the 'Around the Region' section of OSME *Bulletin* 29 (Autumn 1992), of this species in Kuwait, by A. Ross, was of a female in summer plumage, off Shuwaikh (no date given). This record was rejected by KORC.

Common Scoter *(Melanitta nigra)*

A raft of 200 'all-black' birds was seen by S. Howe, who believed that they were 'possibly' Common Scoter, from a dhow between Ras Al-Ardh and Failaka Island on 6 November 1970. This record was listed by the ANHFSG (undated) as being of this species. However, later, the observer believed that the birds could have been Coots (*Fulica atra*). P. R. Haynes (1979) stated 'Unlikely - only record may have been Coot'.

A large group of Common Scoters would normally contain some browner females/juveniles.

Velvet Scoter *(Melanitta fusca)*

A record of 'Two, locality unknown, 10 January. C. W. T. Pilcher, MaShehab [sic]' appeared in the 'Around the Region' section of OSME *Bulletin* 29 (Autumn 1992), and was later described (Pilcher and Shehab, 1994). However, in a personal communication to G. Gregory, M. Shehab stated that he had not seen the birds and was not involved with the record. Confusion, in bad light conditions, with a pair of Gadwall (*Anas strepera*), which were observed repeatedly in the same spot afterwards, seems likely. A record of a group of Velvet Scoters in Bahrain (the only other Gulf record) was rejected, no doubt for the same reason.

Wilson's Storm-Petrel *(Oceanites oceanicus)*

M. Dryden (1982) wrote that he saw a small flock of storm-petrels with black legs at sea on a trip to Kubbar Island. However, there are insufficient details for a specific identification. Wilson's Storm-Petrel is the most likely species to occur, but confirmation is required before adding it to the Kuwait bird list.

African Darter *(Anhinga rufa)*

This species was recorded by both the ANHFSG (1975) and by P. R. Haynes (1979) as being seen at Mufattah in March 1969.

S. Howe stated 'One 95% certain observed by Etchécopar/Montford (March 1969) near Umm Al Maradim, our only record'. However, R. D. Etchécopar said that he had not seen the bird and was not even in Kuwait until mid-April 1969 (Warr, undated).

The identities of the bird and of the observer(s) are clearly uncertain.

Indian Pond Heron *(Ardeola grayii)*

This species was said by R. Meinertzhagen (1954) and by F. Hue and R. D. Etchécopar (1970) to occur in Kuwait. It was listed by the AHNFSG (1975) as being seen by R. D. Etchécopar at Kuwait City/Bay, with no date stated. However, this ornithologist stated that 'I have never seen it' (Warr, undated). H. Heinzel, R. Fitter and J. Parslow (1979) listed it as occurring in 'Mangroves in Kuwait', but there were no mangroves in Kuwait at that time (they have since been reintroduced, but are still small).

A record of three birds seen by P. W. G. Chilman on 13 March 1977 flying low over the water between Kubbar Island and the mainland was submitted on a Rare Bird report form, but was rejected by the panel.

There are no available descriptions, if indeed any were written, supporting various further records of this species in Kuwait.

All claims of the occurrence of this species in Kuwait clearly involve an incorrect assumption that it must occur or confusion with Squacco Heron (*A. ralloides*).

Goliath Heron *(Ardea goliath)*

There have been a number of reports of this species, which maintains, or maintained, a small population in the marshes of southern Iraq. These include: two at Araifjan on 12 January 1973, nine off Ras Al-Ardh on 19 September 1973, one at Kuwait City on 23 December 1973, 30 near Mina Saud on 12 April 1974, one off Ras Al-Ardh on 10 May 1974 and four near Fintas on 17 April 1977. No thorough descriptions were written and confusion with Purple Herons (*A. purpurea*) is likely.

Red Kite *(Milvus milvus)*

Records of one at Ahmadi on 16 March 1954 and two there on 28 February 1955 were submitted by V. A. D. Sales on a Rare Bird Report form. These records were accepted by two of the panel but rejected by a third. A record of one seen by J. P. Hunt at Sulaibikhat on 28 April, who recorded no Black Kites (*M. migrans*), was rejected by the panel (Warr, undated). This species was not listed by the ANHFSG (1975), but appeared in P. R. Hayne's list (1979).

All these records probably involve confusion with the 'Black-eared' subspecies (*M. migrans lineatus*) of Black Kite.

Tawny Eagle *(Aquila rapax)*

The computer list of the ANHFSG (1975) contains records of single birds seen at Ahmadi by S. Howe and R. Stafford on 19 November 1971, at Ahmadi by R. P. Blacker on 3 March 1972, and at Khadima by 'BDTG' on 28 March 1974. No thorough descriptions were written, and there is the distinct possibility of confusion with juveniles of various other species of *Aquila*.

Eleonora's Falcon *(Falco eleonorae)*

Records of two at Ahmadi on 24 March 1966 and one to four there on 22-24 April 1966 were submitted by V. A. D. Sales on a Rare Bird Report form, and this record, although rejected by the panel, was listed by the ANHFSG (1975). A bird possibly of this species was seen by G. Nicholls on 17 May 1975, but he later stated 'I am happy for this to be rejected' (Warr, undated). P. R. Haynes (1979) listed the species as an 'Accidental or rare Passage Migrant', but commented that the records were 'open to doubt'.

It seems most probable that these records refer to Sooty Falcons (*F. concolor*), which have been recorded six times in Kuwait in recent years.

European Golden Plover *(Pluvialis apricaria)*

All or almost all of the Kuwait records of this species probably refer to Pacific Golden Plover (*P. fulva*), which is now regularly recorded in all Gulf states. (The former Lesser Golden Plover (*P. dominica*) was recently split in two species, and Pacific Golden Plover is the one which occurs in Kuwait. European Golden Plover was commonly called just 'Golden Plover' in the past.)

Kuwait records of European Golden Plover include ten records in 1971, four in 1972, one in 1973 and one in 1974. On 15 December 1977 L. Corrall recorded one 'Golden or Lesser Golden Plover' at Prison Pool. C. W. T. Pilcher wrote of European Golden Plover in Kuwait: 'Vagrant. I have seen Golden Plovers on two occasions only and on the first there was no doubt about their being Golden Plovers. More recently a single bird recorded as Golden Plover but could have been Lesser' (Warr, undated). None of these records is supported by an adequate description, if indeed any was written, and it is best to regard all of them as requiring confirmation.

Purple Sandpiper *(Calidris maritima)*

Purple Sandpiper is extremely unlikely to occur in Kuwait. All or most of the past records of this species, regarded as rejected by F. E. Warr (undated), most likely refer to Great Knot (*Calidris tenuirostris*): 18 January 1963 (one), 2 February 1967 (one), 21 April 1969 (one), an unstated date in 1970 (one) and 15 March 1972 (one). All of these birds were seen in Kuwait Bay; the observers were J. Webb, J. D. Etchécopar and V. A. D. Sales. More recent records, some involving quite high numbers, clearly involve confusion with other species of waders.

Great Skua *(Stercorarius skua)*

There is one record of Great Skua on 1 July, year unstated, off Salmiya seen by J. P. Hunt. He described it as 'A large uniform brown skua.' However, he later wrote that 'It is possible that I confused the bird with the Arctic Skua but the reference was to "large" ' (Warr, undated).

Details are lacking and identification is clearly uncertain. A large skua in Kuwait would most probably not be of this species, but of one of the southern forms.

Herring Gull *(Larus argentatus)*
Until recently, all records of large, pale-backed, white-headed gulls in Kuwait were listed as 'Herring Gull (*Larus argentatus*)'. This former species has now been split into a number of new species. There are no acceptable records of the modern species, Herring Gull, in Kuwait.

Armenian Gull *(Larus armenicus)*
There have been numerous records of this species in Kuwait. However, no convincing description has ever been produced, and confusion with Baraba Gulls (*L. fuscus barabensis*) or Caspian Gulls (*L. cachinnans*) with dark bill-bands, seems likely. W. R. P. Bourne, in a personal communication to G. Gregory, stated that Armenian Gulls have a preference for freshwater habitats, and that there were several confirmed records from Iraqi rivers. It is possible that this species has occurred in Kuwait, but confirmation is needed before it can be included in the Kuwait bird list.

Iceland Gull *(Larus glaucoides)*
C. W. T. Pilcher wrote of this species: 'Vagrant. Recorded and photographed by J. Bradley in 1981 or 1982', and later stated that it 'had a red eye-ring'. G. Bundy commented that 'L. cachinnans has a red eye-ring. All-white wings could have been due to wear' (Warr, undated).

Confusion with a Caspian Gull (*L. cachinnans*), with heavily worn primaries, seems likely.

Great Black-backed Gull *(Larus marinus)*
There have been numerous records of this species in Kuwait, in each of the years 1964 to 1974 (except for 1969), and in 1983 and 1984. This species is very unlikely to occur in Kuwait, and clearly there was confusion with the dark-backed Baltic subspecies of Lesser Black-backed Gull (*L. fuscus fuscus*).

Black-legged Kittiwake *(Rissa tridactyla)*
This species is referred to as 'Accidental. Single bird - spring 1991' by C. W. T. Pilcher (undated). However, no description is accessible or was written. There is the possibility of confusion with Little Gull (*L. minutu*s), more likely to occur.

Roseate Tern *(Sterna dougalli)*
A description of a single bird seen by V. A. D. Sales was submitted on a Rare Bird Report form but was rejected by the panel, since the possibility of it being a Common Tern (*S. hirundo*) or Arctic Tern (*S. paradisaea*) was not eliminated.

Tawny Owl *(Strix aluco)*
In the Ahmadi Natural History and Field Studies Group *Newsletter* 16 (1977) there was a report that a 'large tawny owl was sighted'. P. R. Haynes wrote: 'I have a report of a shot (dead) bird from 1978 but the observer is not the world's greatest ornithologist' (Warr, undated). No description was written for either of these records, and confusion with some other species of owl is most likely.

Hume's Owl *(Strix butleri)*

P. R. Haynes (1979) wrote of this species: 'Status unknown - suspected resident. More likely than Tawny Owl.' However, C. W. T. Pilcher (undated) stated that Hume's Tawny Owl was 'Not recorded in Kuwait.' There are no acceptable records for either species in Kuwait.

Green Bee-eater *(Merops orientalis)*

F. E. Warr (undated) considered that the bee-eaters found nesting by V. Dickson on Maskan Island on 7 May 1942 could possibly have been Green Bee-eaters (*M. orientalis*). However, M. C. Jennings (undated) stated that the latter species 'does not nest in colonies or occur in Kuwait', and accepted the breeding record as being of Blue-cheeked Bee-eaters (*M. superciliosus*). Seven birds seen by E. Grieve at Araifjan on 9 March 1973 were not described, and confusion with Blue-cheeked Bee-eaters is likely. P. R. Haynes (1979) stated that records of Green Bee-eaters were 'open to doubt'.

Long-billed Pipit *(Anthus similis)*

C. W. T. Pilcher (undated) stated for this species: 'Accidental. Two records of single birds.' He wrote that 'There is only my one record of a single individual about five years ago but Bryon Wright told me he may have had one in 1985' (Warr, undated). No descriptions were written, and confusion with Tawny Pipit (*A. campestris*) in worn plumage seems likely.

Rock Pipit *(Anthus petrosus)*

The ANHFSG *Newsletter* 3 (1971) reported that several Rock Pipits had been seen at an unstated location in November 1970. This record clearly involved confusion with Water Pipit (*A. spinoletta*). The computer list of the ANHFSG (1975) lumped all records of Rock Pipits and Water Pipits as *Anthus spinoletta*. Since then the species has been split. There are no acceptable records of the modern species Rock Pipit in Kuwait.

Guldenstädt's Redstart *(Phoenicurus erythrogaster)*

This species was listed in *The Birds of the Western Palearctic* (Cramp, Simmons, and Perrins, 1977-1994) as 'Accidental', and by P. A. D. Hollom, R. F. Porter, S. Christensen and I. Willis (1988) as 'Vagrant', in Kuwait. F. E. Warr (undated) commented: 'Source unknown'. This species has never been recorded in Kuwait.

Blackstart *(Cercomela melanura)*

This species was listed in *The Birds of the Western Palearctic* (Cramp, Simmons, and Perrins, 1977-1994) as 'Accidental', and by P. A. D. Hollom, R. F. Porter, S. Christensen and I. Willis (1988) as 'Vagrant', in Kuwait. F. E. Warr (undated) commented: 'Source unknown (not from the list compiled for BWP by P. R. Haynes).' C. W. T. Pilcher (undated) wrote that 'There are no records of this species in Kuwait'.

Eastern Pied Wheatear *(Oenanthe picata)*

A record of one seen by V. A. D. Sales at Ahmadi from 1 to 31 December 1967 was described on a Rare Bird Report form but was rejected by the panel, on the grounds of not being sufficiently distinguished from other similar species.

Scrub Warbler *(Scotocerca inquieta)*

A record of one seen by W. Stuart and L. Corrall at Abdali Farms from 9-10 February 1979 was submitted on a Rare Bird Report form but was rejected by the panel, with a comment that it could have been a Graceful Prinia (***Prinia gracilis***). This latter species was first found in Kuwait there.

B. Wright (1995) wrote of this species: 'One small party of either this or the preceding species [Graceful Prinia] recorded in April 1985.' Again, this record is much more likely to refer to the latter species.

Aquatic Warbler *(Acrocephalus paludicola)*

B. Wright (1995) wrote of this species; 'No recent records though old Ahmadi Natural History Society records may exist.' There have been no records of this species in Kuwait.

Thick-billed Warbler *(Acrocephalus aedon)*

A record of one seen by V. A. D. Sales, probably at Ahmadi, on 7 May 1966 was listed, but with no date, by the ANHFSG (1975). P. R. Haynes (1979) wrote of this species: 'Accidental? No recent records - overlooked?' However V. A. D. Sales stated that this record 'has been causing me some concern with my conflicting statements. I know I listed it and gave you the date but I'm puzzled why I can find no notes about it as in my mind's eye I can still see the bird and I have some recollection having looked it up, this is why I thought my son may have had the notes but all he has is some vague recollection about it. I've spent several hours today before writing checking various sources without success, very frustrating, so it will have to be a non starter' (Warr, undated).

It is clearly best to require confirmation of the occurrence of this species in Kuwait.

Paddyfield Warbler *(Acrocephalus agricola)*

B. Wright (19950 said of this species; ' No recent records though old records may exist in the Ahmadi Natural History Society transactions. Status not described with regard to Kuwait (Cramp 1992).' There have been no records of this species in Kuwait.

Melodious Warbler *(Hippolais polyglotta)*

V. A. D. Sales recorded one in 1955, one in 1959, two in 1963, one in 1965, six in 1967 and two in 1968. These records were submitted on a Rare Bird Report form but were rejected by the panel, on the grounds that other species were not eliminated. Despite this, this species was listed by P. R. Haynes (1979) as an 'Accidental or rare passage migrant'. B. Wright (1995) listed 'One exceptional record from August 1984. What was assumed to be this individual was later found shot.' However, he supplies no description or measurements. For all these records confusion with other species of *Hippolais* is highly likely. C. W. T. Pilcher (undated) wrote that there were 'No acceptable records for Kuwait.'

Spectacled Warbler *(Sylvia conspicillata)*

A description of one seen by V. A. D. Sales at Ahmadi on 28 September 1957 was submitted on a Rare Bird Report form but was rejected by the panel, with a comment that it was rather a weak description. Despite this, this species was listed by P. R. Haynes (1979) as an 'Accidental or rare Passage Migrant'. However, C. W. T. Pilcher (undated) wrote that there were 'No acceptable records for Kuwait.'

Subalpine Warbler *(Sylvia cantillans)*

Descriptions by V. A. D. Sales of single birds at Ahmadi on 3 April 1959 and on 11-12 September 1963 were submitted on a Rare Bird Report form. However, they were rejected by most of the panel, with a comment by one member that Ménétries's Warbler *(S. mystacea)* was not eliminated. Despite this, this species was listed by P. R. Haynes (1979) as an 'Accidental or rare Passage Migrant'. However, C. W. T. Pilcher (undated) wrote that there were 'No acceptable records for Kuwait.'

Sardinian Warbler *(Sylvia melanocephala)*

This species was clearly, in the past, thoroughly confused with Ménétries's Warbler *(S. mystacea)* in Kuwait. V. A. D Sales stated that Sardinian Warbler 'was recorded in every year except 1957, 1958, 1965 & 1966', with 'about 20 in 1963.' Later, he withdrew these records (Warr, undated). S. Howe and R. P. Blacker recorded single birds in Ahmadi, in 1970 on 25 April and 3 May, and in 1971 on 4, 5 and 12 March. It is possible that Sardinian Warbler has occurred in Kuwait (a bird netted by S. Howe on 4 March 1971 could well have been of this species). However, there remains the possibility of confusion with Ménétries's Warbler. P. R. Haynes (1979) listed Sardinian Warbler as a 'Rare or uncommon Passage Migrant', but C. W. T. Pilcher (undated) wrote that there were 'No acceptable records for Kuwait.'

Rüppell's Warbler *(Sylvia rueppelli)*

A description of a female seen by V. A. D. Sales at Ahmadi on 2 January 1958 was submitted on a Rare Bird Report form but was rejected by the panel, with comments that not enough detail was provided. A record of one seen by M. and R. Blacker in Kuwait City on 13 April 1971 was not accompanied by a written description. A description of a bird seen by J. Webb at Khashman on 24 February was written on a Rare Bird Report form, but it is not accessible. P. R. Haynes (1979) commented that records of this species were 'open to doubt'. B. Wright (1995) listed 'One record of an adult female in May 1985', but supplied no description.

For all these records, confusion with Ménétries's Warbler *(S. mystacea)* seems likely.

Cyprus Warbler *(Sylvia melanothorax)*

V. A. D. Sales wrote a description of one on a Rare Bird Report form. Unfortunately this was lost, so the date and location are not accessible. However, the panel rejected the record, stating possible confusion with Ménétries's Warbler *(S. mystacea)*.

Radde's Warbler *(Phylloscopus schwarzi)*

P. R. Haynes (1979) listed this species as a 'Possibly fairly common passage migrant', but added 'but no confirmed records.' He wrote 'No definite records at all but on numerous occasions in 1977 and 1978 I (and others) saw large *Phylloscopus* warblers with a fairly heavy bill and very distinct eye stripe. From the books it seems to fit as Radde's but I'm not claiming it for one' (Warr, undated).

A written description of one seen by J. Gaskell and M. O. Chichester at Wafra Oil Field on 5 October 1998 was rejected by KORC.

Confusion with eastern forms of Chiffchaff (*P. collybita*) or with Mountain Chiffchaff (*P. sindianus*) is possible for these records.

Dusky Warbler *(Phylloscopus fuscatus)*

W. A. Stuart recorded one or two on 26 October 1979 and one on 8 November 1979, but supplied no description. F. E. Warr (undated) rejected the records. B. Wright

(1995) wrote: 'A bird believed to be of this species was photographed by the author.' No date or location is stated, and no description was written or is accessible. Confusion with eastern forms of Chiffchaff (*P. collybita*) or with Mountain Chiffchaff (*P. sindianus*) is possible for these records.

Balkan Warbler *(Phylloscopus orientalis)*

B. Wright (1995) recorded 'A possible in March 1994.' No exact date, location or description is given, and the record is clearly uncertain. The bird was named as Bonelli's Warbler (*P. bonelli*), but this has since been split.

Asian Brown Flycatcher *(Muscicapa dauurica)*

A description of one seen by V. A. D. Sales at Ahmadi on 8 May 1955 was submitted on a Rare Bird Report form but was rejected by the panel, with a comment that the bird was probably not a Spotted Flycatcher (*M. striata*), but that the species could not be determined. The scientific name on the form was given as *Muscicapa latirostris*, a junior synonym.

Collared Flycatcher *(Ficedula albicollis)*

V. A. D. Sales recorded this species four times in 1953, six times in 1966, once in 1967 and twice in 1968. The computer list of the ANHFSG (1975) includes two records in 1970 and one in 1971. P. R. Haynes (1979) described this species as an 'Uncommon Passage Migrant'. However, S. Howe wrote: 'It may be significant that from the time I began to differentiate between *F. a. albicollis* & *F. a. semitorquatus* [sic] the former never appears in our Kuwait record. V. A. D. S. also commented in retrospect he thought all Collared F/C he recorded were *semitorquatus*. Voous now having upgraded it to a species creates a problem, and I would have to say I cannot be sure anymore of *F. a. albicollis*' (Warr, undated).

A written description of a female/first-year Collared Flycatcher seen by J. Gaskell and M. O. Chichester at Wafra Oil Field on 5 September 1998 was rejected by KORC.

All examined *Ficedula* flycatchers trapped or found dead, and all adult males photographed or well observed, from the mid 1980s onwards, have proven to be Semi-collared Flycatchers (*F. semitorquata*). It is possible that Collared Flycatcher has occurred in Kuwait, but a confirmed record is necessary before adding this species to the Kuwait list.

Pied Flycatcher *(Ficedula hypoleuca)*

In the computer list of the ANHFSG (1975) there are two records of this species in 1970, four in 1971, four in 1972 and four in 1974. P. R. Haynes (1979) wrote of this species: 'Fairly Common Passage Migrant. Confusion possible with Semi-collared Flycatcher.' No descriptions were written. Although Pied Flycatcher may have occurred in Kuwait, confirmation is necessary before allowing this species onto the Kuwait list.

Iraq Babbler *(Turdoides altirostris)*

P. R. Haynes recorded an Iraq Babbler at Kuwait City/Bay on 9 May 1974 (ANHFSG, 1975). However, in his list (Haynes, 1979) he states: 'Accidental. Only one sighting - species not clearly identified.'

On 4 June 1999 G. Gregory and P. Robertson observed a *Turdoides* flying around Jahra East Outfall with its bill wide open. Two poor photographs were taken. G. Gregory wrote a description, but the observers were not entirely certain that the bird was of this species.

A group of Kuwaiti hunters reported shooting six birds of this species at Ratqa in March 2002, but no specimen was retained, and no photograph or description was taken.
For all these records, the possibility of Common Babbler (*T. caudatus*) cannot be eliminated.

European Nuthatch *(Sitta europaea)*

V. Dickson wrote that she had seen 'a variety' of this species on 24 April 1939 at an unstated location (Warr, undated). No description was taken, and the possibility of the bird being an Eastern Rock Nuthatch (*S. tephronata*) or a Western Rock Nuthatch (*S. neumayer*) cannot be eliminated.

Western Jackdaw *(Corvus monedula)*

The computer list of the ANHFSG (1975) contains a record of this species by N. Montford with no date or location. S. Howe stated 'Montford's record came as a comment on our draft list as a bird he'd seen not covered by us (ANHG). It was not given in more detail and is totally unconnected with the House Crow' (Warr, undated). P. R. Haynes (1979) listed this species with the comment 'No recent records.'
No description was written, and it seems best to require confirmation before adding this species to the Kuwait list.

Hooded Crow *(Corvus corone capellanus or C. corone sharpii)*

On a Rare Bird Report form, V. A. D. Sales described up to two birds seen at Ahmadi from 23 January to 23 April 1957, and one at Shuaiba on 24 October 1958. Most of the panel considered that the birds were probably House Crows (*C. splendens*). A verbal report of 15 seen on 5 February 1957 by C. Jacques (Warr, undated), and an undated record of one on the computer list of the ANHFSG (1975), seen by 'DHM', were not accompanied by descriptions. Both of these last records also seem likely to have referred to House Crows.

Arabian Golden Sparrow *(Passer euchlorus)*

Descriptions of eight birds seen by V. A. D. Sales at Ahmadi on 30 March 1955 and six there on 6 April 1955 were submitted on a Rare Bird Report form but were rejected by the panel, with comments that various species of escaped birds were not eliminated, and that Arabian Golden Sparrow was non-migratory.

Rock Sparrow *(Petronia petronia)*

A description of one seen by V. A. D. Sales at Ahmadi on 8 May 1955 was submitted on a Rare Bird Report form but was rejected by the panel, on the grounds that there could have been confusion with various species of escaped birds.

European Serin *(Serinus serinus)*

A description of one seen by V. A. D. Sales at Ahmadi on 21 November 1955 was submitted on a Rare Bird Report form but was rejected by the panel with a comment that Siskin (*Carduelis spinus*) was not eliminated.

Pine Bunting *(Emberiza leucocephalus)*

N-A. B. Khalaf stated that he was 'absolutely positive' that he saw one in Salmiya on 1 December 1983, in a written communication to M. C. Jennings, who later commented that he was doubtful about the record (Warr, undated). This bird could well have been a Pine Bunting, but no description was written, and confirmation is needed before allowing this species onto the Kuwait list.

House Bunting *(Emberiza striolata)*

P. R. Haynes (1979) wrote of this species 'Accidental? Few unconfirmed sightings autumn 1978'. The observer, location and exact date were not stated. Later he stated that the above record was rejected (Warr, undated).

C. W. T. Pilcher (undated) noted of this species "Accidental. Two records 7.4.82 (3 birds); 10.3.95 (1). All *E. s. striolata*.' The observer and location are not stated. No descriptions are accessible, if indeed any were written. House Bunting is almost entirely sedentary and is unlikely to occur in Kuwait. The possibility of confusion with other species remains.

Grey-necked Bunting *(Emberiza buchanani)*

In 1986 C. W. T. Pilcher photographed several buntings at Umm Al-Aish, which he considered might be of this species or Cretzschmar's Bunting (*E. caesia*). R. Porter examined the slides and C. W. T. Pilcher looked at skins in the British Museum. They concluded that the birds were probably varying Ortolan Buntings (*E. hortulana*) (Warr, undated). This latter species does vary greatly in plumage, with some individuals resembling, to some extent, the other two species.

Cretzschmar's Bunting *(Emberiza caesia)*

V. A. D. Sales recorded, at Ahmadi, one on 13 September 1955, two on 13 April 1956 and one on 21 May 1963. The computer list of the AHNFSG (1975) contains a record of one seen by 'DAMW' at Mufattah on 13 April 1974. On the strength of these records P. R. Haynes (1979) listed this species as an 'Accidental or rare Passage Migrant'. C. W. T. Pilcher photographed several buntings at Umm Al-Aish in 1986 (see above species). He then wrote of this species 'Accidental. Six records in 40 years' (Pilcher, undated). This implies at least one other record, details of which are not accessible. He later, in a personal communication to D. J. Brooks, commented: 'A puzzling record' (Warr, undated). No full description for any record, apart from that of the birds at Umm Al-Aish, was ever written.

In reviewing all these records, it seems clear that the possibility of varying Ortolan Buntings (*E. hortulana*) has not been eliminated, and that confirmation is required before adding this species to the Kuwait list.

Marbled Duck (*Marmaronetta angustirostris*)
Following the draining of the marshes in southern Iraq, this species started being recorded in Kuwait.

Juvenile Shikra (*Accipiter badius*)
This species is regular in Kuwait, but many birds, such as this one, are shot by hunters.

Male Little Crake (*Porzana parva*)
This species has recently been discovered to breed in Kuwait, a major range extension.

Juvenile Caspian Plover (*Charadrius asiaticus*)
This species is a regular passage migrant through Kuwait.

Black-shouldered Kite (*Elanus caeruleus*)
This species is extending its range in the Middle East. This bird was trapped and kept captive by Kuwaiti falconers.

Hunting falcons (*Falco* sp.)
Some birds are easy to specifically identify, but others are not and some may be hybrids. Escapes are sometimes encountered.

Crab Plover (*Dromas ardeola*)
The breeding colony on Bubiyan Island is probably the largest in the world.

Pacific Golden Plover (*Pluvialis fulva*)
Kuwait is the only Western Palearctic state where this species is regular.

White-tailed Lapwing (*Hoplopterus leucura*)
This species is extending its range in the Middle East.

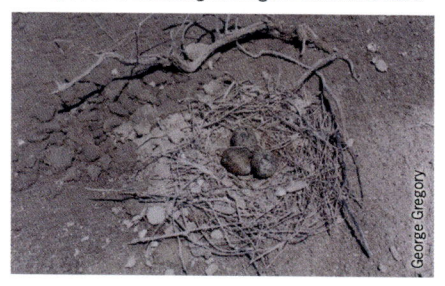

Nests of Slender-billed Gull (*Larus genei*)
Kuwait holds the only breeding colonies of this species in the Arabian peninsula.

Nest of Gull-billed Tern (*Gelochelidon nilotica*)
Large colonies are found in Kuwait, the only state in the Arabian peninsula where breeding occurs regularly.

Colony of Greater Crested Terns (*Sterna bergii*)
This Western Palearctic speciality has been found to breed in large colonies in Kuwait.

Lesser Crested Tern (*Sterna bengalensis*)
Good numbers breed regularly in Kuwait, probably more than in any other Western Palearctic state.

White-cheeked Terns (*Sterna repressa*)
Thousands of pairs of this species breed annually in Kuwait.

Spotted Sandgrouse (*Pterocles senegallus*)
This species has bred irregularly in Kuwait. This female bird was wounded and caged by a Kuwaiti hunter.

Male Chestnut-bellied Sandgrouse (*Pterocles exustus*)
One of about 30 birds which constituted the first Kuwait record. This bird was wounded and caged by a Kuwaiti hunter.

Black-bellied Sandgrouse (*Pterocles orientalis*)
A rare winter visitor to Kuwait. This female bird was wounded and caged by a Kuwaiti hunter.

Female Chestnut-bellied Sandgrouse (*Pterocles exustus*)
The second Kuwait record of a major Western Palearctic rarity.

Bruce's Green Pigeon (*Treron waalia*)
One of two birds that were either escapes or were the first of their species for the Western Palearctic.

African Collared Dove (*Streptopelia griseogularis*)
This species is gradually colonising Kuwait, but has not yet been proven to breed.

Male Namaqua Dove (*Oena capensis*)
This species has recently colonised Kuwait.

Oriental Turtle Dove (*Streptopelia orientalis*)
A rare passage migrant through Kuwait, but probably under-recorded. This bird was wounded and caged by a Kuwaiti hunter.

Juvenile Eurasian Eagle Owl (*Bubo bubo*) A small *ascalaphus* type. Small numbers breed regularly in Kuwait.

White-throated Kingfisher (*Halcyon smyrnensis*) Kuwait is the only state in the Arabian peninsula where this species has bred.

Indian Roller (*Coracias benghalensis*) This species has a limited Western Palearctic range but is a regular winter visitor to Kuwait.

Nest of Black-crowned Sparrow-lark (*Eremopterix nigriceps*) This species now breeds widely in Kuwait.

Juvenile Dunn's Lark (*Eremalauda dunni*) This species is gradually colonising Kuwait, and has been proven to breed.

White-eared Bulbul (*Pycnonotus leucogenys*) This common and easily seen species breeds only in Kuwait in the Western Palearctic.

Red-vented Bulbul (*Pycnonotus cafer*) Kuwait holds the only Western Palearctic breeding population of this somewhat secretive species.

Eastern Orphean Warbler (*Sylvia crassirostris*)
A regular passage migrant through Kuwait.

Southern Grey Shrike (*Lanius meridionalis*)
Kuwait is the only Western Palearctic state where the subspecies *L. m. pallidirostris* (Steppe Grey Shrike) is regular.

Female Woodchat Shrike (*Lanius senator*)
The first known breeding of this species in the Arabian peninsula.

Bank Myna (*Acridotheres ginginianus*)
An adult at the Abdulla Al-Habashi Farm in Jahra, the only known Western Palearctic breeding site.

Male Dead Sea Sparrow (*Passer moabiticus*)
One of only three records in Kuwait of a species that probably is under-recorded.

Male Spanish Sparrow (*Passer hispaniolensis*)
Kuwait is the only state in the Arabian peninsula where this species regularly breeds.

Chestnut-shouldered Sparrow (*Petronia xanthocollis*)
This somewhat secretive species breeds regularly in Kuwait.

Indian Silverbill (*Lonchura malabarica*)
Although regularly recorded, this species has only recently been proven to breed in Kuwait, and probably does so regularly.

Desert Finch (*Rhodopechys obsoleta*)
This species may be about to establish itself in Kuwait.

Red-headed Bunting (*Emberiza briniceps*)
This species is rare in Kuwait on passage and in winter.

Trumpeter Finch (*Bucanetes githagineus*)
This species is gradually colonising Kuwait.

Cinereous Bunting (*Emberiza cineracea*)
A regular passage migrant through Kuwait in small numbers.

REFERENCES AND BIBLIOGRAPHY

ABDULALI, H. (1968-1971) A catalogue of the birds in the collection of the Bombay Natural History Society. *Journal of the Bombay Natural History Society* 65: 182-199 (Introduction and Part 1); 418-430 (Part 2); 696-723 (Part 3); 1969, 66: 251-285 (Part 4); 542-559 (Part 5);1970, 67: 51- 56 (Part 6); 279-298 (Part 7);1971, 68: 127-152 (Part 8); 328-338 (Part 9); 756-772 (Part 10).

AHMADI NATURAL HISTORY AND FIELD STUDIES GROUP (1975) *Computer List of Bird Observations in Kuwait 1956-75*. Unpublished Report.

AL-HADDAD, A. S. and AL-SUDAIRAWI, F. A. (2002) (In Arabic) *Kuwait Birds - A Photographic Record*. Kuwait Centre for Research and Kuwait Studies, Kuwait.

AL-FADHEL, A. (2005) *Birds of Kuwait - A Portrait*. Privately published, Kuwait.

AL-JERIWI, M. and AL-MANSOORI, F. (2001) Colonial breeding of Spanish Sparrow in Kuwait. *Phoenix* 18:7

AL-JRAIWI, M. A. A. (1999) (In Arabic) *Kuwait Birds*. Privately published, Kuwait.

AL NASRALLAH, K. (2004) Kentish plover eggs predated by Long-eared Hedgehog. *Phoenix* 20:9-10.

AL-NASRALLAH, K. (2005) First breeding of Woodchat Shrike in Arabia. *Phoenix* 21: 1.

AL-NASRALLAH, K., AL-AHMED, M.S. and AL-FADHEL, A. (2001) New records of herons nesting in Kuwait. *Phoenix* 18: 5.

AL-NASRALLAH, K. and GREGORY, G. (2003) Bubiyan Island, Kuwait, 2002. *Phoenix* 19: 5-7.

AL-SARAWI, M. A., GUNDLACH, E. R. and BACA, B. J. (1988) *Kuwait: An Atlas of Shoreline Types and Resources*. Department of Geology, Kuwait University, Kuwait.

AL-SUDAIRAWI, F. A. (1984) (In Arabic) *Birds of Kuwait. Wintering birds of the mudflats. KISR Publication # 1362*. Kuwait Institute for Scientific Research, Kuwait.

ANONYMOUS (1972) Birds of Kuwait. *Ahmadi Natural History and Field Studies Group Newsletter 9*.

ANONYMOUS (1978) Field trip to Gurain Hill, Bergan Flint Beds and Subahiyah - 17 February 1978. *Ahmadi Natural History and Field Studies Group Newsletter* 19: 6-7.

BEAMAN, M. and MADGE, S. (1998) *The Handbook of Bird Identification for Europe and the Western Palearctic*. Helm, London.

BOURNE, W. R. P. (1961-1966) Observations on Sea-birds. *Sea Swallow* 14: 7-27; 16: 9-40; 17: 10-39; 18: 9-39.

BRITISH MUSEUM (1901) *Catalogue of Birds' Eggs. Volume 1*. British Museum, London.

BRITISH MUSEUM (1902) *Catalogue of Birds' Eggs. Volume 2*. British Museum, London.

BUNDY, G. and WARR, E. (1980) A Check-list of the Birds of the Arabian Gulf states. *Sandgrouse* 1: 4-49.

BUNDY, G., CONNOR, R. J. and HARRISON, C. J. O. (1989) *Birds of the Eastern Province of Saudi Arabia*. H. F. & G. Witherby, London.

BUTTIKER, W. (1981) *The Wildlife of Saudi Arabia and its Neighbours*. Stacey International, London.

CHICHESTER, M. O. and GREGORY, G. (2000) Yellow-throated Sparrow - A New Breeding Species for Kuwait. *Phoenix* 17:3.

CHILMAN, P. W. G. (1982) Migrants in the Persian Gulf during spring 1979. *Sea Swallow* 31: 25-29.

CLAYTON, D. A. (1991) The Little Owl Athene noctua and its food in Kuwait. *Sandgrouse* 13(1): 2-6.

CLAYTON, D. A. and PILCHER, C. W. T. (1984) *Kuwait's Natural History - An Introduction*. Kuwait Oil Company, Kuwait.

CLAYTON, D. A. and WELLS, K. (1987) *Discovering Kuwait's Wildlife*. Fahad Al-Marzouk, Kuwait University, Kuwait.

CLEERE, N., KELLY, D. and PILCHER, C. W. T. (2000a) Results from a late ringing project in Kuwait, 1995. *Ringing & Migration* 20: 186-190.

CLEERE, N., KELLY, D. and PILCHER, C. W. T. (2000b) Two new bird species in Kuwait. *Sandgrouse* 22(2): 143-145.

CLEERE, N., KELLY, D. and PILCHER, C. W. T. (2004) A mystery *Phylloscopus* warbler in Kuwait. *Sandgrouse* 26(2): 143-146.

COWAN, P. J. (1990) The Crab Plover in Kuwait and the northern Arabian Gulf: a brief review and some new counts. *OSME Bulletin* 25: 6-9.

COWAN, P. J. (2000a) A female See-see Partridge in Kuwait. *Phoenix* 17: 13.

COWAN, P. J. (2000b) The desert birds of south-west Asia. *Sandgrouse* 22(2): 104-108.

COWAN, P. J. and BROWN, G. M. (2001) Prostrate desert gourd plants as apparent cooling sites for larks in heat of day. *Sandgrouse* 23(1): 59-60.

COWAN, P. J. and NEWMAN, D. L. (1998) Bar-tailed Desert Lark Ammomanes cincturus and Black-crowned Finch Lark *Eremopterix nigriceps* breeding in Kuwait. *Sandgrouse* 20(2): 146-147.

COWAN, P. J. and PILCHER, C. W. T. (2003) The status of desert birds in Kuwait. *Sandgrouse* 25(2): 122-125.

COWAN, P. J., PILCHER, C. W. T. and SPENCER, S. T. (2004) Trumpeter Finches *Bucanetes githagineus* in Kuwait: feeding juveniles or courtship-feeding? *Sandgrouse* 26(2): 139-140.

CRAMP, S., SIMMONS, K. E. L. and PERRINS, C. M. (EDS.) (1977-1994) *The Birds of the Western Palearctic. Volumes 1-9*. Oxford University Press.

DICKSON, H. R. P. (1949) *The Arab of the Desert.* George Allen & Unwin, London.

DICKSON, V. (1942) A visit to Maskan and Auha Islands in the Persian Gulf, off Kuwait. May 7th 1942. *Journal of the Bombay Natural History Society* 43: 258-264. (Reprinted in the *Ahmadi Natural History and Field Studies Group Newsletter 7* (November 1971): 6-13.)

DICKSON, V. (1970) *Forty Years in Kuwait.* George Allen & Unwin, London.

DICKSON, V. (undated) (*Private correspondence, now in British Museum*). Unpublished letters.

DRYDEN, M. (1982) Kuwait's Wildlife. *Wildlife* 24: 186-189.

EVANS, M. I. (1994) *Important Bird Areas in the Middle East*. BirdLife International (Bird Conservation Series No.2), Cambridge University Press.

EVANS, M. I., PILCHER, C. W. T. and SYMENS, P. (1991) Impact of the Gulf War on birds. *OSME Bulletin* 27: 1-6.

GALLAGHER, M. D., SCOTT, D. A., ORMOND, R. F. G., CONNOR, R. J. and JENNINGS, M. C. (1984) *The distribution and conservation of seabirds breeding on the coasts and islands of Iran and Arabia. ICBP Technical Publication* 2: 421-456.

GALLAGHER, M. D. (1971) The Crab Plover in the Gulf. *Gulf Bird-watchers Newsletter* 19: 6-7.

GASKELL, J., AL-NASRALLAH, K., GREGORY, G. and ROBERTSON, P. (2001) White-throated Kingfisher - A New Breeding Species for Arabia. *Phoenix* 18: 2.

GORIUP, P. D. (1997) The world status of the Houbara Bustard *Chlamydotis undulata. Bird Conservation International* 7: 373-397.

GREGORY, G. (1987) Recent Bird-watching in Kuwait. *Twitching* 350-351 (Part One).

GREGORY, G. (1988) Recent Bird-watching in Kuwait. *Birding World* 1: 31-32 (Part

Two); 139 (Part Three); 325-326 (Part Four).

GREGORY, G. (2000a) Primary moult in Egyptian Nightjar *Caprimulgus aegyptius* on autumn migration in Kuwait. *Sandgrouse* 22(2): 113-117.

GREGORY, G. (2000b) Recent Breeding News from Kuwait. *Phoenix* 17: 9-10.

GREGORY, G. (2001) Recent Breeding Data from Kuwait. *Phoenix* 18: 8-9.

GREGORY, G. (2002) The captive origin of bird species in Kuwait. *Sandgrouse* 24 (2): 122-129.

GREGORY, G. (2003a) Recent Breeding Data from Kuwait. *Phoenix* 19: 21-24.

GREGORY, G. (2003b) Some moult data for raptors in Kuwait. *Sandgrouse* 25(2): 126-131.

GREGORY, G. (2004a) Breeding Birds in Kuwait, 2003. *Phoenix* 20: 21-23.

GREGORY, G. (2004b) (*Consultant's Reports for January to December 2004.*) Reports to the Kuwait Institute for Scientific Research.

GREGORY, G. (2005a) (*Consultant's Reports for January to March 2005.*) Reports to the Kuwait Institute for Scientific Research.

GREGORY, G. (2005b) Breeding Birds in Kuwait in 2004. *Phoenix* 21: 24-27.

GREGORY, G. and AL-NASRALLAH, K. (2001) The establishment of Bank Mynah *Acridotheres ginginianus* as a breeding species in Kuwait. *Sandgrouse* 23(2): 134-138.

GREGORY, G. and ROBERTSON, P. (2000) White-winged Black Tern - a New Breeding Species for Arabia. *Phoenix* 17: 2.

GREGORY, G., ROBERTSON, P. and THOMAS, B. (2001) Reduction of bird shooting in Kuwait. *Sandgrouse* 23(1): 34-38.

GRIFFITHS, W. A. C. (1975) *A Bibliography of the Avifauna of the Arabian Peninsula, the Levant and Mesopotamia; with Addendum No 1 (December 1978) and Addendum No 2 (December 1979).* Army Birdwatching Society Periodic Publication.

HARRIS, A., SHIRIHAI, H. and CHRISTIE, D. (1996) *Birder's Guide to European and Middle Eastern Birds.* Macmillan, London.

HARRISON, C. (1982) *An Atlas of the Birds of the Western Palearctic.* Collins, London.

HARRISON, C. J. O. (1983) The Occurrence of Saunders' Little Tern in the Upper Arabian Gulf. *Sandgrouse* 5: 100-101.

HAYNES, P. R. (1974) Birds. *Ahmadi Natural History and Field Studies Group Newsletter* 14: 13-15.

HAYNES, P. R. (1978) Notes on the distribution and status of the Birds of Kuwait. *Ahmadi Natural History and Field Studies Group Newsletter* 19: 13-30.

HAYNES, P. R. (1979) Notes on the status and distribution of the birds of Kuwait. *Ahmadi Natural History and Field Studies Group Newsletter* 20: 1-34.

HEINZEL, H., FITTER, R. and PARSLOW, J. (1979) *The Birds of Britain and Europe with North Africa and the Middle East*. Collins, London.

HOLLOM, P. A. D., PORTER, R. F., CHRISTENSEN, S. and WILLIS, I. (1988) *Birds of the Middle East and North Africa*. T. & A. D. Poyser, London.

HUE, F. and ETCHECOPAR, R. D. (1970) *Les Oiseaux du Proche et du Moyen Orient*. Boubee, Paris.

HUME, A. O. and OATES, E. W. (1890) *Nests and Eggs of Indian Birds*. R. H. Porter, London.

JENNINGS, M. C. (1981) *Birds of the Arabian Gulf*. George Allen and Unwin, London.

JENNINGS, M. C. (1986a) Breeding exotics. *Phoenix* 3: 2.

JENNINGS, M. C. (1986b) Recent Reports. *Phoenix* 3: 4-5.

JENNINGS, M. C. (1986c) Spanish sparrows nearly bred in Kuwait. *Phoenix* 3: 5-6.

JENNINGS, M. C. (1986d) The Distribution of the Extinct Arabian Ostrich *Struthio camelus syriacus* Rothschild, 1919. *Fauna of Saudi Arabia* 8: 447-461.

JENNINGS, M. C. (1989) Kuwait 50 years ago: Col. H. R. P. Dickson's game register. *Phoenix* 6: 4-5.

JENNINGS, M. C. (1992) Alexandrine Parakeet, Arabia's newest breeding parrot? *Phoenix* 9: 4.

JENNINGS, M. C. (1994) New exotic breeding species. *Phoenix* 11: 4-5.

JENNINGS, M. C. (1995) *An Interim Atlas of the Breeding Birds of Arabia*. National Commission for Wildlife Conservation and Development, Riyadh.

JENNINGS, M. C. (2004) Exotic Breeding in Arabian Cities. *Phoenix* 20:2-4.

JENNINGS, M. C. (undated) (*Computer List of Breeding Bird Records in Arabia*.) Unpublished document.

JONSSON, L. (1992) *Birds of Europe with North Africa and the Middle East*. Helm, London.

JONES, D. A. (1986) *A field guide to the shores of Kuwait and the Arabian Gulf.* Kuwait University, Blandford Press.

KELLY, D., CLEERE, N. and PILCHER, C. W. T. (2001) Notch factor - a technique for separating Marsh Warblers *Acrocephalus palustris* from Reed Warblers *A. scirpaceus* on spring migration. *Ringing & Migration* 20: 289-291.

LOUGHLAND, R. (2004) (*Reports on the Bubiyan Project.*) Reports to the Kuwait Institute for Scientific Research.

MEINERTZHAGEN, R. (1954) *Birds of Arabia.* Oliver and Boyd, Edinburgh.

NAKAMURA, K. 1974. Observations on the seabirds in the Arabian Gulf. *Transactions of the Tokyo University of Fisheries* 1: 13-16 and Appendix Table 2: 108-112.

PHILBY, H. St. J. B. 1920. Across Arabia from the Persian Gulf to the Red Sea. *Geographical Journal* 56 (6): 446-468.

PILCHER, C. W. T. (1986) A Breeding Record of House Crow in Kuwait with Comments on the Species' Status in the Arabian Gulf. *Sandgrouse* 8: 102-106.

PILCHER, C. W. T. (1987) *Kuwait's Avifaunal Survey 1985-87.* Report to Kuwait Environment Protection Council.

PILCHER, C. W. T. (1988a) Future breeders and exotics in Kuwait. *Phoenix* 5: 4-5.

PILCHER, C. W. T. (1988b) Kuwait Avifaunal Survey. *Phoenix* 5: 18.

PILCHER, C. W. T. (1989a) Sites of Interest: Kubbar Island, Kuwait. *Phoenix* 6: 8.

PILCHER, C. W. T. (1989b) Oriental scourge - Indian House Crow. *Phoenix* 6: 10.

PILCHER, C. W. T. (1994a) Kuwait's Jahra Pool Reserve under threat. *Phoenix* 11:18.

PILCHER, C. W. T. (1994b) The Palm Dove in Kuwait and an unusual nest. *Phoenix* 11:14.

PILCHER, C. W. T. (2000) *Kuwait List, Notes for Birds of the Western Palearctic (Concise Edition).* Unpublished manuscript, mainly about 1996, updated to 2000.

PILCHER, C. W. T. (undated) *A Checklist of the Birds of Kuwait.* Unpublished manuscript.

PILCHER, C. W. T., GREGORY, G., TYE, A. and AHMED, M. S. (1990) Additions to the country list produced by the Kuwait Avifaunal Survey, 1985-7. *Sandgrouse* 12: 31-36.

PILCHER, C. W. T. and SEXTON, D. B. (1993) Effects of the Gulf War oil spills and well head fires on the avifauna and environment of Kuwait. *Sandgrouse* 15:6-17.

PILCHER, C. W. T. and SHEHAB, M. A. (1994) First record of Velvet Scoter (*Melanitta fusca*) in Kuwait. *Sandgrouse* 16(1): 53-54.

PILCHER, C. W. T., STUART, W. A. and SPENCER, S. T. (1997) Graceful Warbler colonization of Kuwait. *Sandgrouse* 19(1): 65-67.

PORTER, R. F., CHRISTENSEN, S. and SCHIERMACKER-HANSEN, P. (1996) *Field Guide to the Birds of the Middle East.* T. & A. D. Poyser, London.

RAMADAN, E., AL-NASRALLAH, K. and GREGORY, G. (2004) Bubiyan Island: a rich Kuwait avifauna. *Sandgrouse* 26(1): 23-26.

REED, M. and CROSS, T. (1995) *Kuwait Ringing Expedition.* Privately published.

REED, M. and CROSS, T. (2001) The first Dunnock *Prunella modularis* in Kuwait. *Sandgrouse* 23(1): 61-62.

ROWLANDS, G. (2001) Little Crake - A New Breeding Species for Kuwait. *Phoenix*18: 20.

ROWLANDS, G. and GREGORY, G. (2000) Greater Sandplover - a New Breeding Species for Kuwait. *Phoenix*17: 24.

SALES, V. A. D. (1965) Terns on Khubbar Island, Persian Gulf 1958/59. *Sea Swallow* 17: 81-82. (Reprinted as: Terns on Kubbar Island, Arabian Gulf 1958/59 in the *Ahmadi Natural History and Field Studies Group Newsletter* 7 (November 1971): 14-16.)

SALES, V. A. D. (undated) (*Notes on bird records in Kuwait.*) Unpublished documents.

SILSBY, J. D. (1980) *Inland Birds of Saudi Arabia.* Immel, London.

SNOW, D. W. and PERRINS, C. M. (EDS.) (1998) *The Birds of the Western Palearctic. Concise Edition.* Oxford University Press.

SVENSSON, L. (1970) *Identification Guide to European Passerines.* Privately published, Stockholm.

TAHA, F. K., OMAR, S. A., CLAYTON, D. A., AL-BAKRI, D., AL-MUTAWA, S. and NASSEF, A. (1982) *Selection and Criteria for Establishment of National Parks/Nature Reserves in Kuwait.* Kuwait Institute for Scientific Research, Kuwait.

TAVARES, J., Si PESSOA, P. and BRITO Y ABREU, F. (2000) The first breeding record of Bearded Tit *Panurus biarmicus* in Syria. *Sandgrouse* 22: 145-146.

TICEHURST, C. B., BUXTON, P. A. and CHEESMAN, R. E. (1921-22) The birds of Mesopotamia. *Journal of the Bombay Natural History Society* 28(1-4): 197-237, 269-316, 325-249, 371-390.

TICEHURST, C. B., COX, P. and CHEESMAN, R. E. (1925) Birds of the Persian Gulf islands. *Journal of the Bombay Natural History Society* 30: 725-733.

TICEHURST, C. B., COX, P. and CHEESMAN, R. E. (1926) Additional notes on the avifauna of Iraq. *Journal of the Bombay Natural History Society* 31: 91-119.

WARR, F. E. (1983) *A List of Birds of Kuwait*. Privately published.

WARR, F. E. (1988.) *Checklist of Arabian Birds*. Privately published (unfinished).

WARR, F. E. (undated) *(Handwritten notes on bird records in Kuwait.)* Unpublished document.

WEBB, J. (1974) Brown-necked Raven. *Ahmadi Natural History and Field Studies Group Newsletter*: 14: 17.

WRIGHT, B. (1994) First record of Bearded Tit *Panurus biarmicus* in Kuwait. *Sandgrouse* 16(1): 62-63.

WRIGHT, B. K. (1995a) The Status of Warblers in Kuwait. *OSME Bulletin* 34: 1-7.

WRIGHT, B. K. (1995b) Observations on copulating Crab Plovers *Dromas ardeola* in Kuwait. *OSME Bulletin* 34: 14-15.

INDEX OF COMMON NAMES

Accentor, Black-throated	141	Crow, Hooded	196
Avadavat, Red	187	Crow, House	172
Avocet, Pied	73	Cuckoo, Common	114
Babbler, Common	167	Cuckoo, Great Spotted	114
Babbler, Iraq	195	Curlew, Eurasian	88
Bee-eater, Blue-cheeked	122	Curlew, Slender-billed	88
Bee-eater, European	122	Darter, African	189
Bee-eater, Green	192	Dotterel, Eurasian	79
Bittern, Great	45	Dove, African Collared	111
Bittern, Little	45	Dove, Eurasian Collared	110
Blackbird, Common	150	Dove, European Turtle	111
Blackcap	161	Dove, Laughing	113
Blackstart	192	Dove, Namaqua	113
Bluethroat	143	Dove, Oriental Turtle	112
Brambling	177	Dove, Rock	109
Bugerigar	186	Dove, Stock	109
Bulbul, Red-vented	138	Drongo, Black	186
Bulbul, White-eared	138	Duck, Ferruginous	39
Bulbul, Yellow-vented	186	Duck, Fulvous Whistling	188
Bunting, Black-headed	183	Duck, Long-tailed	188
Bunting, Cinereous	181	Duck, Marbled	38
Bunting, Common Reed	183	Duck, Tufted	39
Bunting, Corn	184	Dunlin	85
Bunting, Cretzschmar's	197	Dunnock	140
Bunting, Grey-necked	197	Eagle, Bonelli's	62
Bunting, House	197	Eagle, Booted	62
Bunting, Little	182	Eagle, Golden	61
Bunting, Ortolan	181	Eagle, Greater Spotted	60
Bunting, Pine	196	Eagle, Imperial	61
Bunting, Red-headed	183	Eagle, Lesser Spotted	60
Bunting, Rock	181	Eagle, Short-toed	55
Bunting, Rustic	182	Eagle, Steppe	61
Bustard, Macqueen's	71	Eagle, Tawny	190
Buzzard, Common	59	Egret, Cattle	47
Buzzard, Crested Honey	53	Egret, Great	48
Buzzard, European Honey	53	Egret, Little	48
Buzzard, Long-legged	60	Egret, Western Reef	47
Chaffinch, Common	177	Falcon, Barbary	67
Chiffchaff, Common	165	Falcon, Eleonora's	190
Chiffchaff, Mountain	165	Falcon, Red-footed	64
Chukar	184	Falcon, Sooty	65
Cisticola, Zitting	153	Fieldfare	151
Coot, Eurasian	70	Finch, Desert	179
Cormorant, Great	42	Finch, Trumpeter	179
Cormorant, Pygmy	43	Flamingo, Greater	52
Cormorant, Socotra	43	Flycatcher, Asian Brown	195
Courser, Cream-coloured	75	Flycatcher, Collared	195
Crake, Baillon's	69	Flycatcher, Pied	195
Crake, Corn	69	Flycatcher, Red-breasted	166
Crake, Little	68	Flycatcher, Semi-collared	167
Crake, Spotted	67	Flycatcher, Spotted	166
Crane, Common	71	Francolin, Black	185
Crane, Demoiselle	71	Gadwall	36
Crane, Grey Crowned	185	Garganey	38

Godwit, Bar-tailed	87		Lapwing, Sociable	80
Godwit, Black-tailed	87		Lapwing, Spur-winged	80
Goldfinch, European	178		Lapwing, White-tailed	81
Goose, Greater White-fronted	35		Lark, Bar-tailed	125
Goose, Greylag	35		Lark, Bimaculated	127
Goose, Lesser White-fronted	188		Lark, Calandra	127
Goshawk, Northern	57		Lark, Crested	129
Grebe, Black-necked	41		Lark, Desert	125
Grebe, Great Crested	40		Lark, Dunn's	125
Grebe, Horned	41		Lark, Greater Hoopoe	126
Grebe, Little	40		Lark, Greater Short-toed	128
Greenshank, Common	90		Lark, Lesser Short-toed	128
Gull, Armenian	191		Lark, Temminck's	131
Gull, Black-headed	94		Lark, Thick-billed	126
Gull, Caspian	97		Lark, Wood	130
Gull, Great Black-backed	191		Linnet, Common	178
Gull, Herring	191		Magpie, Common	187
Gull, Iceland	191		Mallard	36
Gull, Lesser Black-backed	96		Martin, Common House	133
Gull, Little	94		Martin, Eurasian Crag	132
Gull, Mediterranean	93		Martin, Rock	132
Gull, Mew	96		Martin, Sand	131
Gull, Pallas's	93		Merganser, Red-breasted	39
Gull, Slender-billed	95		Merlin	64
Harrier, Hen	56		Moorhen, Common	69
Harrier, Montagu's	57		Myna, Bank	174
Harrier, Pallid	57		Myna, Brahminy	187
Harrier, Western Marsh	56		Myna, Common	174
Heron, Black-crowned Night	46		Nightingale, Common	142
Heron, Goliath	189		Nightingale, Thrush	142
Heron, Grey	49		Nightjar, Egyptian	118
Heron, Indian Pond	189		Nightjar, European	117
Heron, Purple	50		Nuthatch, European	196
Heron, Squacco	46		Oriole, Eurasian Golden	169
Hobby, Eurasian	65		Osprey	62
Hoopoe, Eusian	123		Ostrich	188
Hypocolius, Grey	139		Ouzel, Ring	149
Ibis, Glossy	51		Owl, Barn	115
Ibis, Sacred	51		Owl, Eurasian Eagle	115
Jackdaw, Western	196		Owl, European Scops	115
Kestrel, Common	63		Owl, Hume's	192
Kestrel, Lesser	63		Owl, Little	116
Kingfisher, Common	121		Owl, Long-eared	116
Kingfisher, Pied	121		Owl, Short-eared	117
Kingfisher, White-throated	120		Owl, Tawny	191
Kite, Black	54		Oystercatcher, Eurasian	72
Kite, Black-shouldered	54		Parakeet, Alexandrine	185
Kite, Red	189		Parakeet, Rose-ringed	113
Kittiwake, Black-legged	191		Partridge, See-see	184
Knot, Great	81		Pelican, Dalmatian	44
Knot, Red	83		Pelican, Great White	44
Lanner	66		Peregrine	66
Lapwing, Northern	81		Phalarope, Red	92
Lapwing, Red-wattled	80		Phalarope, Red-necked	92

Pigeon, Bruce's Green	185	Sandpiper, Broad-billed	85
Pintail, Northern	36	Sandpiper, Common	91
Pipit, Blyth's	134	Sandpiper, Curlew	84
Pipit, Buff-bellied	136	Sandpiper, Green	90
Pipit, Long-billed	192	Sandpiper, Marsh	89
Pipit, Meadow	135	Sandpiper, Purple	190
Pipit, Olive-backed	135	Sandpiper, Terek	91
Pipit, Red-throated	136	Sandpiper, Wood	90
Pipit, Richard's	133	Scoter, Common	188
Pipit, Rock	192	Scoter, Velvet	188
Pipit, Tawny	134	Serin, European	196
Pipit, Tree	135	Shearwater, Audubon's	41
Pipit, Water	136	Shelduck, Common	36
Plover, Caspian	78	Shelduck, Ruddy	35
Plover, Common Ringed	77	Shikra	58
Plover, Crab	73	Shoveler, Northern	38
Plover, European Golden	190	Shrike, Isabelline	169
Plover, Greater Sand	78	Shrike, Lesser Grey	170
Plover, Grey	79	Shrike, Masked	171
Plover, Kentish	77	Shrike, Red-backed	170
Plover, Lesser Sand	77	Shrike, Southern Grey	170
Plover, Little Ringed	76	Shrike, Woodchat	171
Plover, Pacific Golden	79	Silverbill, Indian	177
Pochard, Common	39	Siskin, European	178
Pratincole, Black-winged	76	Skua, Arctic	92
Pratincole, Collared	76	Skua, Great	190
Prinia, Graceful	153	Skua, Long-tailed	93
Quail, Common	39	Skua, Pomarine	92
Rail, Water	67	Skylark, Eurasian	130
Raven, Brown-necked	173	Skylark, Oriental	130
Redshank, Common	89	Snipe, Common	86
Redshank, Spotted	89	Snipe, Great	86
Redstart, Black	144	Snipe, Jack	86
Redstart, Common	144	Sparrow, Arabian Golden	196
Redstart, Eversmann's	144	Sparrow, Chestnut-shouldered	176
Redstart, Guldenstädt's	192	Sparrow, Dead Sea	175
Redwing	152	Sparrow, House	175
Reedling, Bearded	186	Sparrow, Rock	196
Robin, Black Scrub	142	Sparrow, Spanish	175
Robin, European	142	Sparrowhawk, Eurasian	58
Robin, Rufous-tailed Scrub	141	Sparrowhawk, Levant	59
Robin, White-throated	143	Sparrow-lark, Black-crowned	124
Rockfinch, Pale	176	Spoonbill, Eurasian	51
Roller, European	122	Starling, Common	173
Roller, Indian	123	Starling, Rosy	174
Rook	172	Starling, Wattled	187
Rosefinch, Common	179	Stilt, Black-winged	72
Ruff	85	Stint, Little	84
Saker	66	Stint, Temminck's	84
Sanderling	83	Stonechat, Common	145
Sandgrouse, Black-bellied	108	Stone-Curlew	75
Sandgrouse, Chestnut-bellied	107	Stork, Black	50
Sandgrouse, Pin-tailed	108	Stork, White	50
Sandgrouse, Spotted	107	Storm-Petrel, Wilson's	189

Swallow, Barn	132		Warbler, European Reed	155
Swallow, Red-rumped	133		Warbler, Garden	161
Swamp-Hen, Purple	70		Warbler, Great Reed	157
Swan, Mute	34		Warbler, Greenish	163
Swift, Alpine	118		Warbler, Hume's Leaf	164
Swift, Common	119		Warbler, Icterine	160
Swift, Little	120		Warbler, Marsh	156
Swift, Pallid	119		Warbler, Melodious	193
Teal, Common	37		Warbler, Ménétries's	163
Tern, Arctic	102		Warbler, Moustached	155
Tern, Black	105		Warbler, Olive-tree	160
Tern, Bridled	103		Warbler, Oriental Reed	158
Tern, Caspian	98		Warbler, River	154
Tern, Common	101		Warbler, Paddyfield	193
Tern, Greater Crested	99		Warbler, Radde's	194
Tern, Gull-billed	97		Warbler, Rüppell's	194
Tern, Lesser Crested	100		Warbler, Sardinian	194
Tern, Little	104		Warbler, Savi's	154
Tern, Roseate	191		Warbler, Scrub	193
Tern, Sandwich	101		Warbler, Sedge	155
Tern, Saunders's	104		Warbler, Spectacled	193
Tern, Whiskered	106		Warbler, Subalpine	194
Tern, White-cheeked	102		Warbler, Syke's	158
Tern, White-winged	106		Warbler, Thick-billed	193
Thrush, Blue Rock	149		Warbler, Upcher's	160
Thrush, Dark-throated	151		Warbler, Willow	166
Thrush, Dusky	150		Warbler, Wood	165
Thrush, Mistle	152		Warbler, Yellow-browed	164
Thrush, Rufous-tailed Rock	149		Waxbill, Zebra	187
Thrush, Song	151		Weaver, Streaked	187
Tit, Eurasian Penduline	169		Wheatear, Black-eared	146
Tropicbird, Red-billed	42		Wheatear, Desert	146
Turnstone, Ruddy	91		Wheatear, Eastern Pied	192
Vulture, Egyptian	54		Wheatear, Finsch's	147
Vulture, Eurasian Black	55		Wheatear, Hooded	148
Vulture, Eurasian Griffon	55		Wheatear, Hume's	148
Wagtail, Citrine	137		Wheatear, Isabelline	145
Wagtail, Grey	137		Wheatear, Kurdish	147
Wagtail, White	138		Wheatear, Mourning	147
Wagtail, Yellow	137		Wheatear, Northern	145
Warbler, Aquatic	193		Wheatear, Pied	146
Warbler, Asian Desert	163		Wheatear, Red-tailed	148
Warbler, Balkan	194		Wheatear, White-crowned	148
Warbler, Barred	161		Whimbrel	88
Warbler, Basra Reed	157		Whinchat	144
Warbler, Blyth's Reed	156		Whitethroat, Common	162
Warbler, Booted	158		Whitethroat, Lesser	162
Warbler, Cetti's	152		Wigeon, Eurasian	36
Warbler, Clamorous Reed	158		Woodcock, Eurasian	86
Warbler, Common Grasshopper	153		Woodpigeon, Common	110
Warbler, Cyprus	194		Wren, Winter	139
Warbler, Dusky	194		Wryneck, Eurasian	124
Warbler, Eastern Olivaceous	158		Yellowhammer	180
Warbler, Eastern Orphean	162			

INDEX OF SCIENTIFIC NAMES

Accipiter badius	58	Apus apus	119
Accipiter brevipes	59	Apus melba	118
Accipiter gentilis	57	Apus pallidus	119
Accipiter nisus	58	Aquila chrysaetos	61
Acridotheres ginginianus	174	Aquila clanga	60
Acridotheres tristis	174	Aquila heliaca	61
Acrocephalus aedon	193	Aquila nipalensis	61
Acrocephalus agricola	193	Aquila pomarina	60
Acrocephalus arundinaceus	157	Aquila rapax	190
Acrocephalus dumetorum	156	Ardea cinerea	49
Acrocephalus griseldis	157	Ardea goliath	189
Acrocephalus melanopogon	155	Ardea purpurea	50
Acrocephalus orientalis	158	Ardeola grayii	189
Acrocephalus paludicola	193	Ardeola ralloides	46
Acrocephalus palustris	156	Arenaria interpres	91
Acrocephalus schoenobaenus	155	Asio flammeus	117
Acrocephalus scipaceus	155	Asio otus	116
Acrocephalus stentoreus	158	Athene noctua	116
Actitis hypoleucos	91	Aythya ferina	39
Aegypius monachus	55	Aythya fuligula	39
Alaemon alaudipes	126	Aythya nyroca	39
Alauda arvensis	130	Balearica regulorum	185
Alauda gulgula	130	Botaurus stellaris	45
Alcedo atthis	121	Bubo bubo	115
Alectoris chukar	184	Bubulcus ibis	47
Amandava amandava	187	Bucanetes githagineus	179
Amandava subflava	187	Burhinus oedicnemus	75
Ammomanes cincturus	125	Buteo buteo	59
Ammomanes deserti	125	Buteo rufinus	60
Ammoperdix griseogularis	184	Calandrella brachydactyla	128
Anas acuta	36	Calandrella rufescens	128
Anas clypeata	38	Calidris alba	83
Anas crecca	36	Calidris alpina	85
Anas penelope	36	Calidris canutus	83
Anas platyrhynchos	36	Calidris ferruginea	84
Anas querquedula	38	Calidris maritima	190
Anas strepera	36	Calidris minuta	84
Anhinga rufa	189	Calidris temminckii	84
Anser albifrons	35	Calidris tenuirostris	81
Anser anser	35	Caprimulgus aegyptius	118
Anser erythropus	188	Caprimulgus europaeus	117
Anthropoides virgo	71	Carduelis cannabina	178
Anthus campestris	134	Carduelis carduelis	178
Anthus cervinus	136	Carduelis spinus	178
Anthus godlewskii	134	Carpodacus erythrinus	179
Anthus hodgsoni	135	Cercomela melanura	192
Anthus petrosus	192	Cercotrichas galactotes	141
Anthus pratensis	135	Cercotrichas podobes	142
Anthus richardi	133	Ceryle rudis	121
Anthus rufescens	136	Cettia cetti	152
Anthus similis	192	Charadrius alexandrinus	77
Anthus spinoletta	136	Charadrius asiaticus	78
Anthus trivialis	135	Charadrius dubius	76
Apus affinis	120	Charadrius hiaticula	77

Charadrius leschenaultii	78	*Emberiza schoeniclus*	183
Charadrius mongolus	77	*Emberiza striolata*	197
Charadrius morinellus	79	*Eremalauda dunni*	125
Chettusia gregaria	80	*Eremophila bilophus*	131
Chettusia leucura	81	*Eremopterix nigriceps*	124
Chlamydotis macqueeni	71	*Erithacus rubecula*	142
Chlidonias hybridus	106	*Euodice malabarica*	177
Chlidonias leucopterus	106	*Falco biarmicus*	66
Chlidonias niger	105	*Falco cherrug*	66
Ciconia ciconia	50	*Falco columbarius*	64
Ciconia nigra	50	*Falco concolor*	65
Circaetus gallicus	55	*Falco eleonorae*	190
Circus aeruginosus	56	*Falco naumanni*	63
Circus cyaneus	56	*Falco pelegrinoides*	66
Circus macrourus	57	*Falco peregrinus*	66
Circus pygargus	57	*Falco subbuteo*	65
Cisticola juncidis	153	*Falco tinnunculus*	63
Clamator glandarius	114	*Falco vesperinus*	64
Clangula hyemalis	188	*Ficedula albicollis*	195
Columba livia	109	*Ficedula hypoleuca*	195
Columba oenas	109	*Ficedula parva*	166
Columba palumbus	110	*Ficedula semitorquata*	167
Coracias benghalensis	123	*Francolinus francolinus*	185
Coracias garrulus	122	*Fringilla coelebs*	177
Corvus corone	196	*Fringilla montifringilla*	177
Corvus frugilegus	172	*Fulica atra*	70
Corvus monedula	196	*Galerida cristata*	129
Corvus ruficollis	173	*Gallinago gallinago*	86
Corvus splendens	172	*Gallinago media*	86
Coturnix coturnix	39	*Gallinula chloropus*	69
Creatophora cineracea	187	*Gelochelidon nilotica*	97
Crex crex	69	*Glareola nordmanni*	76
Cuculus canorus	114	*Glareola pratincola*	76
Cursorius cursor	75	*Grus grus*	71
Cygnus olor	34	*Gyps fulvus*	55
Delichon urbica	133	*Haematopus ostralegus*	72
Dendrocygna bicolor	188	*Halcyon smyrnensis*	120
Dicrurus macrocercus	186	*Hieraaetus fasciatus*	62
Dromas ardeola	73	*Hieraaetus pennatus*	62
Egretta albus	48	*Himantopus himantopus*	72
Egretta garzetta	48	*Hippolais caligata*	158
Egretta gularis	47	*Hippolais icterina*	160
Elanus caeruleus	54	*Hippolais languida*	160
Emberiza bruniceps	183	*Hippolais olivetorum*	160
Emberiza buchanani	197	*Hippolais pallida*	158
Emberiza caesia	197	*Hippolais polyglotta*	193
Emberiza cia	181	*Hippolais rama*	158
Emberiza cineracea	181	*Hirundo daurica*	133
Emberiza citrinella	180	*Hirundo fuligula*	132
Emberiza hortulana	181	*Hirundo rustica*	132
Emberiza leucocephalus	196	*Hoplopterus indicus*	80
Emberiza melanocephala	183	*Hoplopterus spinosus*	80
Emberiza pusilla	182	*Hypocolius ampelinus*	139
Emberiza rustica	182	*Irania gutturalis*	143

Ixobrychus minutus	45		Numenius phaeopus	88
Jynx torquilla	124		Numenius tenuirostris	88
Lanius collurio	170		Nycticorax nycticorax	46
Lanius isabellinus	169		Oceanites oceanicus	189
Lanius meridionalis	170		Oena capensis	113
Lanius minor	170		Oenanthe alboniger	148
Lanius nubicus	171		Oenanthe chrysopygia	148
Lanius senator	171		Oenanthe deserti	146
Larus argentatus	191		Oenanthe finschii	147
Larus armenicus	191		Oenanthe hispanica	146
Larus cachinnans	97		Oenanthe isabellina	145
Larus canus	96		Oenanthe leucopyga	148
Larus fuscus	96		Oenanthe lugens	147
Larus genei	95		Oenanthe monacha	148
Larus glaucoides	191		Oenanthe oenanthe	145
Larus ichthyaetus	93		Oenanthe picata	192
Larus marinus	191		Oenanthe pleschanka	146
Larus melanocephalus	93		Oenanthe xanthoprymna	147
Larus minutus	94		Oriolus oriolus	169
Larus ridibundus	94		Otus scops	115
Limicola falcinellus	85		Pandion haliaetus	62
Limosa lapponica	87		Panurus biarmicus	186
Limosa limosa	87		Passer domesticus	175
Locustella fluviatilis	154		Passer euchlorus	196
Locustella luscinioides	154		Passer hispaniolensis	175
Locustella naevia	153		Passer moabiticus	175
Lullula arborea	130		Pelecanus crispus	44
Luscinia luscinia	142		Pelecanus onocrotalus	44
Luscinia megarhynchos	142		Pernis apivorus	53
Luscinia svecica	143		Pernis ptilorhynchus	53
Lymnocryptes minimus	86		Petronia brachydactyla	176
Marmaronetta angustirostris	38		Petronia petronia	196
Melanitta fusca	188		Petronia xanthocollis	176
Melanitta nigra	188		Phalacrocorax carbo	42
Melanocorypha bimaculata	127		Phalacrocorax nigrogularis	43
Melanocorypha calandra	127		Phalacrocorax pygmeus	43
Melopsittacus undulatus	186		Phaethon aethereus	42
Mergus serrator	39		Phalaropus fulicaria	92
Merops apiaster	122		Phalaropus lobatus	92
Merops orientalis	192		Philomachus pugnax	85
Merops superciliosus	122		Phoenicopterus roseus	52
Miliaria calandra	184		Phoenicurus erythronotus	144
Milvus migrans	54		Phoenicurus erythrogaster	192
Milvus milvus	189		Phoenicurus ochruros	144
Monticola saxatilis	149		Phoenicurus phoenicurus	144
Monticola solitarius	149		Phylloscopus collybita	165
Motacilla alba	138		Phylloscopus fuscatus	194
Motacilla cinerea	137		Phylloscopus humei	164
Motacilla citreola	137		Phylloscopus inornatus	164
Motacilla flava	137		Phylloscopus orientalis	195
Muscicapa dauurica	195		Phylloscopus schwarzi	194
Muscicapa striata	166		Phylloscopus sibilitrax	165
Neophron percnopterus	54		Phylloscopus sindianus	165
Numenius arquata	88		Phylloscopus trochiloides	163

Phylloscopus trochilus	166		Sterna repressa	102
Pica pica	187		Sterna sandvicensis	101
Platalea leucorodia	51		Sterna saundersi	104
Plegadis falcinellus	51		Streptopelia decaocto	110
Ploceus manyar	187		Streptopelia orientalis	112
Pluvialis apricaria	190		Streptopelia roseogrisea	111
Pluvialis fulva	79		Streptopelia senegalensis	113
Pluvialis squatarola	79		Streptopelia turtur	111
Podiceps auritus	41		Strix aluco	191
Podiceps cristatus	40		Strix butleri	192
Podiceps nigricollis	41		Struthio camelus	188
Porphyrio porphyrio	70		Sturnus pagodarum	187
Porzana parva	68		Sturnus roseus	174
Porzana porzana	68		Sturnus vulgaris	173
Porzana pusilla	69		Sylvia atricapilla	161
Prinia gracilis	153		Sylvia borin	161
Prunella atrogularis	141		Sylvia cantillans	194
Prunella modularis	140		Sylvia communis	162
Psittacula eupatria	185		Sylvia conspicillata	193
Psittacula krameri	113		Sylvia crassirostris	162
Pterocles alchata	108		Sylvia curruca	162
Pterocles exustus	107		Sylvia melanocephala	194
Pterocles orientalis	108		Sylvia melanothorax	194
Pterocles senegallus	107		Sylvia mystacea	163
Ptyonoprogne rupestris	132		Sylvia nana	163
Puffinus lherminieri	41		Sylvia nisoria	161
Pycnonotus cafer	138		Sylvia rueppelli	194
Pycnonotus leucogenys	138		Tachybaptus ruficollis	40
Pycnonotus xanthopygos	186		Tadorna ferruginea	35
Rallus aquaticus	67		Tadorna tadorna	36
Ramphocoris clotbey	126		Threskiornis aethiopicus	51
Recurvirostra avosetta	73		Treron waalia	185
Remiz pendulinus	169		Tringa erythropus	89
Rhodospiza obsoleta	179		Tringa glareola	90
Riparia riparia	131		Tringa nebularia	90
Rissa tridactyla	191		Tringa ochropus	90
Saxicola rubetra	144		Tringa stagnatilis	89
Saxicola torquatus	145		Tringa totanus	89
Scolopax rusticola	86		Troglodytes troglodytes	139
Scotocerca inquieta	193		Turdoides altirostris	195
Serinus serinus	196		Turdoides caudatus	167
Sitta europaea	196		Turdus iliacus	152
Stercorarius longicaudus	93		Turdus merula	150
Stercorarius parasiticus	92		Turdus naumanni	150
Stercorarius pomarinus	92		Turdus pilaris	151
Stercorarius skua	190		Turdus philomelas	151
Sterna albifrons	104		Turdus ruficollis	151
Sterna anaethetus	103		Turdus torquatus	149
Sterna bengalensis	100		Turdus viscivorus	152
Sterna bergii	99		Tyto alba	115
Sterna caspia	98		Upupa epops	123
Sterna dougalli	191		Vanellus vanellus	81
Sterna hirundo	101		Xenus cinereus	91
Sterna paradisaea	102			